How to Service and Repair Your Own Car

How to Service

A Popular Science Book

and Repair Your Own Car

by Richard Day

Drawings by
Lloyd P. Birmingham

POPULAR SCIENCE PUBLISHING COMPANY, INC.

HARPER & ROW
New York, Evanston, San Francisco, London

Library of Congress Catalog Card Number: 72-97173
SBN: 06-011003-1

Second Printing, 1974

Designed by Jeff Fitschen

Manufactured in the United States of America

I dedicate this book
to the guy or gal who enjoys
tinkering with cars
for fun, knowledge or economy.

Acknowledgments

Thanks are due to many people and organizations for their help with this book.

First and foremost, my gratitude to Edward L. "Red" Rust of Peotone, Ill., a mechanic of long experience, for his technical editing and helpful suggestions on many chapters. Special appreciation is also extended to Walter Alley, Manager of Training, Midas-International Corp., for up-to-date and practical information that has been incorporated throughout the book. Also, thanks to Alex Markovich, who copy edited the manuscript and made many helpful suggestions along the way.

Others who have helped with information and illustrations include:

AC Spark Plug Division, General Motors Corp.; Allied Radio Corp.; American Bosch Marketing; American Motors Corp.; Miles Bacon; Bear Manufacturing Co.; John Coxeter and John Winge of The Bendix Corp.; Champion Spark Plug Co.; Ed Naudzius of Chevrolet Division, General Motors Corp.; Chrysler Corp.

Also, Delco-Remy Division, General Motors Corp.; Edward and Colleen Dionne; Dodge Division, Chrysler Corp.; Fred Welty, E.I. Dupont de Nemours and Co.; G.E. "Bud" Adams and others of Ford Division, Ford Motor Co.; The Gates Rubber Co.; General Electric Co.; General Motors Corp.; The Goodyear Tire and Rubber Co.; Grey-Rock Division, Raybestos-Manhattan Inc.

Also, Hunckler Products, Inc.; K-D Manufacturing Co.; Kent-Moore Corp.; R.J. Lannen, Micro-Poise Engineering and Sales Co.; Monroe Auto Equipment Co.; Montgomery Ward; Moog Industries, Inc.; National Auto and Truck Wreckers Association, Inc.; National Safety Council; T-P-H Division, Parker Hanifin; Paul's Automotive; Pendleton Tool Industries, Inc.; H.K. Porter Co.; The Prestolite Co.

Also, Ronald R. Moalli, Raybestos-Manhattan, Inc.; Rubber Manufacturers Association; Sears Roebuck and Co.; Sun Electric Co.; 3M Co.; Norman R. Cooper, Union Carbide Corp.; Uniroyal, Inc.; Walker Manufacturing Co.; and Western Auto Supply Co.; and V. Paul Williams.

Contents

Italics indicate step-by-step photographic sequences.

Introduction

This book is intended to be a working manual that begins where your car owner's manual leaves off. It is meant to be propped on the fender or opened on the workbench. It is aimed at car owners who want to know more about their cars and save on servicing expenses—and perhaps get some enjoyment from their tinkering.

You need not know everything about an automobile before you can take care of it. You can pick up what needs knowing as you go along.

Some repairs are easy and some are complicated.. The book covers a lot of the former and a few of the latter. If you do not understand a particular repair, take the car to a pro. I will let you know when I feel a job is beyond the tools and abilities of the average do-it-yourselfer.

Besides information on making repairs, I have included advice on shopping for professional car repairs. Such advice should enable you to avoid incompetent and overly expensive shops.

Everyone who works around cars should be aware of certain hazards. Among these is the danger of improperly used or ungrounded electrical tools. Some liquids that you may use are flammable or explosive. A car that is lifted off the ground becomes a potential hazard for anyone underneath. Working in an enclosed area with a running engine exposes you to deadly exhaust fumes. And the moving parts of a running engine can catch and tear anything—including flesh and bones—that gets in their way.

I have tried to anticipate these and other risks that are implicit in auto repairs and warn you about them. But the responsibility for safety is yours. Repairing a car is probably a lot safer than driving one—but even so, be careful.

Most important, if you lack confidence in performing a safety-related repair, such as a brake job, ask a pro for advice, or let him do it.

As you gain experience in fixing your car, you will be able to catch safety problems before they become dangerous. For example, the Troubleshooting Chart on pages 344-347 gives many hints on what to look for when brakes start to go sour. Some symptoms might pass unnoticed by the average motorist.

In the book, I have emphasized American cars made within the last ten years, but I have also included information on imports. Much of the data also applies to cars that are more than ten years old. Ideally, you should also have a copy of the factory service manual for your car; it takes up where this book leaves off. You will not need the manual for many operations, but it is helpful in such areas as locating grease fittings and providing various specifications.

I suggest you begin by reading the opening chapters on the economics of car repair and tools. The rest depends on your car. What does it need? A tune-up? Exhaust system repair? Cooling system service? That becomes the next chapter to read. Go to it!

Richard Day

How to Service and Repair Your Own Car

Economics of Car Repair

Repairing your own car is bound to save you money, as well as give you satisfaction. For any car that's beyond its warranty will eat up about $250 a year in repairs — and some will need even more. The money to be saved, then, can be considerable; of course, how much you save depends on how much you can do. Happily, you don't need to know a great deal about your car. You can learn by doing.

Three major collections of parts make up your car: the engine, the chassis, and the body. The engine powers the car, the chassis supports it, and the body makes it comfortable. If some part loosens, gets out of adjustment, becomes dirty, or wears out, it may not perform its function. Most repairs consist simply of finding the problem part and adjusting, cleaning, repairing, or replacing it. Car repairs most often involve the engine, because it is the most complex component and the one that does the most work. Chassis parts are the next most troublesome, and body parts require the least attention.

Getting Professional Help

If your car requires major repairs — a job such as valve reconditioning, transmission overhaul, or collision repair — you probably will have to shop around for a reputable garage.

Make it a practice to deal with established shops, never with someone who drops by your house. The longer the firm has been in business, the better. Affiliation with a national organization may or may not be a good sign. Some new car dealers, for example, do excellent work; others concentrate on selling cars and let their service departments slide. Membership in a national organization such as the Independent Garage Owners Association is a good sign; IGOA is working hard to develop a reputation for quality work among its members.

Mechanics. Good mechanics may be found in all types of service establishments, large and small, national chains and independent shops, all-around shops and specialized ones.

1

Shops that send their mechanics to service schools to learn new methods of car repair are good bets. That costs the shop money, and you pay for it, but you benefit through speedy, competent work. Often diplomas from service schools are displayed prominently in the shop.

Getting good service once at a shop does not always mean you will get good service next time. Often, top- and bottom-level mechanics work in the same shop. Keep your eyes open. The top man is the one all the others consult on problems. Ask for that man to work on your car.

Costs. These will vary, depending on how long the repair takes and on the cost of necessary parts. Labor is charged for in three ways: by the estimate, by the hour,

flat-rate manual and your shop charges a rate of $12 an hour, your charge for labor totals $52.80.

If you are given a firm estimate, that is what you pay, whether the mechanic takes one hour or 10 hours to do the job. The flat-rate method of pricing labor is preferable for the customer in three situations: (1) when dealing with an unknown shop; (2) with problem-laden jobs, such as engine overhaul or muffler replacement; (3) on old cars with corroded fasteners.

When you pay for labor strictly by the hour, you get no firm estimate — though a ballpark figure may be cited if you ask. The mechanic does the job and keeps a record of time. If a job happens to take, say 3.5 hours, you pay $42 labor. But if the

Prices for state-required inspections are often posted.

and by the job. The mechanic and shop sometimes split the labor charge 50-50 or 60-40. Even if they do not, each is earning about half of the repair labor charge.

When a service manager gives you an estimate on labor, he bases it on the number of hours that such a repair normally takes. He looks up the job in a book called a flat-rate manual, which catalogs every conceivable kind of repair and tells how long it takes a properly equipped mechanic to perform it, in hours and tenths. The service manager then multiplies that time by the shop's hourly rate. For instance, if removing and replacing an engine is supposed to take 4.4 hours according to the

mechanic runs into trouble and needs 6.5 hours for the same job, you pay $78.

Per-hour billing is better if you know the mechanic is sharp. A good mechanic can almost always beat the flat-rates, especially on common work such as engine replacement and valve jobs. The per-hour method also works in your favor in terms of quality work. The mechanic knows he will be paid for all the time he spends, so he takes the time to be thorough.

When paying for labor by the job, you know all ordinary costs in advance. Common work — brake relining, wheel alignment, engine overhaul, smog valve inspection — have established prices in many shops. The garage owner knows from past experience how much parts and labor will cost. Though you probably would pay less by the hour, it is hard to get such repairs priced any other way. Suppose, 'for example, that you get regular alignments (as you should) and your car's front wheels are aimed pretty close to where they should be. One quick adjustment may put them right. But you probably will have to pay the same as the owner of a car that has its wheels way off.

Parts. When your car is repaired by a garage, the shop owner gets all parts at discounts of 20 to 50 percent. Shops consider it their right to charge you full list price for parts, and they resent customers who furnish their own parts. The shops' profits on auto parts permit them to stock an ample supply of common parts. This means you do not have to wait for delivery or for someone to be sent for parts that are not stocked.

Doing It Yourself

The money you save by repairing your car in your own garage, then, comes from two sources: labor charges and the shop owner's profit on parts. To ensure this dual savings, be careful when you set about to order replacement components.

New parts. If you do it yourself, you can try to get the discount on parts. Almost every good-sized town has at least one auto parts jobber who will sell at some sort of discount, perhaps 20 percent, to a customer who acts like a professional—in other words, a customer who does not take up the parts man's time with questions about the car repair. By all means ask for a discount if it is not offered.

Another way to get a parts discount is by buying from mail order catalogs from companies such as Sears Roebuck, Montgomery Ward, or Spiegel. The problem

there is that you either have to anticipate the parts you will need—which is rarely possible—or lay up your car for a week or longer until the parts arrive. J. C. Whitney is an excellent source for antique and other hard-to-find parts. If the catalog does not list what you want, call or write. They may be able to get it for you. Retail chain stores such as Wards, Sears, Western Auto, Pep Boys, and J. C. Penney sell parts over the counter, but only the better selling items (spark plugs, polishes, lubricants, tune-up kits, batteries, and tires) are stocked.

All new car parts are sold by part numbers. You need not know the part number; the dealer can look it up. However, you must supply all the information about your car. Begin with the name of the part. Then give car year, make,. and model. Depending on what part is needed, you may be asked for the number of cylinders and cubic inch displacement.

If you are buying a paint or body item, the trim and paint codes may be required. Engine parts may need an engine or factory number. Rear axle parts probably require the rear axle code. Transmission parts require the transmission code. Engine codes are given on the metal identification plate on the left front door pillar and on the top left corner of the dash.

Sometimes, bringing in the old part is the only way to be sure of getting the proper replacement. For instance, some replacement positive crankcase ventilation valves come in differing sizes not related to year of car or engine size. In addition, differing grades of replacement parts are available. For instance, you can get original equipment shock absorbers or pay more and get longer-lasting, better handling but harder-riding heavy-duty ones. If you are in doubt, replace with original-equipment parts.

Unused auto parts usually can be returned for a refund if they do not fit or are not needed. Some dealers make a nominal

Factory identification plate carries the information you will need to correctly order replacement parts.

Replacement parts are tagged so you can match them with the original equipment.

charge for such returns; in any case, you will need your receipt. Many mail-order stores guarantee satisfaction or a refund.

Some replacement auto parts are available only at your car dealer's parts department. Getting a discount there is almost impossible. You get factory-authorized replacement parts in most, but not all, cases from a new-car dealer. Those are not necessarily better than well-known independent brands.

Rebuilt parts. These are fine if you get them from a reputable dealer, because poorly reworked parts are no bargain. Authorized car-manufacturer rebuilt parts usually are excellent. Those rebuilt by established parts-reconditioning firms in your area should be too. Membership in the Automotive Parts Rebuilders Association is a good sign; the emblem should appear on the box the parts come in.

A properly rebuilt component gets the full treatment. It is dismantled and all the parts to be reused are cleaned and made rust-free. Faulty or missing parts are replaced. Finally, the component is assembled and tested. If all those steps have not been done, the part, by law, may not be labeled "rebuilt" or "remanufactured." If the box says "repaired" or "re-conditioned," it is suspect. Such terms have no legal definition.

You should consider buying any of the following rebuilt components: carburetor; distributor; generator; alternator; voltage regulator; radiator; water pump; fuel pump; oil pump; brake cylinder; brake shoes; power brake unit; starting motor; starter drive; starter solenoid; clutch disk; clutch assembly; transmission; shock absorbers; engine.

Usually, you are allowed to trade in your old component. When you buy a rebuilt part, either bring your old component with

Looking as good as new, this rebuilt carburetor was cleaned, fitted with new parts and gaskets and even tested before packaging.

you or arrange to bring it in later for credit. It's usually best to have both the old and the rebuilt part on hand when you tackle the job. Rebuilt parts may come without fittings, arms, plates, and other attachments; you can remove those from the old part before trading it in.

Actually, you can rebuild a fuel pump, carburetor, or brake cylinder yourself and save money. The only cost would be for replacement of worn parts and new gaskets. Rebuilding kits containing all the parts you need are often available for a fraction of the cost of the rebuilt part. But fuel pumps and carburetors, though not large, are complicated. Many of the new fuel pumps are not designed to come apart for rebuilding. Brake cylinders must be honed during rebuilding—and a hone is expensive. You may be wise simply to buy a rebuilt unit. Do-it-yourself rebuilding of other parts is definitely out, for doing the job right requires highly specialized tools. Furthermore, you have no way of testing the finished job without putting it on the car. The modern rebuilt auto part is one of the best buys there is — take advantage of it.

Used parts. Sometimes it pays to install used parts from a wrecking yard rather than new or rebuilt ones. That is particularly true in fixing an old car that may not last the life of better parts.

On the whole, used parts usually cost less than half as much as new ones. Parts you could buy used are: engine; transmission; all manner of housings and castings that get no wear; air-conditioning components; wheels; differential; replacement body, fender and door panels; and window glass (windshields are often excessively scratched or pitted). Don't buy a used radiator except from a low-mileage wreck; most are as corroded inside as your old radiator. Avoid buying used tires, brake-lines, and other safety-related parts that deteriorate with time.

When buying a used engine, examine the car it is in. If it is a low-mileage car that was in a collision, chances are the engine is in good shape. If the car itself is in poor shape, it probably was junked because of a worn-out engine. If the engine is still in the car and you can run it, do so. If you cannot start the engine but it will crank over, at least make a compression check to see that rings, pistons, and valves are sound.

In parts of the country, you can browse through a wrecking yard's stock of reusable parts.

Even if the auto wrecking yard does not have a car exactly like yours, a part from another make or model may fit. The dealer probably has a book called the "Hollander Manual" that lists interchangeable parts. Many Ford parts, for example, fit Mercurys; and some Plymouth parts fit Dodges and Chryslers. Some General Motors parts also are interchangeable among various models and years.

A part sold by an auto wrecking yard usually is guaranteed to be in working order. But if the part should break down after several weeks, too bad. And even if you get a refund on a defective part, you have still lost the time you spent installing and removing the part. Check a used part as carefully as possible before you buy it.

Used parts have no fixed prices. Don't hesitate to haggle with the wrecker if his price seems too high. Consider it a good sign if a wrecker belongs to the National Auto and Truck Wreckers Association.

Wrecking yards are a good place to pick up replacement parts which do not receive much wear, such as this light ring.

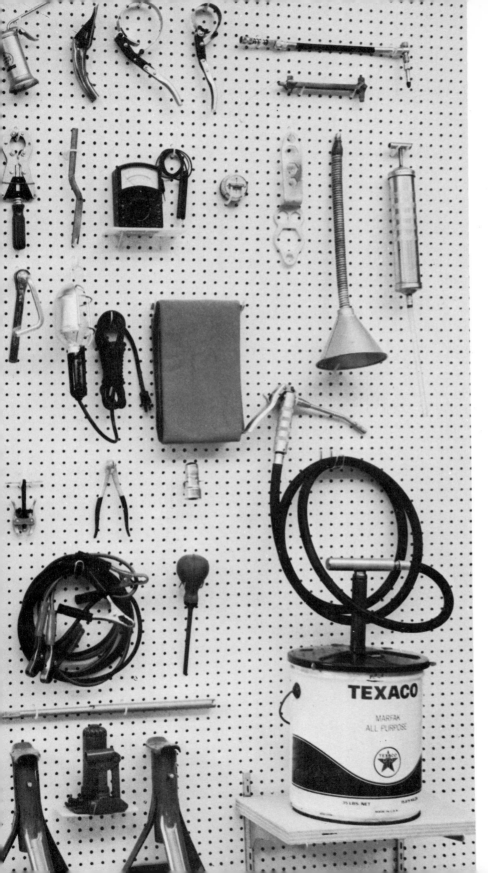

2

Tools

Having the right tool saves time and gets the job done easier and better. True, with a little resourcefulness you sometimes can get around the lack of a tool by substituting another — but why do things the hard way?

A sensible plan is to start with the basic tools, the ones you absolutely must have. Anticipate work you will be doing and get equipped for it when you are tool-shopping. Avoid cheap, flimsy tools — in the long run, they are no bargain.

Grouped below is a comprehensive assortment of tools under five headings: Hand Tools, many of which you may already have in your home workshop; Power Tools; Fasteners; Chemical Tools; and heavy-duty Garage Tools, which are designed especially for making under-car repairs easier and safer. Specialty tools, such as the brake-adjuster, will be examined in later chapters. To work on many foreign-made cars and a growing number of domestic ones, you'll need tools in metric sizes.

HAND TOOLS

Screwdrivers

Always use a screwdriver whose blade is the right size for the screw slot; that preserves the screw as well as the screwdriver. A 6-inch screwdriver is a handy size. If possible, also get a 3-inch and a 10-inch model. A 1½-inch "stubby" model with a regular-sized blade is useful in tight places.

Phillips-head screwdriver. Three sizes — 4-, 6-, and 8-inchers in No. 2 size — will handle nearly any automotive Phillips-head screw. You also can get a handy 1½-inch Phillips "stubby" No. 2.

Reed and Prince screwdriver. Similar to the Phillips-head, but more pointed. If you run across a cross-slotted screw head that your Phillips does not fit well, it more than likely calls for a Reed and Prince screwdriver.

9

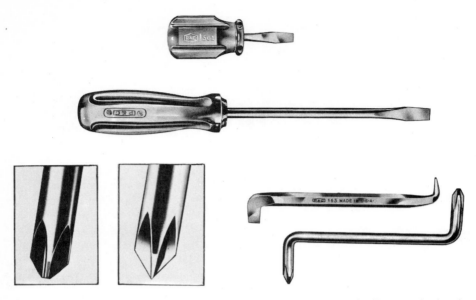

Assortment of screwdrivers includes (*from top left*): stubby, standard, offset standard and offset Phillips; the tips in the insert are the Phillips (*left*) and the Reed and Prince.

Offset screwdriver. Useful when clearance for a regular screwdriver is insufficient, offset screwdrivers come with both standard and Phillips blades. The blades are at right angles to the shank, which is also the handle.

Never use a screwdriver for checking high-amperage electrical circuits. For example, don't arc across battery-to-starter circuits; the current will melt the screwdriver tip. However, high-voltage, low-amperage spark plug current will not hurt a screwdriver.

Never use a screwdriver to substitute for a chisel or any other tool. If you must hammer on a screwdriver, get one whose metal shank extends through the handle. Light-duty prying with a screwdriver is okay; but pry too hard and you may bend the shank. Some heavy-duty screwdrivers have a square shank strong enough to let you turn it with a wrench. But never use pliers on any screwdriver.

If a screwdriver blade suffers minor damage, you can save it by grinding it on an emery wheel. A correctly ground screwdriver blade has practically parallel sides. Since it costs more to make them

Correctly ground screwdriver blade (*left*) tapers to a blunt tip, which fits snugly into a screw slot for maximum leverage. Badly dressed blade (*right*) can easily slip out of, or damage, the screw slot.

this way, most new screwdrivers have blade sides that taper gradually toward the body. Dress your screwdrivers on an emery wheel (or with a mill file) so the faces taper in slightly for a short distance behind the tip. Ground that way, a screwdriver will stay in the slot even under severe strain. Grind the screwdriver tip straight and at a right angle to the shank. Every few seconds, dip the blade in water to cool it, for excessive heat from grinding can take the temper out of the blade.

Pliers

Slip-joint pliers. Dual-purpose jaws that hold either flat or rounded objects make this tool most useful for auto work. Most have cutter jaws for snipping wire. Such combination pliers come in 5- to 10-inch overall lengths. The most useful mechanic's sizes are the 6- and 10-inchers. Look for drop-forged ones; they are stronger.

Diagonal-cutting pliers. Useful for cutting wire and for working with cotter pins which are used to lock some automotive fasteners.

Battery pliers. Often the nuts that secure battery terminals to the battery posts corrode to the point where no wrench will grip them; battery pliers, with their offset handles, let you grip and turn those nuts without contacting the battery case.

Long-nose pliers. Looking like regular pliers that have gone on a diet, the jaws of these tools are long and slim and tapered toward the ends. You may be able to get along without them for months—until you come to a delicate handling, bending, loosening, or tightening job that cannot be done with any other tool. Handling small ignition parts, bending the ends of springs, and picking up dropped nuts and washers are just a few of the jobs that long-nose pliers do well. Some come with built-in wire-cutters, but those without cutters are generally more popular among professional mechanics.

Two handy pliers: the slip joint (*top*) and the interlocking joint.

Long-nose pliers, designed to grasp thin objects, are useful in auto work.

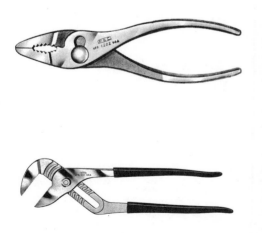

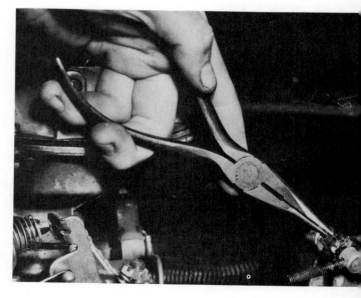

Locking plier/wrench. In some ways, this is not a plier at all. It has jaws something like those of slip-joint pliers, but the opening of the jaws is controlled by a knurled knob. Locking pliers have such a powerful grip that they can be used for turning even rounded and badly corroded fasteners. The size of a locking plier/wrench is measured according to its overall length. The 6- and 10-inch sizes make a good combination.

Interlocking-joint pliers. These work somewhat like slip-joint pliers, except that the slip feature is enlarged. That enables them to open to 2 inches or more with the jaws parallel. Interlocking rings on some models keep the setting from slipping in use. Such pliers are useful where a large plier opening is needed.

Avoid using pliers on hardened steel. That dulls their teeth and loosens their grip. Never use pliers on nuts or bolts that you can turn with a wrench. Pliers chew off the fasteners' corners, making them impossible to grip later with a wrench.

Wrenches

Socket wrench. This tool is basic to all auto repair. The business end of each socket is shaped to fit over the nuts and bolts used to hold auto parts together. The opposite end has a square hole into which the handle's square shank is inserted. A spring-loaded ball in the shank makes a snap-lock action. Once on, the socket cannot fall off; but you can remove the socket by simply pulling it.

Socket wrenches come in several lengths. The standard length is best for most jobs. Deep and extra-deep sockets let you reach nuts that are set down over protruding bolts (as in some exhaust-system U-bolt clamps). A box-end wrench can be used instead.

The size of the square shank is called the socket's "drive." Mechanics' sockets come in ¼-, ⅜-, ½-, and ¾-inch drive. Small auto jobs call for the flexibility of ¼-inch drive. Big auto jobs call for the strength of ½-inch drive. Hold off buying the in-between, ⅜-inch drive until you already have ¼- and ½-inch sets. The ¾-inch-drive sockets are for trucks.

The ratchet handle that accepts individual sockets of various sizes lets you loosen or tighten a nut or bolt quickly. The ratchet can be swung rapidly in wide sweeps or even spun clear around if there is enough room.

An assortment of accessories is available for socket wrenches.

Optional *handles* supplement the ratchet.

Ratcheting socket wrench handle (*immediately below*), with sockets (*center row*) and screwdriver attachments (*bottom*).

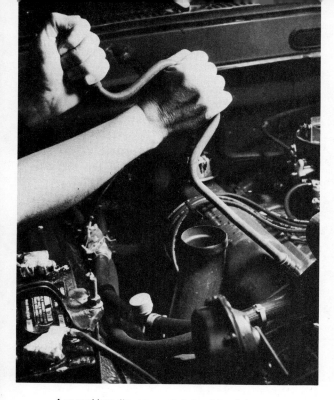

A speed handle, or crank, is best for doing repetitious loosening or tightening; it is not as good when you need a great deal of leverage.

A hinged offset—or swivel—handle is useful for breaking (loosening) tight nuts. To loosen a tightly threaded fastener, the hinged offset handle is swung at right angles to the socket for maximum leverage. Once the nut is loose, the handle can be swung in line with the threads and twisted quickly like a screwdriver.

A sliding offset handle lets you slide the handle to one end for leverage or center it for faster turning. Because it is shorter, it may work in places where a hinged offset handle will not. When fitted with an extension bar, the sliding offset handle becomes a "T" handle.

A crank handle is best for small, repetitious work—for example, removing or tightening numerous fasteners of the same size, such as oil pan or rocker arm cover bolts. Use it like a woodworker's brace and bit. Coupled with a universal joint socket attachment, the speeder handle can reach

where other wrenches cannot. The universal joint lets you hold the handle at an angle to the nut.

Sockets come with hex, double-hex and double-square openings. Hex, or six-point, openings have six sides and are least likely to slip and damage a hexagonal nut or bolt head when forced, especially if the nut or bolt head is rounded. Double-hex, or 12-point, sockets fit ordinary hex-head bolts and nuts in 12 different positions. Their advantage comes when working in cramped quarters; if you can swing the socket only 30° ($1/12$th of a turn), the socket can be repositioned easily for the next swing. With a single-hex socket you need at least a 60° swing. Double-hex sockets are used most often in large sizes. Single-hex, preferred for soft brass or aluminum nuts, are used most often in small sizes.

Double-square sockets are for use on square nut and bolt heads. They permit as little as a 45° swing.

A *spark plug socket* is usually a deep, cushioned $5/8$- or $13/16$-inch socket to prevent the insulator from breaking when you remove or install the plug. Removing all of the spark plugs in some modern V-8 engines is almost impossible without a spark plug socket.

Screwdriver attachments are useful accessories for a socket wrench set. One end fits the square drive of the socket handle and the other is shaped to fit either standard or phillips screws. A screwdriver attachment lets you use your socket handles to screw fasteners as well as nuts and bolts. Other socket set extras include: a long extension for reaching out-of-the-way nuts; a flexible T-bar for breaking and turning; a crossbar for a hinged offset handle to get greater torque when the handle is used out straight; and adapters that allow you to convert socket handles from one size drive to another.

Torque Wrench

To use a torque wrench, first clean and oil the threads of the nut or bolt so all the torque goes into tightening, not into overcoming friction. Run the threads fairly tight with a convenient wrench, then slip the socket onto your torque wrench and increase the torque gradually until the needle reads the right amount of torque. A 0- to 100-foot-pound torque wrench is the most useful for home auto repairs.

A ratcheting torque wrench handle lets you tighten a fastener quickly and then bring it to specified tightness without switching handles. Often, the handle of such a wrench swivels so you can swing it up out of the way of an obstruction.

Torque wrench. A must for the auto hobbyist, especially for engine work. A torque wrench has a gauge or dial that tells how tightly you are securing a nut or a bolt. Some models freewheel when the desired twisting force is reached.

Auto parts are designed to take a certain amount of twisting force — or torque — without distorting. Gaskets are designed to seal under a certain pressure; bolts themselves can withstand so much stress without breaking; and, of course, fasteners that are too loose may loosen still more and allow leaks. That is why a torque wrench is so important.

Open-end wrench. The jaws of these useful tools are parallel and open on one side to slip easily over a bolthead. An open-end wrench sometimes can be used where there is no access for a socket, as on fuel and brake line fittings, where the tubing prevents most other wrenches from being used. An open-end wrench can handle a hex or a square nut or a bolt head.

The standard open-end wrench has a different-sized opening at each end of the handle. One with a $7/16$-inch opening at one end and a $3/8$-inch opening at the other, for example, is called a $7/16 \times 3/8$ open-end wrench. The smaller the opening, the shorter the length of the handle. That

Open-end wrench, best bought in a set.

helps avoid overtightening of small nuts and allows application of greater torque to large ones.

The jaws of most open-end wrenches are set at a 15° angle to the handle. By turning the wrench over after a swing, you can work a hex nut where the wrench can swing only 30°. Some open-end wrench jaws, instead, are set at a 22½°, or even a 75° or a 90° angle.

Always be sure that the wrench is not loose on the bolt or nut; taking care here prevents rounding the corners of the fastener. When there is a tough pull, as when loosening a corroded nut, seat the wrench squarely on the sides of the nut. Better yet, use a socket or a box-end wrench for hard turning.

An *adjustable open-end wrench* is handy on several counts. Sometimes you need two open-end wrenches of the same size to hold both ends of a bolt to prevent it from turning. One of them can be the ad-

Open-end wrench is ideal for grasping fittings—like these on a fuel line—which pliers would round off.

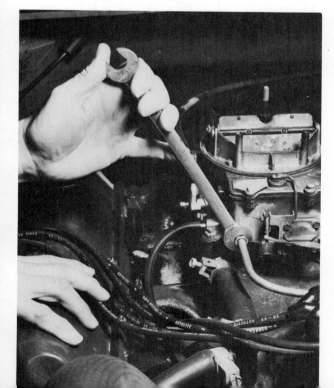

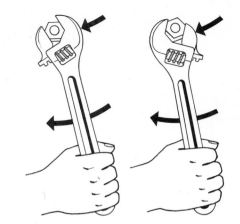

Correct use of an adjustable open-end wrench (*left*) places the stress on the fixed jaw. Incorrect use (*right*) places the load on the movable jaw.

justable one. An adjustable open-end also can handle nuts that are worn off smaller than their original size; and it is handy when you are not sure which size to take under the car with you.

Adjustable wrenches are not intended for rough service. Their weak point is the movable jaw. Get in the habit of using them in such a way that most of the force is taken by the fixed jaw—that means turning so that the movable jaw leads and the fixed jaw trails. The only exception to that rule should be when quarters are cramped and you must invert the wrench every other turn. On hard turning, tighten the wrench after you put it on the nut. Never work with it loose. A 6-inch and a 12-inch adjustable open-end give you a good grasp of things. The kind with click-stops on its adjustment worm will not slip between bites, as others sometimes do.

Box-end wrench. While slower to use than open-ends and sockets, the box-ends can be used like sockets to break loose stuck threads. They also operate in close quarters. The box wraps completely around the fastener, preventing slippage. A single-hex box-end wrench grips best. But the

Box-end Wrench

double-hex, or 12-point, is more maneuverable in tight quarters. Normal procedure is to break the threads with a box-end and then run them off with an open-end. In tightening, run with an open-end and tighten with a box. For that reason we recommend a set of combination open-end/box wrenches, ones with one open end and one box.

The ends of most box wrenches are set at a 15° angle to the handle to get the handle up and away from surfaces and lessen the chance of skinning your knuckles. Some box-end wrenches have the box offset somewhat to gain additional finger clearance. You can also buy flat box-end wrenches without any angle or offset.

Ratcheting Box-end Wrench

Standard Adjustable Wrench

A *multiheaded box wrench* is a single tool that fits eight sizes of fasteners. Forget it unless extreme economy or a compact tool set is what you want. Multiheaded tools slow you down, they do not work in tight quarters, and they are not as strong as individual wrenches.

Another tool you probably will not need if you have a set of box-end wrenches is the *adjustable box-end wrench*.

A *ratcheting box-end wrench* is another tool the pros use. It resembles a box wrench except that its ends have no offset or angle. Place one side up and the wrench tightens; turn the other side up and it loosens. A short swing is all you need to run a nut on or off. Each end fits a different-sized nut. Since the handles of such wrenches are relatively short and can take only so much torque, they are not intended for breaking loose tight threads. Use a regular box wrench for that, and then switch to a ratcheting wrench.

Other types of handy wrenches include:

Flex-head wrench. A worthy addition to any tool box. A conventional flex-head wrench has a different-sized socket at each end. A combination flex-head wrench has a socket at one end and an open-end wrench of the same size at the other. The sockets swivel so that after half a turn the handle can be flipped over for another half turn. Such wrenches take the place of box-end wrenches in most ordinary jobs and work faster.

Set-screw wrench. Often called allen wrenches or socket screw keys, these are L-shaped bars of six-sided steel that fit the hex sockets of set-screws. You should have a set of 13, from .050 inch to 3/8-inch. Hold the long handle of the set-screw wrench for tightening and breaking set screws. Hold the short end for running.

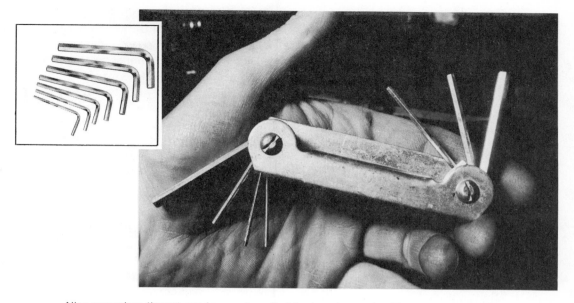

Allen wrenches (*insert*) are frequently called for in auto repairs. They can be purchased as a handy set (*above*).

Pipe wrench. For emergency use on round, not hex or square, objects. The teeth always leave their mark on the object to be turned, so be careful. A 6- or 8-inch pipe wrench is handiest. Pipe wrenches grip in only one direction. Keep the adjusting nut oiled.

Quality of wrenches varies. For $2 you can buy one wrench or a whole set. We recommend buying the very best that you can afford. A good wrench usually is stronger and more comfortable to use than a cheap one. It probably will have a smoother finish that cleans easier. It may be guaranteed against breakage. A problem that we occasional mechanics have with tools is rust—especially if the tools are stored in a damp garage. High-quality tools resist rusting, another reason for spending more.

Pull on a wrench; pushing is risky because the wrench may break loose unexpectedly and make you bang your knuckles on some part of the car. If you must push, be careful. Pad the parts with a soft cloth. Or, push the wrench with the base of your palm, holding your hand open.

A final word of caution: Never slip a pipe or bar over a socket handle or any other wrench to get greater leverage. You may overstress the tool and ruin it.

Miscellaneous Tools

Hammer. The type needed for auto repairs, the *ball peen,* can be used for riveting, chiseling, breaking, and general metalwork. Such hammers are classified by the weight of the head. Common sizes are 4, 6, 8, and 12 ounces, and 1, 1½, and 2 pounds. Buy at least a 12-ouncer. A 1½-ounce hammer is useful for light work such as cutting gaskets out of sheet stock. You place gasket material over the part and tap around the edges; the edges will cut through the gasket material.

Another hammer that is good for mechanical work is plastic-faced. Caps of tough plastic snapped over the faces prevent damage to machined surfaces.

The handle of a hammer should not be used for pounding. It will soon split. Use scrap wood instead. Also, do not use the handle for prying; it may break. Keep your hammers clean by rinsing them in fuel oil to remove dirt and grease.

Measuring Devices. The carpenter's rule or tape has limited applications in auto repair because its 1/16- or 1/32-inch graduations are inadequate. A *6-inch steel rule* is more useful because it has 1/64-inch graduations (equal to about 0.016 inch). The 6-inch rule, or scale, comes in both rigid and flexible models. The thinner it is, the better, since the divisions will be closer to the work. For work on imported cars or the Ford Pinto and Chevrolet Vega, you may find it easier to use a *metric rule,* since fasteners in these vehicles are measured in millimeters (2.54 mm equals 1 inch).

Hacksaw. This saw is intended for cutting metal. A 24-tooth-per-inch blade is best suited for most auto repair work. For fine cutting, as with exhaust system piping, a 32-tooth replacement blade may be preferable. A hacksaw is basically an emergency tool—if a part will not come off in the usual way, it can be sawed off. Old, corroded tailpipes and mufflers often need to be cut away. Stubborn, rusted-on bolts can also be cut off and replaced.

Cold chisel. Another emergency tool, it has a fairly blunt edge for use on metal. If you have ever been faced with a badly corroded license plate bolt, you know the spot for a cold chisel. A hacksaw will not reach into the license recess in most cases. Keep the chisel correctly sharpened. Hit it with a ball peen hammer.

A cold chisel also can be used to split stubborn nuts that will not break loose from their threads. Once split, the nuts usually can be removed easily. Often the nuts on an exhaust manifold, which cor-

Three useful files (*from top*): round file, 8-inch mill file and three-cornered file.

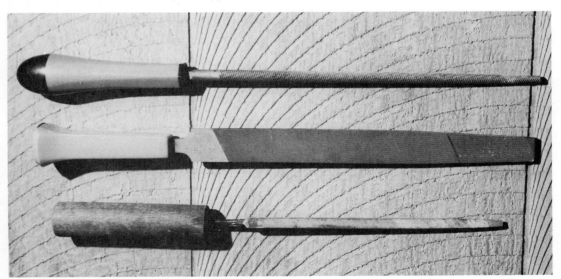

Impact driver, with an assortment of tips, is used to loosen jammed fasteners. This reversible model can also be used to tighten fasteners.

rode rapidly, are made of brass so they can be chiseled off. A ½-inch-wide cold chisel is useful for most jobs.

Like a screwdriver, a cold chisel is sharpened on a grinding wheel. It is much easier than dressing a screwdriver. Set the tool rest at an angle to put a 65° blunt point on the chisel. Then run the chisel back and forth against the spinning abrasive wheel, first with one side against the wheel, then the other. Finish with both ground faces the same width and the edge square across.

Files. You should get the flat mill, round rat-tail, and three-cornered files. The mill file is for dressing down flat parts and is the first one to buy. The three-cornered file can mark parts and clean up damaged threads. The round file is useful for removing burrs left after sawing through a pipe; it might be handy in muffler-tailpipe work but is limited for other uses.

Impact driver. This handy tool makes

easy work of loosening stuck screws — Phillips or regular. You hold the thick steel shank in your fist and pound on the flat top with a ball peen hammer. The lower end holds a screwdriver bit of the desired type and size. When you hammer on the top, the bit end turns powerfully. The screwdriver cannot slip readily because the hammer blows force it into the slot. An adjustment collar lets you set the impact driver for both loosening and tightening.

Nut-cracker. A life-saver when a corroded nut must be removed. The cutting end of the nut-cracker has two hardened-steel chisel-pointed bits that dig into a nut and split it in two. Nut-cracking is better than sawing or chiseling because it preserves the threads of the bolt. All you need is a new nut.

Screw extractor. Used to remove the shaft of a screw whose head has snapped

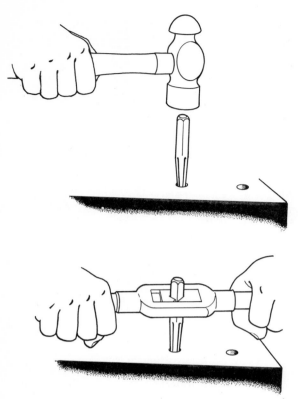

To use a stud extractor, drive it in (*top*); then, turn it with a tap wrench.

off. Often nothing is left sticking out that you can grab hold of. When that happens, whether it be a screw, a bolt, or a stud, you need a screw extractor. Center-punch the broken fastener as near to its center as you can. Then choose a drill bit slightly smaller than the solid portion of the fastener. Drill a hole that is deep enough to insert the extractor. Tap it in firmly with a hammer. Put a wrench — better yet, a machinist's tap wrench — on the square upper end of the extractor and turn. As you do, the fluted sides of the screw extractor bite hard into the hole.

Magnetic pickup tool. This is extremely useful for retrieving dropped nuts, bolts, and other parts from tight places.

Center punch. Use this tool to start the drill in the right spot when you drill through metal. It also is useful for upsetting, or deforming, threads to keep a nut from working loose. Once its threads have been deformed, a nut should not be reused when removed. Replace it with a new nut. The bolt probably should be replaced too.

Scraper. Similar to a putty knife but with a stiffer blade and a square-cut edge. Some are made like a wood chisel. Use a scraper to remove old gasket material before installing a new gasket. Every bit of the old gasket should be scraped from both mating surfaces. A putty knife will serve as a scraper, if necessary; or you can sacrifice an old wood chisel. Do not use a screwdriver. It may gouge machined surfaces.

Thickness gauges. Sometimes called feeler gauges, a set is comprised of thin strips of steel, each several thousandths of an inch thick. The thickness designation is etched on each strip. The strips are bound at one end so they fold out as needed. By sandwiching two or more thin strips, you can create any thickness from the thinnest strip — usually .002 inch — to the total thickness of all the strips. A handy size contains 15 blades from .002 to .025 inches. Some contain metric sizes, too. Thickness gauges are used for checking clearances on distributor points, and even for precision carburetor adjustments on some cars.

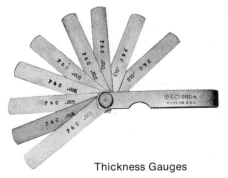

Thickness Gauges

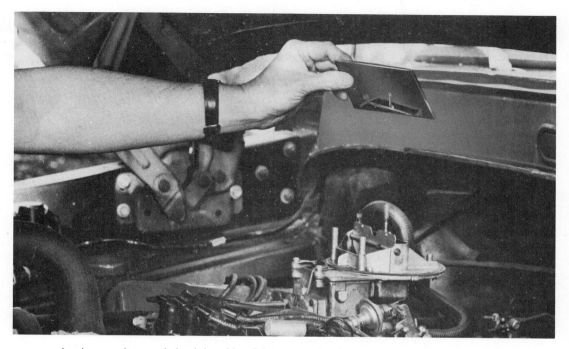

A mirror makes such back-breaking jobs as peering into a carburetor much simpler.

Mechanic's trouble light. This serves as both a light and an extension cord. The heavy-duty, oil-resistant cord that good trouble lights have should last for years. Replacement light bulbs should be the kind rated for rough service; ordinary bulb filaments cannot take punishment. Do not use a trouble light on a wet floor or around a wet car—the risk of shock is high. Likewise, never use one to run portable power tools that require three-wire grounding extensions. The two-wire, ungrounded trouble light receptacle leaves you unprotected.

Mirror. The ordinary kind that girls carry in their handbags makes an excellent auto repair tool. Use it to see into tight corners, like the bottom of the water pump, fuel pump, or carburetor float bowl. An old rear-view mirror will do.

Stethoscope. Doctors use stethoscopes to listen to the sounds of the body; mechanics use them to listen to the sounds of the engine and other automotive systems. A mechanic's stethoscope has a long steel prod instead of a disk-shaped listening device. The prod is touched to various parts of a running engine to listen for clicks, clunks, grinds, and other noises that indicate the condition of engine bearings, pistons, water pump, spark plugs, fuel pump, distributor, valve train, transmission, differential, wheel bearings, and other moving parts. A stethoscope does not cost much, and you can get one used.

Goggles. A wise safety measure whenever you work under a car is to wear goggles; they keep debris out of your eyes—especially when you turn or pound anything. Wear goggles, too, when using a grinder or when chiseling, to keep flying metal and abrasives out of your eyes.

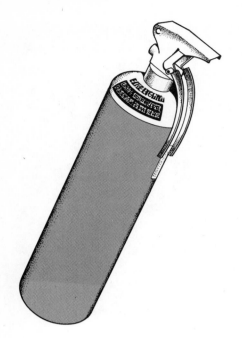

Every shop should have a dry-powder fire extinguisher, which is effective on most types of fires, including electrical.

Fire extinguisher. Mounted on the wall of your garage, an extinguisher is also worthwhile. Use the dry-powder type. The larger the extinguisher, the bigger the fire it can put out.

POWER TOOLS

Electric drill. A ¼- or ⅜-inch drill and a set of bits are indispensable to the auto mechanic. It is useful for removing rivets, installing accessories, refitting parts, removing broken bolts, and any number of projects. You need not buy an industrial-duty drill for home use, though the better home models have speed control triggers and are reversible.

Your set of *bits* may be in one of two types: numbered or fractional sizes. Numbered sizes run from No. 0 (large) to No. 60

(small). Probably better for your use is a set in fractional gradations from 1/16 to 1/4 or 3/8 inch. (The largest size depends on how big a bit your electric drill chuck can handle.)

Start the drill in a center punch mark to keep it from drifting off target. Small bits, such as the 1/16-inch, break easily if bent or if they catch while drilling.

Bench grinder. Another power tool you will find necessary. The most practical is the self-propelled type with a motor between its two ends. This allows you to put a medium-grit emery wheel on one shaft and a rotary wire brush on the other. Use the emery wheel for sharpening tools and general grinding, and the wire brush for cleaning parts such as spark plugs.

Impact wrench. This drives sockets and can tighten or loosen lugs or nuts effortlessly in a fraction of the time it takes by hand. An impact wrench is handy for rotating tires or when multiple nuts of the same size must be removed or installed, especially if the nuts are large and tight. For safety's sake, use an impact wrench only in a grounding electrical outlet with a three-pronged plug and receptacle.

FASTENERS

Most cars made in the United States use fasteners measured in fractions of an inch. The Ford Pinto, the Chevrolet Vega, and most imported cars, however, generally use metric fasteners, measured in millimeters.

The most-used automotive fastener is the threaded one: the nut, the bolt, the screw, and the stud. Nearly all threaded fasteners use right-hand threads; you turn right to tighten, left to loosen. A few are made left-handed because they are used to fasten a component (such as a wheel) that rotates. Left-hand threads make the normal rotation tend to tighten, rather than

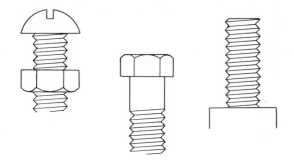

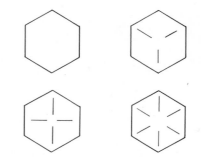

Common fasteners include the screw (*left*), the bolt (*center*), and the stud (*right*).

Bolt-head strength is signalled by the lines on it; the more lines, the stronger.

loosen, the fastener. Wheel lugs that have left-hand threads are usually marked with an "L" on the end of the stud.

Threaded fasteners are sized first by diameter of the threaded portion and next by the number of threads per inch. The more threads per inch, the finer the thread is said to be. Two finenesses are found on most U.S. cars; the coarser is used on most common nuts and bolts found in hardware stores while the finer is the SAE (Society of Automotive Engineers) thread. Keep a wide assortment of screws, nuts, and bolts in your workshop so you do not have to interrupt jobs with trips to the hardware or parts store.

Bolts and screws also are classified according to type of head. Bolt heads sometimes are marked with radial lines to indicate their strength. No marking means the bolt is of intermediate strength. Three lines mean it is of minimum commercial strength. Four or five lines indicate medium commercial strength and six lines tell you it is of the highest commercial strength. These markings indicate how hard you can tighten the bolt without breaking it. You may upgrade bolt quality during replacement, if you wish, but you should never replace a bolt with one of lower quality.

Screw fasteners. These are bolts without nuts; either self-tapped or threaded holes in the parts serve as the nuts. Such screws come with slotted, Phillips, hex, or other heads. Sometimes, a lockwasher under the head keeps the screw from loosening. Hex-headed screws often are called bolts even though they have no nuts.

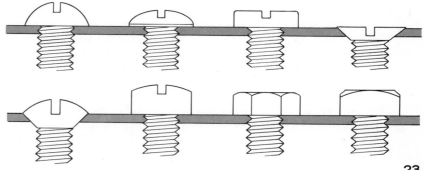

Screws come in a variety of heads to suit a variety of purposes.

23

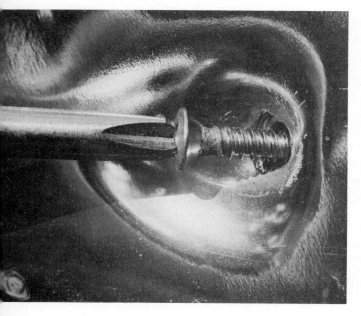

Sheet metal screws have special metal-grasping threads; on cars, they are used to secure moldings.

Sheet metal screws. Unlike ordinary wood screws, these taper only at the tip. The diameter of the rest of the threaded portion is constant. Sheet metal screws thread into drilled holes in sheet metal, creating their own threads. If the self-tapped holes become enlarged, a larger-diameter sheet metal screw often can be substituted.

Stud. A headless bolt, this may be made integrally with the part or threaded into it. A nut is installed to clamp the desired parts together. Studs and nuts are used, for example, to hold the carburetor to the intake manifold.

Lockwasher. Mounted between a nut and a bolt, it acts like a tiny spring, keeping tension on the assembly and preventing it from loosening.

Locknut. One type contains a ring of soft fiber that hugs the threads to resist turning except by wrench. Another form of lock-

nut consists of two nuts, one tightened on top of the other.

However, locknuts have one drawback: their action is not positive. Steering linkage and other critical spots for fasteners must have a more failsafe method of locking. One such method is with *castellated nuts*—nuts with slots in them resembling castle towers. A split, round metal pin called a cotter pin fits between two slots in the nut and through a hole in the bolt. The two halves of the pin are bent in opposite directions around the nut to lock it.

Whenever you remove fasteners with locking devices, replace them the same way they came off. Replace lost or broken lockwashers with ones of the same type and size. Cotter pins in critical locations, such as on front wheel bearing nuts and steering parts, always should be replaced with new cotter pins.

Cotter pins are used to secure nuts that, for safety reasons, must not loosen, such as on front wheel bearings (*below*) and on steering parts.

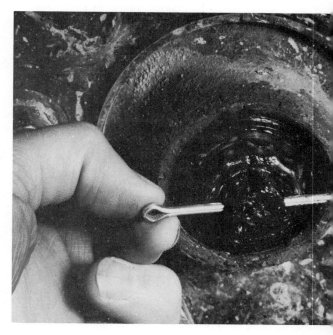

Rivet. The rivet is not a common automotive fastener. But if you ever have to undo one, drill it out. Rivets can be replaced most easily with pop-rivets; for this, you will need a pop-rivet tool and set of soft pop-rivets. Line up the hole, insert the rivet in the tool, push the end of the rivet all the way into the hole, and squeeze the tool handle. When tight, the rivet breaks off at the surface. Except for being hollow, a pop-rivet looks like a regular rivet.

Pop-rivet Gun

CHEMICAL TOOLS

Special-purpose lubricants, cleaners, cements, sealants, and other chemical products sometimes are every bit as useful as a screwdriver or a wrench. Such "tools" are sold by auto parts jobbers, chain stores, service stations, hardware stores, and mail order houses.

Chemical tools come in several forms. The cheapest way to buy is in bulk; most costly are the aerosols.

Motor oil. The oil that is used in the engine of your car is good for general lubrication of heavy moving parts, distributors, generators, hinges, and electric motors of over $\frac{1}{4}$ hp. Squirt the oil on and wipe off the excess.

Light machine oil. Also called household oil, it comes in applicator cans, aerosol sprays, drop-oilers, and in bulk. Use it on light moving parts, in motors of less than $\frac{1}{4}$ hp, and for rust-protection of tools and auto chrome. Apply it and work it in; then wipe off the excess. For rust-protection, spray it on lightly and spread it with a cloth.

A full array of chemical tools—lubricants, sealers, adhesives and cleaners—can make automotive maintenance and repair much easier.

Penetrating oil. Used for freeing rusted parts, especially nuts and bolts. You can also apply it as general light lubrication. It comes in applicator cans, aerosol sprays, drop-oilers, tubes, and bulk. Squirt penetrating oil onto the joint and tap to work in. The longer you let it penetrate, the better. Repeat the application, if necessary. Applying penetrating oil is a good night-before project for almost any car repair.

White grease. Also called lithium grease, this is used to lubricate sliding metal-to-metal parts such as hinges, bearings, slides, latches, linkages, and cables. White grease also protects against rust and corrosion. Apply the lube between moving parts and wipe off the excess in exposed locations. For corrosion protection, wipe on a thin coat. An advantage of white lube is that it will not wash away or dry out.

Stainless stick lube. Used for coating the exposed parts of door latches and strikers. Remove the cap and rub the stick over the contacting parts to leave a film of lubricant. Also known as door lube.

Moisture-displacing penetrating lube. Helps keep locks from freezing in cold weather. It is also good for cleaning moving parts and preventing rust on tools. And sprayed onto wet wiring, a wet coil or a wet distributor cap, it can quickly dry the component and enable the spark to get through—and the engine to start. To use moisture-displacing lubricant as a lube, shake the can and spray the parts. Sprayed

into a wet lock, it flushes out dirt and water and leaves the inside of the lock clean and lubricated.

Liquid locknut. Applied to threads before installing a nut or bolt, it hardens in an hour and holds the fastener in place—even when the nut is subjected to vibration. The fastener can still be removed when desired. This locknut comes in tubes.

Chemical hand-protector. Comes in a jar and works like liquid gloves. Apply it to your hands—especially under and around the fingernails, where grease tends to collect—before starting work. Rub until the chemical disappears. After the job is finished, wipe off excess dirt and wash away the hand-protector—and the remaining grime. The protection from grease, oil, and paint lasts three to four hours.

Hand-cleaner. This chemical helps remove dirt when you have not used hand-protector. Apply it to your hands and work it in thoroughly. Then wipe it off or rinse your hands in water. The cleaner takes off dirt, grease, oil, tar, gasket cement, rubber cement, and other materials. It comes in cans, tubes, and handy wall applicators.

Degreaser. Also called engine cleaner, it removes grease from engines, tools, concrete floors, and other surfaces. It comes in applicator cans and aerosols as well as in bulk. Before using it, scrape off heavy deposits. Spray degreaser liberally onto the warm engine or other surface and let it

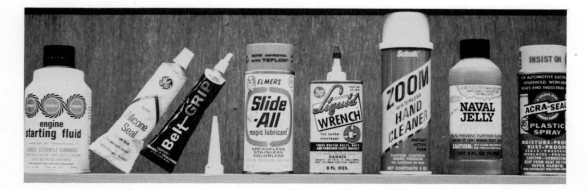

soak in—but not long enough to dry. Brush and scrape if necessary and then hose off with water. Do not get degreaser on your hands; it leaves them feeling like leather.

Gasket cement. Basic to engine repair, it forms a tight seal, filling irregularities in metal parts and preventing metal-to-metal contact. There are three types—adhesive, nonhardening, and hardening. *Adhesive* is most useful. Apply it to both of the cleaned mating surfaces, as well as to the gasket surfaces. Let it dry until tacky, and then position the gasket in place. Position it right the first time; once down it is tough to remove. Assemble the parts and bolt them together. *Nonhardening* gasket cement should be used only on metal surfaces, not on gaskets. New *gasket-in-a-tube* compound—there are several brands— may be used in place of gaskets and gasket cement. Follow directions on the package.

Trim cement. Also called weatherstrip adhesive, this material fastens weatherstripping, fabric, and insulation to metal. It also mends convertible tops and seals radiator hose joints. Apply to both cleaned mating surfaces, then press and hold the surface together for a few minutes.

Silicone rubber sealant. Real rubber in liquid form, silicone rubber sealant sets quickly and seals windshield, rear window, and firewall leaks permanently. It also beefs up shrunken weatherstripping. Available colors include clear, white, black and aluminum. Each tube comes

with a tapered plastic applicator spout. Apply a bead under the lip of the rubber windshield molding or along the desired surface and let it cure before closing the door or touching the bead.

Rubber lubricant. Makes rubber suspension parts work quieter and smoother. Use it around the beads of tires to ease mounting and dismounting. The chemical is also useful for cleaning rubber, vinyl, and leather. It comes in applicator cans. To lubricate cleaned rubber fittings, simply squirt it on. For cleaning, rub into a lather and wipe or flush off.

Belt lubricant. This substance quiets a squeaky fan belt or other automotive drive belt by preventing slippage. Put several drops of it onto the inside edges of the moving belt. It will be distributed in seconds and the belt noise should stop. Belt lubricant comes in tubes and sticks.

Powdered graphite. Whether the dry or the solvent type, this is best for lubricating locks. It comes in applicator cans and plastic squeeze bottles. Graphite also is good for manifold heat control valves and for making wheel lugs easy to remove.

Silicone lubricant. Best for lubricating sliding surfaces such as window channels, and for quieting squeaky weatherstripping on doors. Use it, too, to reduce corrosion on battery terminals. It is greaseless, stainless, and colorless and is not affected by solvents. It comes in tubes and aerosol

sprays. Spray a light film onto the clean, dry surface and work the moving parts. A white coating indicates that the application was too heavy. Brush off any excess.

Solvent cleaner. There are three types: carburetor cleaner, automatic choke cleaner, and PCV (positive crankcase ventilation) valve cleaner. The three are somewhat interchangeable, but for best results use the proper type. The cleaner comes in bulk, applicator cans, and aerosol sprays. To remove fuel and other deposits, spray the cleaner onto the part and work it in. For the PCV system, remove the valve from its hose or fitting and spray it liberally. Keep cleaning until the liquid comes out clear.

Naval jelly. Naval jelly comes in plastic bottles and is used to remove rust from tools, trim, and other metal surfaces. No scraping, sanding, or wire-brushing is necessary. Just brush the jelly liberally onto the rusted parts. Wait, and then rinse off with water. Protect the parts with oil to prevent further rusting.

Starting fluid. This fluid aids in starting an engine in very cold weather. Remove the air cleaner from the carburetor and spray the fluid into the carburetor throat while a helper tries to start the engine. Engage the starter in two-second bursts. If several bursts do not do the job, give up — letting too much chemical accumulate in the carburetor could cause an explosion. Do not breathe the fumes; starting fluid contains ether.

Ignition sealer. Used to waterproof high-voltage ignition components; once the sealer is properly applied, you can drench a running engine with water from a garden hose without causing the engine to stall or misfire. Ignition sealer comes in applicator bottles and aerosol sprays. Spray a fine mist onto the cleaned ignition wiring, coil, and distributor cap. Ignition sealer also protects chrome trim.

Gas and oil leak-sealer. It works from the outside, so draining the tank is not necessary. It comes in stick form; simply rub it vigorously over the leak.

Exhaust system sealer. This compound seals exhaust pipe, muffler, and tailpipe joints. It comes in tubes. Apply a thin layer to about one inch of surface on both the male and female parts of the joint. Then assemble the parts and clamp.

Speedometer cable lubricant. As its name implies, this lubricant is designed especially for speedometer cables. It comes in dispenser containers. To use it, disconnect the speedometer cable at the speedometer by unscrewing the retainer ring and pulling the housing and cable free. Puncture the dispenser and let the whole container of lubricant flow down into the speedometer cable housing between the cable and housing. Replace the housing, inserting the cable into its recess in the speedometer. Snug the retainer ring finger-tight.

GARAGE TOOLS

Garage tools do not differ much from mechanic's tools, but in professional auto service they usually are furnished by the garage. That is why we list them separately.

Bench vise. A basic mechanic's tool, the bench vise should be attached firmly to the workbench. Get a vise with a swiveling, locking base and with soft metal jaw attachments so parts held in the vise will not be scarred. A 4-inch jaw is best for the home mechanic.

Jack stands. At least two are essential when you must raise a car and work underneath. Do not substitute stones or blocks

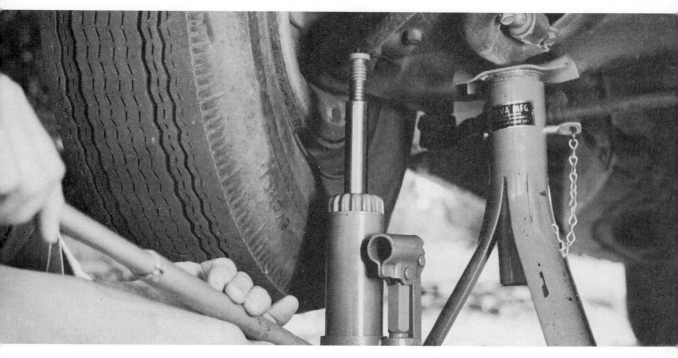

Ideal jacking: use a 1½-ton hydraulic jack (*left*) to lift the vehicle, then position a jack stand (*right*) to firmly support the car.

Wheel ramps are a more convenient way to raise the car—you just drive onto them. But they are useless for any job in which the wheels must hang free.

With a set of creeper wheels, a plywood board and several strips of wood, you can make your own garage creeper.

under the wheels; they can break or slip out, allowing the car to drop and crush you. Even worse is trusting a jack alone; jacks can slip or let go. To use a jack stand, jack up the car to the height you want it. Then raise the telescoping jack stand post and lock it at a point where it will fit under the frame or axle of the car. Never jack or block under the center of the rear axle; the axle may bend. Rear axle jacking and blocking should not be done inboard of the point where the springs are attached. Front axle jacking should be done at the heavy frame crossmember between the front wheels. (That raises the whole front end of the car.) Or, to raise just one side, jack under a heavy part of the lower suspension arm on that side. Block there, too.

Most standard-equipment jacks are inadequate for regular service work and quickly wear out. A *1½-ton hydraulic jack,* if correctly positioned, is less likely to slip than a common bumper jack. This machine is quite inexpensive.

Wheel ramps. A pair of wheel ramps can substitute for jack stands when the car must be raised but access to the wheels is not required. Ramps cost more than wheel stands, but they save time since the car can be driven onto them without jacking.

Garage creeper. Simply a board on casters, this device makes it easy to slide under a raised car. To change your position, push against the floor with your heels or pull on the undercarriage with your hands. You can make your own creeper by buying a set of creeper casters and mounting them on a plywood base. But if you do not have a paved garage floor, forget the creeper; lie on a sheet of plywood or hardboard instead.

CHECKLIST OF TOOLS
(metric sizes also may be needed)

Hand Tools

Screwdrivers—3″, 6″, 10″
Phillips screwdriver—No. 2
Slip-joint pliers—6″, 10″
Long-nose pliers
Socket wrench, 1/2″ drive—7/16, 1/2, 9/16, 5/8, 11/16, 3/4 standard-length double-hex sockets;
  1/2, 5/8 standard-length double-square sockets;
  Ratchet handle; Hinged offset handle, 4″ extension; Speeder handle.
Socket wrench, 1/4″ drive—1/8, 5/32, 3/16, 7/32, 1/4, 9/32, 5/16, 11/32, 3/8, 7/16 standard-length single-hex sockets;
  1/4, 5/16, 3/8 standard-length double-square sockets;
  Hinged offset handle, 2″ extension.
Spark plug socket—13/16″ (for most cars)
Torque wrench, 1/2″ drive—0-100 ft/lbs.
Combination open-end/box-end wrenches—1/4, 5/16, 3/8, 7/16, 1/2, 9/16, 5/8, 11/16, 3/4
Adjustable open-end wrench—6″, 12″
Allen wrenches—set of 13, 0.50″ to 3/8″
Pipe wrench—8″
Locking plier/wrenches—10″, 6″
Ball peen hammer—12 oz.
Rule—6″
Hacksaw—32-tooth, 24-tooth blades
Cold chisel—1/2″
Files—8″ mill, 3-cornered, round
Nut-cracker
Screw extractors, set of four, No. 2 - No. 5
Magnetic pick-up tool
Center punch
Scraper
Thickness gauges—set of 15, 0.002″ to 0.025″
Trouble light
Mirror
Stethoscope
Goggles
Fire extinguisher—dry type

Power Tools

Electric drill—1/4″ or 3/8″;
  Bits from 1/16″ to 1/4″ or 3/8″
Bench grinder—with emery wheel and wire brush

Fasteners

An assortment of common fasteners—screws, nuts and bolts

Chemical Tools

Motor oil
Light machine oil
Penetrating oil
White grease
Stainless stick lube
Moisture-displacing penetrating lube
Liquid locknut
Hand-protector
Hand-cleaner
Degreaser
Gasket cement
Trim cement
Silicone rubber sealant
Rubber lubricant
Belt lubricant
Silicone lubricant
Fuel cleaner
Naval jelly
Starting fluid
Ignition sealer
Gas and oil leak-sealer
Exhaust system sealer
Speedometer cable lubricant

Garage Tools

Bench vise—4″ jaws
Jack stands—two
1 1/2-ton hydraulic jack
Wheel ramps—two
Creeper
Fender cover

3

Engine Tuning: An Introduction

Every engine needs a regular tune-up. Otherwise it will waste precious gallons of fuel. Besides that it may run roughly, be hard to start, and give off smog-producing emissions. A well tuned engine lasts longer, too.

Most car makers call for a complete tune-up every 10,000 to 12,000 miles, or once a year. The sensible time to do it is in the fall, while the weather is still pleasant and before you have any cold-weather starting problems.

Even if you perform tune-ups regularly, you may want to make periodic spot checks to see that everything is up to specifications. One good time for this is just before taking a long trip with your car. During such a check, you do not clean, adjust, or replace anything unless the check shows it is necessary. When you do a tune-up, though, do a complete one. If you do not check every system, you cannot be sure your engine is operating at its best. Every automobile engine has five basic systems:

breathing, fuel, ignition, starting, and charging. All five are covered in the following chapters.

Equipment

The modern auto engine is complex; the more equipment you have, the more types of jobs you can tackle.

If you enjoy working with good equipment, you may want to set up your own engine-care clinic. That could cost $500 or more, but you could do tune-ups on neighbors' and friends' cars to help you pay for the equipment.

(Local zoning may prevent you from doing tune-ups for others in your home garage. Check. Maybe the zoning ordinances merely prevent you from putting up a sign. Also check into whether you need a license to do automotive work for others. No local law should prevent you from working on your own car, however.)

For an ideal home engine-care clinic you will need the following, listed in order of importance: thickness gauges; spark plug cleaning tool; spark plug socket; distributor point file; vacuum gauge; compression tester; battery hydrometer; battery charger; tachometer-dwell meter; electronic distributor tester (or a timing light, which is considerably less expensive); ignition oscilloscope; high tension pliers; battery-starter tester; exhaust gas analyzer; alternator-generator-regulator tester; battery post switch; remote starter button; alternator-generator unit.

Many top manufacturers of testing equipment for professional mechanics also produce smaller, lower-priced units for home garage use. The big professional testers can take more punishment and serve a number of different voltages. Less expensive models may be acceptable for occasional use; but never buy cheap, low-quality testers.

To save money, you might consider combination testers, which perform several tests that normally require a number of different units. For instance, you can buy an ignition analyzer that is supposed to do much of the work of the ignition oscilloscope, the tach-dwell tester, the battery-starter tester, and the generator-alternator-regulator testers. But for operating a real engine-care clinic, we advise against most such combination instruments. You can do a quicker and better job with the individual units. The only possible exception is a volt-ammeter combination for checking the starting system and charging system; it could substitute nicely for the battery-starter tester and generator-alternator-regulator tester, both of which are volt-ammeters. Although a battery post switch is not a necessity, it simplifies hooking up the tester for generator-alternator use. We recommend it as a great time-saver.

Be careful to avoid duplication. For instance, some ignition tach-dwell units

Full complement of testers can cost some $550, but you can perform good tune-ups with just some of these instruments and tools.

include a provision for testing ignition output, but the oscilloscope does that job better. You probably would not want both.

An important word of warning: In several states, anyone who performs tune-up services on an engine equipped with an exhaust emission device must be authorized or licensed by the state. All cars since 1968 — and some earlier models — have such devices. If your state is one of these and your car has an exhaust emission control system, take your car to an authorized shop for all tune-up work to stay within the law.

Before using your new testers, get thoroughly acquainted with them, Read the instructions that come with each one. Often they give interesting side-checks you can make. Such checks may not be needed every tune-up, but they could be helpful in fixing your engine or learning more about it.

Keep the equipment looking new by coating the cases periodically with auto wax. Clean dirty test leads with waterless soap or solvent. Never use gasoline to clean equipment. It is hard on the rubber and removes the protective antistatic coating from the instrument windows. For accurate test results, see that all pointers return to zero when the tester switches are turned off.

Minimum Equipment

If engine-tuning is to be only an occasional pursuit, you may want to do it with simpler, less-costly equipment. However, you cannot do as complete a job that way. For example, without a volt-ammeter, you will not be able to check your charging system. The instrument panel indicator light is not much help; all it tells is whether or not the charging system is charging, not how much.

Minimum equipment and tools for a tune-up include: a compression tester; an ignition timing light; thickness gauges; a battery hydrometer; a spark plug socket; a spark plug cleaning and gapping tool; a distributor point file; and various basic mechanic's tools. All of these can be bought for less than a total of $20 (not including the basic tools).

With this limited equipment, special problems (such as a weak ignition coil, an out-of-adjustment generator regulator, or a shorted spark plug wire) may be impossible to diagnose. Still, you can perform ordinary tune-ups and take special problems to a shop.

Minimum tune-up equipment includes: 1) ignition timing light; 2) spark plug socket; 3) point file; 4) thickness gauges; 5) battery hydrometer; 6) spark plug cleaning-gapping tool; 7) compression tester.

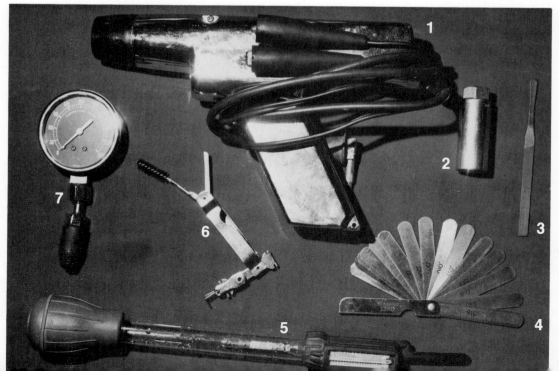

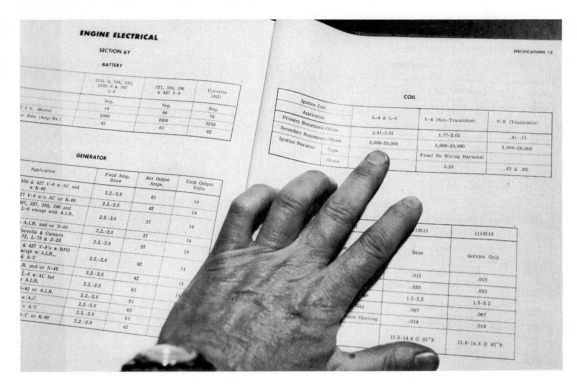

Specifications for the various tune-ups are found in your car's service manual, which should be available from the dealer.

Factory Specifications

To do a tune-up, you will also need the automobile manufacturer's specifications on test items such as engine compression, ignition timing, distributor-point dwell, charging voltage, and more. Using "average" specifications for those would make as much sense as buying a pair of average-sized shoes.

Some specifications are listed in the owner's manual that comes with the car. Others can be gotten from any large auto repair manual, such as "Motor's," "Chilton's," or "Glenn's." Almost every library has one of those. The ultimate source for specifications is the manufacturer's service or maintenance manual (also known as the shop manual) for your car. You can buy a copy from your dealer.

Tune-up Procedures

The entire tune-up procedure may take you a whole weekend the first time you go through it. When you become familiar with the engine, the equipment, and the procedure, you should be able to complete an average tune-up in about two hours. Often an entire system can be okayed with one simple tester hookup. That lets you skip the more detailed hookups that are necessary to pin-point problems. For example, you may not need to check the charging system if the battery is found to be properly charged.

Tune-up tasks should be done in a logical sequence. For example, adjusting the carburetor idle is useless until you complete all your ignition system adjustments, since ignition corrections may affect idle

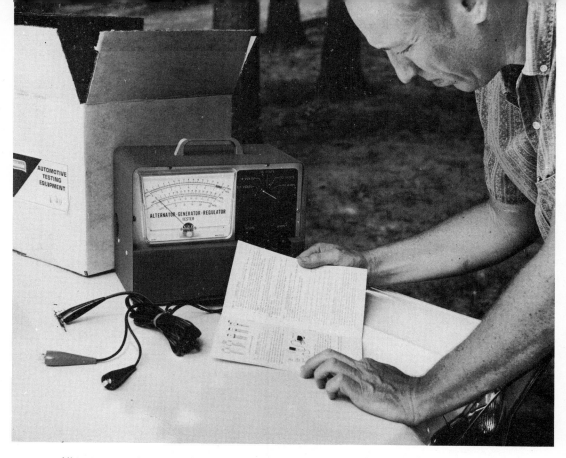

All testers—such as this charging system instrument—come with instructions. Familiarize yourself with each tester before you use it.

speed. The following is a logical procedure for the complete tune-up: 1. compression; 2. spark plugs; 3. manifold vacuum; 4. ignition dwell; 5. ignition power series; 6. ignition timing; 7. carburetion; 8. antipollution system; 9. battery; 10. starting system; 11. charging system. Specific instructions for making the various tests and corrections follow in later chapters.

4

Engine Tuning: Compression

An automobile engine must breathe properly to develop full power and efficiency. Most engine breathing problems involve major repairs — some possibly too costly to warrant keeping the car. Repairs to breathing must be made before tuning the other, easier-to-repair engine systems. Two easy checks for proper engine breathing include a compression test and a vacuum test. Both require simple, inexpensive equipment. This chapter deals with the compression test.

Before that test, however, some basic engine theory:

Nearly all automobile engines operate on what is called the four-stroke cycle. The strokes are intake, compression, power, and exhaust.

A piston moves up and down in each cylinder, with three or four piston rings pressing against the walls of the cylinder to keep gases from leaking past. The piston is attached to the rotating engine crankshaft by a connecting rod. The connecting rod simply converts the back-and-forth (reciprocating) motion of the piston into rotary motion. At the top of the cylinder is the combustion chamber, which is closed except for two valves, intake and exhaust. The valves control the flow of gases. A spark plug ignites the combustible fuel/air mixture at the right instant to produce an "explosion." Power is derived from the force generated by the burning gases.

The *intake stroke* begins with the piston at the top of its travel. As the piston moves downward, it creates low pressure, or partial vacuum, in the cylinder. Outside air pressure forces fuel/air mixture in through the open intake valve.

The *compression stroke* begins with the piston reversing and moving upward, with the intake and exhaust valves closed. The piston thus forces the fuel/air mixture up into the combustion chamber, compressing the mixture to the pressure designed by the engine manufacturer.

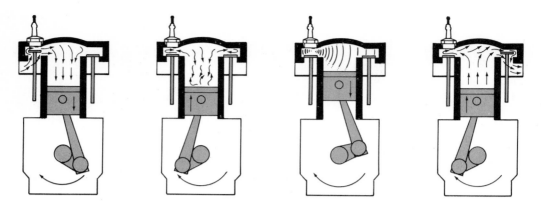

Four-stroke cycle (*left to right*): intake draws in fuel and air; compression pressurizes the mix; power ignites the mix; and exhaust vents the gases.

The *power stroke* is the one that actually moves the car. As the piston nears the top of its stroke, a spark jumps the gap in the spark plug and ignites the compressed charge. The burning fuel/air mixture expands, increasing the compression pressure and pushing the piston down. Power developed is transmitted to the crankshaft, through the transmission, driveshaft, and differential and on to the wheels.

The *exhaust stroke* begins as the piston moves upward again and the exhaust valve opens. The piston forces the burned gases out of the cylinder and into the exhaust system.

The four-stroke cycle is repeated over a thousand times a minute at highway driving speeds. Each cylinder is at a different stage of its four-stroke cycle, resulting in a smooth flow of power.

For the engine to develop full power, it must meet the manufacturer's specifications for compression. The cylinder should have no leakage. Leakage can occur past the piston rings, past the intake or exhaust valves, and past the cylinder head gasket. An engine with leakage in one or more cylinders may idle roughly because of its uneven power strokes. It also will suffer a reduction in power and fuel economy.

Severe leakage past the piston rings can allow oil to get into the combustion chamber and foul the spark plugs.

Testing Compression

Testing compression is the first step in tuning the engine. You need a compression tester—simply a pressure gauge or barometer—to measure combustion chamber pressures through the spark plug openings.

To test compression, run the engine until it reaches normal operating temperature. Turn the engine off. Remove the spark plug wires from the plugs. (First number each wire with a bit of masking tape so you can replace the wires in the proper order.) The spark plugs are located at the ends of the heavily insulated spark cables (four, six, or eight depending on number of cylinders). Remove them properly by twisting the rubber boots and pulling at the same time. If you simply pull on the wire, you may break the delicate carbon track conductor inside. If a conductor breaks, it greatly hampers the flow of electricity to the spark plug.

With the wires off, slip a spark plug socket wrench over each plug and loosen it one turn. Socket accessories may be

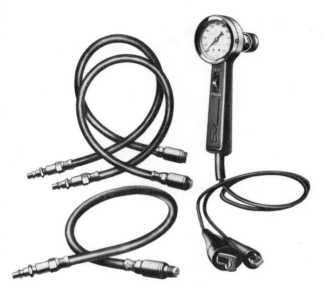

Good quality compression tester has several adapter hoses (*left*) and a remote starter.

useful if your plugs are hard to reach. A hinged, offset handle, teamed with a short extension and spark plug socket, work well on most engines. Avoid twisting the socket sideways; this puts pressure on the brittle ceramic insulation of the plug.

Replace the cables on the loosened spark plugs, start the engine, and run it at a fast idle to blow out any loosened carbon from around the plug bases. (If allowed to remain in the cylinders, carbon particles might lodge under a valve seat and give a false, low compression reading.) Then switch off the engine, remove the spark plug cables again, and remove the plugs. All spark plugs should be out when you test compression. Otherwise the reading will not be accurate unless the throttle is held open. (*text continued on page 44*)

Spark Plug Removal and Installation

1. Gently wiggle off the rubber boot that covers each plug; never yank on the cable.

2. Clean the recess before you remove the spark plug; this keeps dirt out of cylinders.

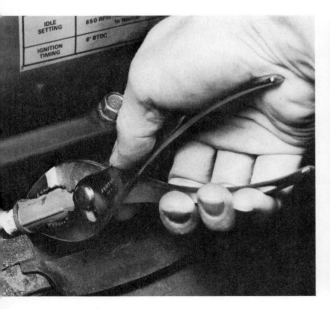

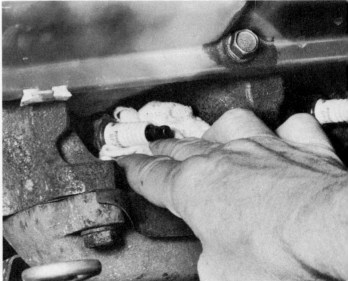

3. To speed spark plug removal, team a cushioned spark plug socket (*right*) with a ratcheting handle (*below*).

4. Keep the removed plugs in the correct order with some type of holder.

42

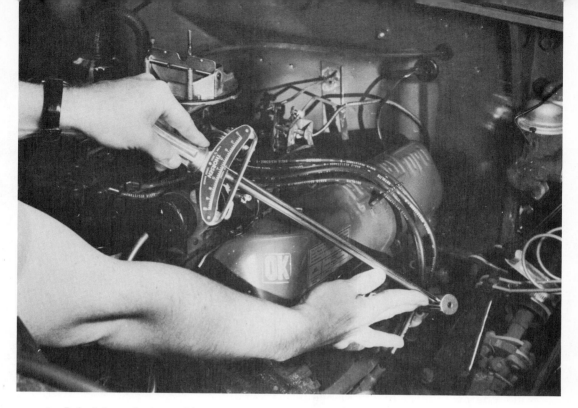

5. Install spark plugs with a torque wrench or a ½-inch-drive ratchet wrench; with the latter, do not overtighten.

6. Finish the installation by wiggling the rubber boot back on. Make sure that each boot is completely seated.

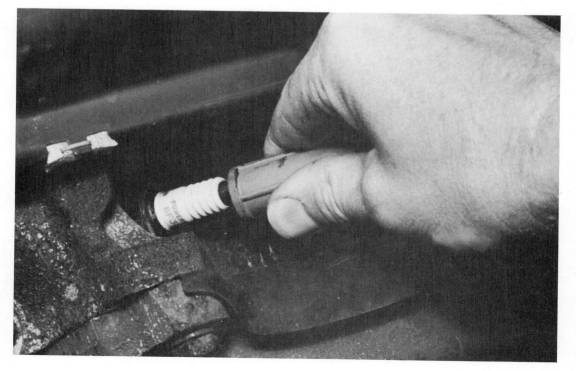

The high-tension lead between the coil and distributor should be grounded during the test. It is easy to find, even if you are not familiar with it. Trace back along the spark plug wires to where they all converge, at the distributor cap. The high-tension cable emerging from the center of the distributor cap is the coil lead. Pull it out and touch its metal tip to some clean metal part of the engine. Grounding the coil protects you from getting a shock if your hand should touch a spark plug lead, and it protects the insulation of the coil from possible damage by high voltage build-up.

Some compression testers are held by hand in the plug opening. Others screw in. If the plug openings are easily accessible, almost any tester will work. If they are located at the bottoms of tubes, as on some Chrysler engines, you need an adaptable tester.

If your compression tester has adapters that fit into the spark plug holes, thread the proper adapter into the first or front spark plug on an in-line engine and work your way back. On a V-engine, do the left front cylinder first and work your way back along the left cylinder bank. Then test the cylinders on the right side of the car, from front to back.

Check that the parking brake is on and the transmission is in neutral or park. If your compression tester has a remote-control switch to crank the engine, use it. The tester clips should be connected to the positive battery post and to the small terminal on the starter solenoid. (The positive battery post is larger than the negative one, and sometimes it is marked with a "+" symbol.) To find the solenoid, follow the battery cable leading from the positive battery post; it leads to the solenoid.

Lacking a remote control, have a helper work the starter switch for you. Be sure,

Connect the compression tester and crank the engine through four compression strokes; the pressure reading should rise quickly.

before each cranking, that all parts of your body and clothing are clear of the fan, pulleys, and belts. Crank until four full compression strokes have passed the tester. A valve inside the tester holds the compression until you read and release.

Repeat the compression test on all cylinders, recording the readings.

Interpreting the Readings

If the fourth-stroke readings for all cylinders are within the specified range for your car and they do not vary by more than the specified amount, compression is all right. Suppose the compression pressure for your engine is specified at 125 to 155 pounds per square inch (psi) with a maximum variation between cylinders of 25 psi. If your compression readings came out like the following, you would have an engine in good breathing condition and worthy of the best tune-up you can give:

Cylinder #1 – 135 psi   #5 – 135 psi
      #2 – 130 psi   #6 – 135 psi
      #3 – 130 psi   #7 – 140 psi
      #4 – 135 psi   #8 – 130 psi

All cylinders rate close to each other, and none is as low as the minimum specified pressure.

But you would know you had serious breathing problems in the engine if the readings went as follows:

Cylinder #1 – 155 psi   #5 – 155 psi
      #2 – 125 psi   #6 – 155 psi
      #3 – 150 psi   #7 – 150 psi
      #4 – 155 psi   #8 – 150 psi

While the number two cylinder is not below the specified pressure, it is below the permissible range of pressures. Something is wrong with its breathing.

Here is another example of an engine that would flunk its compression test:

Cylinder #1 – 130 psi   #5 – 125 psi
      #2 – 115 psi   #6 – 130 psi
      #3 – 130 psi   #7 – 125 psi
      #4 – 120 psi   #8 – 125 psi

In this case the variations between cylinders are within the tolerance range, but two cylinders, numbers two and four, fall below the minimum specified pressure. Chances are the engine is pretty well along in miles and needs major work.

Reading compression as it builds can tell you something about what repairs an engine needs. Compression that is low on the first stroke and builds up on the following strokes, but never reaches normal, tends to indicate piston ring leakage. To double-check, squirt a tablespoon of motor oil into the cylinder through the spark plug opening, crank several times to spread the oil, and test again. Oil seals the piston rings. A much higher second read-

Perform the test on all cylinders and record the readings. Compare these figures against each other and against specifications.

ing confirms piston ring trouble.

Compression that is low on the first stroke and stays low spells valve leakage. The reading will not change much when tested with oil in the cylinder.

If you get low readings on two adjacent cylinders, suspect cylinder head gasket leakage between the two.

Pressure readings much higher than specified point to carbon buildup in the cylinders. That reduces the effective volume of the cylinders, making the mixture compress into a smaller space than it is supposed to. That condition is harmful to the engine and should be taken care of by removing the head and scraping away the carbon deposits.

Any compression deficiencies must be corrected before you can do a successful tune-up. It is not a job for the average do-it-yourselfer. Take your readings with you to the shop so you can tell the repairman what is wrong and where.

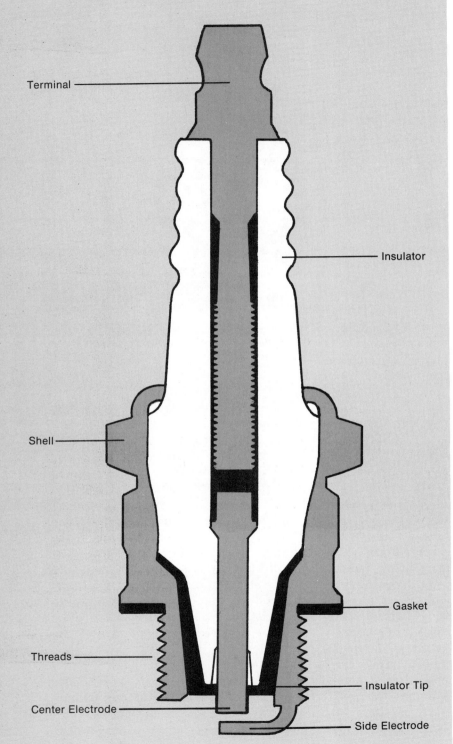

Terminal

Insulator

5

Shell

Gasket

Threads

Insulator Tip

Center Electrode

Side Electrode

Engine Tuning: Spark Plugs

While the spark plugs are out for a compression test, you should examine them closely. Spark plugs to a large extent determine how smoothly the car runs at low speeds in traffic, how quickly it accelerates, and how well it runs at high speeds on the freeway. If just one spark plug in a V-8 engine misfires half the time, at 50 mph it wastes some 7 percent of your fuel. That means that a car that normally gets 12 mpg will drop to 11 mpg because of the misfiring plug.

Spark plugs perform two vital functions in an engine. They conduct high-tension electricity created in the ignition system to the insides of the combustion chambers. And they provide a pair of spaced electrodes that the electric current can jump across to ignite the air/fuel mixture. The spark plug does not create the spark, it only provides a place for the spark to occur.

Voltage, in electricity, is like pressure in water. It's a measure of how much push there is. In order to fire, a spark plug must be supplied a certain minimum electrical voltage, called the plug's firing voltage. Firing voltage varies with plug design, how clean it is, how worn it is, combustion chamber temperature, how much load the engine is under, and how much fuel is mixed with the air. When the engine is under a full-throttle load, firing voltage goes way up. When your foot is off the accelerator pedal, firing voltage goes way down. It can vary from about 4000 to 18,000 volts. If the firing voltage is higher than available voltage that is being produced by the rest of the ignition system, the plug will misfire. It is like trying to squirt a stream of water across your yard. If the water pressure is too low, you just cannot do it.

In a modern engine, available voltage should be about 20,000 volts to prevent misfiring. Below 18,000 volts, the spark plugs will begin to misfire under maximum load conditions such as full-bore acceleration. The plugs usually get the blame, but more often a weak ignition system with low available voltage is the culprit. Installing new spark plugs may eliminate the misfiring for a while; the new plugs require less firing voltage simply because they are clean and new. Eventually, however, the new plugs become worn and dirty, and their firing voltage increases above the available voltage. Then, they too misfire.

Some mechanics say you should clean your car's spark plugs at 5000 miles and replace them at 10,000 miles. Most mechanics, however, feel that cleaning or replacing only when necessary makes better sense. How long a set of plugs lasts depends on the quality of the plugs, the condition of the engine, and the type of driving. Some spark plugs won't last 5000 miles. Others have gone more than 40,000 miles. If your old plugs can be cleaned and gapped to work satisfactorily, you stand to save more than a dollar apiece.

SPARK PLUG IGNITION

Ignition of the air/fuel charge may occur in one of three ways.

Normal ignition, in which a correctly timed spark jumps across the gap and sets off the charge, gives maximum engine power and economy.

Tracking ignition occurs when the spark jumps from one "island" of spark plug deposit to another along the spark plug insulator tip and ignites the fuel charge at some point along the way. While the charge does not actually misfire, the effect is to retard ignition timing. Engine power and gas economy are lost, probably without the driver realizing it.

Preignition occurs when a surface inside the combustion chamber gets hot enough to ignite the fuel charge even without a spark. The source of preignition may be

Types of spark plug ignition: normal (*left*), in which sparking occurs at the gap; tracking (*center*), in which sparking occurs within the plug; and preignition (*right*), in which there is no sparking.

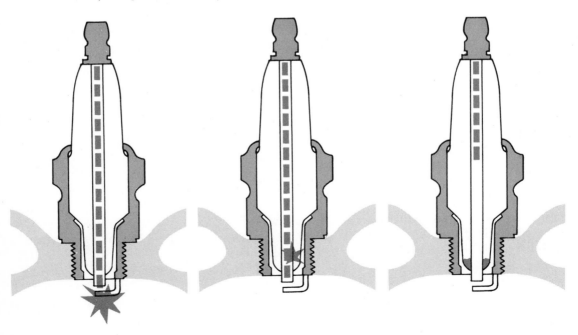

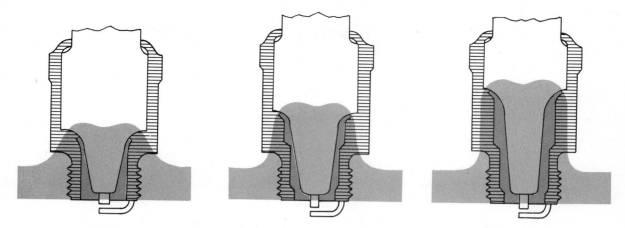

Heat range of a plug refers to the distance that heat must travel from the sparking tip to a cooling medium. The spark plugs above are, from left to right, called "cold," "normal" and "hot."

an overheated spark plug, a red-hot valve, or glowing carbon deposits. Depending on how severe preignition is, the driver may or may not be aware of the problem. When preignition gets so bad that the entire air/fuel charge actually explodes at once, it is called detonation. When you can hear it, detonation sounds like marbles dropping into an empty coffee can. Preignition causes loss of power and performance. Detonation can ruin the engine in a hurry.

SPARK PLUG CHARACTERISTICS

Spark plugs must be the right type for the engine and for the kind of driving you do. They should run reasonably hot at low speeds to burn off deposits and keep from fouling; yet, they should run cool enough at high engine speeds to keep from overheating and causing preignition. The effective firing temperature range is from 750 to 1750 degrees, the temperature at which preignition begins.

To suit different engines and varying types of driving, spark plugs are made in different *heat ranges*. Heat range has nothing to do with how hot a spark is given off. A spark plug's heat range refers to its ability to transfer heat from the super-hot firing tip of its insulator to the spark plug seat on the engine, and then to the engine's cooling system. The rate of heat transfer is controlled mostly by the distance that heat has to travel from tip to cooling medium. A spark plug with extra short heat travel distance is called a cold plug. A spark plug with an extra long heat travel distance is called a hot plug. In-between plugs are termed normal.

Cold plugs are best used for continuous, high-speed operation. Racing cars often use cold plugs. Hot plugs are used for short-trip driving with lots of idling. They burn off combustion deposits that might tend to foul them. Normal heat range plugs are used for average driving at both slow and fast speeds. A salesman whose car is on the road at highway speeds much of the time might require cold plugs for his car's engine. A commuter who drives two miles to the train station, parks all day, and then drives two miles home might need hot plugs. Most of us get the best service from normal heat-range plugs. Switch plugs only if the normal ones do not give proper performance.

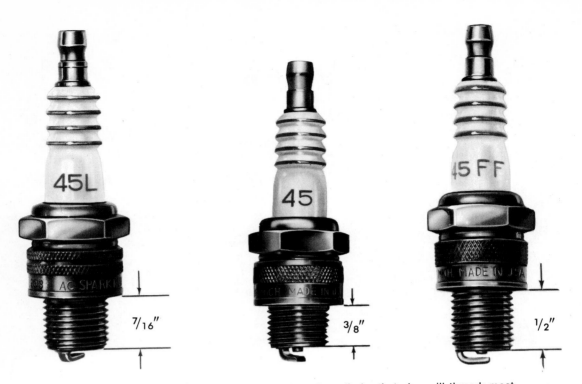

Reach of a spark plug determines how far into the cylinder that plug will thread; most American cars take plugs with a ⅜-inch reach.

Car manufacturers usually specify the spark plug that is normal for the engine. U.S.-made plugs use heat range number designations. Low numbers refer to cold plugs, high numbers to hot plugs.

If spark plugs are of the wrong type or are in poor condition, the compressed air/fuel mixture is not ignited efficiently. Then, only part of the fuel goes into creating power. The rest runs out through the exhaust system or past the piston rings where it dilutes oil in the crankcase.

The *reach* of a plug is as important as its size and heat range. Reach refers to distance from the tip of the threads to their base and is the distance the plug reaches into the cylinder. A plug that does not enter the cylinder far enough will not give efficient ignition. If the plug reaches into the cylinder too far, it may be struck by the piston or valve during engine operation. Most U.S. cars use ⅜-inch-reach plugs.

You need not use the recommended brand plugs. To switch, you merely consult a spark plug conversion chart. Stores that sell plugs will look up the proper plug number for you, once you give them your engine's specifications. For example, the normal heat-range plug for a recent Ford Maverick, according to the owner's manual, is the Autolite BF-82. According to the conversion charts, you can substitute a Champion F-14Y or UF-14Y, an AC 85TS, or a Prestolite 18F82.

The conversion charts, unlike the owner's manuals, also show hotter and colder heat ranges available. One-step-colder plugs include the Autolite BF-42, the Champion F-11Y, the AC 84TS, and Prestolite 18F42.

Finally, the spark must be of the proper length to fire the mixture efficiently at various engine speeds; this is controlled by the width of the *spark plug gap*. If the gap is too narrow, the engine may run roughly at idle and at low engine speeds. If the gap is too wide, the spark may not be able to leap across, particularly under full throttle, and the engine will misfire. The best gap width is a compromise between idle and high-speed, full-load operation, determined for each engine by the car manufacturer. Gaps should be adjusted at each spark plug servicing.

A round wire gauge does a more accurate job of gapping than a flat thickness gauge. Bend the flat side electrode to adjust the gap. Never bend the round center one; you may crack the brittle insulator tip surrounding it. Do your bending with the notched bar on the cleaning-and-gapping tool, never with pliers or by hitting the plug on a hard surface. Spark gaps should be adjusted so that the right-thickness wire drags a little as you snap it through.

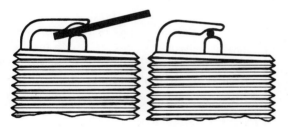

Check spark plug gap with a round wire gauge. As you pull the wire through, there should be a slight resistance.

Most cars built today use spark gaps of .030 to .035 inches. The factory generally gaps new plugs within that range. If your car requires a different gap, you will have to reset the gaps on new plugs before you install them. It is wise to check the gaps anyway.

A note: All spark ignition engines radiate radio frequency (RF) energy into the atmosphere. The intensity of the RF radiations depends on the quality of the ignition systems and the degree of RF sup-

pression built into them. Engines with defective wiring, solid-wire spark cables, or nonresistor spark plugs give off RF radiation serious enough to interfere with nearby radio, TV, and other electronic reception. The car's own radio is also affected. The Federal Communications Commission requires some type of RF suppression in all auto engines. Modern car engines have carbon track resistance inside the insulation of the wiring. Some cars count on resistor spark plugs to help with the job. If your car manufacturer specifies resistor plugs, replacing with nonresistor plugs will unbalance your ignition system. Resistor plugs also are less likely to foul and misfire. They can be used on any engine.

SPARK PLUG PROBLEMS

Misfire of the charge can occur with any of the following:

• When spark plug electrodes are gapped or worn so badly that they are too far apart, available voltage may not be sufficient to fire them. Cleaning and regapping or replacing the plug is called for.

• When combustion deposits have bridged the gap between electrodes so that the voltage is drained away without creating a spark, the plug misfires. A bridged plug usually can be cleaned. A resistor spark plug fights off such misfiring longer than a standard plug. If misfire plagues you, switch to resistors. Each contains a 10,000-ohm resistance inside the plug, which allows firing voltage to be built up before ignition "oomph" has been sapped.

• Dirt or moisture on the insulator or boot of the plug can cause the spark to shoot over the outside surface of the insulator instead of jumping the gap inside the plug. Called flashover, that condition makes the plug misfire. Wiping the insulator clean and drying it are the cures.

Misfiring of spark plugs can occur in five common ways:
1. Gap too wide—no spark;
2. Dirty electrodes—no spark;
3. Dirty insulator or spark plug boot—spark occurs outside;
4. Cracked insulator— spark short-circuits;
5. Cracked insulator tip— no spark.

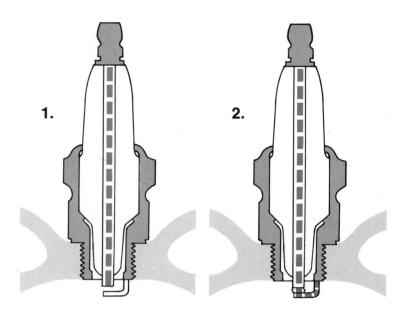

• High voltage may short-circuit through a crack in the insulator of a spark plug and fail to produce a spark across the gap. Such a plug must be replaced. Most cracks in plugs occur during removal or installation. Buy a cushioned, deep spark plug socket wrench to help prevent breakage.

• Electrically conductive deposits on the insulator tip surface inside the plug will drain away voltage and make the plug misfire. The fix is cleaning or replacement.

Inspect your car's spark plugs as you perform a compression test. Lay them out on the bench corresponding to their positions in the engine; then, if a compression problem is spotted in one cylinder, you can easily pinpoint the spark plug involved.

A visual check of the spark plugs can tell you a great deal about engine conditions. For example, a normal spark plug contains a light beige or gray deposit. It shows a small amount of electrode wear, about .001 inch per 1000-2000 miles of driving. Those clues indicate that the plug is of the correct heat range and that the car has re-

ceived mixed high- and low-speed driving. Such a spark plug can be cleaned, regapped, and put back in the engine. If you have a V-8 that requires removal of half the accessories just to get a wrench on the spark plugs, forget cleaning. They are usually so worn that you should replace the plugs every time you have them out.

Clues to Sick Plugs

A *worn insulator* or eaten-away, pitted electrodes means that a new set of spark plugs should be installed.

A *wet, oily deposit* on a plug is caused by crankcase oil leaking past the piston rings, valve guides, or fuel pump diaphragm and into the cylinders. Break-in of a new or rebuilt engine may produce such a condition temporarily. Oil-fouled plugs usually can be degreased, cleaned, gapped, and reinstalled. While hotter heat range plugs will reduce future oil-fouling, in severe cases the only cure is an engine overhaul.

A *fluffy black deposit* indicates carbon-fouling. It comes from too-rich carbure-

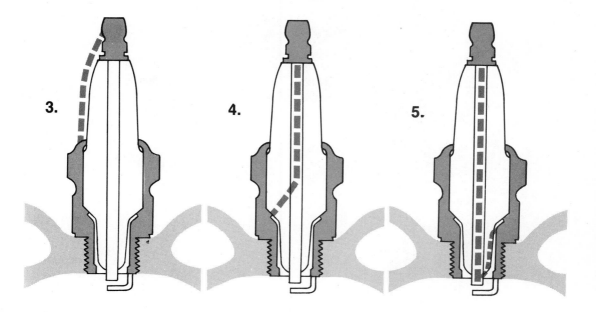

3. **4.** **5.**

tion, overchoking, a sticking manifold heat control valve, or a clogged air filter element. Misfiring can be aggravated by a weak ignition system. Carbon-fouling also may result from low-speed driving and long periods of idling, which keep plug temperatures so low that normal combustion deposits are not burned off the plugs. In such a case, hotter spark plugs are called for.

Only *one carbon-fouled plug* out of an entire engine usually means the compression in that cylinder may be low due to poor piston rings. Or, later ignition system checks may turn up a shorted spark plug cable to that cylinder.

A *burned* or *blistered insulator nose* and badly eroded electrodes indicate plug overheating. That may be caused by improper heat range, overadvanced ignition timing, or running on fuel of too low octane. Lean air/fuel mixtures, a stopped-up cooling system, or sticking engine valves can cause that problem too. The tune-up checks you will perform should pick up any of those conditions. If you find no

such cause for the problems, switch to a colder heat range plug.

A *red, brown, yellow,* or *white coating* that forms on the spark plug insulator is a by-product of combustion, resulting from additives in fuel and oils. Usually, scavenger deposits, as they are called, have no ill effect and are quite normal. Sometimes, however, they can cause misfiring at high engine speeds under heavy loads. If the insulator is not too heavily coated, the plug can be cleaned, gapped, and put back in. Occasionally, even after cleaning, an invisible path for an electrical short circuit remains and a plug still misfires. Then you must replace the plug. (Under some operating conditions, scavenger deposits melt and form a *shiny yellow glaze* over the insulator. When hot, that glaze is a good conductor of electricity; the spark follows the deposits instead of jumping the gap, and the plug misfires. You can prevent the formation of such glazed deposits by avoiding sudden loads such as wide-open-throttle acceleration after a long period of slow-speed driving or idling. Once

Normal Use

Scavenger Deposit, Glazed

Oil-Fouled

Scavenger Deposit, Unglazed

Burned Electrodes

Carbon-Fouled

Spark plugs show the use—or abuse—they have undergone.

formed, the glaze is almost impossible to remove, and the plugs must be replaced.)

A *chipped insulator* can be caused by heat shock from preignition. Over-advanced ignition timing or too-low octane fuel can also cause the insulator to crack. Another possible cause is improper plug gapping methods in which a side force is put on the insulator tip. Replace the plug and correct the problem during your tune-up.

Improper installation of the plugs can cause poor heat transfer from plug to engine and, in turn, plug overheating. Full

contact between the plug and the engine is vital. Dirty threads in the engine head, which make the plug seize in its threads before it is fully seated, can prevent such contact. So can insufficient tightening during installation. To cure the problem install a new plug of the proper heat range. Make sure it is fully seated and properly tightened.

Cycle-Cleaning

A little known on-the-car plug-cleaning tip may save you from early spark plug trouble. Called cycle-cleaning, it removes most unglazed lead deposits that frequently cause spark plugs to short out at high speeds and under rapid acceleration.

To cycle-clean plugs, get out on the highway and speed up gradually until you reach the point where the engine begins to misfire. Then slow down a bit to where the misfiring just stops. Run at that speed for a mile or two. This lets the misfiring plug burn away the offending lead deposits. Repeat the procedure at a higher speed until you can accelerate from the slowest speed to the highest legal speed without a misfire.

Cycle-cleaning is especially effective on an engine that has been run on short trips at slow speeds, a practice that allows unglazed lead deposits to form on the spark plugs.

PROPER PLUG SERVICE

Plugs that can be cleaned, gapped, and replaced should get the following treatment:

Proper removal is all-important. Use care not to break the insulators. When all the plugs are out, wipe the spark plug openings clean, being extremely careful to keep dirt from tumbling down into any of the cylinders.

Check the spark plug gaps. If they have opened more than .008 to .010 inches over the specified figures, the plugs probably are due for replacement. If the plugs are dirty and worn but still serviceable, wipe the insulators clean and wire-brush around the bases and threads by hand or with a power brush. Do not wire-brush the plug's insides. To clean the insides you must either scrape or sandblast.

A garage that has a spark plug sandblaster generally charges about 25 cents each to clean your plugs, once you have them out of the car. See that the mechanic does the job right. Oily or greasy plugs should be degreased before sandblasting so the abrasive particles do not lodge in the grease. Each plug should be rocked back and forth in the sandblaster while getting short abrasive blasts. This lets the abrasive get into all dirty areas of the plug without wearing down the insulator in one spot. Abrasive-blasting should be followed by air-blasting to blow out the abrasives.

Blast-cleaning is a last-ditch method of recycling a spark plug, but the process can wear off insulation.

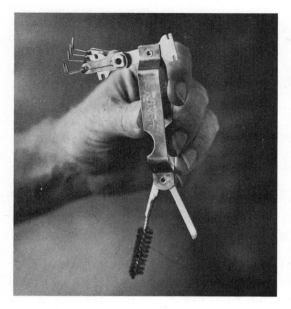

Handy spark plug cleaning tool has (*from top left*) wire gauges for gapping, an electrode bending bar and a brush and scraper for cleaning.

The do-it-yourself plug-cleaning method is to scrape the combustion deposits off with the small tool provided in some cleaning and gapping sets. Some car makers recommend that system over sandblasting, which tends to wear down the electrodes.

After cleaning, each plug should be tapped against something solid, with the electrodes point downward, to knock out any loose abrasives or scrapings.

Whatever cleaning method you use, file both electrodes flat and parallel to each other, removing all worn, rounded edges. Open the gaps to get the file in. Filing is the most important spark plug cleaning step because sharp, square edges are easier for the spark to jump across than the rounded edges left by wear and sandblasting. For that reason, a sandblasted plug often has a higher firing voltage than before it was cleaned. Filing of electrodes is a good plug-stretcher.

When you remove a spark plug, check it carefully for cracks or other signs of wear (*left*); all plugs pulled from the same engine should look similar. If you plan to reuse a plug, scrape all deposits off the firing end (*right*).

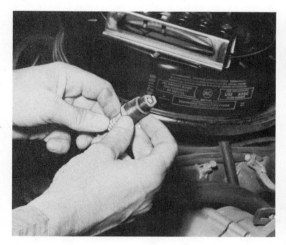

You should also test old spark plugs before reusing them to make sure that they do not have cracked insulators or unremoved, glazed-on deposits. Most spark plug sandblasters are fitted with testers to let you see how the plug fires under air pressure. Remember that these testers can be misused by unscrupulous mechanics to sell lots of new plugs.

Sometimes the plugs are tested before cleaning. Don't fall for that. The only way to test spark plugs is after cleaning. And make sure the electrodes have been filed flat.

Do not test a plug with dirty, damp, or oil-coated upper insulator. Those conditions may cause "flashover" from terminal to shell. (The shell is the metal portion of the plug.) Clean the insulator with a solvent-moistened cloth.

Do not attempt to correlate the indicator pressure reading with the cylinder compression reading. The voltage required in the engine is much lower than the firing voltage required under the same pressure of dry compressed air in the indicator.

Do not discard plugs that exhibit blue light just above the shell. Blue light is a corona discharge or evidence of a high-tension field. It does not affect plug performance or indicate a plug defect.

Do not discard a used or new plug that sparks from the terminal to shell (flashover). Sparking from terminal to shell merely indicates that excessive voltage has been applied and that the insulator is in good condition. Flashover will not occur in engine operation if the upper insulator is clean and dry. But if a used plug sparks through the upper insulator to the shell, it has a cracked or broken upper insulator and should be replaced with a new plug.

When just one plug needs a replacement, you may wonder whether the whole

After cleaning the tip, dress both electrodes with an ignition file until they have square edges (*left*). Then, clean dirt, rust and abrasive particles from the outside of the plug with a wire brush (*right*), but do not brush the electrodes.

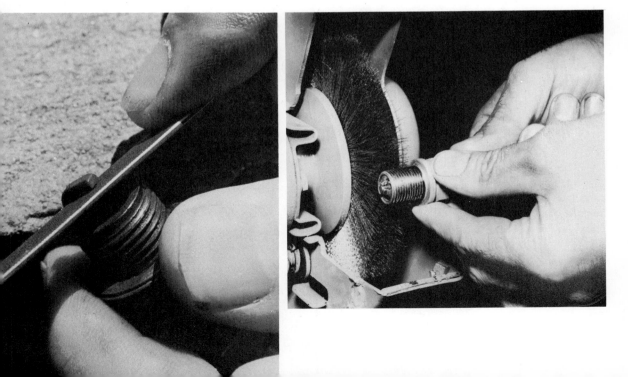

Check the gap with a wire gauge of the correct specification.

If the gap is incorrect, adjust it with a bending bar; then, recheck.

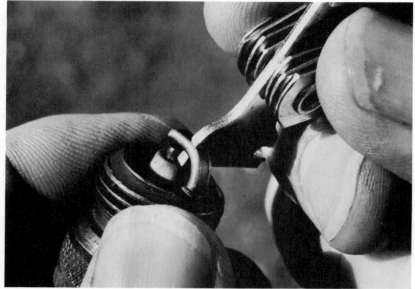

This compact gapping tool has slide-out gauges, bending bar and file.

set should be replaced. Generally, if the set has 10,000 miles of service behind it, or if the plugs were tough to get at, you should replace them all. Otherwise, replace the one bad plug and get your full use from the rest.

CORRECT INSTALLATION

Before you install spark plugs, put a few drops of oil on their threads. If the threads in the cylinder head are dirty, clean them by twisting a cloth into the spark plug openings. Wipe each plug seat. Plugs installed in engines with aluminum cylinder heads may need lubrication with an anti-seize compound; follow the advice of the car manufacturer.

In most cases, tightening of spark plugs is not so critical as to require a torque wrench. Turn the spark plug socket finger-tight. Then, tighten the plug about half a turn more with the wrench; this gives a gas-tight seal. Spark plugs without gaskets —tapered-seat ones—should be tightened only firmly enough to get a gas-tight seal.

If you have a torque wrench and want to be more accurate, follow the SAE recommendations in the accompanying table.

The torque values in the table apply only when the plug and the cylinder head threads are clean and the spark plug has been installed finger-tight with a new folded-type seat gasket. Preferably, spark plugs with solid gaskets should be installed with a torque wrench. Ford products have used tapered-seat spark plugs without any gaskets since 1955.

To help your spark plugs as well as your engine last longer, don't use regular fuel in an engine designed to run on premium (check your owner's manual). In a standard-transmission car, making the engine lug instead of shifting to a lower gear shortens engine and plug life.

| Spark plug thread type | With Torque Wrench | | Without Torque Wrench |
	Cast Iron heads	Aluminum heads (foot pounds)	Cast iron or aluminum heads
10 mm	12	10	¼ to ⅜ turn
12 mm	18	16	¼ turn*
14 mm	25	22	½ to ¾ turns*
14 mm taper-seat	15	15	½ to ¾ turns*
18 mm	35	25	½ to ¾ turn
18 mm taper-seat	17	15	½ to ¾ turns
⅞ in.	40	30	¼ to ½ turn

* Spin-out type gasket must be installed to have full contact against the plug seat.

6

Engine Tuning: Manifold Vacuum

After your engine has passed a compression test and had its spark plugs serviced, it is ready for a manifold vacuum test. This is made with an inexpensive instrument called a vacuum gauge. A usable one costs about $5.

In testing engine intake manifold vacuum, you are again measuring breathing—this time, the decrease in air pressure caused by the pistons as they move downward in the cylinders. The amount of vacuum developed depends on engine speed, engine load, and the condition of the pistons, rings, valves, and exhaust system. Any weaknesses, restrictions or leaks in the breathing system affect the vacuum gauge reading. So do other factors, such as ignition timing.

Testing Manifold Vacuum

To test manifold vacuum, warm the engine to operating temperature. Connect the vacuum gauge to the intake manifold —the large cast-iron part on which the carburetor is mounted. In some models you may have to drill and tap a hole through the manifold for the fitting. The manifold should be removed for that operation so that metal filings do not get into the engine.

Or, you may need to install an adapter which comes with the vacuum gauge. If your car has power brakes or vacuum-operated windshield wipers (mostly on old cars and on recent American Motors models), installing the adapter should be no problem. Look for a metal line or rubber hose leading from the manifold to the power brake cylinder or the vacuum-operated windshield wiper motor. If the car has vacuum windshield wipers, it also may have a built-in vacuum booster on the fuel pump. In that case, the vacuum line will lead to the fuel pump. Be sure to attach the vacuum gauge to the line between the manifold and the fuel pump; attaching it between the fuel pump and windshield wiper would register boosted vacuum, which is meaningless in engine tuning.

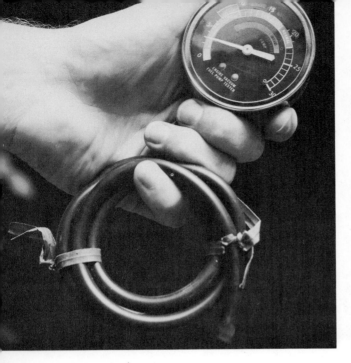

Some vacuum gauges contain pressure as well as vacuum scales so they can be used for fuel pump testing; the chapter on fuel system tuning tells how.

The instructions packed with some vacuum gauges are overly optimistic about how much a vacuum gauge can tell about your engine. Measurements other than those listed here are suspect.

If the engine idles badly, adjust the idle to specified speed and smooth it out, as described in the chapter on fuel system tuning. (You may gloss over some of the finer points.)

Typical vacuum gauge (*left*) comes complete with hose and adapters.

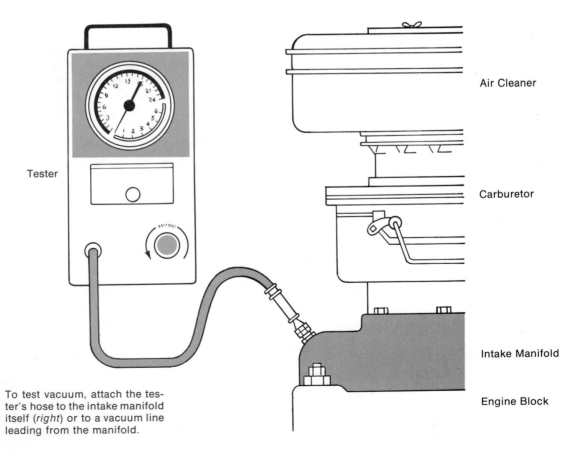

Tester

Air Cleaner

Carburetor

Intake Manifold

Engine Block

To test vacuum, attach the tester's hose to the intake manifold itself (*right*) or to a vacuum line leading from the manifold.

With the warm engine idling, the vacuum gauge should register a fairly steady 15 to 21 inches. Late-model engines with high-lift camshafts (the rotating parts inside the engine that make the valves open and close at the right time) generally show a slightly lower, more pulsating vacuum than older engines. Deduct 1 inch for each 1,000 feet of elevation.

Interpreting the Readings

Sticking valves are indicated by a dropping back of the vacuum pointer. Valves stick because of gum and varnish deposits on their sliding stems, sticking valve lifters, weak valve return springs, bent valve stems, carbon build-up, or other causes. The cure may be as simple as adding a can of special oil to the engine. Choose a reputable brand that promises to free sticking valves. If that does not work within several hundred miles, see your garageman for a mechanical cure.

An *incorrect air-fuel mixture* makes the pointer float up and down. You can take care of that later, during the fuel system tune-up.

Late ignition or *late valve timing* shows up as a too-low vacuum reading. So does mechanical drag, compression problems, or a vacuum leak in the intake manifold for vacuum-operated accessories. Finding and fixing late valve timing is a shop job; so is correcting poor valve adjustment and finding excessive mechanical drag.

An *unsteady vacuum reading* points to incorrect distributor point spacing (take care of that later), or poor valve adjustment (a shop job—fortunately, not common). Needle unsteadiness also may indicate a carburetor in poor condition (remember for later) or uneven compression (the compression test would have indicated that). Manifold air leaks also can cause vacuum needle unsteadiness—more on that later.

A *restricted exhaust system* also can impair engine breathing. An engine that can-

Normal manifold vacuum range is marked on this gauge, which can also be used to check fuel pump pressure.

not exhale properly cannot make room for all of the incoming charge it is capable of handling. To check for an exhaust restriction, run the engine up to 2000 rpm and hold that speed for 10 seconds. A restriction will cause the vacuum reading to drop slowly until it is less than it was at idling speed. In that case look for a stuck manifold heat control valve (see the chapter on exhaust system servicing).

A *pinched exhaust pipe* or a *plugged muffler* also can create an exhaust restriction. A pinched pipe is easy to see. A plugged muffler is hard to diagnose unless you remove it and repeat the test again. Do that if all the other possible causes of exhaust restriction have been eliminated.

Manifold Leaks

Any engine that registers low manifold vacuum should be checked for leaks in the intake manifold. With an oil can, squirt a mixture of kerosene and motor oil around all intake manifold joints while the engine idles. Notice any changes in engine speed.

A neater way is to open the gas valve of a propane torch without lighting the escaping gas. Feed the gas around the intake manifold joints as the engine idles; if the propane gas encounters any opening in the manifold, it will be drawn in by engine vacuum and you will notice an immediate increase in idle speed. A tachometer is handy for that test. Wherever

To check for leaks, open the valve of a propane torch, but do not light it. Idle the engine and pass the torch near the intake manifold; if the engine speed increases, there is a leak.

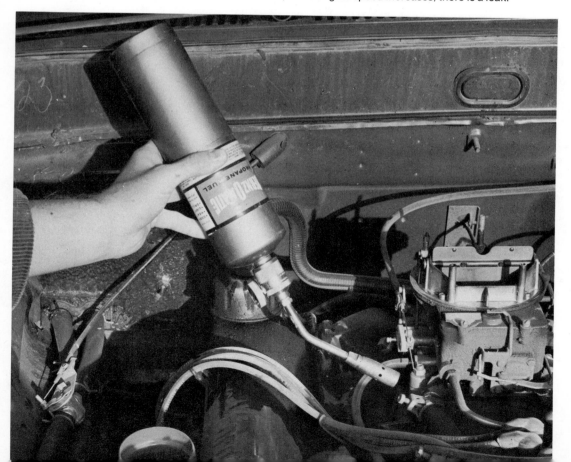

you are aiming the torch at that moment is where the leak is.

The biggest manifold joint is at the base of the carburetor. Others occur where air/fuel mixture is fed into the cylinders. Check for leaks at all hoses and lines leading away from the intake manifold toward the power brake, windshield wipers, fuel pump, and other vacuum-operated accessories.

Leaks between metal parts of the manifold and the carburetor or engine block often can be fixed simply by tightening the bolts nearest them. Fix a cracked, leaking hose end by removing the hose, cutting off the last inch or so and replacing the hose. If the hose is not long enough to do that, the entire hose may have to be replaced. Leaks at tubing joints usually respond to a tightening of the fittings. A leaky manifold-to-engine joint that cannot be eliminated by tightening requires removal of the manifold. So does a cracked manifold. In these cases, see a mechanic.

If you cannot fix a leaking carburetor-to-manifold joint by tightening, remove the carburetor (covered in the chapter on fuel system tuning) and install a new gasket. Repeat the manifold vacuum test after you have made repairs.

Engine Tuning: Ignition

The purpose of the ignition system is to take relatively low battery voltage (12 to 13 volts), step it up to a high, spark-producing voltage, and distribute the spark to the spark plugs sequentially.

Most no-starts and on-the-road engine troubles can be traced to some fault in the ignition system. Yet, if this system is kept in top shape with regular tunings, it is as reliable as most other parts of the car.

Conventional ignition systems are comprised of:

• The distributor, which houses *points* that initiate the spark, a *condenser* that controls the spark, and a *rotor* that distributes the spark to the cylinders;
• The coil, which boosts the battery current to spark-producing proportions;
• The ignition switch;
• The cables and wires that run between these components, and that connect them to the battery.

Electronic ignition. With greater demands being placed on late-model ignition systems in terms of reliability and the prevention of excessive emissions, electronic ignition has become standard on many recent cars. Some GM and Chrysler models got it first; it will doubtlessly be used in other models as well.

Such systems are simpler to service than the regular points-coil-condenser systems —and, they need service less often.

The *Delco-Remy* system looks, and works, much like a conventional distributor. But instead of points, it has a magnetic pick-up assembly. This component induces a high voltage in a built-in coil. The high voltage is then directed, by an all-electronic module, to the correct spark plug.

Thus, there is no sparking in the electronic system itself.

The unit requires no periodic lubrication; engine oil and an oil-filled reservoir do the job for you. Nor does the unit need any other service, unless it malfunctions.

The *Chrysler* system also looks like the standard ignition system. The distributor, though, has a double primary wire.

In this set-up, current step-up and direction is performed by a transistor. Again, there are no points within the unit.

Periodic checks for timing and dwell are unnecessary, though possible. And since the internal components do not normally wear, you need only inspect the wiring, and clean and change the spark plugs, to maintain the system.

All testing and servicing of electronic ignition units should be left to qualified mechanics—these systems can easily be damaged by incorrect hook-ups.

DISTRIBUTOR

The distributor houses breaker points, which are opened and closed by a cam. One point is stationary, one is movable. If the engine has six cylinders, the cam has six sides, or lobes. In an eight-cylinder engine the cam has eight lobes.

Every time a lobe passes under the fiber rubbing block on the movable point, it separates the points, breaking the circuit and creating a spark.

The distributor cam rotates half as fast as the engine crankshaft, so a spark is produced for each cylinder during every other revolution of the engine. By careful adjustment of point position, the sparks can be timed to occur exactly when they are needed inside the combustion chamber.

Precise spark timing is important. If the spark comes too early, serious preignition can cause engine damage. If the spark comes too late, the engine will lose power and give poor fuel mileage. In either case, poor acceleration and overheating may occur.

The distributor not only creates the spark by opening and closing the points; it also acts as a switch, routing the spark to

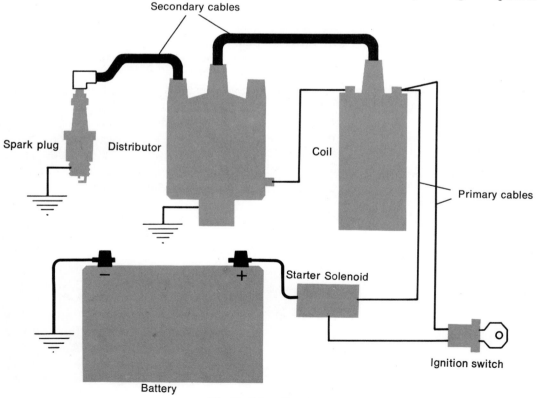

The Ignition System

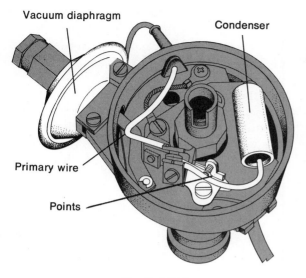

Vacuum diaphragm

Condenser

Primary wire

Points

The Distributor

fore the piston reaches the top of its travel (top dead center, or TDC). To give full power, all burning should take place before the piston goes 10° to 20° past TDC.

It takes .003 seconds for the air/fuel mixture to ignite sufficiently to push downward on the piston. Therefore, to complete the process in time, the fuel must be ignited early. The initial spark advance, as it's called, does that.

Higher engine speeds require an even greater advance, since the piston is moving more rapidly. To get that advance, most distributors are built with *centrifugal advance* mechanisms.

To match the spark advance to the engine load, many distributors contain a *vacuum advance* unit. This is a disk-shaped vacuum chamber attached to the outside of the distributor. Its spring-

the proper high-tension cable and on to the spark plug. This distribution is the job of the rotor, which is driven by the same shaft that drives the cam.

The stepped-up current needed for sparking comes from the coil, via a wire from the secondary terminal in the coil to the center tower of the distributor.

As this high-voltage surge comes, it is accompanied by an induced low voltage (the process is called self-induction). This low voltage tends to arc across the points as they separate, causing, among other things, point burning.

To prevent this phenomenon, a condenser—a small, round metal can—is included in the circuit.

The condenser has the ability to soak up extra self-induced current. Connected across the points, it acts as an electrical shock absorber. The condenser not only prolongs point life, it helps produce a quick, hot spark.

Advances. Spark timing at idle occurs several degrees of crankshaft rotation be-

Centrifugal advance mechanism relies on the movement of weights to vary spark advance according to engine speed.

loaded vacuum diaphragm is linked to the breaker plate, the base that supports the breaker points. The other side of the vacuum chamber is connected to the carburetor through a vacuum line.

With an increase in engine vacuum at the carburetor, the unit's diaphragm moves against the spring and its linkage to pull the breaker plate and attached points, and thereby advance the spark.

Practically all modern automobile distributors contain both centrifugal and vacuum advances. Many old cars had only centrifugal advance. A few old Fords had only vacuum advance.

Many cars today have dual-diaphragm distributors to minimize air pollution. To check whether your car does, look for two hoses leading to the distributor. One comes from the intake manifold, the other comes from the carburetor.

The system works by retarding spark timing at idle. The hoses are all too easy to switch. If they are switched, you will get noticeably poor engine performance and high exhaust emissions.

See that the hose from the carburetor leads to the advance side of the diaphragm and the hose from the manifold leads to the retard side.

Distributor Disassembly

Do not remove the distributor from the car unless it needs more than routine breaker point service or replacement.

Remove the distributor cap by unsnapping the two clips that hold the cap to the body, or by turning the two lock-screws on top of the cap. Unsnapping clip-type fasteners is easy if you insert the blade of a large screwdriver between each clip and the cap's body, near the upper end of the clip, and twist.

Without removing any of the wires, lift the cap to one side, out of the way.

On top of the distributor you will see the rotor, a black component with a center spring contact. Most rotors simply lift straight off the distributor shaft. GM V-8s have round rotors that are fastened with two screws; remove the screws and lift off the rotor.

Now you can get at the distributor breaker points.

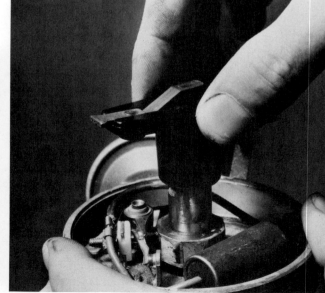

To service a distributor, begin by unsnapping the clips (*left*) that hold the cap to the mechanism's body (a few caps are fastened with screws). Then, lift off the rotor (*right*). Some GM rotors are secured by screws.

Points

With your finger or a small screwdriver, hold the movable point apart from the stationary one and examine the point contact surfaces. Points that have gone several thousand miles or more will have a rough surface, often showing some transfer of metal from one point to the other. That is normal, and no cause for point replacement, since the roughened surfaces have an even greater contact area than a new, unworn set of points. Normally, a set of points will go at least 10,000 miles.

External-adjustment distributors, such as the Delco window-adjusting unit, have their point openings preset at the factory. Normally, no adjustment is necessary. However, if you suspect a faulty adjustment, check it with a thickness gauge.

A few makes of cars, notably Chrysler products, use dual breaker points. One set gives an early point close. The other stays closed after the first set opens and provides the correctly timed spark. Such systems pose no unusual problem.

Service. To take out a set of points, first remove the insulated ignition and condenser wires from them.

Some point sets transfer their electrical current through the tension spring, which slips under the terminal nut—the one coming through the distributor housing. Such points come out when you simply loosen the terminal nut and take out the point hold-down screw that threads into the breaker plate below.

Some point sets have one mounting screw plus an eccentric gap-adjusting screw. Others have two hold-down screws with slotted openings that permit point gap adjustment when the screws are loosened. In either case, the fasteners must be removed to get the points out.

If the point contacts are burned, the points may be cleaned with several

Cleaning Points

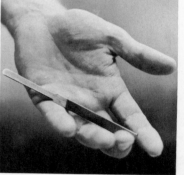

Compare the build-up of metal against a 0.020-inch thickness gauge (*above*). If the metal transfer matches or exceeds the thickness of the gauge, replace the points. If the points are reusable, take a distributor point file (*right*) and burnish the point surfaces (*below*). Do not file off the deposits.

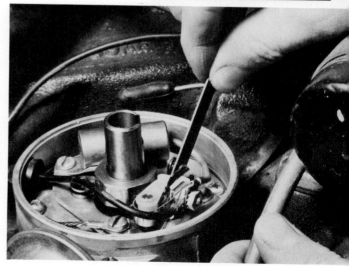

strokes of an oil-free, fine-cut contact-point file. Don't use emery cloth; the abrasive grains may stick to the point surfaces and cause further burning. Remove scale and dirt, but do not dress or smooth the point surfaces.

Burned points. If the points are burned, try to find out why. The cause may be improper point adjustment, a defective condenser, oil or other foreign material on the points, or too-high voltage at the points.

High voltage comes from a poorly adjusted charging system regulator (see the chapter on the charging system), or (rarely) from shorted resistance in the ignition circuit. The latter check calls for a tester.

Oil inside the distributor may work up from the crankcase. Even vapors from the crankcase will cause rapid point-burning. If oil is the cause, you should see a smudgy line on the breaker plate under the points. A clogged positive crankcase ventilation (PCV) system, plugged crankcase breather pipe, or over-oiling of the distributor also can bring oil to the distributor points.

If the contacts are poorly adjusted so that they open insufficiently, they will heat up from the excess flow of electricity.

Check the point gap with your thickness gauges. (Detailed information on point gapping appears later in this chapter.) Too-close point spacing also brings on rapid arcing between the points, and possibly engine misfiring because of low secondary voltage.

If none of the preceding proves to be the cause of point-burning, see whether the condenser is tightly fastened down. A loose mounting can create high series resistance in the condenser, and bring on point-burning. So can a defective condenser. If a defective condenser seems to be the cause for burned points, replace it.

If the transfer of metal exceeds .020 inch—compare it with a .020 thickness gauge—replace the points. Also replace them if most of the tungsten contact covering is gone, or if the points do not meet fully and squarely.

Pitted points—even slightly pitted ones—cannot be adjusted with a thickness gauge. Unless you adjust them with a dwell meter or some other method, you must replace them.

Installation. If you can clean the old points, reuse them. If not, buy a new set.

If there is an oil streak (*arrow*) on the breaker plate surface, replace the points and trace the source of the leak before proceeding any further.

To remove points, unfasten the hold-down screws. Take out the condenser and its wires, noting their positions so you can replace them easily.

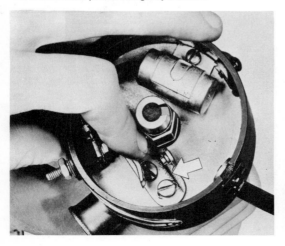

Distributor Reassembly

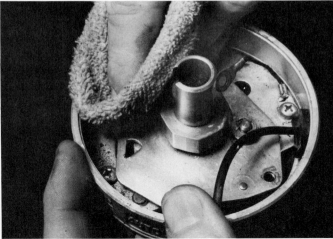

1. Before reinstalling the distributor parts, spread distributor cam lubricant lightly around the cam. Do not over-lubricate.

2. Place a drop of oil in any breaker plate hole marked "oil." Then thoroughly wipe off the breaker plate until it comes clean.

3. After the points and condenser are in place, check the distributor shaft. If it has a felt washer inside, place three drops of oil in it.

4. Finish by lightly oiling the moving parts of the vacuum advance mechanism. Place a drop of 20-weight oil on the vacuum pivot arm post.

You can get a new set at a car dealer's parts department, auto parts jobber's, or almost anywhere car parts are sold. Buy just the points, not the much-promoted tune-up kits that contain points, condenser, distributor cap and possibly rotor.

Smear some oil, with your fingertip, around the breaker point pivot post before installing the points.

On distributors with an accessible centrifugal advance mechanism, place a drop of oil on the pivot post of each weight.

Next, a light coating of high-temperature distributor cam grease should be smeared onto the cam. Excess lube will be thrown off at high speeds and temperatures, and will be deposited on the points, causing rapid burning. If the distributor has a cam lubrication wick or roller, cam grease is not needed. The wick should be adjusted to rub lightly against the cam. A replaceable wick should be installed at each point servicing. Some wicks are switched end for end once, then replaced the next time.

Before you install the new points, wipe the breaker plate clean.

Place the points over their pivot post. Then, insert the attaching screw or screws that hold their base tightly to the breaker plate. Don't tighten the screws until the point gap has been adjusted.

Carefully replace ground, condenser, and primary lead wires (if any) as they were originally. Make sure the wires will not interfere with the moving cam or points, and will not restrict movement of the breaker plate.

The condenser also should be positioned so it will not restrict breaker plate motion.

If there is a felt washer inside the end of the distributor shaft, put three drops of oil on it. It lubricates the joint between the two separate portions of the distributor shaft and the centrifugal advance mechanism.

The vacuum pivot arm post, if there is one, should get a drop of oil, too.

Point tension. One-piece point sets are correctly tensioned when made. If the breaker points are two-piece units, as on all older cars and some newer ones (such as Chevy fours and sixes), the point tension should be checked with a small, inexpensive spring scale.

Too much tension makes the rubbing block wear too quickly, changing the point gap. Not enough tension lets the points bounce at high engine speeds, causing loss of power.

Hook one end of the spring scale to the movable point arm at the contact of the closed points, and pull at a right angle to the arm until the points just separate. Compare the reading with the manufacturer's specifications. Check tension whether you reuse the old points or install new ones.

To adjust tension in the slotted type of point sets, remove the terminal nut and lockwasher, and take off the pigtail wires from the condenser and ignition primary wires. With a tiny open-end wrench from

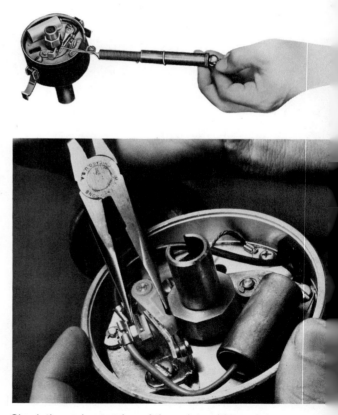

Check the spring tension of the points with a point-tension scale (*top*). On bend-adjust points, use pliers to work the spring (*above*). On slotted points, slide the spring to adjust tension.

an ignition wrench set, loosen the small nut that holds the tension spring.

Loosen sufficiently so that you can slide the spring in its slot. To lessen tension, slide the spring toward the breaker pivot arm. To increase tension, slide it away from the pivot arm. Tighten the nut and check tension again.

To adjust tension on bend-adjust springs, use a pair of pliers. Pinch the spring together to lessen tension. To increase tension, remove the movable point arm and spring, and bend the spring and arm away from each other. Release and check.

For best high-speed performance, keep tension toward the higher tolerance. For around-town puttering, set tension toward the lower tolerance for longer rubbing block life.

Point alignment. Check every new set of points you install for proper meeting of the contacts. (You may need a magnifying glass.) An off-center or nonparallel condition requires bending the fixed contact arm. Never bend the fragile movable contact arm. Preassembled contact sets should not need alignment when the breaker arm spring is all the way down on the attaching screw.

Point gap. Breaker points must be adjusted so that they open exactly the right amount when the cam lobe passes under the rubbing block. If they open too far, they will not stay closed long enough at high speed to saturate the coil with electricity. A weak spark and poor high-speed engine performance will result. Too close an adjustment causes hard starting and pitting and burning of the point surfaces.

To make the adjustment, turn the distributor shaft so that the points open to their widest.

Look up the point gap specifications; often, you will be asked to gap a new set

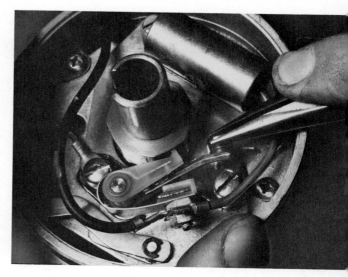

Correct point alignment is vital for a hot spark and long point life. Adjust alignment by bending the stationary point with a pair of pliers.

of points about .003 inch wider than a used set, to compensate for rapid rubbing block wear in the early hours of point life.

Insert the correct thickness gauge between the points. You should feel a slight drag on the feeler as you pull it squarely through the point opening.

To change the adjustment, loosen the locking screw or screws and turn the off-center adjusting screw. Some point sets, instead of having an eccentric screw, have a slotted hole between the point base and breaker plate. Insert a screwdriver into that hole so its sides engage the slots. Then, turn one way or the other to open or close the gap.

When the gap is correct, tighten the mounting screws and recheck. It may take several tries to get everything right.

Finishing up. The last step in a point installation should be a thorough cleaning of the contact surfaces with carburetor cleaner or lighter fluid. Be sure you remove all traces of grease and oil—most early point failures come from oil on the contacts. Dry by running a strip of clean cloth between the contacts.

Gapping Points

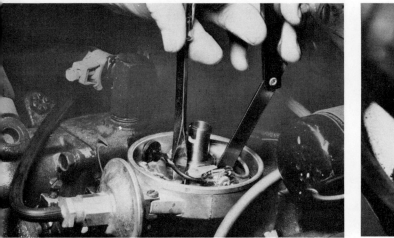

On distributors with an adjusting screw, insert a correctly sized thickness gauge between the points. Then, turn the screw until the gauge drags slightly as it is pulled out.

On distributors with an adjusting slot, first loosen the hold-down screw. Then, insert a screwdriver tip into the slot. Move the tip until the points are correctly gapped.

External adjustment distributors should need no adjustment of points. If they do, handle it as follows: Start and idle the engine. Using an allen wrench, turn the adjusting screw behind the sliding "window" clockwise until the engine begins misfiring. Then turn the screw a half turn counterclockwise, remove the wrench and close the window. Dwell can be set even more accurately using a dwell meter.

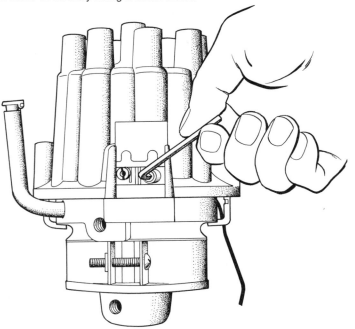

Condenser

To remove the condenser, take out the small screw, or screws, holding it to the breaker plate. Its pigtail wire is already free from the points. Wipe the breaker plate clean before installing the new condenser.

A condenser may be completely tested on a condenser tester, but buying such a tester is impractical for most do-it-yourselfers. Take the suspect condenser to a shop for testing. Three checks should be made: insulation resistance (leakage) and breakdown test; series resistance test; and capacitance test.

If there was rapid metal transfer on the old points — say, .020 inch in less than 10,000 miles — that would be cause to replace the condenser, since it failed to do its job of preventing point arcing.

But do not install a new condenser simply as a precautionary measure. Condensers seldom go bad, and a new one is just as likely to be faulty as the old one. Too many mechanics replace the condenser with every set of points. This is a waste of money.

Centrifugal Advance

While you work on the distributor, check the centrifugal advance mechanism. Grasp the upper end of the distributor shaft. See if you can turn it against the centrifugal advance retaining spring, in the same direction that the distributor rotates. (Replace the rotor on the shaft if it helps you to turn.)

Let go of the rotor gently to see whether it settles back to its retard position without hesitating or sticking. Now, try to turn the shaft in the opposite direction. If it settled all the way back on its own spring tension, you should not be able to turn it backwards. If the shaft feels as if it is turning back another notch, the centrifugal advance may be binding. Though that is

Condensers rarely fail. But if you must remove one for testing or for replacement, simply unfasten the hold-down screw and lead wire.

rare, a professional distributor analyzer bench-test is advisable. Checking the distributor's advance with a timing light will pinpoint the problem. (Instructions on that check appear later in this chapter.)

Vacuum Advance

Whether the vacuum advance mechanism turns the whole distributor or only the breaker plate, you can test vacuum advance without any equipment.

First, remove the vacuum hose at the distributor. Then, turn either the breaker plate (most common) or the distributor itself, depending on which one is advanced by the vacuum unit. Move it as far as it will go toward the vacuum advance unit. Hold it there while you seal off the vacuum opening in the unit with your thumb.

Now, let go of the breaker plate. It should stay where it is until you take your thumb off the opening. Then, it should immediately and smoothly return to its initial position, without binding.

If the breaker plate moves back while

Testing Advance

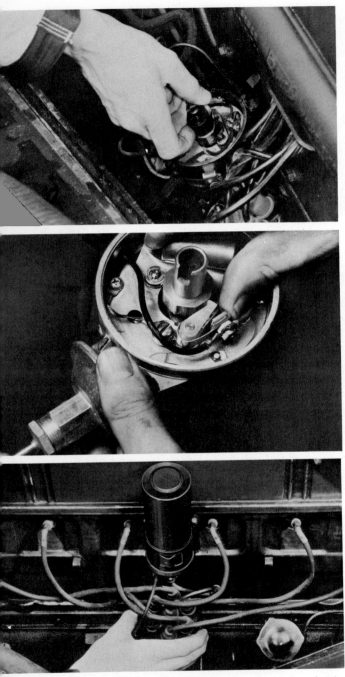

your thumb is on the opening, the diaphragm in the vacuum advance unit is probably leaking. Replace the unit by removing the two screws on its side, unclipping the diaphragm link from its hole, and lifting the unit off.

Without testing equipment, checks of the centrifugal and vacuum advance do not tell you how much advance either function gives; you only learn whether the systems are working. Later, with the use of a timing light, you can learn about how much advance each is actually giving.

Rotor and Distributor Cap

Every ignition tune-up should include an inspection of the rotor and distributor cap.

First, wipe the rotor clean with a dry cloth. Then look for cracks, chipped spots or carbonized tracks where spark could leak away. Also look at the top of the metal rotor strip. Some burning at the rotor tip is okay; just scrape it down to bare metal. Never file a rotor tip, for that increases the gap that each spark must jump.

See that the spring or carbon brush atop the rotor has enough tension to make good contact with the center terminal inside the distributor cap.

If the rotor has a built-in resistor between the center contact and tip, examine that for cracks. Look for signs of mechanical contact between the rotor tip and the distributor cap's secondary terminals. They should come close, but not touch.

If anything is wrong with the rotor, replace it.

The distributor cap requires the same cleaning and thorough inspection. Cracks and carbonized tracks are more common on distributor caps than on rotors.

Push on each high-tension cable coming into the distributor cap towers. If a cable is not in all the way, the spark may have to

Even without equipment, you can make simple checks on the different distributor advances. See that there is no binding on the centrifugal mechanism *(top)*, the vacuum advance *(center)* or the vacuum advance of a distributor-rotated unit *(bottom)*.

Rotor and Distributor Cap Care

Inspect the rotor tip for signs of burning. Scrape— but do not file—the tip clean.

Wipe the cap thoroughly. Oil, grease, dirt and road salt can lead to voltage leaks.

The rotor contact button inside the distributor cap should be free of burning and carbonized tracks. Sand lightly to clean.

With a spark plug tool, clean the spark cable terminal contacts inside each cap opening.

Cracks in the distributor cap can be safely patched with silicone rubber sealant.

jump between the end of the wire and the metal contact inside the tower, causing misfiring. Eventually, such arcing can erode the tower, with resultant high-voltage electrical leakage.

The insides of the towers should be clean and bright looking. Check them, removing and replacing the wires one at a time to keep them in the right order. Clean dirty tower contacts by scraping with a small screwdriver or a small wire brush.

The terminals inside the cap also should not be badly burned or corroded. Clean them if necessary. Check the rotor button at the center of the cap for wear, chips, or cracks.

Defects that cannot be fixed require replacement of the distributor cap.

Distributor Reassembly

With the points in place and adjusted, install the rotor. Make sure that its indexing tab slips down into the notch in the top of the distributor shaft. GM round rotors have round and square recesses that fit over round and square posts on the rotor shaft.

Install the screws that secure the rotor. Finish by snapping on the distributor cap.

REMOVING AND REPLACING A DISTRIBUTOR

Before you remove the distributor, disconnect the battery ground cable so that no one can crank the engine. Then, remove the distributor cap. With a piece of masking tape, make a mark—on the engine, fender shield, radiator, or some other clean area—directly in line with the rotor. Put another mark in line with the distributor vacuum advance unit. Be sure you know later which mark is which.

Remove the distributor hold-down bolt and clamp, and unfasten the primary lead from either the distributor or the coil.

Remove the vacuum tube from the distributor advance unit. The distributor body then should lift out of the engine block.

To replace the distributor, first line up the vacuum advance unit and the rotor with their respective marks. If the distributor rotor is turned by helical gears, the rotor will have to be started about 30° one way or the other from its in-place position. You will see which way, and how much, by several test insertions of the distributor.

When the rotor aligns with its mark and the distributor is fully seated, check the alignment of the vacuum advance unit against its mark.

Install and tighten the hold-down bolt and clamp. Install the primary lead wire and distributor cap, but do not put on the vacuum advance tube yet. Start the engine and go through the basic ignition timing procedure described earlier in this chapter. Reinstall the vacuum advance tube, and you are done.

If you should lose the proper distributor-engine relationship while the distributor is out (the only way that can happen is if

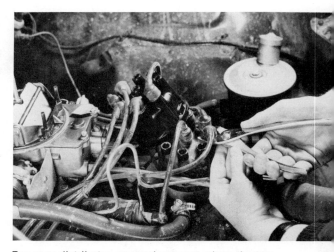

For easy distributor cap replacement, place the two caps side-by-side. Align the No. 1 towers and transfer the cables one at a time.

someone cranks the engine), remove the No. 1 spark plug. Hold your finger over the spark plug opening, and have someone nudge the starter. The coil primary should be grounded by a jumper, so that you will not get a shock and so that the engine will not start.

When you feel air coming out of the spark plug opening, and the ignition timing marks become aligned, you have reached the No. 1 firing position.

Now, replace the distributor so that the rotor is aligned with the No. 1 cylinder's tower on the distributor cap. At that point, both engine and distributor are in the No. 1 firing position. Complete the installation as described above, forgetting about the tape mark for the rotor.

THE COIL

When you turn on the ignition switch, battery electricity flows to the coil. The coil actually consists of two coils of wire: one of fairly heavy wire, the other of fine wire. The secondary fine-wire circuit is wound over the primary heavy-wire circuit, but the two circuits are insulated from each other.

As long as electricity is flowing steadily through the primary circuit, there is no effect in the secondary circuit. But when primary current flow stops suddenly, as when the distributor breaker points open, a momentary high voltage is created in the secondary wires. It is caused by the rapidly collapsing magnetic field cutting across the many secondary wires. The voltage produced by this action is more than enough to jump across the spark plug gaps.

An ignition system coil rarely goes bad. However, you should give it the same clean-up and check-up that the distributor rotor and cap receive. If you see cracking, carbon tracking, or tower erosion, replace the coil. Check that the primary connec-

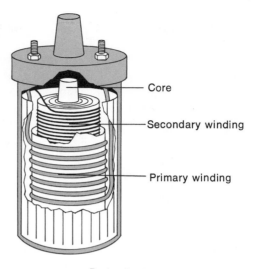

Parts of a Coil

tions are tight not only at the coil, but also at the distributor, resistor (if any), and ignition switch. The insulation on the leads should be sound.

Indications of a faulty coil include hard starting and misfiring at high speed and under heavy load when the engine is hot. Sometimes, a coil will perform and test out perfectly when cold, but will deliver a weak spark after it is heated during operation.

Thorough testing of a coil is a job for an ignition oscilloscope, a special coil tester, or a volt-ohm-milliammeter (VOM). Coil tests with a VOM are covered later in this chapter. If you lack those instruments, and if the coil is suspect, take it to a garage for full tests.

Polarity. A little-noticed ignition system problem—reversed coil polarity—can rob your engine of nearly half its firing power, even though all ignition system components are tip-top.

Spark plugs fire most easily when the electrons leap from their center electrodes to their ground electrodes, since the center electrodes are hotter, and thus more conducive to flinging off electrons.

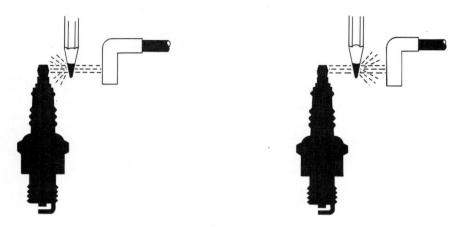

To test coil polarity remove a spark plug boot. Position a lead pencil point between the plug and the boot and idle the engine. The flare of sparks should aim towards the plug (*left*), not towards the boot (*right*).

The center electrodes should therefore be negative in the circuit. Besides loss of power, reversed coil polarity causes high-speed misfiring and poor fuel economy.

Most cars today have negative-grounded electrical systems. Yours does if the cable leading from the smaller, or negative, battery post goes to the engine block or car's frame. All hookups described in this book are for negative-grounded systems. If your car has a positive-ground system, reverse the hookups described here.

In a negative-ground system, the primary distributor lead should connect to the negative (−) terminal of the coil. Sometimes that terminal is labeled "Dist" for distributor. The battery lead should connect to the positive (+) terminal, which is sometimes labeled "BAT" for battery. One problem with coil polarity is that coils are not always properly labeled. To check whether polarity is correct, remove any spark plug cable by the boot. If the metal terminal is recessed, straighten a paper clip except for one curve, and shove that curve up into the

boot. The clip should contact the metal terminal, with the wire end sticking out.

Hold the end of the cable with a spring clothespin to avoid getting a shock while the engine idles. Bring the paper clip close enough to either the spark plug terminal, or to some clean part of the engine, to let it spark. Then, put the lead point of a pencil in the path of the spark.

A flare of sparks on one side of the pencil should aim toward the plug. If the sparks aim toward the cable, ignition polarity is reversed. Switch the coil primary leads, no matter how they are labeled, and check again.

IGNITION SWITCH

This component rarely fails; but if it does, there may be no spark nor any sign of primary electricity at the coil of the distributor.

When the points are closed, the switch is easy to check. Remove a wire and scratch it on its terminal: No spark, no electricity.

You can temporarily bypass a defective

When removing a spark cable from a running engine, use insulated high-tension pliers or a clothespin for safety: the cable is carrying 20,000 volts.

The badly burned spark cable boot above could cause misfiring. It should be replaced, and the other cables carefully scrutinized for wear.

ignition switch with a length of wire—an ignition-testing jumper, with alligator clip leads, is ideal. Attach one clip to the battery positive terminal, and the other to the coil's battery primary terminal.

This should allow you to start the engine and drive to a mechanic who can fix or replace the faulty switch.

CABLES

There is another oft-troublesome portion of the ignition system that is not commonly checked—the spark cables.

Cracks in the cable insulation can permit electrical leaks to deplete available voltage. More common, in today's cars a carbon track resistance conductor inside a cable may part, perhaps because of rough removal of the spark plug boots. Then, its resistance becomes so great that the cylinder served by that cable does not get sufficient spark to fire part or all of the time.

If everything in the ignition system up to this point checks out, and the engine misfires, cable trouble is a safe bet.

Working with cable. Be careful with resistance cable. It has a braided nylon inner core that is impregnated with current-carrying carbon. Pulling or bending sharply can separate the terminal or cable and increase resistance.

To remove the cable from the distributor cap or coil tower, first loosen the nipple. Then, grasp both the upper portion of the nipple and the wire and pull straight out. To put the cable back into the tower, push the wire straight in until it seats at the bottom of the tower recess. Then, slide the nipple all the way down over the tower.

Visual checks. Spark plug *boots* should not be brittle or swelled. Each should fit snugly over the terminal of the plug. Look for carbon tracking inside each of the boots. Never pierce the spark plug boots

Cleanliness of high-tension voltage cables is vital to engine performance. Clean them periodically.

Crossed cables look sloppy, but they are deliberately routed this way to prevent crossfire.

to connect tester adapters into the wire; that sets the boot up for future electrical leaks. Use an adapter, such as the straightened paper clip described previously.

Keep *cables* clean. Accumulations of oil, grease, and road salt make them become brittle and prone to cracking. Water and dust enter the cracks and partially ground the high-voltage current. As a result, not enough current reaches the spark plugs, and the engine misfires.

Unseen problems. Not all cable problems show up during a visual inspection.

A *broken conductor,* for instance, does not. The nontester method for finding a defective cable is to twist and pull off each cable at the spark plug in turn, and test for a spark to ground with the engine idling. Hold the cables with a spring clothespin. If some cables produce a good, cracking spark, and others do not, you have found the problem.

Another cause of insulation deterioration is *corona* — the magnetic field that forms around each wire as high-voltage current surges through it. The field is so strong that it breaks down (ionizes) the air around the cable, converting oxygen in the air into ozone. Ozone is a corrosive form of oxygen that attacks the cable's insulation.

Corroded or burned terminal connections can cause misfire without showing on the outside. Peer down into each spark plug boot. Again check each cable terminal at the distributor end.

Crossfire — one spark plug firing by induction when the one next to it fires — is a problem on some late model engines. It occurs between consecutive-firing cylinders whose spark cables are next to each other. Crossfire can be minimized by careful routing of cables to keep the troublemakers apart.

The spark cables on your car's engine may pass through a separating block that holds them away from each other. Moreover, the cables are not routed to the spark plugs in the same order they are fed through the separating block. While that may seem like sloppy assembly, it is done to prevent crossfire.

An *open conductor* or an abraded wire calls for replacing only that one wire. But if the insulation of any wire is frayed, oil-soaked, spongy, cracked, hard, or brittle, replace the whole set.

Replacement cables. Always get a quality replacement set, not a cheap off-brand. Also, do not replace high-tension resistance wiring with solid wire cables. Your engine would immediately become a source of radio and TV interference. Replacement cables should be the same type and length as the originals. Often, replacement factory cable comes long enough to fit the longest reach. Cut the cable to proper length at its distributor end and install a terminal.

CHECKING IGNITION OUTPUT

You can give your ignition tune-up a final spark test that will tell how the points, condenser, and coil are working.

Remove the center cable (the heavy one between the distributor and coil) from the distributor and hold it 3/16 inch away from

To check ignition output, remove the distributor-to-coil cable and hold it near bare metal. When the engine cranks, there should be a thick spark.

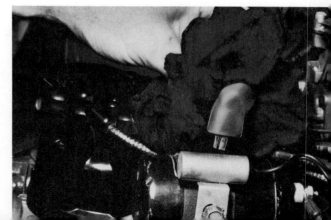

a clean portion of the engine, using a spring clothespin to avoid shock.

Have someone turn on the ignition key and crank the engine. A thick, blue, snapping spark should jump between the lead and the engine. If a thin, weak, reddish or yellowish spark jumps, you still have major ignition problems. (This test does not reveal minor ignition problems.)

It may be time to remove the coil and condenser and take them to a tune-up shop for complete testing. First, though, recheck the distributor points for cleanliness, gap, and correct alignment.

IGNITION TIMING

Now that you have a good spark and are feeding it, undiminished, to each spark plug, make sure the basic spark timing is right. A timing light makes the job easy, but it is not absolutely necessary.

Basic timing is set at idle (or at some other speed specified by the manufacturer) without any centrifugal or vacuum advance. Timing is adjusted by turning the loosened distributor housing in its mount.

Because distributor point spacing affects ignition timing, always adjust the points before you time. Too wide a gap advances timing, too slim a gap retards it.

Without a Timing Light

Turn the engine until the No. 1 piston is at the top of its compression stroke. You can usually do that by turning the fan blade while pressing the fan belt tight. "Bumping" the starter will work too, if you are careful to ground the coil high-tension cable so the engine does not start.

Cylinder sequence. You can identify No. 1 because the distributor rotor will be aimed right at its cable tower. Also, the following rules apply to most cars:

Before you can make any timing adjustments, you must be able to rotate the distributor. To do this, loosen the hold-down clamp.

In all U. S.-made in-line fours and sixes, the front cylinder is No. 1.

Some foreign-built cars call the rear cylinder, the one next to the firewall, No. 1.

On Ford V-8 engines, the No. 1 cylinder is the front one on the passenger side. The Nos. 2, 3 and 4 cylinders follow it on the same side, while the Nos. 5, 6, 7 and 8 cylinders are arranged, front-to-rear, on the driver's side.

On all other V-type engines—both sixes and eights—the No. 1 cylinder is on the driver's side. On those cars, all the odd-numbered cylinders are also on that side, and all even-numbered cylinders are on the passenger side.

Timing marks. Engines contain a variety of ignition timing marks. Most of them are located on the crankshaft drive pulley at the front of the engine. (Look for a single, double, or triple pulley that drives the generator, fan, water pump, power steering, and air conditioner belts.)

The top dead center position is variously labeled "O," "TDC," or "DC." The

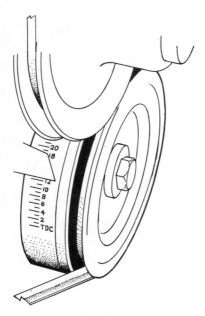

Timing Marks and Pointer

degrees of advance markings are splayed out ahead of the top dead center indication; they are marked off either in degrees or simply with a reference line.

If degree markings are on the pulley, an engine-mounted timing pointer, about an inch long, aims at them. If the degree markings are on the engine-mounted pointer, the pulley contains only a steel pin or reference mark. In any case, you usually will have to look up the manufacturer's specifications to tell which mark to use for timing. It may depend on the grade of fuel you use.

In a few engines, the timing mark is viewed through an opening near the flywheel, at the rear of the engine. A pointer in the opening aims at the timing marks, which are etched into the flywheel, next to the starter drive gear teeth.

When the No. 1 cylinder is close to top dead center, the engine's timing marks should be aligned by turning the crankshaft slightly one way or the other.

Timing with paper. With the timing marks in firing position, remove the distributor cap and rotor. Open the breaker points and slip a strip of cigarette paper between them, letting the points close on the paper. Then, loosen the distributor hold-down clamp. (Most are either between the distributor body and the engine or around the lower part of the distributor, fitted like a horseshoe.)

Once the bolt is loosened, the distributor may be rotated in either direction. Turn it in the retard direction (in the same direction the rotor shaft will turn against centrifugal advance) until the points are fully closed.

Now, slowly rotate the distributor housing toward advance, while pulling gently on the cigarette paper.

Stop turning as soon as the points open enough to release their hold on the paper. That is the position at which the No. 1 cylinder would fire. Tighten the distributor clamp without moving the housing. The engine is now correctly timed.

Timing with cigarette paper: Place the paper between the points. Rotate the distributor until the points are fully closed. Now, rotate the other way as you tug against the paper. When the paper pulls out, timing is set.

Timing with test light. A nonsmoker's method for timing calls for a test light. Make it by taking a replacement dome light bulb, and soldering lengths of wire to its base and center contact. Alligator clips on the ends of the wires make the test light that much easier to use (Other uses for the same test light are covered in later chapters on various electrical systems.)

Remove one end of the primary wire leading from distributor to coil, and put

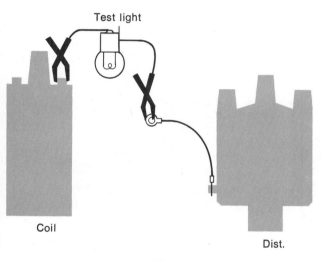

Test light

Coil

Dist.

Test Light Timing Hook-Up

the light across the gap between the terminal and the end of the removed wire. The test light will burn whenever the points close, and go out whenever they open.

Bring the engine to firing position for the No. 1 cylinder with the timing marks aligned. Loosen and rotate the distributor housing and retard it. The light will glow. Then, turn the distributor housing toward advance until the light just goes out. Stop there and tighten the housing clamp bolt. The basic timing is set.

With a Timing Light

The advantage of a timing light over the preceding methods is that you need not preset the engine to its No. 1 firing position; you can just let it idle. Furthermore, a timing light allows you to check the centrifugal and vacuum advance mechanisms, too.

Either a neon or a stroboscopic timing light can be used.

A simple *neon timing light* may cost as little as $10.00. However, its light will be weak. You will have to work in a fairly dark garage—or use the light at night—to see the timing marks. Even then, the marks will have to cleaned, and maybe even chalk-marked, for you to see them.

A neon timing light needs all the power it can get, so the No. 1 spark plug is not fired when such a light is hooked up.

To use a neon timing light, simply attach its two leads between the removed No. 1 spark cable and a good engine ground.

A *power timing light* is better. It uses either battery power, or electricity from a wall receptacle, to boost the spark sufficiently to fire a stroboscopic flashtube. The flashtube gives the same brilliant flash that a photographer's electronic flash gun does. With a power timing light, you can see the timing marks indoors or out, and whether they are clean or somewhat dirty. A power timing light has the added advantage that the spark cable is not disconnected; thus, the engine runs on all cylinders while being timed.

The handiest power timing lights use battery power. A good one costs from about $20 to more than $50.

To use a power timing light, plug it into a handy receptacle, or connect its slim red primary lead to the positive battery post and its slim black primary lead to the

Timing With a Timing Light

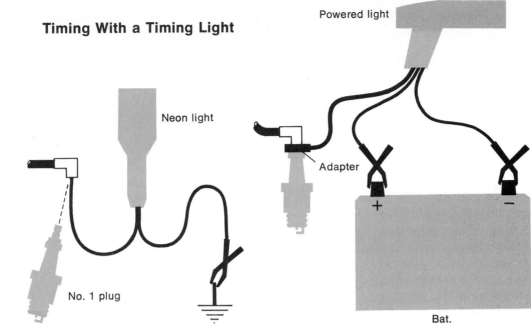

Neon light

No. 1 plug

Neon Timing Light Hook-Up

Powered light

Adapter

+   **−**

Bat.

Power Timing Light Hook-Up

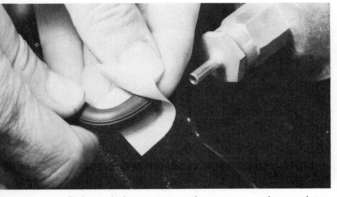

Before timing, remove the vacuum advance hose from the distributor and plug its end with tape.

As the engine idles, shine the timing light on the timing marks.

The timing marks—here, chalked for visibility—will appear to stand still. Rotate the distributor until the proper mark aligns with the pointer.

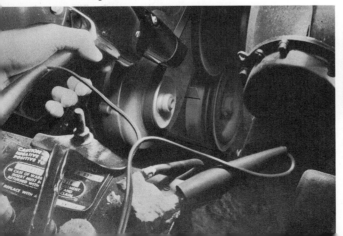

negative battery post. In either case, its heavy high-tension lead conducts into the No. 1 spark cable circuit, using the adapter furnished. One end of the adapter fastens to the plug terminal, while the other end reaches up into the spark cable boot.

Timing. Connect your timing light to the No. 1 spark cable so that every time the cylinder fires, the light flashes. The duration of each flash is so brief that when the light is directed onto the spinning timing mark, the mark seems to stand still. Because it "stands still" only at actual firing, the mark shows exactly where the spark is occurring in terms of the timing pointer and its reference marks.

Be careful to keep the timing light—and your hands—away from moving engine parts. Those parts may look stationary under the quick flashes of light, but do not be fooled. In fact, some timing marks are so inaccessible that you may want to remove belts and stop the moving parts before you snuggle the light in closer.

Start the engine and set the speed as specified for ignition timing adjustments (most often, idling speed). Disconnect all distributor vacuum lines if that is called for. If it is, as is usually the case, stick a piece of masking tape over the tube ends to keep vacuum from leaking into the engine.

Aim the flashing timing light at the timing marks. If the marks do not line up according to specifications, loosen the distributor hold-down clamp and turn the distributor housing one way or the other until they are correctly aligned.

For instance, if your car manufacturer calls for a basic timing advance of 6° before top dead center (sometimes called 6° BTDC), rotate the distributor until the 6° advance mark lines up with the pointer. With a timing light, you need not figure out which way to turn the distributor—the illuminated timing marks will show you

whether you are heading in the right direction.

Testing Advance

To check the operation of the timing advance mechanisms—centrifugal and vacuum—leave the vacuum lines to the distributor disconnected.

Centrifugal advance. Check the centrifugal advance first. Adjust the idle speed back to specifications if it was changed for basic timing. Aim the timing light at the timing marks while you or a helper accelerate the engine from idle in quick, brief bursts. With each burst of speed, the timing should advance. Afterward, as the speed returns to idle, the timing should go back to its initial position.

If degree marks on the pulley go far enough to let you read timing advance— say, 30°—you can compare the advance at various engine speeds with that called for in the specifications.

You will need a tachometer to measure engine speed accurately. Run the engine up to 2000 revolutions per minute (rpm) and note the amount of advance. Compare it with your engine's specified maximum centrifugal advance. Trouble with centrifugal advance mechanisms is rare; but if timing does not advance properly, you should take the car to a shop to have the distributor removed, tested, and adjusted.

Vacuum advance. Most advance problems come from the vacuum advance. To test it, reconnect the vacuum line, or lines, to the distributor, and run the timing advance test again. If the advance is now greater than before, the vacuum advance is probably okay.

Compare the advance at 2000 rpm with the specified maximum total advance for your engine. If the advance does not meet the specifications closely, replace the vacuum advance diaphragm. It is a simple job

The stroboscopic timing light, though more expensive, is easier to use.

described earlier in this chapter. Usually, the job does not require removal of the distributor.

Modern advances. Seemingly complex systems have been added to 1968 and later engines to vary the spark timing in the interests of reduced exhaust emissions.

One is Ford's distributor modulation valve. A tiny alternator (an alternating current generator) on the speedometer shaft controls distributor vacuum, and thus spark advance. The device is found only on certain engine-transmission combinations where the manufacturer had trouble maintaining a low carbon monoxide content in the emissions.

Another type is a water-jacket-mounted thermostatic valve that adjusts spark timing according to engine temperature. Hot-burning combustion chambers are necessary for lowered exhaust emissions; but when they get too hot, they need cooling off. Speeding up the idle through a spark advance does the job.

American Motors' post-1969 valve typically switches the vacuum source from the carburetor to the intake manifold when engine temperature reaches 235°. Manifold vacuum is higher than carburetor vacuum, so spark advance is increased to speed up the idle.

The valve's operation is checked with a tachometer on a warmed-up engine. On the American Motors valve, if idle speed drops 200 rpm when the hose at the lowest port is removed and plugged, the valve should be replaced.

If the speed holds, cover the radiator and run the engine until the temperature indicator reaches the high end of the operating band, but no higher. The valve is doing its job if engine speed then increases by 200 rpm. If it doesn't, replace the valve.

Let the engine temperature return to normal before switching off the engine.

ADVANCED IGNITION TUNING

Regular service of ignition components and simple timing, as described above, should be enough to keep your ignition system in tip-top shape.

But if you enjoy the jigsaw puzzle aspects of electrical work, you can—with additional test equipment—do further tests that are at once easier and more precise.

Specifically, there are three useful ignition testers:

• The VOM, or volt-ohm-milliameter;
• The tachometer-dwell, or tach-dwell, meter;
• The ignition oscilloscope.

The VOM is an all-purpose tester; we will describe specific VOM ignition tests in this chapter, and suggest other electrical tests with this instrument in later chapters.

The tach-dwell meter and ignition oscilloscope invariably come with complete testing instructions. For that reason, we will only discuss these testers in general.

VOM

For almost anything you do with electricity, whether on your car or around the house, this instrument is extremely handy.

It measures the level of volts (units of electrical pressure), ohms (units of resistance to electrical flow) and amperes (units of electrical flow—a milliampere is $1/1000$ ampere) that are present in a circuit.

Because electrical current, pressure, and resistance are inter-related, current flow through the meter indicates all three values.

With a VOM, you can make go-or-no-go checks of primary wiring, coil, distributor points, spark cables, ignition switch, ground circuit, distributor cap, rotor, built-in primary resistance, and more. To check a condenser, however, see your mechanic.

A VOM ranges in price from $5 to $20, depending on quality. A more costly unit generally has more scales, is more sensitive, and has a larger, easier-to-read dial.

Separate scales are provided on the dial to let you read the various values. Most VOMs can measure up to several thousand volts A.C. or D.C., about half an ampere of current, and up to one to ten megohms of resistance. (A megohm is 1000 ohms.)

The VOM's selector switch is much like the channel selector on your TV set. Before you take a reading, you turn the switch to the proper position for factor and value.

The VOM has two leads, one red and one black, which plug into sockets on the instrument. The red lead should always go into the socket labeled either volts, ohms, milliamperes, output, or "+." The black lead should go into the common, negative or "−" socket. Getting into the habit of polarizing the test leads correctly during hookup makes your electrical testing that much easier.

Volt-ohm-milliammeter, called the VOM, is a handy instrument for most electrical testing. It generally comes with test prods.

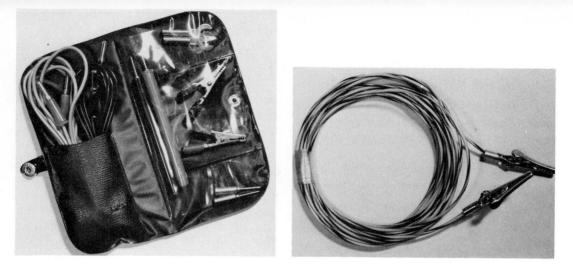

VOM accessories that make tests easier include a lead kit (*left*) that contains extra-long leads, plugs, alligator clips and test prod tips, and a jumper wire (*right*). Make the jumper yourself with No. 16 (AWG) wire and alligator clips.

Using the VOM. The instructions that come with your VOM will tell you how to zero the pointer. Do that with the meter either vertical or horizontal, depending on how you are going to use it.

Tap on the case gently to normalize the needle during the zero adjustment. The movement of a VOM is delicate, and easily damaged by jarring.

When you measure a live circuit without knowing how high a reading to expect, set the selector switch on its highest scale to prevent possible damage. Then, with the test leads hooked into the circuit, turn the selector to lower settings until you get a significant needle swing.

If the needle tries to swing to the left, below the zero point, the test prods have been used with the wrong polarity. Reverse them. On ohm readings, you do not have that problem.

Never take an ohm reading of a live circuit—you can easily blow the meter. Make sure that the circuit is dead before you read its resistance. Similarly, never forget to set the selector switch properly before reading a live circuit.

Just to play safe, get into the habit of turning the meter selector out of the ohms position as soon as you are through taking ohm readings. Place the selector on some high volts position, where it cannot be harmed by accidental connection to a source of electricity.

For the tests, you should have a short No. 16 (AWG) jump wire with alligator clips on both ends (about $2) to double as a helpful test-lead for your VOM. Sometimes, the alligator clips are more convenient than the prods that come with the VOM.

Our testing instructions apply to nearly all U. S. cars with 12-volt, negative-ground electrical systems. If your car has a positive-ground system, reverse the red and black lead hookups shown in the drawings. If your car has a six volt system, the primary circuits, primary meter settings, and readouts will vary from those we give, so you cannot use them.

One caution before you start: Never try to make primary circuit tests on an engine with transistorized ignition. A wrong hookup can blow the system in a flash. Secondary circuit checks, however, can be made on any ignition system.

Here are the tests in the order you should make them:

(text continued on page 99)

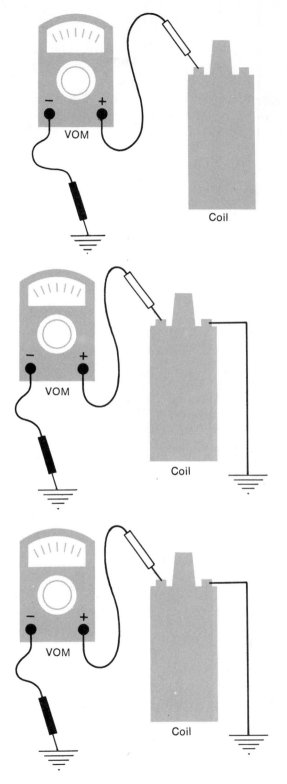

Coil Primary Voltage

Battery voltage. With the VOM at the 12 DC volts position and the meter hooked up, make sure all accessories are off. Turn the ignition switch on. If the VOM needle falls short of 12 volts, nudge the starter to get the points open. The meter should now read normal battery voltage. Low readings could mean: low battery, a ground between coil and distributor or inside the distributor, a ground between coil and battery.

Running voltage. Add a jumper between the coil's distributor primary terminal and ground. Flip the ignition switch on and off several times. Each time the switch is on, the needle should be between 5 and 7 volts. Fluctuating readings could mean a faulty ignition switch. Less than 5 volts could mean a loose battery-to-coil connection. More than 7 volts could mean a loose coil-to-distributor wire.

Cranking voltage. Using the same hook-up, turn the ignition switch to "start." The meter should read about 9 volts (in Fords, about 7 volts). The cranking voltage should be greater than the running voltage just tested. If it is not, the bypass switching system in the coil may be faulty, the starter may be drawing too much current from the battery, or the battery may be too weak to hold a sufficient voltage during cranking.

Primary Voltage Drop

Running circuit. With the VOM at the 12 D.C. volts position and all accessories off, flip the ignition switch on and off. The meter should read between 5 and 7 volts (on some Fords, 4.5 to 6.9 volts). This reading should be the same every time the switch is on. A too-high reading means excessive resistance between battery and coil—look for corroded terminals. A too-low reading means faulty primary resistance, a job for a mechanic.

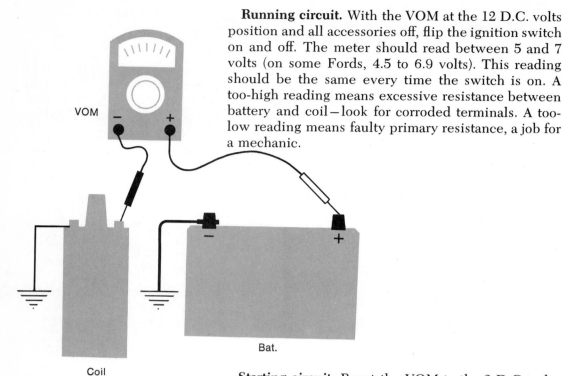

VOM

Coil

Bat.

Starting circuit. Reset the VOM to the 3 D.C. volts position. The meter will read off the scale to the right. Turn on the ignition switch. The needle should drop to 1 volt or less (1.5 volts or less on some Fords). Excessive voltage drop may result from a loose connection, excessive resistance or faulty bypass switch. Pin-point the problem with individual voltage drop tests between each part of the circuit.

VOM

Coil

Bat.

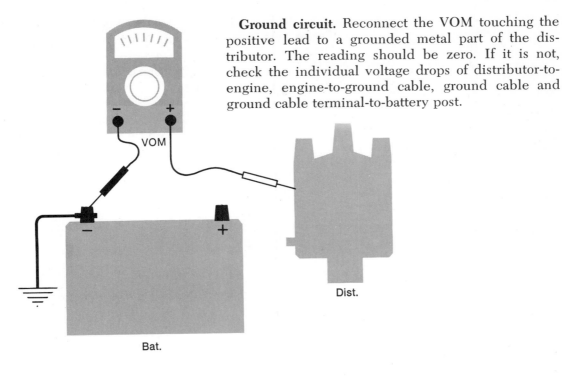

Ground circuit. Reconnect the VOM touching the positive lead to a grounded metal part of the distributor. The reading should be zero. If it is not, check the individual voltage drops of distributor-to-engine, engine-to-ground cable, ground cable and ground cable terminal-to-battery post.

VOM

Dist.

Bat.

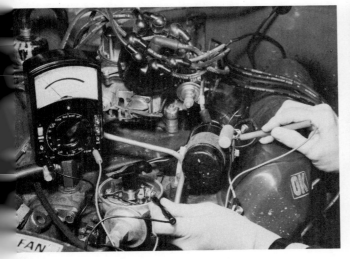

To test individual voltage drop, use the prods to isolate one segment of a circuit. Here, the drop between coil and points is being measured.

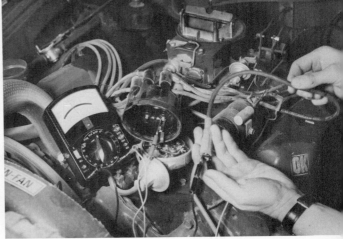

Spark cable resistance is measured with the VOM set on RX100 ohms. Alligator clips on the leads makes this connection easier. When you perform this test, wiggle the cable. If the reading fluctuates, the cable has a broken conductor.

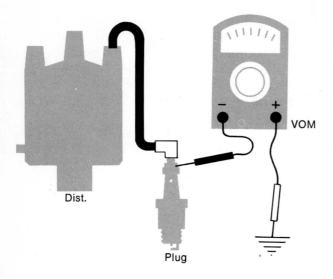

Dist.

Plug

VOM

Coil polarity. To achieve this hook-up, separate the spark plug boot from the plug terminal with a paper clip. Set the VOM to the highest D.C. volts position. As the engine idles, contact the black prod to the now-accessible plug terminal. If the meter reads up-scale, the polarity is correct. If the meter tries to sink below zero, the coil's polarity is reversed.

Distributor voltage drop. Set the VOM on 12 D.C. volts. With all accessories off, turn the ignition switch on. Nudge the starter to open the points. The meter should read the battery voltage. If it is above 12 volts, the points are either burned or not closing, or there is a ground in the coil-to-distributor wire or within the distributor. If there is a problem, find it. Then, nudge the starter to close the points. The meter should read zero. Switch the VOM to the lowest D.C. volt position. The meter should not exceed 0.1 volts (on Fords, 0.25 volts). The lower the reading, the better. If it is too high, perform individual voltage drop tests of the components.

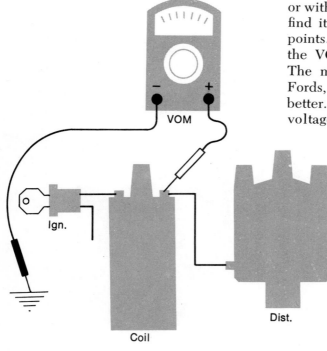

VOM

Ign.

Dist.

Coil

Coil Tests

Primary to case. Primary windings must be fully insulated; if not, primary current leaks out instead of producing a hot spark. With the primary wires disconnected and the VOM set to the highest ohm position, touch the prods as shown in the diagram. Be sure to hold the prods by their insulated grips. If the reading is not infinity, replace the coil.

Coil

Primary resistance. Set the VOM to its lowest ohm position and touch the prods as shown. The reading should be about 1.5 ohms. This is so low that inexpensive testers may not indicate it accurately. If the reading is more than 3 ohms, replace the coil.

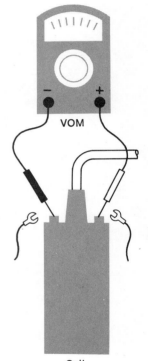

Coil

Secondary cable removed

Secondary resistance. Turn the VOM to the RX100 setting. Remove the coil-to-distributor primary wire. Press one test prod into the coil tower until it contacts the metal terminal fully. Compare the reading against the manufacturer's specifications (these vary considerably from one make to another). If the reading is outside the specifications, replace the coil.

Coil

Resistance Tests

Check resistance of resistor spark plugs with the VOM set on ohms. The reading should be between 10,000 and 20,000 ohms on most of these plugs.

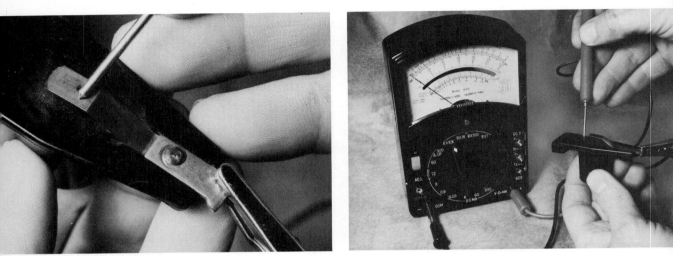

With the VOM set for low ohms, test the distributor rotor. From tip to contact spring (*left*), there should be zero resistance. Next set the VOM on high ohms. With one prod on the tip and the other probing all insulated surfaces (*right*), the meter should read infinite resistance. If the rotor fails these tests, replace it.

With the VOM set for low ohms, test the distributor cap. Test every terminal from outside to inside (*left*). There should be zero resistance. Next, with the VOM set on high ohms, test every terminal against its surrounding insulated surface (*right*). Resistance should be infinite. If the cap is clean and fails these tests, replace it.

Tach-Dwell Meter

The tachometer-dwell meter is a two-in-one instrument that measures engine rpm while showing whether the gap of the distributor points is correct. It can also show whether or not a distributor is worn out.

A tach-dwell meter is sometimes more convenient for setting point gap than a thickness gauge. It is also a good running check on your thickness gauge setting.

The tachometer itself has many uses during the tune-up procedure.

The dwell portion of the meter, as its name implies, measures the dwell—the angle through which the distributor shaft rotates while the points are closed. Dwell is the time, in distributor degrees, during which the coil soaks up electricity from the battery between firings.

Dwell is always measured in distributor degrees—and not engine degrees, which are double. During the time the distributor rotates 30°, the engine rotates 60°. The degrees-of-dwell, also called the dwell angle, cam angle, or simply dwell, is measured electrically by a correctly adjusted dwell meter.

A dwell range for each engine is specified by the car manufacturer. It is greatest for a four-cylinder engine and least for eight; the more cylinders there are, the greater is the time between firings. The greater the gap, the less the dwell and vice versa.

Delco window-adjustment distributors are beautifully built for setting the dwell while the engine is running and hooked to a dwell meter. The dwell on other distributors is set with a thickness gauge and readjusted with the engine off and the distributor cap and rotor removed.

Tach-dwell meter electrically measures the length of time the distributor points are closed. This specialized instrument greatly speeds tune-ups.

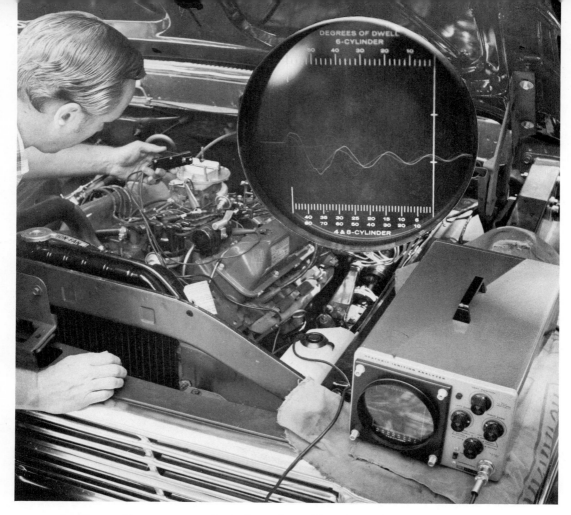

Ignition oscilloscope can evaluate the entire ignition system in minutes. The read-out (*insert*) is in the form of an oscillating "trace."

Ignition Oscilloscope

An oscilloscope checks out the entire ignition system in minutes, with just one easy hookup. With that tester, you need no separate ignition analyzer.

An oscilloscope lets you see ignition system functions such as firing voltage, spark duration, dwell, coil, condenser, and breaker point action as well as maximum ignition output. You can check spark plugs, ignition cables, rotor, distributor cap—everything—in minutes.

The only disadvantage of an oscilloscope is its high initial cost. A low-cost way is to assemble a kit; for instance,

Heath Company sells a $100 package that you should be able to put together with no special knowledge of electronics. An acceptable oscilloscope already assembled costs about three times as much.

This tester is simply an instant-reading voltmeter with a memory. A regular voltmeter takes a second or so for the needle to reach a reading and settle on it. When you hook a voltmeter to a rapidly varying voltage, as when you test ignition output, you get only an average reading of ignition voltage.

In an oscilloscope, a beam of electrons, rather than a needle, indicates the voltages. As the electron beam hits the front of the scope, a phosphor coating, like that on a TV screen, glows wherever the beam strikes it. Electronic circuits swing the beam back and forth horizontally across the screen.

The glow remains long enough for the moving electron beam to create a straight line across the face of the oscilloscope tube. Ignition system voltage makes the beam bounce up and down, resulting in a wiggly line that is called a trace.

The trace is actually a measurement of ignition voltage plotted against time. It tells the whole story of your car's primary and secondary ignition system. Voltage readings of the primary and the secondary systems produce different patterns, because a different voltage registers for each.

Since the secondary trace gives a far better insight into ignition problems, it is the one most often measured.

A normal, healthy ignition system produces a typical trace on the scope screen. When you become familiar with the normal trace, you will know that something is wrong when the trace looks different— each ignition problem changes the trace, creating a distinct but abnormal pattern.

TROUBLESHOOTING

When you have ignition trouble on the road, where you cannot do a complete tune-up, follow these tips:

No-start. First, make sure the trouble is in the ignition system. Remove the high-voltage cable from the distributor's tower

IGNITION TROUBLESHOOTING

SYMPTOM	CAUSE	CURE
No spark from coil	Points dirty, burned, not closing	Check points, clean or replace if necessary
	Condenser defective	Replace if in doubt
	Coil defective	Test with VOM, replace if faulty
No spark at plugs	Rotor or distributor cap defective	Check, replace if necessary
	Faulty spark cables	Test with VOM, replace any that is defective
Spark at plugs, but will not start	Faulty spark plugs	Clean or replace
	Ignition timing off	Adjust timing
	Problem outside of ignition system	See other chapters on tuning

No-Start Remedies

If your car is hard to start, short across the points with screwdriver. A good spark means worn points.

Emergency cleaning of points can be done with the abrasive striking surface of a matchbook.

In cold or damp weather, make sure such ignition parts as the distributor cap are free of moisture.

Make sure the primary terminals on the coil and distributor are tightly fastened.

and hold it about ³/₁₆ inch from a ground while someone tries to start the car. To avoid shock, either hold it by the insulation, or prop the cable in position with the end of a screwdriver, holding the handle of the tool.

If there is no spark, or the spark is thin and weak, you have an ignition problem.

Remove the distributor cap and take off the rotor. Turn the engine until the points open. Short across them with a screwdriver while you watch for a fat, blue spark at the coil wire. If there is a spark now, the points are most likely the cause of the problem.

Have someone crank over the engine while you watch the points open and close. If they do not seem to be opening the right amount, adjust them. Better too wide than too narrow for a hard-to-start condition.

When you get home, you can make a more accurate adjustment with thickness gauges or a tach-dwell meter.

If the points open and close about right but seem oily, dirty, or burned, clean them by drawing the corner of a handkerchief between them. Then, file them with a fingernail file, the striking surface of a matchbook cover, or a knife or screwdriver. Wipe the points again and try the spark once more.

Moisture on ignition parts also can prevent starting by drawing off current needed to fire the cylinders. To get going, wipe the spark plug insulators, cables, and the distributor cap with a dry cloth. Also wipe the coil tower and coil-to-distributor cable.

If the engine then fires on one or two cylinders, at least you have made progress. Next, remove the distributor cap and wipe it dry on the inside. Wipe the rotor too, being careful not to bend or break the spring contact. Replace everything and try again. If the cause was moisture, the

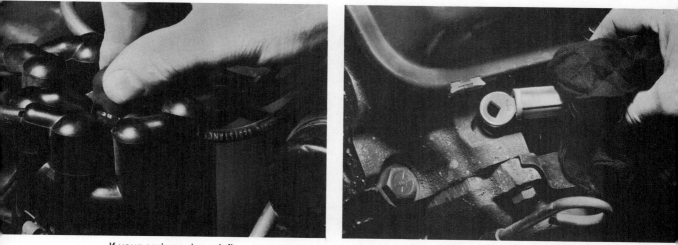

If your car's engine misfires constantly, check to see that all spark cables are fully seated (*left*). In addition, with a key or bent paper clip, test to make sure there is a spark (*right*).

engine should start. And once it starts on a few cylinders, it should soon fire on the others.

As a final attempt to get some spark, look for a loose or broken primary wire to the coil or distributor.

In nine cases out of ten, you can clear up a case of no-start if the trouble is in the ignition system. But if a bad coil or condenser, badly fouled plugs, or some other unusual problem causes the no-start, you cannot do much without tools and testers.

Misfiring. An engine that misfires on one or more cylinders should not be driven far. Raw, unburned gasoline in those cylinders washes oil off the cylinder walls, which then may become scored by the piston rings. Find and fix the misfiring, or get professional help, promptly.

If the cylinder misfires all the time, the problem is easier to solve. Remove one spark plug wire at a time with the engine idling. The idle should slow down and get noticeably rougher each time you remove a cable to a cylinder that is firing.

When you reach the cylinder that is not firing, though, you will detect no difference in the idle when you pull that cable off.

Be sure that the cable in question is pushed all the way down into the distributor tower, and that it makes contact with the metal terminal inside.

Switch off the engine. Bend a hairpin or paper clip and fit it up into the spark cable boot with the end sticking out. Restart the engine and hold the cable about 3/16 inch from a ground.

If you do not see a spark, chances are the spark cable is defective. If there is a good spark, the plug must be the culprit.

Misfiring under load indicates weak ignition. It may get so serious that the car can barely move. Keep the engine going and firing as long as you can while proceeding toward service; once you stop the engine, it may not start again. Shift down to a lower gear if the engine will not pull in high.

If you stall completely, check for a spark. If the spark is weak or nonexistent, try the checks outlined earlier. Condenser and coil troubles often cause such symptoms. You usually need the services of a mechanic to cure these ills.

8

Engine Tuning: Fuel System

The fuel system starts at the gasoline tank, continues through the fuel line, the fuel pump, through the fuel filter into the carburetor, and ends at the engine's intake valves, where the air/fuel mixture enters the cylinders.

We will examine the problems and remedies for each of these components separately, following the route that the gasoline takes.

FUEL TANK

The fuel tank needs little attention. It is filled through a large pipe. As the tank fills, air trapped in the top of the tank is vented through a tube leading back to the filler neck. Some fuel tanks are vented to let air in as the gasoline flows out or to let air out as warming fuel expands. Fuel tanks in 1971 and later models have evaporative emission controls and are not vented. (See the chapter on antipollution system service.)

Vents. Fuel vents rarely act up. If your car has a vented gas cap and it is not working, the engine will soon run out of fuel and the car will stop. If removing the gas tank cap gets you started again, the problem is in the cap or the integral vent.

To reduce fuel evaporation, and thus fuel tank emissions, some gas tanks have pressure systems. These allow about 2 psi of pressure to build up inside the tank before any venting occurs. In such a tank, you might hear a hiss as you remove the cap. Do not condemn the fuel tank vent.

If the gas tank cap is the self-venting type, it should rattle when you shake it. If it does not, it probably should be replaced. If the gas cap has no vent holes, your car should have an internal tank vent. Look in the service manual to make sure the right cap has been installed. Never use a nonventing cap on a nonvented fuel tank. Some provision must be made to let air in and out of the tank.

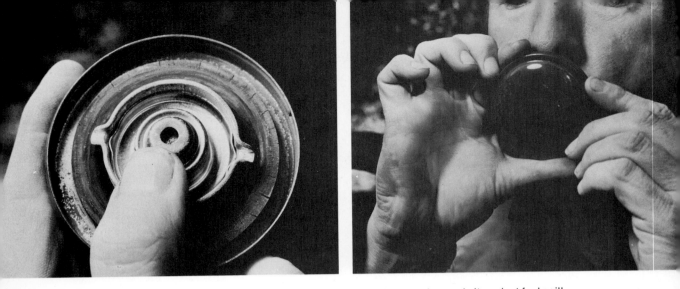

Vented gas tank cap (*left*) has a hole and valve in the center that seals it against fuel spill-over, but allows air in and out. If you cannot blow through a cap, it is either unvented or a defective vented cap.

Fuel gauge. Almost all fuel tanks have some provision for indicating fuel level, usually a self-contained float-rheostat. The rheostat has a resistance that varies with float position. When the float rides low, resistance is low; when the float rides high, resistance is high. The fuel gauge is simply a milliammeter that reads out cur-rent flow through the rheostat as tank fuel level. Trouble with any part is rare, but the tank unit fails more often than the gauge. Some fuel tanks must be removed to get at the tank unit. For electrical tests for a defective fuel gauge, see the later chapter that deals with automotive wiring and lighting.

The Fuel System

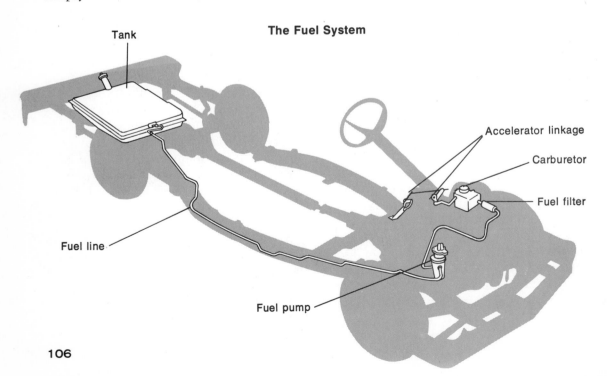

Tank

Accelerator linkage

Carburetor

Fuel filter

Fuel line

Fuel pump

Test the fuel line for leaks by connecting a vacuum gauge to it at the tank end. The reading should equal that of the fuel pump vacuum test.

FUEL LINES

Fuel system lines are mostly of steel tubing. Many older cars use a flexible line between the steel fuel line and the fuel pump inlet. Newer cars have replaced the flex line with a flexible loop of steel line; this minimizes the number of joints in the system. A single steel pressure line leads from the pump pressure outlet to the carburetor float bowl inlet. Compression fittings make up all joints between lines and tank, pump, and carburetor. In rare instances, a fitting will work loose or a line will develop a leak.

FUEL PUMP

Engine performance at all speeds requires sufficient fuel at the correct pressure. Insufficient fuel pressure makes the engine starve, perhaps even stall. Too much pressure floods the engine with fuel. A potential trouble spot is the fuel pump. Most last a long time—often 100,000 miles or more—without service. But they can fail any time.

The fuel pump sucks gasoline from the fuel tank and pumps it into the carburetor float bowl. Most fuel pumps work by mechanical action. A lever arm rides on a cam inside the engine. As the engine rotates, the cam does too, cranking the fuel pump lever back and forth and moving a flexible diaphragm up and down inside the pump chamber. When the dia-

Fuel pumps are usually noted for their longevity. But if one acts up, it is usually because of the failure of one of the five components illustrated below.

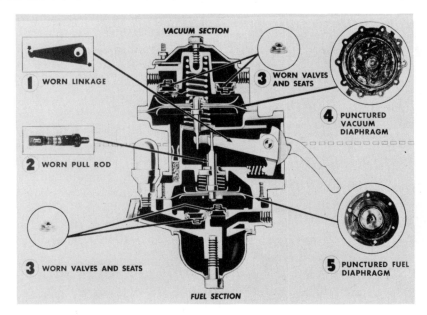

phragm moves away from the chamber, it draws fuel in through the suction side of the pump. The suction valve opens with the inflow of fuel and the pressure valve closes. The valves keep fuel flowing in one direction. When the diaphragm moves toward the chamber, the suction valve closes, pushing the charge of fuel past the open pressure valve and out toward the carburetor float bowl. When the diaphragm wears out, the valves do not function properly. When the lever wears excessively, the pump may fail.

For fuel pump tests, you will need a vacuum gauge.

Fuel pump volume test. This should be made while the pump seems to be working satisfactorily, not after it fails and leaves you stranded at the side of a road.

Using an open-end wrench, disconnect the fuel line running from the pump to the carburetor at the pump outlet and attach a rubber hose to the pump outlet. One of the adapters furnished with your vacuum gauge may help this hookup. You also can

To test fuel pump volume, unhook the fuel line at the carburetor and aim it into a container. Start the engine. You should collect a pint in 30 seconds.

use the rubber hose from the vacuum gauge, if you can remove it.

Get a bottle with a capacity of at least one pint and with 1-ounce graduations; hold the bottle under the hose to catch the fuel as it is pumped out. Then start the engine. (It will idle for several minutes on the fuel in the float bowl.) Fuel should flow freely through the rubber hose into the container. When the fuel in the container reaches the 4-ounce mark, submerge the end of the hose in the fuel and watch for bubbles. Bubbles indicate leaks in the fuel pump or in the suction side of the fuel delivery system (the fuel lines between the gas tank and the pump).

See how long it takes for one pint of fuel to be delivered by the pump, and compare this time with the manufacturer's specifications. Most pumps should deliver a pint in 30 seconds or less. Low volume indicates a defective fuel pump or a restricted or leaking tank-to-fuel pump line.

After the volume test, find a safe way to dispose of the collected fuel. If it is perfectly clean, pour it back into the gas tank.

Fuel pump pressure test. Even if the pump passes the volume test, check for pressure; a weak pump can still produce an adequate volume of fuel when it is not under pressure. Temporarily reconnect the fuel pump-to-carburetor line and run the engine for 10 seconds to refill the carburetor float bowl. Then, remove the line again at the pump and install the adapter — this time, along with the vacuum gauge — on the outlet opening of the pump, where the rubber line was connected during the volume test. Start the engine and let it idle. When the vacuum gauge needle stops climbing, compare the reading with the specifications for your fuel pump. (For some models, the directions call for an engine speed that is higher than idling speed.)

To test fuel pump pressure, connect the gauge to the pressure side of the pump. To test vacuum, connect the gauge to the suction side of the pump.

A common pressure range is 3½ to 4½ pounds per square inch (psi). The specifications for most Ford products call for 4 to 6 psi.

Too little pressure can be caused by vacuum leaks in the fuel lines or a weak fuel pump that is about to fail. A weak fuel pump pressure reading also may be caused by a worn fuel pump pushrod. To get at the pushrod, you have to remove the fuel pump.

Too much fuel pump pressure can cause an overly rich carburetor mixture, flooding problems, and poor gasoline mileage. The best cure is to install a fuel pressure regulator on the pump-to-carburetor fuel line. (Replacing an overpressure fuel pump is not always successful; the replacement pump — whether new or rebuilt — often produces the same result.)

Instructions for fuel pump pressure-testing once told you to switch off the engine at the end of the pressure test and see whether the pump would hold its rated pressure. Such a test no longer is valid; modern fuel pumps are built with a bleed-back feature. This prevents the pump from holding pressure against the float needle of a stopped engine and possibly flooding the carburetor with fuel. A small opening inside the pump lets pressure bleed back from the pressure side to the nonpressure side of the pump.

If you noticed bubbles during the volume test, make a vacuum test to learn whether the air is entering the fuel system from the fuel pump or through the tank-to-pump fuel line. Reconnect the fuel line and idle the engine for 10 seconds to refill the float bowl. Shut off the engine, disconnect the fuel line at the inlet of the fuel pump, and attach your vacuum gauge to the pump with the proper adapter. Then start the engine and idle it.

If peak vacuum is below 10 inches, the air leak is in the fuel pump itself. Switch off the engine and watch the vacuum reading. It should hold if the fuel pump is in good shape. Replace the fuel line back on the pump inlet and tighten the connection.

If the fuel pump vacuum test failed to find the problem, remove the fuel line from the gas tank and hook the vacuum gauge to the end of the line. Run the engine and note the vacuum reading. A low reading indicates a leak in the long fuel delivery line between tank and fuel pump. A new line must be installed — a tough job that you might prefer turning over to a shop. If you do the job yourself, do not use copper tubing.

Vacuum booster test. If your car was built before the advent of electric windshield wipers, it may have a vacuum booster on the fuel pump. A vacuum booster fuel pump looks like two fuel pumps, one above the other; one pumps fuel, the other pumps air. The purpose of the booster is to operate the windshield wipers when hard acceleration leaves too

Fuel Pump Service

To remove a fuel pump, take off both fuel lines and the cap screws that hold it to the engine. Discard the gasket between pump and engine. When you replace the pump, install a new gasket.

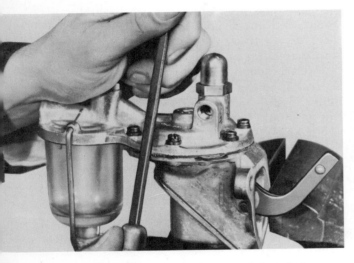

File marks across both pump halves before you disassemble them. This helps to align them later.

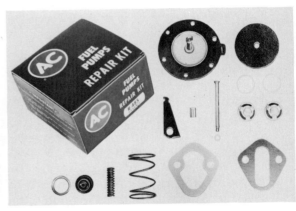

A good fuel pump rebuilding kit should include gaskets, diaphragm, valves and springs.

When you replace a fuel pump, be sure to place the pump's lever arm correctly on the pushrod or cam.

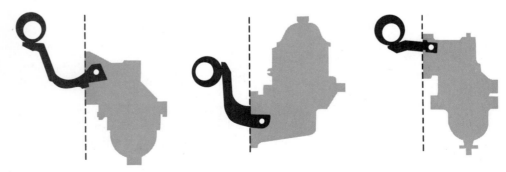

little manifold vacuum. Before such boosters, windshield wipers tended to stall under hard acceleration.

To test the vacuum booster, disconnect the vacuum line at the booster pump vacuum inlet. Then, connect the hose from your vacuum gauge to the inlet. With the engine running at a fast idle—about 1,000 rpm—the vacuum gauge should generally show 8½ inches or more of vacuum. Stop the engine and watch the gauge needle for several seconds. It should fall off slowly. Rapid falling indicates air leaks in the pump, pump valves or tester connections.

The fuel pump and the vacuum booster are separate mechanisms. One can fail without affecting the other; but when one fails, both should be replaced as a unit.

Repair or replace? Late-model fuel pumps are not designed to come apart for service; replacement is the only fix. Older pumps can be rebuilt with new gaskets, springs, valves, and other parts from a rebuilding kit. But unless you enjoy such tinkering, we suggest that you buy a new or rebuilt pump. In this instance, rebuilt pumps from a reliable dealer are as efficient as, and less costly than, new ones. Be sure to use a new pump mounting gasket between the pump and the engine.

Under no circumstances should a defective fuel pump or vacuum booster be left on the engine. If the problem is something like a ruptured diaphragm, which creates an opening between crankcase and intake manifold on many engines, oil vapor will be drawn into the engine. This fouls spark plugs, valves and other parts. What's more, the PCV anti-emissions system will be totally disrupted.

Removing a fuel pump is a simple nuts-and-bolts operation. Fuel pumps that work directly off a special cam lobe will lift out with no problems. Pushrod-operated pumps should be lifted to the top of the opening and then tilted back; this lifts the pump arm off the pushrod inside the engine. When replacing a pushrod-operated pump, you may need to stuff heavy grease around the rod to hold it in place while the pump is being positioned over it.

FUEL VAPOR SEPARATOR

Some late-model, high-performance V-8s have a fuel vapor separator between the fuel pump and the carburetor to help prevent vapor lock. The separator, a metal can about the size of the fuel pump, has three lines coming out of it. It includes a filter screen, inlet fitting, outlet fitting, and metered orifice.

Fuel is pumped into the separator until the unit is filled. The outlet tube picks off fuel from the bottom of the can and routes it to the carburetor for burning. Any fuel vapor caused by excessive heat rises to the top of the separator and is forced out the metered orifice, through the return line, and back to the fuel tank. There, it condenses back into liquid fuel.

Check first to see that the fuel vapor separator unit is correctly installed. The inlet and return fittings should be at the bottom of the unit, and the outlet fitting should be at the top.

Test for a restricted or plugged screen with a fuel volume test through the unit. Disconnect the fuel line at the carburetor, place a container under the end of the fuel line, start the engine, and let it idle. In one minute of idling, one quart of fuel should be delivered. If less fuel comes out and if the fuel pump and lines are not at fault, replace the unit.

If you experience vapor lock in spite of the unit, remove the return hose to make sure the metering orifice is open. If it is clogged, clean it with a bent paper clip. The fuel line back to the tank, if clogged, can be cleared with air pressure. But first remove the gas tank filler cap.

FUEL FILTERS

Even the smallest particles of dirt can clog the tiny passages that run through a carburetor. Therefore, one or more filters are usually included in the fuel system.

The first filter may be on the fuel pickup tube, where gas flows from the bottom of the gas tank into the fuel line.

Many early-model fuel pumps come with sediment bowls attached. The glass bowl is held to the pump by a screw-tightened bail. To remove the glass bowl, loosen the nut on the end of the bail and swing the bail out of the way. Clean the bowl and the fine copper screen immediately above it. After you have replaced them and tightened the bail nut, run the engine to check for leaks. Modern fuel pumps often contain fine brass screens to hold back the larger particles.

Cartridge-type fuel filters should be changed at the manufacturer-recommended intervals. Loosen the filter element by turning it counterclockwise until it falls free. Many times the fuel filter cartridge is on so tight that you need a wrench to get it off. The special wrench for this purpose looks much like an oil filter cartridge wrench, but is smaller. Install the new one by turning it clockwise; give it half a turn after the rubber gasket has made initial contact.

To service the fuel inlet filter, disconnect the fuel line at the carburetor with an open-end wrench. Often, the inlet fitting on the carburetor must also be removed to get at the filter element, which is a porous brass tube. When removing the filter, note the positions of the washers, gaskets and springs. Wash the filter in carburetor solvent, shake it dry and blow air through it. Install the parts as they came out.

In addition, a fine porous bronze filter is installed in the fuel line at the carburetor float bowl on some models. Make sure this is clean.

Because they continually strain out impurities in the gasoline, all fuel filters need periodic cleaning or replacement. More than just dirt can foul a filter. Water—from gas tank condensation, or from leaky service station storage tanks—can block filters, too. The proper schedule for such service appears in your owner's manual.

CARBURETOR

The carburetor is the most complex part of the engine. It has to provide the engine with the proper amount of air/fuel mixture depending on speed, load, temperature, and throttle opening.

A carburetor works on the venturi principle; that is, when air flowing through a tube comes to a narrow, restricted spot in the tube, it speeds up, creating a partial vacuum at that point. Venturi-created vacuum draws gasoline into the moving air and atomizes it into a readily combustible, vaporous air/fuel mixture. As this mixture is drawn into the cylinders and burns, it expands, providing the power to move the pistons and, in turn, the car.

The carburetor's tube is called a barrel. Each barrel contains one or more venturis. Sometimes, tubular venturis are placed one inside another. A carburetor with just one barrel, or tube, is called a single-barrel carburetor. Single-barrel carburetors usually are found on four-cylinder engines. Big-bore V-8s usually have two- or even four-barrel carburetors.

In carburetors with one or two barrels, the barrels work full time. High-performance, four-barrel carburetors have two primary barrels that run the car at ordinary speeds and two secondary barrels that cut in at high speeds. That gives smooth, economical operation at low speeds plus full breathing and high power at high speeds. The secondary barrels may be actuated mechanically by linkage from the primaries, by vacuum, or by electricity.

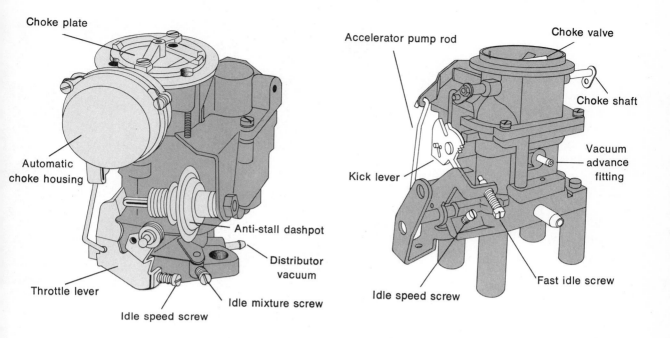

Choke plate

Automatic
choke housing

Throttle lever

Idle speed screw

Anti-stall dashpot

Distributor
vacuum

Idle mixture screw

Accelerator pump rod

Kick lever

Idle speed screw

Choke valve

Choke shaft

Vacuum
advance
fitting

Fast idle screw

Two Types of Carburetors

Leave adjustments of four-barrel car- buretors — including all-important syn- chronization — to a carburetor specialist.

A carburetor consists of several com- ponents and systems. In the order in which fuel enters, they are: the float system, the main metering system, the idle system, the power and pump systems, the choke sys- tem and the antistall dashpot.

In the following section, we will discuss each of these components and systems *in the order in which they should be ad- justed.* The initial step in a carburetor tune-up is to check the idle system; the final step is an exhaust analyzer test.

Idle System

The idle system keeps the engine run- ning when your foot is off the accelerator. A throttle plate in the carburetor, called a butterfly, is connected to the accelerator pedal. The butterfly is a valve that con-

trols the amount of air entering the engine. The flow of air, fast or slow, controls the amount of fuel drawn in through the main metering system. At idle, the butterfly is closed and the air flow is so slow that it cannot create enough venturi vacuum to draw fuel from the main metering system. The engine would die were it not for the idle system, which feeds fuel to the engine around the closed butterfly. Engine vacuum provides the needed suction.

The *idle speed screw* governs idle speed. That screw either rides the throttle shaft or bears against an arm extending from it. Its effect is to keep the throttle butterfly from completely closing.

Your car may have a *hot-idle solenoid,* a device that kicks up the idle speed when the engine is overheated. This device — which cannot be adjusted — must be off when you adjust idle. To be sure, find it — at the side of the carburetor base — and unhook it.

Do not confuse this with the *throttle stop modulator,* which is also a solenoid. Both are mounted at the side of the carburetor base, and both have plungers that contact the throttle arm and are fed by wires. Many 1969 and later models, especially those with air conditioning and automatic transmissions, have throttle modulators. Their purpose is to prevent dieseling, or the running of the engine after you switch off the ignition.

A pointed needle, called an *idle mixture screw,* seats against the port and controls the flow of idle fuel to the engine. One idle mixture screw is used per barrel.

A few carburetors also have an *idle air screw* that admits additional air when idling. Most carburetors, however, get idle air through the barely-open throttle butterfly.

Part of the idle system is an *off-idle system.* As the throttle is opened, the off-idle system helps make a smooth transition from idle to the point where the main metering system begins to function. Like the main metering system, the off-idle system has no adjustments. Problems there are rare.

The first step in adjusting the idle is to remove the air cleaner from the carburetor (unless the idle-adjustment instructions say to leave it on), connect a tachometer to the engine, and switch the tachometer to the low-rpm scale. Without a tachometer you cannot set idling speed to specifications or adjust for minimum exhaust emissions.

With the car resting level, warm the engine to operating temperature. Automatic transmissions should be in the drive position. In some models, the headlights should be switched on to load the charging system, or the air conditioning should be operating; check your shop manual for such special instructions.

Tachometer is vital for adjusting idle. With the engine at the specified speed, set idle by turning the idle speed adjusting screw.

Adjusting idle speed. The stop screw that governs idle speed is at the side of the carburetor, where it limits the amount that the throttle valve can close. Have a helper step on the accelerator pedal and then release it slowly. Check which screw on the carburetor contacts a stop just as the throttle closes. That is the correct one. Do not be fooled by the fast-idle screw—it looks the same but is part of the choke linkage. The fast-idle screw closes on a stepped or curved plate that is moved by the manual or automatic choke control. (More on the fast-idle screw later in this chapter.)

Turn the idle speed adjusting screw with a screwdriver, inward to increase the idling speed and outward to slow it down. Bring the idle to specified speed.

Adjusting the throttle stop modulator. The modulator is energized whenever the ignition switch is on; it holds the throttle open to maintain the normal idle speed.

When you switch off the ignition, the solenoid is de-energized and the throttle can close against its stop screw in the normal way. In that position, if the engine were to try to keep running, its idle speed would drop several hundred rpm—which would effectively kill the engine. You can check the action by watching its plunger while a helper shuts off the engine. The plunger should retract, letting the throttle close. Do not try to repair the unit. If it malfunctions, replace it.

When you adjust the idle on an engine with a throttle modulator, adjust both the normal and the lower idle speeds to specifications. But do not confuse the normal idle speed with the engine's fast-idle specifications. The two are very different. The normal idling speed probably will not be specified at more than 700 rpm, while the fast idle generally should be much higher.

Adjust the normal idle speed by turning the energized throttle solenoid in its threaded mounting bracket (GM engines) or screwing the shaft in and out (Ford engines). Get the lower idling speed by disconnecting the solenoid wire at its bullet connector to de-energize the solenoid while the engine is running. Then, adjust the throttle stop screw in the normal way. To finish, reconnect the wire.

Many air-conditioned 1971 and 1972 GM cars have no such slow-idle provision. Instead, the air conditioner clutch engages briefly upon engine shut-down to stall the engine if it should try to diesel.

Adjusting idle mixture. Now switch your attention to the idle mixture adjusting screw. (Two- and four-barrel carburetors have two such screws.) They usually are located at the front or back of the carburetor at its base; in some single-barrel carburetors, the idle mixture screw is at the side. Try to turn the screw with your fingers to get a good feel of what you are doing. If you cannot, use a screwdriver. Some idle mixture screws are so inaccessible that you will need a special screw-

Idle mixture adjusting screws are often difficult to reach. Some (*left*) have a limiting stop to prevent a too-rich setting, which would negate an emission-control system. A flexible screwdriver (*right*) helps you reach the idle mixture screw.

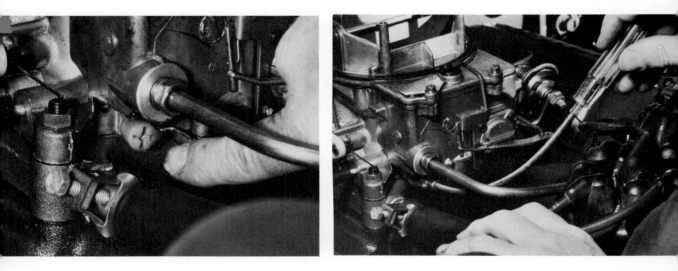

driver, with a flexible shaft and a surrounding shoulder on the tip, to prevent slipping.

If the idle mixture screws are badly out of adjustment, screw each one in until it just seats, without forcing it. Then screw it outward 1½ turns. That adjustment should come close enough to allow the engine to start and idle while you perform an idle adjustment.

Turn the screw slowly inward until the engine runs roughly from too lean a mixture. Note that position. Then, turn the screw outward until the engine lopes from too rich a mixture. The best idle mixture setting is usually half-way between the lean and rich positions.

If there are two idle mixture screws, adjust the second one in the same way. Then go back over both for a finer setting. Afterward, check the idling speed and readjust it if necessary. More adjustment of the idle mixture screws may be needed. Keep repeating all the steps until you get the desired result. If it helps you, use a vacuum gauge in setting the idle, adjusting for the highest vacuum reading.

On some engines with exhaust emission controls, color-coded plastic limiter caps are mounted over the idle mixture screws. The caps have tabs that limit the adjustment of the screws, preventing an overrich idle mixture. The trouble is that the caps usually allow only an extremely lean idle to meet federal emissions specifications. Often, to get a smooth idle, the caps must be removed so the screws can be opened more—a solution that we cannot in good conscience recommend. In strict anti-pollution states like California, if the limiters are missing you are subject to a fine.

Adjusting idle air. An idle air adjustment—usually by means of a larger screw above the mixture screws—is used in some cars. Open the screw until the engine runs at its smoothest. You then may need to readjust the idle speed and mixture slightly for a smooth idle at the proper speed.

Choke System

When a cold engine is started, it needs a richer air/fuel mixture than after it has warmed up. That is because the heavy components of raw gasoline condense on the cold manifold passages. To richen the mixture of easy-vaporizing light fuel components, a choke system is needed. The choke is a big butterfly valve at the top of the carb. When closed, it lets engine vacuum suck gasoline in quantity out of the float bowl and into the manifold.

If your engine has a *manual* choke, look down into the carburetor throat to see that the choke is fully open when the choke control knob on the dashboard is pushed all the way in. Also, see that the choke closes completely when the choke knob is pulled all the way out. If the butterfly does not open fully, position the choke knob within ⅛-inch of the dashboard.

To adjust a manual choke cable, loosen the screw, adjust the travel of the wire with a pair pliers, and tighten the screw.

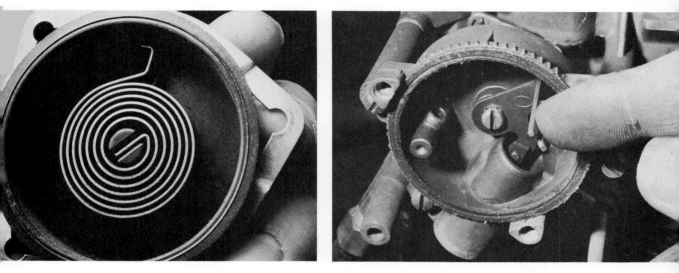

Automatic choke consists of a bimetallic coil spring (*left*) that winds and unwinds with temperature changes, and an automatic choke arm (*right*) that moves with spring tension.

Loosen the clamp screw that bears on the end of the choke wire and move the choke lever to full open. Then tighten the screw.

If the choke butterfly is not closing completely and the arm hits the end of the cable housing, loosen the cable clamp and pull the cable all the way back. Retighten the cable in that position, and recheck the operation of the choke.

Most modern chokes are *automatic*, with the amount of choking depending on engine temperature or vacuum. Working in conjunction with the choke is a fast-idle cam that swivels in front of a throttle stop screw. They hold the throttle butterfly open a bit while the engine is cold and choked. On most carburetors, both the choke and the fast-idle screw are adjustable. As the engine warms, the automatic choke receives heated air from a heat stove on the exhaust manifold. The heat uncurls a bimetallic coil spring, which opens the choke. The choke should be closed when cold and fully open in a running engine. With the choke open, the fast-idle cam (which is linked to the choke butterfly) is out of the way of its stop-screw, and idle speed is normal.

An automatic choke usually needs no adjustment if the car does not have cold-starting or hot-running problems. As a double-check, remove the air cleaner when the engine is fully warmed up and see that the choke has opened fully. Then, with the engine shut off, push the choke closed to check its action. While you do so, hold the throttle part way open to keep the fast-idle cam from getting in the way.

If you notice sticking or hesitation, spray some carburetor solvent, PCV valve cleaner, or automatic choke cleaner on all moving parts of the choke, including the butterfly shaft. Wipe the parts clean with a cloth and apply a little fine machine oil to them. If it still sticks and you cannot find the cause, see a professional mechanic.

Linkage. To correct *sticking linkage* on automatic chokes, look for the choke rod which connects the choke lever to another lever lower down. Sometimes the choke rod is direct; that type is easy to see on the side of the carburetor. Sometimes the linkage is indirect, working through a countershaft and other levers. Locate this type by working the butterfly manually and watching what else moves as it does.

On some automatic chokes, the control linkage is also bent to effect a choke adjustment. In some Chrysler-built cars, the automatic choke is mounted in a well in the exhaust crossover passage of the intake manifold. Its choke butterfly is controlled through a rod leading between the two. Rarely does choke linkage need adjustment. If it does, try bending the choke rod with pliers to lengthen or shorten it. Make your bends where they will not hinder movement of the rod.

Adjust chokes with *outside-mounted control units* by bending the offset portions of their control rods to lengthen or shorten them. Bending the rod to shorten it leans the choke adjustment. Bending to lengthen richens the adjustment. If you shorten the rod, make sure that the choke butterfly is fully closed when the choke rod is pulled all the way up against its stop.

To check the adjustment, remove the small clip that retains the choke rod in the butterfly lever. Remove the rod from the lever and lift the choke rod until it hits the stop inside the control unit and closes the butterfly choke. Check the alignment of the rod with the rod's hole in the butterfly lever. On many single-barrel carburetors, the bottom of the rod should line up with the top of the hole. On many two-barrel carbs, the center of the rod should line up with the top of the hole. Bend the rod to achieve the correct position, and then reinstall the rod and retainer. Move the rod through its normal travel to check for binding.

Automatic chokes with vacuum-break units can have their *vacuum-break linkage* adjusted. That should be done with the engine running to create a vacuum. Re-move the choke rod from the butterfly lever as described above. Install a rubber band on the choke lever so that it tries to close the choke butterfly. Open the throttle slowly until the choke closes. It will not close completely because of the vacuum-break unit's interaction, but it should close until the highest step of the fast-idle cam is under the adjustment screw. (Fast-idle adjustments are described later in this chapter.) At that speed, insert a drill bit of the gauge specified for your car between the choke butterfly and the carburetor air horn. If necessary, adjust the vacuum-break by bending the rod or tang until the choke butterfly just touches the drill rod.

Types of chokes. Some models use a *thermostatic spring choke*. The thermo spring is coiled around the choke shaft. The choke may or may not be linked also to a vacuum-break piston that opens the choke somewhat upon engine start-up. Usually, the thermostatic spring is covered by a black plastic cover that has an index mark molded onto it. That mark is supposed to line up with a reference mark on the carburetor. In some cases it is the center reference mark; check the specifications for your carburetor.

To change the adjustment, loosen the three screws that clamp the choke cover and turn the cover until the index mark aligns with the proper reference mark. If the specifications say "one notch lean," turn the cover in the direction of the "lean" arrow until the index mark is opposite the first reference mark on the lean side. Tighten the three clamp screws.

Choke thermostatic spring operation is governed by heating during warm-up. If the choke control unit is not mounted in a heat sink in the exhaust manifold, then engine heat is brought to it by vacuum up a heater tube. In some models the tube starts at the air filter, runs to the choke-

To adjust the automatic choke, loosen the three fastening screws and turn the black plastic cover cap until you meet the specifications.

The plastic cap has a notch, while the carburetor body has a series of bumps. This particular automatic choke is centered.

Hose from the hot-water heater is routed past the cover to keep the coil warm and thus prevent over-choking after a brief engine shut-down.

heating stove on the exhaust manifold, and then is routed to the choke itself. Engine vacuum from the carburetor passages pulls cold air from the air filter and runs it over the heat stove and over the thermostatic spring coil in the choke. If anything keeps the heated air from reaching the thermostatic spring, the choke may fail to open fully. Remove an end of the heater tube and blow through it to make sure it is not clogged. Also clean the choke air screen if it is clogged. A rusted-out heat tube could let cold air enter and mix with the heated air; inspect the tube for leaks. The circular gasket behind the choke cover plate also could let in cold air if it is not in place.

To keep the automatic choke from closing too soon after the engine is shut down, a heater hose is routed near the choke cover in some cars. Hot coolant inside the hose keeps the choke open as long as the engine is warm.

Another type of automatic choke uses a *thermostatic coil* as a sensor. This coil is mounted on the exhaust manifold, sitting directly on the exhaust crossover passage on some V-8s. Automatic choke coils move the rods either up or down, depending on the engine, to close their chokes. Inspect yours to see how it works. A rod connects a thermo-spring to the choke butterfly. A vacuum-break unit partially opens the choke butterfly after starting. During warm-up, the thermo spring opens the choke butterfly gradually until it is completely open when the engine is fully warmed.

If a faulty choke coil unit throws the automatic choke system out of whack, replace the thermostatic unit. To do that, first remove the cover and the thermo spring screw. Once you have replaced the spring, you may have to readjust the choke rod. Also, the tang may face upward or downward when the coil is installed. Make a mental note of the position of the old one when you remove it.

An automatic *electric choke* consists of an electromagnet in a housing, a choke arm, and a rod leading to the choke butterfly. When the starter is operated, the electromagnet closes the choke through its linkage. When the engine starts and the starter is switched off, the electromagnet releases. The choke then would open completely were it not for a thermostatic spring. The spring holds the choke partly closed until the engine warms it sufficiently to open the choke fully. Check the operation of the electromagnet by holding a screwdriver near the electromagnet housing while a helper cranks the engine. The metal screwdriver blade should be drawn to the housing by the electromagnetic force and released when the starter goes off. If it is not, see that the electromagnet is getting power. Replace the unit if it is defective.

Some automatic-choke carburetors have *unloaders.* When the throttle is opened wide, the unloader kicks the choke part way open to let you crank the engine and get rid of excess fuel caused by overchoking, a condition called flooding. A flooded carburetor smells of fuel and may even be wet on the outside. If your carburetor does not have an unloader for the automatic choke, one way to get rid of flooding is to remove the air cleaner and manually hold the choke butterfly open while someone else cranks the engine with the starter. Alternatively, you can wait 10 to 15 minutes and try starting without pumping the accelerator.

Adjust the unloader with the engine off and the air cleaner removed. Hold the throttle wide open by moving the linkage from under the hood. See if a small tab on the throttle lever along the base of the carburetor contacts—or nearly contacts—any

part of the automatic choke linkage. Such a tab is called the unloader tab. Adjustment is made by bending it so that wide-open throttle pushes the choke part way open. The carburetor manufacturer may specify how far the choke butterfly should be opened by the unloader.

Speaking of wide-open throttle, check the *throttle control.* When the accelerator pedal is floored, the throttle should open fully. Ask a helper to step on the accelerator pedal while you watch the throttle lever. If the lever does not open all the way against the stop on the carburetor, adjust the length of the throttle control. Then make sure that throttle return spring pressure will bring it all the way back to idle.

Fast idle is provided in all carburetors to speed the idle when the automatic or manual choke is closed or partially closed, and to keep the engine from dying while it is warming up. On some models, the fast-idle speed is adjustable. Some carburetors have one fast-idle speed, others have several. When there are more than one, the fast-idle specification refers to the fastest. On the few carbs with nonadjustable fast-idle, the proper slow-idle speed adjustment also gives the correct fast-idle speed.

Fast-idle speed is controlled by a cam that moves in relation to the choke. A rod often connects that fast-idle cam with the choke linkage; as the choke closes, the fast-idle cam is moved to bring its step under the throttle stop screw. Locate the screw by tracing the choke linkage to the fast-idle cam. The screw which rides that cam is the fast-idle adjustment screw. With both the throttle and the choke in the closed position, that screw contacts the highest step of the fast-idle cam.

To adjust the fast-idle, warm the engine fully and attach a tachometer. All accessories should be shut off and the transmission should be in neutral. With the engine off, open the throttle and move the highest step of the fast-idle cam under the adjusting screw. Let the throttle close to hold it there. Then start the engine without touching the throttle. Turn the fast-idle screw in to increase idle speed, out to decrease it.

Fast-idle adjustment may change as an engine wears in. Check it with every tune-up.

The specified adjustments do not always provide the most desirable choking, especially in high-mileage engines. If the cold engine needs too much pumping of the accelerator pedal to catch on, or if it runs lean when cold and dies when you step on the gas, the setting is too lean. On the other hand, if the engine floods without starting, runs with a lope during warm-up, and emits heavy black smoke from the exhaust, the setting is too rich. Move the choke adjustment a slight amount at a time until you get the best results.

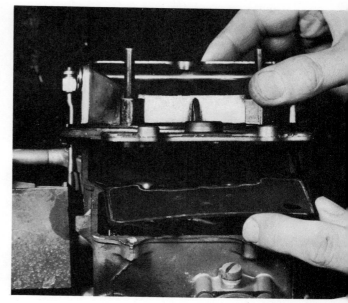

On some carburetors, like the one above, you can get into the float bowl by removing the top cover plate and air horn. If you have no such access, leave float bowl adjustment to a shop.

Float System

The float bowl provides a place where several ounces of fuel are stored at a constant level, ready to be drawn into the venturi and mixed with air preparatory to burning. As the engine runs, fuel flows into and out of the float bowl continuously. The fuel always must stay at the same level in the bowl. If the level should rise, fuel would flow too freely into the venturi and feed the engine too rich an air/fuel mixture—one in which the ratio of air to fuel is too low. If the float bowl level should drop, the mixture would become too lean—too low on fuel—and the engine would starve. The air/fuel mixture should be between 11 to 1 and 14 to 1. The engine will not run well on a richer or leaner mixture.

The necessary level in the float bowl is maintained by a float valve. A hollow float rides on top of the fuel. A tab on one end of the float pushes a pointed float needle into a seat in the end of the line coming from the fuel pump. As the fuel level climbs, it lifts the float—and thereby closes off the supply of incoming fuel, the same as the float on a toilet tank. When the fuel level drops, the float lowers, releasing the needle from its seat and letting more fuel in. In action, the process is smooth and fuel stays at about the same level. Adjustment to the fuel level is usually within do-it-yourself scope.

However, if gaining access to the float requires removing the top of the carburetor, think twice. In some carburetors, removing the top involves components such as metering rods and vacuum pistons, which can be hard to replace properly.

The diagrams of the carburetor in your service manual can help you decide if you want to take on float adjustment.

Adjusting Float Level

Measure fuel level from the top surface of the bowl to the surface of the fuel. Do this after the engine has been turned off, but before the fuel has had a chance to evaporate.

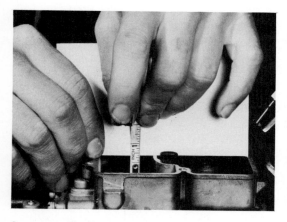

Some specifications state the distance from the top of the bowl to the top of the float. For such a measurement, use a file card to mark the top of the bowl.

When you adjust the float arm, do it gently. Hold the float and the float arm and bend slowly. Never pry the float up—that can jam the needle.

Specifications may cover either float level or fuel level, sometimes both. If both are given, the fuel level specification is merely a check on the float level setting.

You will first have to take off the air cleaner to get at the chamber. To reach the float chamber, remove the screws around the cover. Then, with the float exposed, you can check its adjustment.

Float in cover. If the float is part of the cover, turn the cover upside down so that gravity closes the float against its needle. Do not press against the float to close it; you may press the float needle so hard into its seat that an accurate adjustment will be impossible. That is not a problem with the old brass needles, but the newer nylon and neoprene needles take on a groove from the seat; they require some time to return to shape. Meanwhile, they will give a false adjustment.

Measure from the bottom of the float to the cover's gasket seat. (Since you are holding the cover upside down, the float's bottom is at the top.) To change the float level, bend the tab on the float with a screwdriver or pliers—without forcing the needle into its seat. The proper tab is the one that contacts the end of the float needle as the float rises.

Float in carburetor. If the float is in the carburetor rather than in the cover, measure from the top of the float bowl to the top of the float. To make the float rise fully, you will have to pour gas into the bowl. Compare with the manufacturer's specifications and bend the tab if necessary. Float adjustment should be as accurate as you can make it, for it affects engine operation, emissions, and fuel economy.

Occasionally, a float or needle sticks in the closed position, usually because of needle-seat wear. Then, no fuel can get into the float bowl, and fuel starvation stalls the engine. The needle starts life with a smooth taper from body to point, but thousands of contacts with the seat wear a groove around the needle. When the groove gets deep enough, it either shuts off fuel entirely or lets fuel run over the top of the float bowl. In either case, your engine runs poorly or not at all. If the needle shows wear, assume that the seat is worn too and replace both. Do not overtighten the seat in the carburetor body or you may strip the threads. The gasket should seal the joint without overtightening.

Needle and seat replacement is a simple matter. Replacements, available for all models of carburetors, do not cost much.

Fuel level specifications. These are different from float level specifications. Generally, they represent distance from the top surface of the carburetor to the top surface of the fuel—the level reached as the engine runs. Some carburetors have sight holes or transparent covers to let you see the fuel level. Others have holes for inserting a dipstick measure. If after a float level adjustment the engine does not act right, you can check the fuel level. The cause may be fuel inside the float. In that case, see a pro or install a rebuilt carburetor.

After the float adjustment, use a rag to clean out dirt, water, and anything else besides clean fuel left in the float bowl. To do that, you must first remove the float's hinge pin and lift the float out. The needle may come with it.

Gummy or dark-colored varnish deposits from evaporated fuel should be removed with carburetor cleaning solvent. Clean the outside of the carburetor too, once the cover is put back on. Before you install the cover, make sure that the float is not binding. And be careful not to bend it during installation.

Main Metering System

This is installed in the float bowl to feed fuel from the float bowl to the venturi in proper quantities. It consists of a metering jet, which is a carefully sized hole, and a tube leading from the float bowl and metering jet to the venturi.

One popular make of carburetor also has a metering needle—a tapered pin that lifts out of the jet to increase fuel flow as the throttle is opened.

Each carburetor barrel has a main metering system. No adjustments can be made to that system. Not much can go wrong with it unless a piece of dirt lodges in it and restricts the flow of fuel.

Power and Pump Systems

The power system increases fuel flow when the throttle is wide open. The engine cannot draw enough fuel through the main metering system to develop full power under wide-open throttle. The power system, incorporated into the carburetor, bypasses the metering jet and increases fuel flow into the venturi. The power system may be activated mechanically by the throttle valve's wide-open position or by a vacuum-controlled valve inside the car. Other than replacement of the power valve, no work is possible on the power system.

The accelerator system injects a squirt of raw fuel directly into the carburetor throat when you step down on the gas pedal. It takes a fraction of a second for the main metering system or power system to take hold. The engine would falter except for that squirt of raw fuel. The accelerator system is simply a piston pump, much like a tire pump, that is worked by gas pedal movement. Step on the gas pedal and it squirts. Release, and it refills with fuel.

Some carburetors, especially pre-emission control models, have an adjustment

Accelerator pump arm with more than one hole allows for adjustment of the stroke. A shorter stroke leans the mixture, a longer one richens it.

to govern the amount of fuel injected. Most of them have two or three holes in an arm coming off the throttle shaft. The proper setting is the one that eliminates hesitation during acceleration; the climate may well determine which hole you use. The summer position is the one closer to the throttle shaft, the one that allows less movement when the throttle moves. The winter position allows greater movement.

If the engine coughs or dies momentarily every time you step on the gas pedal, a richer setting, with greater movement, is called for. If the engine hesitates and black smoke pours from the exhaust when you step on the gas, a leaner setting, with less movement, is called for. A few carburetors use vacuum-controlled accelerator pumps. If one of these acts up, there isn't much you can do to adjust it.

Most pumps are either of the piston or diaphragm type. Piston accelerator pump problems are almost always caused by incorrect adjustment or worn or folded-over pump leathers. Diaphragm pump failure is usually through leakage.

If even the richest setting does not cure a lean accelerator pump, that component needs service. Kits are available to rebuild these pumps, but that job is best left to the pros. The do-it-yourself way is to install a completely rebuilt carburetor, especially if your car suffers from other carburetor problems.

Antistall Dashpot

The antistall dashpot is a round gadget found on carburetors for new engines and on older ones with automatic transmissions. Its purpose is to return the throttle to idle position gradually rather than letting it close quickly. That keeps the engine from dying if you should gun it and then change your mind and stop quickly.

After every idle speed adjustment, check the adjustment of the antistall dashpot if it is outside the carburetor. (Those inside the carburetor are not easily reached.) Each manufacturer specifies the proper clearance between the fully depressed dashpot and the carburetor lever that it touches. To check clearance, push

Antistall dashpot adjustment is vital to good tuning. Turn the dashpot with a wrench while you check the clearance with a thickness gauge.

the dashpot ram in all the way with a small screwdriver.

Dashpot adjustment is easy: usually it involves loosening the lock nut and turning the dashpot to get the necessary thickness gauge clearance. If the dashpot sticks or is adjusted out too far, it can hold the throttle off idle slightly. Even then, replacement of the dashpot is rarely needed.

Exhaust Analyzer

The best way to check a carburetor is with an exhaust gas analyzer. This gadget can tell you if all carburetor systems are functioning properly for smooth running, good performance, top fuel economy, and minimum air pollution.

The analyzer uses exhaust gas samples collected inside the end of the tailpipe. It determines the engine's air/fuel ratio or, in some units, the percentage of combustion efficiency or the percentage of carbon monoxide. Most have more than one scale; this lets you take whichever reading you wish. Some portable units can be attached to the car for on-the-road air/fuel readings. This type of unit has a pickup tube that fastens to the rear bumper, a neoprene tube that reaches into the tailpipe to collect gas, and a meter attached to a 20-foot lead wire.

To make an exhaust gas analysis, fully warm up the engine. Fasten the sensing unit to the rear bumper. Calibrate it on air, then slide the pickup tube into the tailpipe. With dual exhausts, use the tailpipe opposite the manifold heat control valve.

Hook up your tachometer to the engine. Adjust the idle mixture screw or screws to get a smooth idle; the meter should read in the proper idling band. Modern engines with exhaust emission control equipment call for lean idles of less than 14 to 1 air/fuel ratio or 0.9 percent or less carbon monoxide.

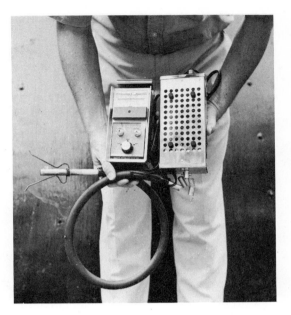

Exhaust analyzer, which tests carburetor efficiency, consists of the meter (*top left*), the sampler (*top right*) and the collector tube. Set up (*below*), the exhaust analyzer tube collects exhaust from the tailpipe and passes it through the sampler, which reports emissions to the meter in the car.

Run the engine up to 1500 to 2000 rpm. At that speed, the air/fuel ratio should be between 14 and 14½ to 1. Too rich a mixture indicates a high float level, leaky power valve, incorrect metering rod adjustment (on carbs that have metering rods), incorrectly sized main metering jet or jets, or plugged air bleeds. All you can do is check the fuel level in the carburetor bowl. The other problems call for a rebuilt carburetor or the services of a carburetor specialist.

A too-lean reading indicates a low float level, incorrect metering rod adjustment, too-small metering jets, plugged high-speed passages, or manifold or carburetor air leaks. You can check the float level and look for air leaks. The rest, again, call for carburetor replacement or a specialist.

A drifting meter reading indicates a worn float needle and seat, fuel pull-over from the high-speed nozzle or accelerator pump jet, improper float level, or a leaky power valve. Again, you can check the float level and inspect the needle and seat for wear.

The action of the accelerator pump is next to be tested. Accelerate the engine quickly to half throttle, then let it drop back to idle.

The effect of the pump-richened mixture will take a moment to register on the exhaust gas analyzer. When it does, the meter needle should swing to the rich side of the scale and then return as the effect passes. If it does not, the accelerator pump either is not working or is out of adjustment.

Carburetor and intake manifold leaks also show up on the analyzer. With the engine idling, squirt a mixture of kerosene and engine oil onto areas of possible leakage such as the carburetor flange and the intake manifold gaskets. Watch the meter needle for a swing toward the rich side,

indicating ingestion of the kerosene-oil mixture.

Test the air cleaner for restriction with the engine running at 2000 rpm. With the air cleaner off, the meter should read in the lean portion of the scale. Install the air cleaner with the engine running, being careful to stay clear of rotating parts. With the air cleaner on, the exhaust analyzer needle should not move more than a quarter of one division toward the rich side of the air/fuel scale. If it does, the filter cartridge should be cleaned and tested again. If the meter still shows a rich reading, replace the filter element.

Reset the idle speed as specified by the manufacturer and make a road test. Run the engine up gradually from low speed to about 2500 rpm. (You can make the same test in the shop, but with less accuracy.) The carburetor's switchover from its idle system to its main metering system should show a gradual leaning on the meter needle. A sudden leaning or richening of the mixture, accompanied by engine vibration, is the tip-off to a sick carburetor.

On the road, hard acceleration should shove the needle all the way to the rich side. A steady speed of 25 to 30 mph should produce a mixture reading of 13½ or 14 to 1. A richer reading indicates excessive friction in the drive line, probably dragging brakes.

Rebuilt Carburetors

A dirty carburetor is insensitive to idle adjustments. When adjustments do not correct the trouble, you must either clean the carburetor or trade it in for a rebuilt. Initially, you could try one of the on-the-car cleaning kits. The solvent container hangs under the hood and feeds through the carburetor to remove hidden varnish deposits. The kit costs about $4.

Carburetor cleaning kits do not claim to

correct dirt-clogged passages or worn, maladjusted parts; disassembly, thorough cleaning, parts replacement, and careful reassembly are needed for that. You should not try it. Even professional mechanics usually buy a rebuilt carburetor. Pay the deposit and hang onto your old carburetor until you complete the installation. Get a new carburetor mounting gasket, too.

Removing the old carburetor is a straightforward operation involving the unfastening of assorted hardware. When installing the rebuilt unit, change over all the parts from your old carburetor that are missing on the new one. (Those may include the fuel line fitting, antistall dashpot, manual choke lever, and vacuum line fitting.) Remove the old mounting gasket, clean the manifold gasket surface and install the new gasket. Set the carburetor on the manifold and tighten the nuts a little at a time all around. Hook up all connections as they came off. Service all fuel filters to keep your new carburetor clean.

A rebuilt carburetor has a dry float bowl. You will have to crank the engine long

To remove a carburetor, take off all the nuts that fasten the base to the intake manifold. Then, remove all other lines and connections.

enough for the fuel pump to fill the bowl. You can prime the carburetor by pouring a shot glass of gas into the carb throat.

Most rebuilt carburetors are tested and adjusted before you get them, but they still need a fine idle speed and mixture adjustment when the engine warms up. The float level, however, should already be set properly.

AIR CLEANER

An air filter is mounted over every carburetor. Its purpose is to keep airborne abrasives out of the engine while offering a minimum resistance to vital air flow. Running an engine without such a filter allows dirt in and causes moving parts to wear rapidly. Since an engine breathes 10,000 gallons of air for each gallon of gasoline consumed, lots of air passes through the air filter during its lifetime.

A corrugated paper-type filter that is dirty acts like a choke; it increases the amount of fuel used and reduces engine performance. A damaged paper filter accelerates wear on cylinder walls, pistons, and piston rings. An oil-wetted or an oil-bath air filter that is dirty does not restrict air flow. Instead, it permits dust to enter the engine. No matter what type of air filter is used, it needs servicing—just how often depends on driving conditions. Cars driven on dusty, unpaved roads require the most frequent air filter service.

Paper filter. Inspect a paper-element air filter cartridge by holding it up to bright sunlight. If you cannot see the light through the folds of paper, the element is dirty. If the dust coating is dry, tap the filter repeatedly on a hard surface to knock off the accumulated dirt. Rotate the element after each tap until the entire surface has been cleaned. Try the light test again.

Air Cleaner Service

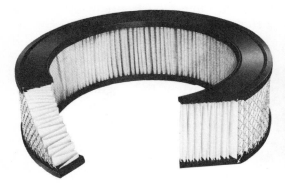

Paper-element filter uses porous paper to trap particles before they can enter the engine. A dirty filter should be replaced.

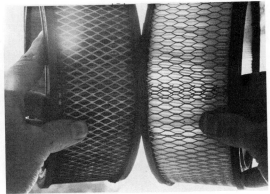

Light test helps you check filter condition. An old element (*left*) lets no light through; it should be replaced. The other filter is acceptable.

To clean a dirty element, tap it sharply on a flat surface. If you have access to compressed air, blow air through from inside out.

Before you reuse a paper-element filter, check it carefully for tears. A hole this small will pass many abrasive particles into the engine.

If it still does not pass, ask a service station attendant to blow compressed air through the filter from the inside out. If the element still does not pass the light test, buy a new one.

Some cars run crankcase fumes from the PCV system through the air filter. That cuts down on emissions, but it can quickly clog a paper filter with oil. A paper filter cartridge that is coated with oil must be discarded. Breaks or cracks in the element also call for replacement.

Some paper filters have mesh wrappers for protection from PCV oil vapors. Such a wrapper can be removed and cleaned in solvent and replaced. The paper cartridge itself, however, should not be cleaned in solvent.

Polyurethane filter. A polyurethane foam element also can be cleaned and re-used. Remove the element, submerge it in kerosene and agitate. Wring it out gently. Repeat the process until the kerosene comes out clean. Pour oil on the element and wring to distribute it evenly. Squeeze out excess oil (too much restricts air flow), reinstall the element in its mesh and replace the cartridge in the air cleaner.

Polyurethane elements are not harmed by oil vapors from a PCV system. If your PCV system keeps fouling paper filter cartridges, switch to a polyurethane cartridge.

Dry or wet-type paper or polyurethane cartridges must seat snugly against the top and bottom of the air cleaner so that dusty air cannot by-pass the element. Inspect the soft, rubbery gasket material on the cartridge to see that it is leakproof.

Polyurethane foam and porous paper are about equally good at trapping dust; oil-wetted mesh cleaners are the least efficient.

Oil-wetted filter. Oil-bath air cleaners are thorough and especially desirable for driving on dusty roads. With an oil-wetted or oil-bath air cleaner, the usual cleaning procedure is to take it apart and wash it in gasoline (do this outdoors). When the mesh is clean, coat it with engine oil, shake out any excess, and reassemble the air cleaner. Also, fill the oil reservoir to the proper level with the specified weight of engine oil. It is the oil that traps dust particles.

Do not submerge the large silencing chamber in solvent. It can fill with gasoline and take a long time to empty, causing an over-rich fuel mixture in the meantime.

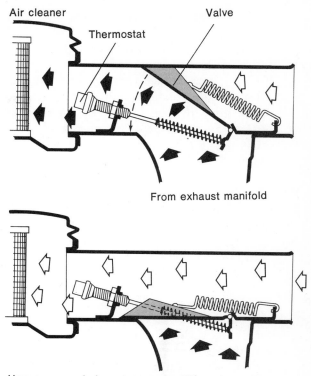

How a warmed-air system works: When the engine is cold (*top*), the bimetallic thermostat closes the valve against outside air. Hot air from the exhaust manifold enters the engine through the air cleaner. When the engine has heated (*bottom*), the thermostat opens the valve to outside air.

Check the operation of a warmed-air system by peering into the air intake when the engine is cold (the valve should be closed to outside air) and again when the engine is warm (the valve should be open to outside air). Clean sticky valves with degreaser.

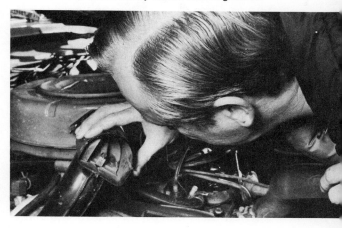

Warmed-air systems. The warmed-air intake system has been adopted by a number of car manufacturers. Around the air filter is an air cleaner enclosure that quiets air rushing into the engine by smoothing out pulsations. In most recent-model cars, air entering the cleaner housing of a cold engine passes over the exhaust manifold, where it is heated. The cold engine can then gulp warm air and run better. But because hot air does not let an engine develop full power, a thermostatic valve, located between the warm air intake and cold air intake pipes, switches to cool air when the underhood temperature rises.

In an engine with a warmed-air system, the air cleaner has a pipe coming off the side and leading down to the exhaust manifold. Inside the pipe, a flapper valve lets either cold or warm air pass through to the air cleaner. Some flappers work thermostatically, others use vacuum.

Warmed-air systems are quite trouble-free. Check yours only if you have a problem such as poor fuel economy, lack of engine pep, or balky operation while the engine is cold.

To test the system, start the engine cold and peer in at the flapper valve. It should be set to draw warmed air. After the engine has reached normal operating temperature, check that the valve is set to draw direct cool air. Clean a balky valve with engine degreaser. If cleaning does not work, consult a professional mechanic. Fortunately, thermo flap valves seldom malfunction, for no adjustment can be made on them.

The manifold heat system is another system designed to help the car run better. When the engine is cold, hot exhaust gases are routed through intake manifold passages to warm the air/fuel mixture. Warming helps vaporize fuel.

When the engine is hot, a thermostatic valve in the exhaust manifold routes most of those exhaust gases directly out the exhaust pipe. (A little warming is needed even then to prevent stumbling during acceleration.)

Manifold heat control valves, or heat riser valves, are prone to sticking, often in the heating position. The intake manifold then runs too hot, and fuel economy and power suffer.

In a few cars, hot engine coolant instead of exhaust gases is routed through the intake manifold. The purpose is the same.

ON-THE-ROAD TROUBLESHOOTING

Should your car act up while you are on the road, your first step — provided you can do so safely — is to see if you are experiencing fuel system failure or abrupt ignition system failure.

In cars with manual chokes, hand-choking is the best way. When a failure occurs, yank the manual choke out. If the engine gives a spurt of power, the problem is surely in the fuel system. The choke draws out any fuel remaining in the float bowl and the engine runs on that. If choking does not help, the problem probably is in the ignition system.

If your car engine has an automatic choke, you still can distinguish between a fuel-out and an ignition-out. Pump the accelerator pedal rapidly as the car slows. If shooting raw accelerator-pump gas into the carburetor has an effect, fuel system trouble is indicated. If it does not, suspect the ignition system.

Running out of gas. This, the most common fuel system problem, can be the hardest to solve — it may mean a long walk. With some cars, the following trick may help: if the road is clear and it is safe to do so, cut the steering wheel back and forth to make the car swerve within its lane. Keep the engine running even if you must shift to a lower gear. Such swerving

To test for a spark, insert a partially unbent paper clip into the boot. Hold the boot with a clothespin near a good ground. As the engine is cranked, there should be a spark.

may make the remaining fuel in the tank slosh around sufficiently to keep you going to the nearest gas station.

Once you refill the tank, there is a trick that will get you going faster. Since the fuel lines, fuel pump, and carburetor float bowl are all empty, the engine may require up to a minute of cranking to start. Save your battery by using the last few tablespoons of emergency gas to prime the engine. Remove the air filter and pour the gas into the carburetor throat.

If you run out of gas, save some of the refill to prime the carburetor. Pour a little down the carb throat. To avoid fire, replace the air cleaner before you start up.

Replace the air filter before trying to start; it will act as a flame barrier if the engine should backfire. Hold the throttle down as you crank.

Fuel pump failure. This component rarely just lets go; usually, failure is gradual, and you first notice the trouble when the engine is under a strain — say, while going up a hill. As long as you hold the gas pedal to the floor, the engine will run flat or even slow down. Try letting up on the accelerator for a few seconds to let the float bowl refill. If the engine then takes off and runs full blast for a bit, a weak fuel pump is likely.

Unless you have wrenches along, you cannot do much on the road to fix a weak fuel pump (or a fuel line restriction, which produces the same results).

Flooding. Flooding is a problem that you may be able to relieve. Flooding caused by overchoking is covered in the chapter on cold weather starting tips. Another kind of flooding that stalls you just as dead occurs when the carburetor float needle sticks, because of either dirt in the fuel or float needle-seat wear. The float bowl overfills, and excess fuel runs into the carburetor throat and is drawn into the cylinders.

In some cases of stuck-needle flooding, you can set things right just by tapping sharply on the carburetor float directly over the fuel inlet while someone tries to start the engine. You may have to remove the air cleaner first. Tap with a screwdriver handle or a wrench, not something as heavy as a hammer.

Stuck-needle flooding always is accompanied by gasoline odor. Often you can see fuel running out over the outside of the carburetor. As soon as the flow of fuel stops, you will know the needle has seated. It still may take a moment of crank-

Gentle taps on the outside of the float bowl will free a stuck float needle. If you don't have a wrench handy in the car, you can use a rock.

Cure vapor lock—a condition caused by fuel boiling in the lines, pump and float—by pouring cool water over these parts. Keep ignition parts dry.

ing for the float level to return to normal so the engine can start.

If flooding is not cured immediately, give up. Do not chance having a spark ignite the raw gasoline. If you have a dry-chemical or CO_2 fire extinguisher in the car, keep it handy—just in case.

A carburetor that floods once from a stuck needle is almost sure to do it again. At the very least, remove, inspect, and clean the needle and seat the first chance you get.

Vapor lock. This can occur when an en-

gine gets very hot. The fuel in the fuel pump, pressure line, and carburetor float bowl boils, and turns into vapor, and the engine stalls. Vapor lock is rare in late-model cars because of improved fuel system design. In an older model, hot weather, high altitude, and an over-heated engine can help bring on vapor lock. You can simply wait until the engine cools off. Or you can speed the process by opening the hood and removing the air cleaner. If water is at hand, pour some over the carburetor, fuel line, and fuel pump; but do not get any into the carburetor throat or

To isolate no-start troubles to the fuel system, remove the air cleaner and peer into the carburetor (*left*). Pump the throttle lever several times. With each pump, you should see fuel squirting into the carburetor venturi (*right*), one stream for each barrel.

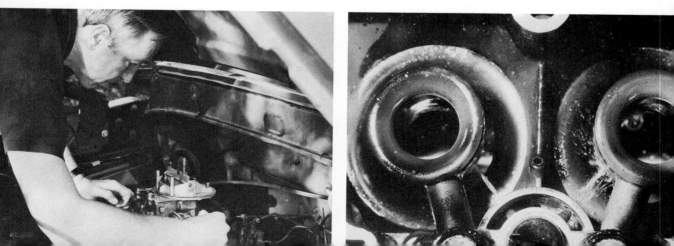

Carburetor flooding can be cleared by holding the automatic choke butterfly open. Crank the engine with the gas pedal depressed to the floor.

On-the-road idle adjustment is easy. If you don't have a screwdriver handy, use a dime. Be sure to adjust the idle to specifications later.

on the ignition cables or spark plugs. Often, wrapping the line from the fuel pump to the carburetor with wet rags effects an immediate cure.

Stalling. Occasionally, a float or needle sticks in the closed position, usually because of needle-seat wear. Then no fuel can get into the float bowl, and fuel starvation stalls the engine. While a helper pumps the gas pedal, look down into the carburetor throat. If no fuel squirts out of the accelerator pump jet or jets, the float bowl is probably dry. Tapping, as for flooding, is the temporary cure. There is no danger of fire from raw gasoline. As soon as the float needle jars loose, the engine will run. Again, make repairs at the first opportunity.

Rough idling. In heavy traffic, a bumpy engine may be caused by percolation, or the boiling of fuel in the fuel bowl. At every stop, shift to neutral and run the engine at a fast idle with the accelerator pedal. The additional cooling may help lower underhood temperatures enough to keep you going. If the engine keeps dying

in traffic, pull off the road, remove the air cleaner, and set the idle screw up enough to keep it running. A dime can double for a screwdriver. When you get home, perform a full idle adjustment. Idle adjustment can also be thrown off by dirt clogging in one of the idle system passages. The roadside cure is to open each idle mixture screw $\frac{1}{8}$ turn.

Poor gas mileage. To recap, fuel system problems that cause low mileage include: oversize carburetor metering jets; too rich an idle mix; dirty air filter; leaking power valve; too high a float level; fuel leaks; overactive accelerator pump; overchoking. The tune-ups described earlier in this chapter should allow you to make proper adjustments.

Factors outside the fuel system that can cut down your gasoline mileage include: dragging brakes, retarded ignition system, cylinder misfiring, poor compression and faulty cooling system thermostat.

Finally, a number of other factors—fast starts, heavy braking at stops, high speeds —can cause poor gas mileage. These you can correct by changing your driving habits.

Engine Tuning: Emission Control Devices

The equipment for reducing air-polluting emissions from the modern automobile extends from one end of the vehicle to the other. It requires little service, but when it does get out of adjustment it can hurt performance and fuel economy as well as the atmosphere.

More and more states are requiring checks of emission control devices. In California, for example, you can be ticketed for subverting an emission control system.

The positive crankcase ventilation system (PCV) is the oldest of the emission control devices. PCV was installed in 1961 models sold in California and in 1963 models sold elsewhere. Gases from inside the engine crankcase, which in pre-PCV models were released into the atmosphere, are routed to the carburetor intake manifold where they are inhaled and burned.

The PCV system gives a positive flow of filtered air through the engine crankcase all the while the engine is running. The flow is regulated by a valve. Modern PCV valves meter the flow according to engine needs. Because it helps to reduce smog, it sometimes is called a smog valve. Many pre-1968 PCV systems were of an open type, using a simple orifice—the oil filler cap—as an intake for PCV air. Since 1968, PCV systems have been closed, drawing in filtered air through a hose between the carburetor air cleaner and the engine's rocker arm cover.

Exhaust controls arrived in 1966 on California vehicles and in 1968 nationwide. Their purpose is to reduce the discharge of unburned hydrocarbons and carbon monoxide—and, starting with 1973 models, oxides of nitrogen—from the engine exhaust.

One type, an integral system, involves changes in the design of the fuel, ignition, breathing, and cooling systems to make the engine run hotter and cleaner. Portions of commonly used integral exhaust control systems are described in the chapters on ignition and fuel system tuning.

Another type of exhaust control, an air injection system, blows fresh, filtered, compressed air into the engine exhaust ports to provide oxygen for additional burning of hydrocarbons and the conversion of poisonous carbon monoxide into harmless carbon dioxide. An air pump, belt-driven by the engine, provides the compressed air. Several valves are incorporated into the system. One is for pressure relief; others are check valves for one-way flow. Often an antibackfire valve is also used.

Fuel evaporative emission controls have been required by law in new cars since 1970 in California and 1971 nationwide. Evaporative emissions occur when fuel tanks are vented into the atmosphere; they account for about one-fifth of the total free hydrocarbons emitted by automobiles. The controls prevent gasoline in the fuel tank and carburetor float bowl from evaporating into the air. Fuel vapors from the gas tank and carburetor are stored until they are consumed by the engine. Two types of evaporative systems are used. One routes fuel vapors into the engine crankcase for storage. The other vents the fumes into a charcoal-filled cannister in the engine compartment for storage. When the engine starts, each system picks up stored fumes and burns them through the carburetor.

Future emissions standards may require further reductions of automobile emissions, even at the expense of fuel economy. Since 1972 models, exhaust gas recirculation systems have become widespread. These channel part of the exhaust gas back through the combustion chambers.

By 1976, among the new equipment that probably will be used is the catalytic exhaust reactor, which removes practically all exhaust pollutants. Lead in motor fuel fouls a reactor rapidly—which is the main reason why lead-free fuels are cur-

Emission Control System

- Fuel-vapor separator
- P C V valve
- Check valve
- Charcoal canister

rently being promoted. Even without an exhaust reactor, lead-free fuels have the advantage of preventing lead particles from entering the atmosphere. Another potential device to meet future pollution specifications is the catalytic converter, a muffler-like cannister that converts most of the remaining hydrocarbon and carbon monoxide emissions in the exhaust into carbon dioxide and water vapor.

One PCV test: As the engine idles, pinch off the hose leading to the PCV valve. The engine speed should drop between 60 and 100 rpm.

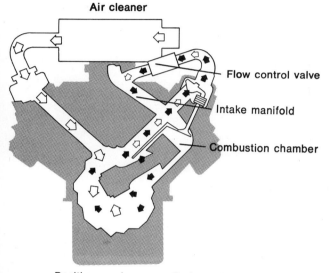

Air cleaner

Flow control valve

Intake manifold

Combustion chamber

Positive crankcase ventilation utilizes fresh, filtered air (*white arrows*) to pick up blowby gases (*black arrows*) for re-burning.

Servicing the PCV System

In time, sludge from crankcase fumes may plug the PCV system so that it no longer can draw pollutants from the engine crankcase. That causes condensation of gases in the crankcase, resulting in formation of acids, sludge build-up, and oil dilution. It also increases exhaust emissions because of carburetor enrichment.

Check your engine's PCV system every 4,000 to 6,000 miles. First, find the rubber hose that leads from the crankcase or rocker arm cover to the base of the carburetor or intake manifold.

Somewhere along that hose is the PCV valve. Some PCV valves slip-fit into their rubber-lined rocker arm cover openings. Others are fastened with spring-type hose clamps on the end of the hose. Still others clamp to the hose at one end and screw into a fitting at the other.

Have the engine idling at operating temperature. With a pair of pliers, pinch the hose so that no gases can get through and listen for a change in idling speed. If the system is operating, engine speed should drop about 60 to 100 rpm. If idling speed does not change perceptibly, the PCV system is plugged. Sudden spells of engine conking out at idle are a sign of a clogged PCV system. If the idle becomes slow or rough, check the PCV valve before making carburetor adjustments.

Another PCV test requires a file card. Remove the oil filler cap and hold the card ¼ inch from the opening. As the engine idles, the card should be sucked toward the opening.

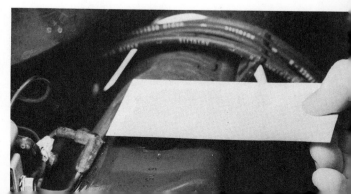

You also can check the PCV system another way. With the engine idling, take off the oil filler cap and hold a file card or a similar stiff piece of paper over the filler opening and about a quarter-inch away. The paper should be pulled against the opening within 10 seconds if the PCV system is working properly.

The PCV system should be cleaned every year or 12,000 miles, whichever comes first, whether or not the system is clogged. Do it even oftener on an engine that has begun to wear out; it releases more gases into the PCV system.

Some PCV valves—the ones that do not come apart—must be replaced rather than cleaned. A new one costs about $2. Cleanable PCV valves should be carefully disassembled and immersed in fuel oil, lacquer thinner, carburetor cleaner, or special PCV solvent. Soak until no brown varnish or grease deposits are left to color the solvent. If the valve has a drilled metering orifice, poke a wire through gently to clean the orifice without enlarging it.

Easiest PCV check is with a valve tester. With the engine idling, press it over the open oil filler. A green light means the system is working.

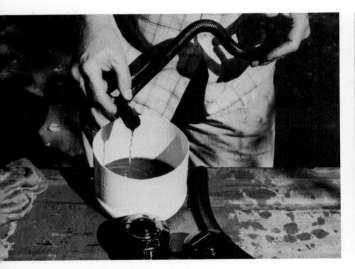

Once a year, or every 12,000 miles, the entire PCV system should be removed from the car and thoroughly cleaned with fuel oil or solvent.

Sludge-clogged hoses that can be reused should be opened with a bent coat hanger. Then, wash out the hose with solvent.

PCV hoses also should be cleaned whenever you service the valve. Remove the hoses and soak them in fuel oil. If a hose is clogged with sludge, run a wire through to open it to solvent. Blow or wipe dry. If a hose contains any hard deposits or is soft and spongy, replace it with a new one. Route the new hoses to avoid low spots that might collect fluids and clog up.

Systems that route gases into a plate at the base of the carburetor often plug up at that point. Remove the carburetor and lift off the plate for thorough cleaning of this portion of the system. Sometimes the air passages can be cleaned without removing the base plate. Squirt in a special carburetor or PCV solvent and work pipe cleaners around to soften and remove the deposits.

Mesh filter screens in the vents or caps should be flushed clean with solvent. They can plug easily, rendering the entire system inoperative.

Your PCV inspection should include a look at the carburetor air filter element. If the element is clogged with crankcase vapors, it too should be renewed.

Some PCV systems have a crankcase ventilation filter inside the air cleaner housing or in a tube leading from it. If your engine has one of these, inspect it and replace if it has served 20,000 miles, more often if your car is exposed to dusty driving conditions.

Servicing Exhaust Controls

Integral exhaust control systems should be serviced along with your annual thorough tune-up. The main steps are as follows:

Check the idling speed. Pinch off the PCV hose and check for a drop in idle rpm. Check basic ignition timing and timing advance (see the chapter on ignition tuning).

Next, measure exhaust emissions (see the chapter on fuel system tuning). Remove the air injector hoses (if any) and watch for a large increase in exhaust emissions, indicating that the injector system is working. Reconnect the hoses. Finally, test for a fairly steady vacuum (see the chapter on manifold vacuum).

Failure in any of these areas calls for a complete tune-up.

Specifications for exhaust control-equipped cars are usually different than for earlier models of the same make. Decals on late-model U.S.-made cars

One-piece PCV valve (*below*) cannot be cleaned; it must be replaced. Slip one end of the valve into a clean hose. Then, insert the other end of the valve into the receptacle in the crankcase (*right*).

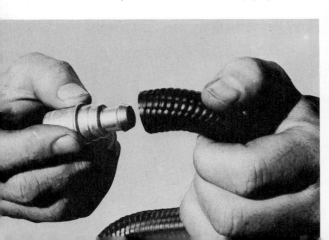

usually list basic ignition timing, dwell angle, plug and point gaps, and idle speed —and, sometimes, instructions for adjusting the idle mixture. With all of the devices described below, no service is possible. Complete replacement is the cure for problems—a shop job in any case.

Chevrolet has a "combination emission control system" in addition to the exhaust controls used on most GM cars. At the heart of the new system is a valve that is part of the carburetor assembly. It has a simple solenoid with a vacuum valve at one end and a hex-head throttle checkrod at the other. When the ignition is switched on, the valve is energized and controlled by the transmission. It allows vacuum spark advance only in the top driving ranges. Its other functions include positioning the throttle plates during deceleration and permitting more complete throttle closure at curb-idle and engine shutdown. In 1972, most GM V-8 engines got a speed control switch for vacuum spark advance only at speeds above 38 mph or engine temperature below 95° and above 230°. The switch is located on the right cylinder head between spark plugs Nos. six and eight.

The latest Chrysler products use two nitrogen oxide (NO_x) control systems, one with automatic transmissions, the other with manuals. Both have special valve camshafts that overlap intake and exhaust valve operation. Thermostats opening at 185° are also used.

Furthermore, both have switches that sense what the transmission is doing; thermal switches that react to outdoor air temperature; and solenoid vacuum valves. The transmission switches stay closed in all but top driving ranges and gears. When the switches are closed, vacuum-controlled spark advance is operational in both transmissions. The transmission switches can be overridden by the thermal

switches to give vacuum-controlled spark during both cool weather and when the engine overheats. Advanced spark speeds the idle, cooling the engine. In 1972 models, some 400- and 440-cubic-inch engines had solenoids that advanced the spark timing $7\frac{1}{2}°$ during engine cranking.

American Motors and General Motors use similar systems for eliminating spark advance in the lower gears.

All 1972 Ford products featured similar devices, called electronic distributor modulators. The system includes a speed sensor hooked in with the speedometer cable, a thermal switch near the front door pillar, an electronic control amplifier, and a three-way solenoid vacuum valve controlling distributor vacuum advance. It prevents vacuum advance below about 23 mph when accelerating and below about 18 mph when decelerating.

Servicing Transmission-Controlled Spark

If you have a vacuum gauge, you can check whether the transmission-controlled spark system is working as it should. The service manual contains full particulars. The general procedure is first to connect the vacuum gauge in the hose between the solenoid and distributor. With the engine running, a rear wheel raised off the pavement, and the car well blocked to prevent rolling, shift the transmission into each gear. (Automatic transmissions have to be driven to permit upshift into high gear.) Caution: If the car has a limited-slip differential, raise *both* rear wheels off the pavement. Take vacuum readings in all gears. If full vacuum is found in every gear, something is wrong. Look for a blown fuse, a wire disconnected at the solenoid or transmission switch, a faulty transmission switch, a temperature override switch energized (disconnect its

Use a vacuum gauge to check the transmission-controlled spark system. Connect it to the hose between the solenoid and the distributor.

entire unit and reset the two idling speeds as described in the fuel system chapter.

To tell whether the speed control switch on a GM car is operating correctly, jack up and block the rear wheels. Hook up an ignition timing light, start the engine, and shift into drive. Engine temperature should be above 95° and below 230°. While a helper gradually runs the engine up to slightly above 38 mph, watch the timing mark with the light to see whether the mark advances as the speed increases above 38 mph. If it does not, replace the speed control switch.

The solenoids on large post-1972 Chrysler Corporation V-8s that advance the spark during cranking can be checked easily. Disconnect the vacuum line from the distributor and hook up a tachometer. Idle the engine. Disconnect the lead wire about 6 inches from the distributor advance solenoid and hook a jumper wire to the lead. Energize the solenoid by touching the other end of the jumper to the positive terminal of the battery for no more than 30 seconds. If the solenoid works, idling speed should increase by about 50 rpm. If it does not, replace the solenoid.

Servicing Air Injectors

The air injection system is entirely separate from the PCV system. A word of warning: Air injection does not reduce the possibility of being poisoned by carbon monoxide for anyone foolish enough to run the engine in a closed garage. It does, however, promote more complete burning of exhaust gases.

Not much can go wrong with an air injection system. To check for air supply, remove one of the air-delivery hoses from the distribution manifold, start the engine, and see if air is being pumped through the hose. Other service consists of inspecting the pump's drive belt or belts every year and tightening or replac-

lead wire and test again), or a faulty solenoid.

If, on the other hand, there is no vacuum in high gear when there should be, look for switched clean-air and vacuum lines at the solenoid, a clogged solenoid, a broken plunger return spring, a broken distributor or manifold vacuum hose, a shorted transmission switch or a wire shorted to ground.

An idle-speed solenoid is easy to check visually by watching it while the engine is switched off. It should back away from the throttle plate, allowing the throttle to close further. If it does not, replace the

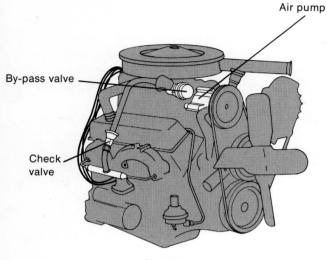

Air Injection System

ing when necessary. Full effectiveness of the system also depends on engine idling speed, ignition timing, and idle fuel mixture.

The filter on the main air pump, usually located behind the drive-pulley wheel, may need service. Check the pressure side of the system with a soapy water solution. Bubbles will form around leaky joints, fittings, or hoses while the engine idles. You can test the check valve by removing it and blowing through it toward the air manifold. You should be able to blow air through, but not suck air back. Badly corroded or burned air injection tubes on the manifold should be replaced by a shop. If the air pump is noisy or locks up, get a new one. Do not try to overhaul it.

Servicing Evaporative Control Systems

If you car is a 1971 model or later (1970 in California), it has a fuel evaporation system.

American Motors V-8s with automatic transmissions, all General Motors products, and all Ford products have charcoal storage systems. The only service needed is replacement of the air filter unit in the bottom of the charcoal storage every 12,000 miles or 12 months. Other parts of the system are not repairable and must be replaced if damaged. Since those systems must be closed to keep in fuel vapors, a damaged or lost fuel tank cap should be replaced right away with a similar cap. American Motors 6s and V-8s with manual transmissions and all Chrysler products have crankcase systems. Normally, such systems do not need maintenance. If fuel or gasoline vapor should escape from the filler cap, check the seal between the cap and the tank filler neck for leakage. Also suspect a defective release valve in the special cap (replace the cap if necessary) or clogged lines between the fuel tank and the vapor separator or between the separator and the crankcase air inlet filter (unblock them). The same condition may occur with a plugged fuel tank expansion chamber inlet hole in the main gas tank. Unblock it if necessary.

Emission Controls for Older Cars

If your car is too old to have positive crankcase ventilation or exhaust emission control, you can install devices to make it more pollution-free. Kits are available for many cars. Some are not yet approved for use in California and thus would not be available in that state.

PCV kits are available for almost any early-model car. They are required on all second-hand, post-1954 autos sold and registered in California. The parts consist of PCV valve, hoses, attachment to air cleaner, sealed oil filler cap, and special carburetor base plate or other fitting into the intake manifold.

You may want to install an exhaust emission control kit on your car. Most kits are made to fit cars from 1955 through 1967. One, the Chrysler Clean Air Package, is available from authorized dealers

Add-On ECS System Adjustments

	Chrysler	Ford	GM
Idling speed	650 rpm (auto. trans.) 700 rpm (man. trans.)	Add 100 rpm to original specs	600 rpm (auto. trans.) 700 rpm (man. trans.)
Air/fuel mixture	13.6:1 to 14:1	14:1 or, preferably, set with Rotunda exhaust analyzer	14:1
Ignition timing	Retard 5° from original specs	Retard 5° from original specs	Set to original specs

for 1955 through 1967 Chrysler products. You can install it yourself, as per accompanying instructions, in a little more than an hour. A complete tune-up should be done at the time of installation.

GM also offers a kit, which is installed as follows: Remove and discard the hose that connects the distributor vacuum advance to the vacuum source. Drain the cooling system partially and slice out a section of the engine-to-radiator upper hose. Install the temperature-controlled vacuum switch between the sections of cut hose, using the kit's hose clamps to make a tight connection. Attach a small-diameter hose, which is also provided in the kit, from the carburetor tapping of the vacuum switch to the engine vacuum source from which you removed the old hose. Run the other small hose from the distributor tapping on the vacuum switch to the distributor vacuum advance unit from which you removed the other end of the old hose. Refill the cooling system. Set the ignition timing, idle speed, and mixture according to the car manufacturer's new exhaust-control specifications (see the accompanying table). Lock the speed and mixture screws in place with snap-

Add-on exhaust emission control kit for older cars is keyed to a thermostatic vacuum switch that is mounted in the cooling system.

caps, tabs, or adhesive furnished with the kit.

Service of your converted system is the same as for a factory-installed exhaust-control system, including once-a-year tuning.

10

Engine Tuning: Starting System

The starting circuit consists of the battery, control switches and connecting leads, and starting motor. The battery provides electrical power that travels through the switches and leads to the motor which, of course, cranks the engine to start it.

Except for the battery, the circuit may well last the life of your car. But when a starting problem does develop, the car is just so much dead weight. A car with an automatic transmission that has no rear oil pump cannot be started by pushing. Neither can an alternator-equipped car with a completely dead battery; alternators have no residual magnetism to enable them to generate power on their own. You are lucky if the problem hits you at home. At least there you stand a good chance of finding and fixing the trouble.

Here, in detail, is how the starting system works: When you turn the ignition key to start position, the *battery* sends a small amount of current through the *starter solenoid*'s secondary circuit. The solenoid is a magnetic switch mounted either on the engine compartment or on the starter itself. The tiny secondary current closes the solenoid's heavy primary circuit contacts and sends high-amperage current through *thick cables* to the *starting motor*. The motor has a small pinion gear in mesh with a large ring gear on the flywheel. As soon as the engine catches, the pinion gear is kicked out of mesh with the ring gear. The starter coasts to a stop soon after you release pressure on the ignition key.

Cars with automatic transmissions have a *neutral safety switch* in this circuit to prevent the starter motor from operating unless the transmission selector is in neutral or park position.

Hard starting may be caused by the ignition, fuel or breathing systems as well as by the starting system. The place to start looking for trouble in the starting system is the battery.

BATTERY

An auto storage battery holds electricity in chemical form for future use. A six-volt battery, found on early-model cars, has three individual cells made up of positive lead plates and negative lead plates that are held apart by insulating plate separators. It also has three caps for replenishing the electrolyte—a solution of dilute sulfuric acid. A 12-volt battery has six cells and six caps.

The *acid strength* of battery electrolyte is measured by specific gravity. Specific gravity is the weight of a solution—in this case electrolyte—compared to the weight of water. Electricity is produced by chemical changes between the electrolyte and the active materials in the dissimilar battery plates. Using electricity from the battery is called discharging, a process that depletes the amount of active materials on the battery plates. Putting current into the battery is called charging. Charging a battery is done by applying a greater voltage across the battery terminals than is produced by the battery. It reverses the chemical process inside the battery, and the amount of active materials on the plates is increased. A battery can produce maximum electricity only when its cells are fully charged—that is, when all of its chemicals are in their active state.

Battery capacity is stated in ampere hours. That measures the capacity of a battery to store electrical energy and deliver

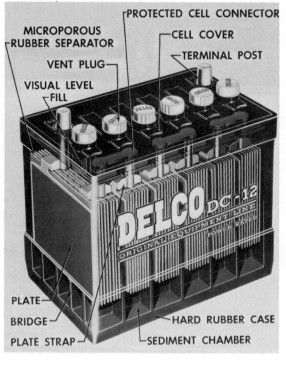

Typical Battery

it when it is called for. One ampere delivered for 100 hours is the same amount of electricity as 100 amperes delivered for 1 hour; both equal 100 ampere hours.

The principal causes of battery failure are overcharging and sulfation. Sulfation occurs in a battery that is operated continuously at a low state of charge.

Periodic Maintenance

Whether a car is driven or not, its battery eventually deteriorates. Proper care and maintenance of the battery and related equipment can prolong battery life. Regular battery service can head off most electrical problems caused by battery failures—including the inconvenience of a no-start.

Electrolyte level. The first rule of good battery care is to keep the cells filled above

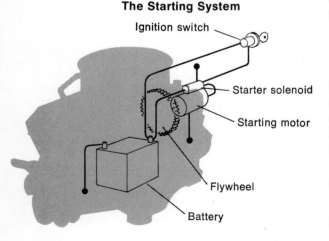

The Starting System

Ignition switch

Starter solenoid

Starting motor

Flywheel

Battery

Battery syringe is the best way to fill the cells of a battery. You can use ordinary tap water if you know that it is iron-free.

bubble over when charging, weakening the battery unnecessarily. It also promotes corrosion of the battery carrier.

Distilled water is not a must. At the factory, batteries are filled with drinking water. However, hard, iron-bearing water is undesirable; if you have such water in your area, buy bottled water for the battery. Do not add acid to a battery, for acid does not evaporate. Nor should you put additives into the battery. Many have been tested, but none seems to do a battery any good. Besides, using an additive voids the battery guarantee.

When a battery uses too much water, it is being overcharged (all cells low). High temperatures and too high a voltage limiter setting can cause excessive water consumption. (More on the voltage limiter in the chapter on the charging system.)

A battery that does not need water after several months of average driving is probably being undercharged. That generally is caused by poor cable connections or too low a voltage limiter setting.

Some batteries are supposed to need addition of water only three times a year. Those have no special design other than a large electrolyte storage capacity over the cells. When you finally add water, you need to add that much more.

the battery's plates. Only that portion of the plates immersed in the electrolyte can take part in creating electricity. Any portion of a plate above the electrolyte level may become irreparably damaged.

Check electrolyte level every 2,000 miles or once a month, more frequently in extremely hot weather and on long trips. If the level drops, add enough colorless, odorless drinking water to bring each cell up to the proper mark. If the cell filler openings have no level indicator, the usual level is 3/8-inch over the tops of the plates. Overfilling lets the electrolyte

Washing the battery. Keep the top of the battery clean. Dirt, acid film, and corrosion around the battery posts let battery current leak away. Leakage is especially serious on 12-volt batteries; it can discharge the battery slowly without your being aware of it. One good cleaning method is to remove the battery from the car and wash it with a dilute ammonia or baking soda solution to neutralize the acid. Keep the neutralizing solution from getting into the cells through loose cell caps or open vent holes in the caps. Flush the battery with water.

Toothpicks inserted into the vent cap openings will prevent suds from getting into the cells as you wash your car's battery.

This battery terminal is so corroded that its current-carrying capacity is seriously affected. The entire cable should be replaced.

You can test the battery for electrical leakage with a voltmeter or VOM. Set the selector to read about 0.6 volt. Put the black lead on the negative battery terminal and move the red test prod over the top of the battery, without letting it touch the positive post or any exposed cell connectors. Electrical leakage will register on the voltmeter. If the reading exceeds 0.5 volt, clean the battery.

The battery cables are of heavy insulated copper wire, with metal clamps on their ends to fit snugly around the battery posts. Corrosion tends to build up between the battery posts and cable terminals, preventing proper electrical contact. Remove and clean corroded terminals. Most non-GM battery terminals are removed by loosening the through-bolts and nuts that clamp them onto the posts. If the nuts have

Check leakage due to corrosion with a VOM. Touch black lead to negative post and red lead to case. The reading should be less than 0.5 volts.

Squeeze-type battery terminals are used in GM cars. To remove such a cable, grip the lugs with a pair of pliers, squeeze, and then lift.

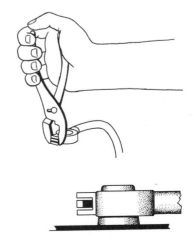

corroded, turn them with a pair of battery pliers. GM battery terminals are self-clamping. Loosen them by pinching the protruding prongs with pliers. In a car with a negative-ground system, always remove the negative cable first to prevent a short circuit when removing the positive cable.

Never pound or pry a terminal; the battery post is fragile. Loosened battery terminals that cannot be lifted easily off the posts must be removed with a battery terminal puller.

The inside of the terminals should be cleaned with a round wire brush, a round file, or sandpaper. Also clean the outside of the battery posts with a wire brush or coarse sandpaper. While you have the terminals off, expand them with a terminal expanding tool, if you have one, so they will go back on the posts without harmful pounding.

Slip the cleaned, expanded terminals back onto their proper battery posts until the tops are flush with, or below, the tops of the posts. On cars with negative-grounded electrical systems, the cable that leads to the starter solenoid goes on the positive post. The negative terminal, even if expanded, will not fit over the positive post. Install the positive cable first. If the through-bolts on the terminals are corroded, replace them.

If a battery terminal is corroded to the point where its strength or electrical contact is suspect, install an entire new cable rather than just a replacement terminal.

After installation, coat the terminals and what you can reach of the battery posts with a thin film of nonmetallic grease or petroleum jelly. This retards future corrosion. Spraying the terminals with silicone lubricant or ignition sealer also works. (Coating the battery posts before installing the terminals impedes the flow of electricity.)

Battery Terminal Care

Tools (*from left*): hydrometer, syringe, carrying strap, battery pliers, terminal puller, expander, post-and-terminal cleaning brush, lubricant, jumper cables.

1. Begin by loosening the terminal clamps with a wrench or with battery pliers, which are better for working on corroded nuts.

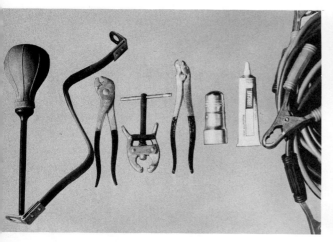

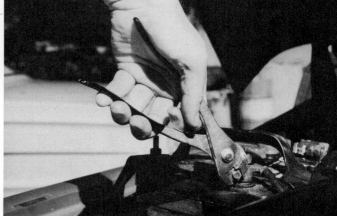

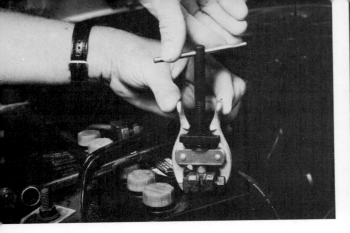

2. Slip the legs of a battery terminal puller under the terminal. Turn the screw to lift the terminal.

3. Loosen the terminal clamp nut and slip an expander into the terminal to stretch it.

4. With the post-and-terminal cleaning brush, scour both parts. Use the male end of the tool—the brush is beneath a cap—to clean the terminal (*left*). Use the female end of the tool to clean the post (*center*). To ward off future corrosion, consider buying inexpensive terminal mats (*right*), which fit between the battery and the terminals.

5. Once the terminal has been reinstalled, either smear non-metallic grease over the parts (*left*), or coat the terminal and post with a spray of silicone lubricant (*right*).

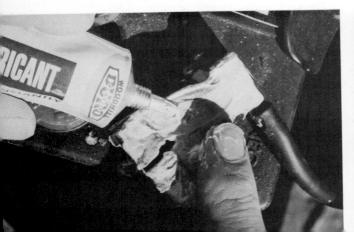

The battery carrier—the holder or tray in which the battery rests—often rusts, its threaded fasteners corrode, and its hold-down clamp loosens. You can buy replacement hold-down clamps and bolts at an auto parts jobber. See that the hold-down is tight, but not too tight (usually 60 to 80 inch-pounds torque). Wire-brush all rust off the battery carrier, and prime the bare spots with an aerosol-spray metal primer. When that dries, paint the parts, preferably with a black, acid-resistant paint.

Battery Carrier Care

1. Begin by unfastening the hold-down clamps. These parts are usually quite corroded—you may need pliers and a wrench to loosen the nuts.

2. With the battery removed, grind off rust and other corrosion deposits on the carrier with an electric drill and a wire brush attachment.

3. Finish by priming all bare metal, and follow with a generous coat of acid-resistant paint.

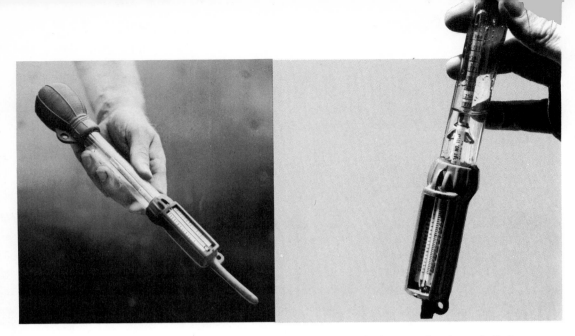

The best battery hydrometer is one with a thermometer at the lower end and a scale that gives temperature corrections. When you use a hydrometer, be careful not to spill electrolyte on yourself or on the car.

Hydrometer Test

A battery that fails should be given a hydrometer comparison test. Too many owners replace a battery prematurely when, often, all it needs is a charge. To tell a good battery from a bad one, first examine the outside and top of the case for cracks and punctures. A battery with a broken case should be replaced no matter how it tests out. At the same time, replace missing or broken cell caps with ones taken from a junk battery.

Then, make a hydrometer test.

A battery hydrometer is an essential tool for every knowledgeable car owner. It measures the specific gravity of the electrolyte in the cells. It consists of a rubber syringe bulb, a glass tube, a rubber pickup tube, and a float calibrated to read specific gravity from 1.160 to 1.320, in gradations of 0.005.

Water has an assigned specific gravity of one (1.000). Temperature affects the specific gravity, so very cold and very hot

Hydrometer Corrections

Temperature of electrolyte (degrees F.)	Add or subtract
160	+.032
150	+.028
140	+.024
130	+.020
120	+.016
110	+.012
100	+.008
90	+.004
80	.000
70	−.004
60	−.008
50	−.012
40	−.016
30	−.020
20	−.024
10	−.028
0	−.032

readings need to be corrected. Battery specific gravity is figured at 80° F. For every 10° of electrolyte temperature above 80, four specific gravity points (.004) must be added to the hydrometer reading. Similarly, for every 10° below 80, four points must be subtracted from the reading. For example, a hydrometer reading of 1.286 taken at 40° F. would be corrected to 1.270 at 80°. (See the accompanying table of hydrometer corrections.)

The best battery hydrometers, which cost but a few dollars, contain a built-in thermometer for measuring the correction factor. The incoming solution flows around the thermometer and gives an automatically corrected reading. Cheaper hydrometers without the thermometer—and often without a point-scaled float—are widely sold. But their markings, such as "full charge," "half charge," and "dead battery," are almost meaningless for accurate testing. Get a good hydrometer.

The test. Remove all of the cell caps. Starting at one end of the battery, squeeze air out of the rubber hydrometer bulb, place the pickup tube in the electrolyte, and release the syringe to bring electrolyte up into the glass tube. Empty and fill the hydrometer several times to bring the thermometer to proper temperature. Hold the hydrometer up to eye level, but be careful not to drip acid on the car or on yourself. If acid should get on something, wash it off immediately with water and neutralize with ammonia or baking soda.

When you take the reading, hold the hydrometer vertically so that the float moves freely without sticking on the sides of the tube. Record the reading for the first cell, and then repeat for each remaining cell.

If the difference between the highest and the lowest specific gravity readings is

Hydrometer Test

Difference between highest and lowest cells	Specific gravity lowest cell (80°F.) corrected	Battery
Less than 50 points	More than 1.230	Good, and satisfactorily charged
Less than 50 points	Less than 1.230	Good, but needs charging
More than 50 points	– –	Defective. Should be replaced

more than 50 points, discard the battery.

If the level of electrolyte is too low to lift the float, add water to bring the cells to their correct level. But do not take your readings until the next day; it takes time for the water and electrolyte to mix. And never add water to a battery in freezing weather if you do not intend to drive the car immediately. The pure water could freeze before it has a chance to mix with the electrolyte, damaging the battery. A discharged battery is especially vulnerable to freezing.

A battery that passes the first hydrometer comparison test but fails in service needs further hydrometer testing. First, bring it to full charge with a battery charger.

Batteries vary in what they will accept as full charge, depending on how they have been used. Most show specific gravity readings of between 1.230 and 1.310. New batteries are designed to be fully charged at 1.260. Batteries built for tropical climates have normal fully charged specific gravities of 1.225. (On such batteries that figure is stamped on one of the posts.)

A battery that is fully discharged will test about 1.150.

For reliable operation, the battery should be in at least a 75-percent state of charge, a specific gravity reading of about 1.230. If, after charging, the lowest cell's specific gravity is less than 1.230, discard the battery.

A reading higher than 1.310 means that one cell was improperly activated when new or that acid has been added at some time subsequently. Short life and poor service will result.

Before discarding a battery, make sure that a light or accessory was not left on to drain the battery and that the charging system regulator is adjusted according to specifications. Also, check the charging system wiring for high resistance and poor connections. (More on these topics in the chapter on the charging system.)

High-Rate Discharge Test

If you have a battery-starter tester (BST), you can perform another tell-tale test on your battery. This expensive but useful device is actually a combination voltmeter, ammeter, and variable carbon-pile resistance load. It has leads to the circuit being tested and selector switches that let you control the readings.

One of the examinations you can perform with the BST—the high-rate discharge test—is considered the "acid test" for a battery.

The test. The instructions for most makes are as follows: Turn the load control knob all the way to the left. Connect the ammeter (large) leads and voltmeter (small) leads to the battery posts, observing polarity—connect reds to the positive post, blacks to the negative post. The clips may be placed on the terminals, but they should touch the battery posts.

With a battery-starter tester, or BST, you can make a quick but informative test to see if the battery in your car is worth saving.

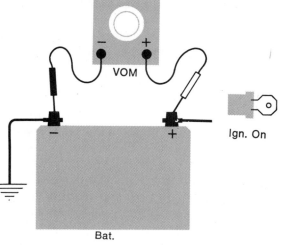

High-Rate Discharge Test Hookup
With Voltmeter or VOM

Set the BST selector switch to the volts-amps position and turn the load control knob to the right until the ammeter reaches triple the amperes of your battery's specified ampere hour rating. Quickly move the selector switch to the volts position and read the meter. It should show not less than 9.6 volts for a 12-volt battery or 4.8 volts for a 6-volt battery. Turn the load control knob back to the left to complete the test. Do not run the high-rate discharge test longer than 15 seconds; it drains a battery rapidly. If, during the test, battery voltage drops below the required minimum with the battery fully charged, get a new battery.

Lacking a BST, you can get similarly informative results with nothing more than a good voltmeter. To test with this instrument, pull the ignition coil wire out of the center tower of the distributor so that the engine does not start. Have a helper crank the engine. After 15 seconds of cranking, battery voltage should be not less than 9.6 volts for a 12-volt battery, 4.8 volts for a 6-volt. A battery that meets either load test and passes the hydrometer test is reliable.

Battery Charging

If a battery becomes discharged and will not start your car—and yet passes the hydrometer cell test—recharge the battery and continue using it. Charging may be done in the car or out.

Charging at 5 amperes for 10 hours provides the same amount of charge as charging 50 amps for one hour; each adds up to 50 ampere-hours.

There are two types of charging: slow and fast. Both are useful at times. Slow charging supplies a small amount of current, say 3 amperes, over a long period of time, perhaps 24 hours. Fast charging provides a high rate of charge, such as 50 amperes, for perhaps 1½ hours. An emergency boost to get an engine started may

take only 30 minutes on a fast charger. Although the engine starts, that should not be considered a sign of a fully charged battery. The battery should be given a complete charge at the first opportunity.

Some new battery chargers and those that have not been used in six months or more need conditioning. Plug the line cord into an alternating current house outlet and let the charger run for 15 minutes. Be sure that the clips are not connected to anything and that they cannot touch each other. Then disconnect the cord. The charger is ready for use.

Before charging a battery, top off the electrolyte in all cells. Also, see that the vent holes are open to let gases escape during charging. If in doubt, loosen or remove the filler caps to provide ample venting.

Hook-up. Connect the charger to the battery before plugging it into an outlet. Correct polarity of the connections is important. An alternator-equipped charging system (used in most cars these days) can be damaged by a wrong hookup. Remove the negative terminal from the battery before connecting the charger. The charger as well as the battery can be damaged by

To connect a battery charger, remove the negative cable. Then, clip the black lead to the negative post and the red lead to the positive post.

an incorrect hookup that is left for long. Always connect the red ("+") battery charger clip to the positive battery terminal and the other clip (sometimes black or marked "—") to the negative terminal, regardless of whether your car has a negative- or positive-ground electrical system. Wiggle the clips so they make good electrical contact.

If the hookup of battery chargers with meters is correct, there will be no reading on the meter until the line cord is plugged in. If the leads are reversed, sparking will occur on chargers without meters as the second terminal is touched to the battery. Switch the leads and try again.

Setting. Before plugging in the charger, see that its voltage selector switch, if any, is set to match the voltage of the battery being charged. If set on 6 volts, a charger cannot hope to charge a 12-volt battery. If set on 12 volts, it could work itself to death trying to charge a 6-volt battery.

Caution. Highly explosive hydrogen gas is given off by charging batteries. The gas forms inside the cells and escapes through the cell vent openings. For that reason, keep cigarettes and other sources of sparks and flames away. An explosion can spray acid over everything in the vicinity—including you. Do not smoke near a charging battery or one that has been freshly charged. Be careful, too, when connecting or disconnecting booster cables; a spark often is created then.

Plugging in. When you plug in the charger, its charging rate will be shown on the meter. Rate depends on both the voltage received from the receptacle and the internal condition of the battery. Higher than normal (117 volt) AC line voltages increase charging rate; lower than normal voltages decrease it. A discharged battery takes a higher charging rate than a partially

charged one. One make of 6-ampere battery charger will charge 8 amps into a discharged battery, 6 amps into a half-charged one, and 3 to 4 amps into a fully charged battery. Other chargers act similarly. When you become familiar with your own charger, you will know that when the meter shows a charging rate of about half the charger's capacity, the battery is fully charged. Check the battery with a hydrometer.

Unusually high meter readings immediately after plugging in a battery charger may be caused by reversed connections. The meter will swing to the far right and stay there until the charger's built-in overload protector cuts out. Then the needle will drop to zero.

Most good chargers have automatic resetting overload protectors. When they cool down, they kick back in, pegging the meter on the far right again. The cycle keeps repeating. To correct that condition, reverse the charger's leads at the battery terminals.

If your charger has no overload protector, do not let it charge for more than a minute with the meter at the extreme right of the scale. When a meter shows that a charger is working 30 percent above its rated capacity, the charger is overloaded. If overloading persists, the charger should be unplugged. The problem may be too-high line voltage, a defective battery, an incorrectly connected charger, or a battery that is overly discharged. Trying to charge a 6-volt battery on the 12-volt setting gives the same symptoms.

A completely discharged battery causes high meter readings too, until it begins to become charged. That is nothing to worry about. It may even make the meter cycle, as in the example above. But after 15 or 20 minutes the cycling should stop, as the battery takes on enough of a charge to offer some resistance. A battery that has one or

Charging Schedule (Passenger Car Sizes)

Battery	Slow charge		Fast charge		Emergency boost	
	Time	Rate	Time	Rate	Time	Rate
12-volt	24 hours	4 amps	1½ hours	40-50 amps	½ hour	40-50 amps
6-volt	24 hours	6 amps	1½ hours	60-70 amps	½ hour	60-70 amps

more defective cells, however, may cycle the charger indefinitely. Such a battery will not accept a charge and must be replaced.

Charging time. To figure charging time, you need to know the size of your car's battery and the charging rate of your charger. Multiply the percentage of charge by the ampere-hour rating of the battery. Divide by the rating of the charger times 100. Here it is in a formula:

$$\frac{\% \text{ of charge} \times \text{battery amp-hours}}{\text{charger rating} \times 100} = \frac{\text{hours to}}{\text{charge}}$$

For example, the time for charging a half-charged 60-amp-hour battery with a 6-amp battery charger would be:

$\frac{50 \times 60}{6 \times 100} = 5$ hours. Add about 25 percent

to the calculated charging time for inefficiency and taper of charging rate. Any battery that will not take a charge must be replaced.

Slow charging. Battery chargers for slow charging are not costly. A charger that puts out about 4 amperes is a good size; with it, you can charge a completely dead average-sized battery in 24 hours. A battery is considered fully charged if all its cells are freely gassing while charging, and if hy-

drometer readings do not increase in three hourly readings.

Low-rate battery chargers are called trickle chargers. They feed about 1 or 2 amperes into a battery. Trickle charging is fine for keeping partially discharged batteries topped off to full charge and for use during extreme cold weather to maintain full battery power. Using one overnight warms a battery internally for better starting on a cold morning. Trickle charging is not recommended for extended use because it, too, can overcharge a battery.

When you attach jumper cables to your car's battery to give it a boost, be sure that you observe the correct polarity (see chart, page 172).

Percent of Charge

Specific gravity (corrected)	Percent of charge	Voltage (12-volt battery)
1.260	100	12.6
1.230	75	12.4
1.200	50	12.2
1.170	25	12.0
1.110	0	11.7

Some of the greatest new home-type battery chargers are self-limiting. That is, they shut themselves off automatically when the battery is fully charged. These may be left on without attention. Ordinary battery chargers should not be left on for more than 24 hours without checking on the state of charge.

Fast charging. This does not harm a battery, if it is done properly. However, it will bring a battery to only about 75 percent charge. A full charge requires additional slow charging.

Fast chargers are large, costly units intended for use by service stations and auto repair shops. If you are stranded with a dead battery, fast charging will get you going even if the old battery is defective. Battery defects show up worst in discharged batteries, and a fast charge can enable a defective battery to perform a while longer. If the fast charge at a station will let you get home, it probably is worth its cost.

Improper fast charging, though, can ruin a battery. Here is what to look for when someone is giving your battery a fast charge:

• The mechanic should check the electrolyte level. If necessary, he should fill the cells with water.

• He should see that the cell vents are functioning.

• He should look up the correct fast-charging rate for your size battery (see the accompanying table of charging rates). The charger's timer should be set for the correct charging rate and time.

• He must make some provision for slowing or stopping the charge if the electrolyte reaches 125°; otherwise, the battery can be damaged. Some fast chargers have a thermoswitch probe that reaches into the electrolyte of one cell. Others have electrical overload controls. Lacking these, a thermometer should be placed in one cell and it should be checked periodically. If electrolyte begins spilling over from any cell, or if the thermometer reaches 125°, the rate of charge must be reduced or the fast charging must be stopped.

Disconnecting. To disconnect a charger after use, first unplug it from the AC outlet. Then unclip its leads from the battery. Most chargers, if left connected to the battery but not plugged in, will discharge the battery slightly. Those that shut themselves off automatically cost more.

Selecting a New Battery

Battery sizes once were a jungle of numbers and terms. Now, battery box sizes are divided into numbered groups. For instance, a Group 24 battery fits most U.S. cars. The salesman need know only the make, model, and year of your car to look up its group number. Look for these factors in selecting a new battery:

A replacement battery should have at least the same *storage capacity* as the factory-installed one. Battery capacity, expressed in ampere hours, appears in the general specifications of your car. Original-equipment battery size is adequate for normal needs, but if you have added extra electrical accessories since you bought the car, use a larger battery.

The best way to handle a battery is to carry it with a battery strap. Before you lift, make sure the clamps are securely locked to the posts.

Cold weather driving, short trips, and driving in heavy traffic also call for a larger battery. (Cold weather decreases battery capacity and increases starting load.) A hot climate can be even harder on a battery than a cold one. For one thing, heat shortens the life of batteries. Moreover, a hot engine may need more cranking to start than a cold one.

(Electrical capacity of a battery sometimes is expressed according to the number of plates per cell or the total number of plates in the battery, but since no standard exists for number of plates, such a figure is meaningless.)

Ampere-hour ratings are based on a 20-hour discharge time. The shorter the discharge period, the tougher the load on the battery. A battery passes the 20-hour test if it can be discharged at 1/20th of its rated capacity for 20 hours and still produce 10.5 volts at the end of the test. That is primarily a test of how much active chemical material there is in the battery; it says nothing about how well that chemical will last or what it will do under stress.

The standards measure the amperage that a new battery can deliver at 7.2 volts for 30 seconds. The higher the amperage, the better the battery.

Another new standard measures a battery's *reserve capacity.* It is based on the number of minutes the battery can deliver an operating load of 25 amperes—about the amount of current needed for ignition, lights, wipers, and defrosters—without receiving a charge from the alternator.

LEADS AND SWITCHES

If the battery checks out all right, the place to look for starting system problems is in the electrical circuit between the battery and starter—because it is easiest to check, not because it gives the most trouble.

First, make a visual check of the wires and cables that comprise the starting circuit. Look for frayed insulation, loose connections, and broken wires. Inspect all connections from the battery to the cranking motor, including the solenoid and the ignition switch. Check the neutral safety switch too. Clean and tighten any faulty connections. If there is still no draw, further testing is needed.

The Jumper Test

Next, using one of a pair of battery jumper cables, jump from the battery's positive post (on negative-grounded systems) to the starter motor's power terminal. There should be a spark. If there is, hold the lead on for an instant and listen for starter action. Make the contact quickly and firmly to avoid excessive arcing. If the starter turns, the problem is somewhere in the wiring circuit to the starting motor. If there is no spark or if the starting motor does not operate, the trouble is likely within the starting motor. Remove it for further testing.

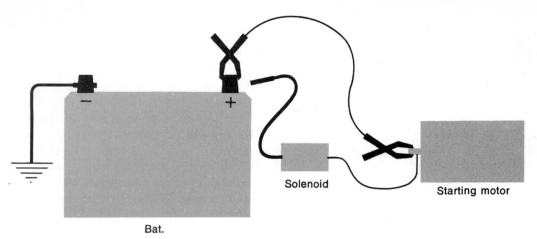

Bat.

Starter Motor Jumper Test

To isolate secondary circuit troubles, try jumping across the various parts of the switching circuit. A light jumper wire can be used for this. Short across the ignition switch, the neutral safety switch, and the switching terminal of the starter solenoid. If the starter operates, the part being shorted out at that time is faulty.

A common cause of no-start troubles is the neutral safety switch. If it works itself out of position, it may not allow the starting system to work properly. Try holding the ignition switch to start position while moving the transmission selector lever around. If the starter works, the switch needs repositioning. Most neutral safety switches are located on the steering column under the instrument panel. Some are in the engine compartment, possibly on the firewall just above the steering column. And some are on the transmission. Adjustment is made usually by loosening the mounting screws and positioning the switch so that it turns on only when the transmission selector is in neutral or park.

Starter-Draw Test

If you have a voltmeter or battery-starter tester, you can trace most starting difficulties quickly. The test to make with a BST is of amperage-draw of the starter. Connect the ammeter leads and voltmeter leads to the battery posts with correct polarity. Follow instructions. With some meters you set the test selector switch to the volts-amps position and the volts-amps selector switch to the volts position. Turn the load control knob all the way left, and remove the high-tension cable of the ignition coil and ground it.

If you have a remote starter button, hook it up. One of the two leads goes to ground (or the positive battery post) and the other goes to the small terminal on the solenoid. That enables the starter to crank when the button is depressed. Otherwise, have a helper in the car crank the engine with the key when you give the word.

As the engine cranks, read the exact cranking voltage on the voltmeter. Stop cranking. Turn the BST's load-control knob to the right until the voltmeter matches the cranking voltage. Now, move the volts-amps selector switch to amps, and read the meter for starter amperage draw. Unless specified otherwise, the reading should be within the green band on the amp scale marked "starter." Turn the load-control knob back to the left to end the test.

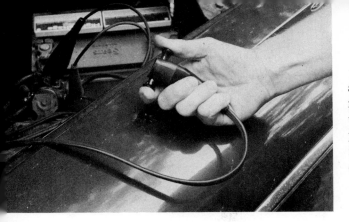

Remote starter button is extremely useful for any tuning tests that require cranking of the engine. When it is properly connected to the starter solenoid, you can turn the engine by just pressing the button.

accompanied by low cranking speed, look for high resistance in the starting circuit wiring or the starting motor. If the circuit passes the voltage-drop tests, the trouble is in the starter. Remove the starter and check it.

Voltage-Drop Tests

Using a voltmeter, you can easily conduct voltage-drop tests of starting circuit wiring. These are handled much the same as ignition system voltage-drop tests. The tests rate the resistance of the insulated and ground circuits to the starter and the starting switching circuit. Proceed as follows:

For an *insulated circuit test,* set the selector on the voltmeter to read in the range of 0.1 to 0.4 volts. Connect the red voltmeter lead to the battery's positive post (not to the terminal). Connect the black lead to the starter terminal. Ground the coil's high-tension cable to prevent starting, and crank the engine.

Unless specified otherwise, the reading should not exceed 0.3 volt with starter-mounted solenoid systems and 0.4 volt with separately mounted solenoid systems. A higher reading indicates excessive resistance in the cables, switches, or connections, which would lower cranking speed and cause hard starting. Test individually with the voltmeter leads across each part of the circuit as the engine is cranked. Individual voltage-drop readings should not exceed the following amounts (half these for 6-volt systems): cable, 0.2 volt; solenoid, 0.1 volt; connection, 0.0 volt.

For a *ground circuit test,* connect the red lead to a good ground on the body of the starting motor and the black lead to the battery negative post. Crank the engine as before. If the voltmeter reading exceeds 0.2 volt, suspect a loose, dirty, or corroded

Interpreting the readings. A good starting system on a large, high-compression V-8 engine takes about 200 amps or more when cranking. A six or a four takes 180 amperes or less. Those starter ampere draws should produce normal engine cranking speeds.

Normal starter draw with a low cranking speed indicates high resistance in the starting circuit. If this is the case, conduct the voltage-drop tests described later.

High starter draw usually indicates trouble in the starting circuit, but it also may be caused by an overheated engine. Let the engine cool for 15 minutes and test again. If amperage is still high, the starting system has shorts or the starting motor or engine is suffering from internal mechanical drag.

Sometimes, excessive current draw is caused by high resistance in the starting circuit, which restricts the flow of current. If so, conduct the voltage-drop tests. If those come out according to specifications, remove the starter and conduct a free-running current-draw test; instructions for your BST should tell you the hookup procedure. That test tells whether the high draw is caused by the starter or the engine.

Low starter draw also is possible. If it is

ground connection or a ground cable too small to handle the load. Any of these conditions could reduce cranking speed and cause hard starting. Clean and tighten the ground cable at both ends. Also tighten the starting motor mounting screws.

You can narrow the problem by testing each portion of the starter ground circuit similarly. Readings with the starter in operation should be no more than 0.1 volt on short ground cables, 0.2 volt or slightly above on long ground cables and zero across each connection.

A *switching circuit test* enables you to diagnose high resistance in the secondary switching circuit. Such a condition can reduce current through the circuit enough for it to function improperly or fail altogether. In time, that burns the solenoid's primary circuit contacts, reducing current flow to the starter.

Set the voltmeter selector as before and ground the coil cable. Connect the red lead to the battery positive terminal. Connect the black lead to the solenoid switch terminal (the small one that is fed from the ignition switch). Crank the starter with

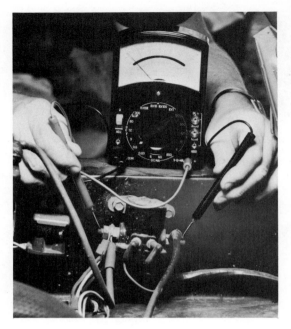

To check voltage drop across the starter solenoid, touch the red lead to the primary battery terminal and the black lead to the other large terminal. With starter turning, reading should be less than 0.4 volt.

To test the starter solenoid, jumper across its terminals. If there is a spark and the engine then cranks but won't normally, the solenoid is probably defective.

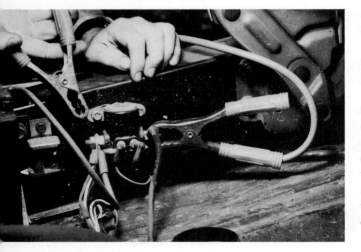

the ignition key—not with a remote starter cord—and watch the voltmeter. Unless otherwise specified, the maximum reading should be 0.5 volt. A higher reading indicates excessive resistance somewhere in the switching circuit. (Some cars, though, normally show more than 0.5 volt resistance. Check your car now, while everything is all right, and note the reading so you can make comparisons later if you should have starter problems.)

The trouble can be isolated by testing the voltage drop in each portion of the circuit with the starter motor in operation. Do not run the starter more than 15 seconds at any one time without allowing it to cool. A reading of more than 0.1 volt across any single wire or switch or more than zero across any connection is an indication of trouble.

Solenoid switches that simply control

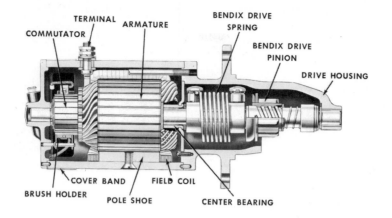

Parts of a Starting Motor

current to the starter are inexpensive to replace with new ones, if they are defective. Those that engage the starter pinion are more costly and are worth repairing, if possible. Take such a switch to a professional mechanic.

If you get an excessively high voltage-drop reading across the neutral safety switch, check the adjustment of the switch.

STARTING MOTOR

The starting motor is a direct-current motor whose shaft has a small pinion gear. That gear meshes with a large ring gear on the engine flywheel. The starter may revolve 20 times for each revolution of the engine to get the engine started.

Usually, this assemblage will last the life of the car; but sometimes it will act up. A starter is located beneath the engine. Even so, in some cars it is easier to remove from above. In either case, remove the ground cable from the battery before tackling the starter. Usually two through-bolts and an end support hold the unit to the engine. Once those are out, the solenoid lead wires (if on the starter) and the

starter cable are removed. The starter then can be snaked out. The starter pinion inside the engine must be moved away from the engine to clear the ring gear as you work the starter out of its opening.

Once the starter is on the bench, try to turn its shaft by hand. Tight, dirty, or worn bearings or a bent shaft will make the starter hard to turn. If you find any such problem, get a rebuilt starter without further checking.

If the shaft turns freely, turn the starter pinion gear on the screw shaft to check for freedom of operation. If it sticks and you had starter drive problems, have the entire drive assembly replaced.

Take the starting motor to a garage or auto electrical repair shop for testing and service. Even if it is not the cause of your problem, once the motor is removed it should at least have its brushes and commutator checked and serviced before you remount it. You can do that part of the job, if you like. (Refer to the section on brush-commutator service for generators in the chapter on charging systems—the job on the starter is similar.) Finally, lubricate the bearings while the starter is apart.

TROUBLESHOOTING STARTING PROBLEMS

SYMPTOM	CAUSE	CURE
No sound when switch turned to start position	Dead battery	Use jumper cables, recharge, or replace battery
	Loose or broken cable connections	Tighten connections or replace cables
	Faulty ignition switch	Test by shorting across starting terminals of switch; replace if defective
	Defective starter solenoid	Test by shorting across terminals of solenoid; replace if defective
	Neutral safety switch faulty or out of adjustment	Test by shorting across switch; adjust or replace switch
Clicking sound when starter switch turned to start position, but engine does not crank	Very low battery	Charge or use jumper cables
	Loose or partially broken battery cable connections	Clean and tighten cable connections at battery, starter solenoid, and starter; replace if broken
	Faulty starter solenoid	Test by jumping; replace if defective
	Locked starter drive	Auto. trans.: loosen starter drive to free. Man. trans.: put shift in high gear and rock car to free
	Locked engine	Remove spark plugs and try to release any trapped water; all repairs are major
	Open starting motor circuit	Remove and repair or install rebuilt starter

Starting motor spins, but engine does not crank	Ice on starter driveshaft keeps pinion from engaging	Try "jogging" techniques described in chapter on cold-weather starting, or push car into heated garage
	Damaged starter drive mechanism	Remove starter and repair drive
	Ring gear teeth missing	Major repairs necessary; turn off key and rotate engine by hand to bring good teeth up, then start, drive to shop for repairs
Engine cranks slowly	Battery partially discharged or damaged	Check battery and recharge or replace
	Excessive starter current draw	Perform starter-draw test; replace starter with rebuilt if defective
	Excessive voltage drop in starting circuit	Perform voltage-drop test; clean connections and tighten
	Starter drive or ring gear misaligned or damaged	Take car to shop for repair
	Engine hard to turn	Engine hot: allow to cool: engine oil too heavy for temperature, use proper weight. Engine cold: install preheater (see chapter on cold-weather starting). Automatic transmission drag, tight bearings, sticking pistons; take to shop for diagnosis and repair
Engine cranks but does not start	Engine needs tuning: fuel, ignition, breathing	See chapters on engine tuning
	Battery too weak to provide good spark when cranking	Check battery condition; replace battery if necessary
	Starter draw too high to leave current for ignition	Perform starter-draw test; install rebuilt starter if necessary

11

Cold-Weather Starting Tips

Professional auto mechanics have a big bag of tricks to get engines started in even the coldest weather. You, too, can make sure your car starts every time by taking the following tips from the pros.

GETTING READY

By first frost, most motorists have already mixed anti-freeze in their radiators. But there are other precautionary measures you should take to insure smooth starting all winter long. Experts say that a spark-ignition engine, if properly tuned for the cold, should start without trouble at temperatures as low as 10° below zero. If your cold starts are unsure, your engine probably needs tuning—see the various chapters covering the different engine systems.

Any tune-up should include checking the *automatic choke* while it is cold to see that it moves smoothly without binding.

The *battery* must be tip-top for reliable starts in cold weather. When the temperature drops, the cranking power required goes up—and the available power of the battery wanes. Today's 12-volt batteries provide fast engine cranking for only about a minute. Remember that fact when trying to start a cold, balky engine.

If your battery is not at full charge, it is not as likely to get you started when the temperature plummets. Do not rely solely on your charging system to keep the battery at full charge during the winter. Use a battery hydrometer (about $1) to check the charge regularly. Use a small battery charger (about $15) to keep your battery at peak charge at all times. Regular charging, by ending replacements, soon saves the price of the charger.

The viscosity of the *oil* used in your engine determines its cranking speed and its capability to start. To fire, a typical modern engine needs a cranking speed of 20 to 35 rpm at 20° below zero. An engine in good shape will fire on 20-weight oil, while one needing work will not start even on lighter, 5-weight oil. Poor compression does not let an engine develop enough power to take hold and run by itself. An engine with poor compression must have a light oil. So must one with a weak battery or starting system.

The lower the numerical rating, the lighter—less viscous—the oil. For example, SAE 30 oil is less viscous than SAE 40 oil. Multiviscosity oils—say, 20W-40—supposedly give the advantages of both the light, 20W oil and the heavy, 40 oil. (The "W" stands for "winter.") Unfortunately, such oils tend to thicken unpredictably below zero degrees. Then, they do not give you the snappy cold-weather cranking that a straight 5W or 10W oil does. The thickening varies by brands. The oil industry recently introduced a 10W-50 oil, which should prove effective for year-round use.

Using an engine oil that is too light is risky for fast driving on warm days. Never use oil lighter than recommended by your car's manufacturer for the temperatures expected.

Clean ignition cables give you an edge in winter starting. Periodic jet-spraying in a car wash helps prevent leakage of high-voltage electricity.

TROUBLESHOOTING

Knowing how to coax a cold engine to life can get you going when other drivers fail. The starting procedure varies with the idiosyncrasies of each engine. As a general rule, hold the accelerator pedal about half-way down and crank the starter. If the engine has not come to life within 10 seconds of cranking, it is probably flooded. Sit and wait a minute. Then ease the gas pedal to the floor and try another 10 seconds of cranking. If that does not work, the engine may be gas-starved. Crank and pump the gas pedal at the same time. If that does not work, begin looking for troubles.

First, make sure you have fuel in the tank. Then, proceed through the following checklist:

• According to a survey by a spark plug company, one-third of the cars that will not start have low ignition output. Remove a spark plug wire and hold it 3/16 inch away from the engine. Have someone work the starter while you watch for a spark. The spark should be thick and fat. If it is thin and weak, your problem could be in the ignition system.

• See if enough electricity is left for a good spark during cranking. Turn on the headlights and hit the starter switch briefly. The lights should dim slightly. If they dim considerably, suspect a weak battery, a poor battery terminal connection, or a sick starter.

• Spark plugs could be the problem. More than half of the no-start cars in the previously mentioned survey needed spark plug cleaning or renewal. Some 12 percent of all the cars with 5000 miles on their spark plugs did not start. With 15,000 plug miles, 41 percent did not start.

• Fuel freeze-up is usually indicated by an engine that starts and runs briefly and then dies and will not start again. A stuck automatic-choke butterfly produces the same symptoms, but accompanied by the signs and smells of raw gas.

To check for fuel starvation, remove the air cleaner and look into the carburetor throat while a helper pumps the gas pedal. Gasoline should shoot out of the accelerator pump jets. If it does not, water frozen in some part of the fuel system could be blocking the fuel flow. Pour hot water carefully onto the carburetor bowl, fuel pump, fuel filter, and low spots in the fuel lines to thaw them. Keep it out of the carburetor and off the ignition system parts.

• If everything checks out properly so far, the balky engine may simply be flooded. A wet carburetor or the odor of gasoline from under the hood is a tip-off. Have a helper try to start the engine with the accelerator floored while you hold the automatic-choke butterfly open with your hand. (The air cleaner must be removed to do that.) If you still get no results, cap the top of the carburetor with your hand as the engine is cranked. That sucks up raw gas to start an underchoked engine.

• A starter drive that won't engage can be maddening. Ford and other cars with Bendix-drive starters sometimes suffer that affliction. Water on the starter shaft freezes or oil on the shaft congeals, preventing the drive gear from sliding into its engaged position. The starter spins but the engine does not budge.

To shake the drive gear loose, turn the ignition key to "start" and back about ten times. In between hits, give the starter time to stop spinning. If the inertia of 10 starts does not free the gear, run the starter continuously for a minute to warm it up. Wait a minute for the heat to reach the gear before trying the inertia trick again. If that does not do it, try another minute of running followed by more starter hits. Sooner or later the heat will reach where it will do some good.

Hot water poured over the carburetor, fuel lines and fuel pump can get you started on a cold day. Be sure to keep inside the carb and spark cables dry.

If you flood the carburetor while trying to start, remove the air cleaner and hold the choke butterfly open. Have a helper crank the engine with the throttle open. The excess fuel should clear quickly.

REMEDIES

One answer to most cold-weather starting problems is a fully charged *spare battery* in your trunk. Hook it up to the regular battery with a pair of jumper cables. You can also hook these cables to the battery of another car.

In any case, make sure that you hook the red jumper cable between both positive battery terminals and the black jumper cable between both negative terminals. Otherwise, reverse flow of electricity through the alternator diodes can burn them out in a flash. Reversed hookup is not good for the batteries, either.

In extreme cases you can hook two weak batteries in series, giving the starter and ignition system a 24-volt blast.

Do not try series jumping on a car with an alternator or you will burn out the alternator diodes.

To make a series hookup, remove the positive battery terminal and switch off all lights and accessories, lest they be damaged. While a helper turns the ignition key to "start" and holds it there, you manipulate one jumper wire to make or break the circuit. That way, voltage drop caused by starting keeps the full 24-volt jolt from blowing out your car's warning light bulbs. (They may blow out anyway, but that is the price of emergency starting.)

Never crank an engine on 24 volts for more than about 5 seconds or you may burn out your starter or overheat the starter cables. Series jumping is not recommended with fully charged, warmed-up batteries; it has been known to snap off starter drives, strip flywheel ring gears, and blow up batteries. Watch it.

If your engine has been properly maintained and will not start after several tries, chances are that the *spark plugs* are fouled with wet gasoline. Flooding allows lead deposits on the plugs to short out the electrodes. As a precaution, carry three cleaned and gapped spare plugs and the necessary tools to install them. If the engine's plugs get fouled, three spares should be sufficient to let a six or V-8 en-

If the spark plugs in your car are in good shape, remove several and place them in the exhaust pipe of a car that is running. When the plugs are hot, reinstall them in your engine, then try to start it.

Squirt of starting fluid into air cleaner intake while the engine cranks may do the trick. Use a screwdriver to open the warmed-air flapper valve. Do not spray more than a few seconds.

A fully charged battery is vital to cold-weather starting. A small charger, left on overnight, may be enough. Be sure to get the hookups right.

On particularly bitter mornings, a spare battery—here, housed in an easy-to-make carrier—and jumper cables can save you a service fee.

gine catch and run. The other plugs soon will come to life.

One mechanic's trick is to remove and heat as many of the plugs as you can take out. If you are at home, put them on the stove in the flame for a minute. Scrape the electrodes clean while you have the plugs out. Reinstalled, hot plugs may help get you going.

Another old cold-weather starting trick is to remove every other plug in the firing order. Let those cylinders pump air, so your starter has less of a compression load to handle. Warm up the engine on half the plugs, then put in the rest, and the engine should start immediately. Follow every other lead from the distributor cap to get the right plugs. Let the unused spark plug cables hang in the air. That gives the other plugs a hotter spark.

Ether injection can get your engine started—sometimes. It is a two-man job; one tries to start the engine while the other sprays ether from an aerosol can into the engine's air-filter opening. Easy-vaporizing ether sometimes can fire the cylinders where gasoline vapors cannot, if the battery is weak or the ignition system is in poor condition. If the engine has been flooded, forget using ether.

Be careful when using ether as a starting fluid. Leave the air filter on the engine to prevent flash-back. Do not give an engine more than a couple of two-second squirts. If that does not get you going, put the ether away; you can blow the engine by using too much ether.

Ether is poisonous, too. Do not inhale it. Do not smoke while you use it. Do not spray it on yourself; besides being toxic and highly flammable, it evaporates so fast it can cause frostbite.

If the cold engine is wet, spray a *moisture-displacing penetrating lubricant* over the spark plug wires and distributor cap. It will get rid of the water and let the sparks get through to the plugs.

Of course, many of these remedies would be unnecessary if you could *heat* your engine before starting. The best way is to install an engine preheater; but if this is not feasible, you can improvise other warming tricks.

Place a 150-watt light bulb on the engine right next to the intake manifold, turn it on, and let it burn all night.

Or, garage the car at night. If the garage is unheated, or the car must stand outdoors, remove the battery and take it indoors at night. Install it just before you're

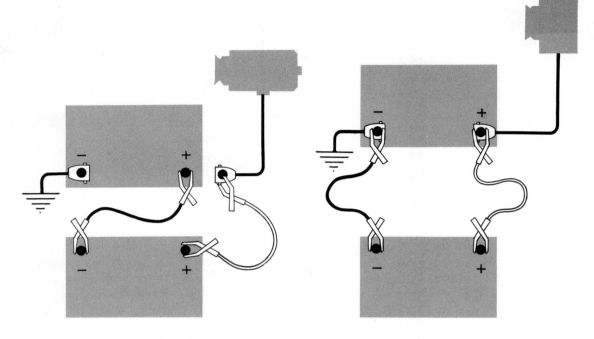

Generator System   Alternator System

Emergency use with weak batteries   Standard hookup for generator and
and generator systems only.   alternator systems.

ready to go. Or keep it on a charger over-night. Charging warms a battery as well as holds it at full charge.

If you have no garage, putting a heavy blanket over the engine and radiator after shut-down will help hold in some of the heat until your next start. Do not forget to remove the blanket before you crank.

PREHEATERS

An hour's time and $15—what it takes to install an engine preheater—can mean the difference between start and no-start on many a cold morning. With the warmth from such a device, the battery and starter have an easier job, and engine wear is re-

duced. Often, you can avoid using a light weight motor oil that cranks easier, but cannot withstand high-speed driving. Another of the preheater's benefits is that your car's heater comes on strong within a minute or two.

You can choose from among many different types of engine preheaters. Most use 120-volt house current to provide heat to some part of the engine. You can also get ones that work on propane, butane, or diesel oil. Those are costly compared with the electrically operated heaters we will discuss.

You can use a preheater all night or only when needed. Allow about 3 hours for a

Required Size of 25-Foot Extension Cord

Heater size	Amps	Wire size (AWG)
500-watt	4.1	No. 18
850-watt	7.1	No. 16
1000-watt	8.3	No. 16
1500-watt	12.5	No. 14

1500-watt preheater to warm a large V-8 engine. To avoid having to get up in the middle of the night to prepare for an early-morning start, plug the preheater into an electric timer. Smaller preheaters should operate all night.

Do not be too concerned about the cost of engine heating. At the national average electrical rate, you can run an 850-watt heater full blast all night for about 23 cents. Using the more economical three-hour fast-warm-up method, you can get by for about 9 cents a night, provided enough electric power is available. Engine heating may be banned in electrically short areas.

High-wattage engine preheaters can draw 10 amperes and more. Never plug one into a light extension cord. Use an extension with at least 16-gauge (AWG) wire. See the accompanying table on extension cord wire sizes.

Finally, never use an engine preheater that plugs into the car's cigarette lighter. Such units run down the car's battery.

Installing an engine preheater is not a difficult do-it-yourself job. When you finish, a short cord and plug are left dangling beyond the grille. Simply plug the cord into an extension cord the night before or several hours before you want to start. By the time you are ready to go, your engine is warm. Of course, a preheater cannot help you get started in a parking lot after work, unless you can rig up some means of getting electricity to your heater.

Types of Heaters

You have a choice among three kinds of engine coolant heaters: tank-type; core-plug; lower-hose. Each has advantages.

Two popular types of preheaters—the tank type (*left*) and the core-plug type (*right*). The tank type contains a thermostat to prevent overheating.

Cold Climate Heater Size (#Watts)

Engine size	3 to 4-hour warm-up (watts)	Overnight
4-cyl.	450	450
6-cyl.	1000	850
V-8	1500	1000

Note: The largest heater can be used on the smallest engine, but it would be neither necessary nor economical.

Recently developed lower-hose preheater is the simplest to install. However, it does not have a thermostatic control.

Most *tank-type* preheaters have thermostats that switch them off when the engine coolant nears operating temperature and switch them on again as the coolant cools. This not only saves electricity, but it prevents overheating in mild weather and protects against heating element burnout. That advantage makes tank-type preheaters best for most cars. Sizes from 500 to 1500 watts are available. The 500-watters are for small engines and for large engines in moderate climates. The 850- and 1000-watters are for cars and light trucks. Preheaters larger than that are too big except for extreme cold weather.

To use a preheater, just plug it in at least three hours before starting. The cost in electricity is just pennies for each start.

Tank-type models come in kit form and operate much the same as a hot water boiler in a house. An electric immersion coil inside a small tank heats the engine coolant. As the coolant heats, it flows by convection up out of the tank and through the engine block. The rising coolant draws cold coolant out of the bottom of the engine and into the preheater. Circulation is continuous without need of a pump.

The *core-plug* type is the next most useful preheater. These electric devices fit into the blocks of most engines through core openings (often misnamed "freeze plugs"). Their heating coils are immersed in the water jacket surrounding the cylinders.

An advantage of the core-plug engine preheater is that two of them can be used to heat both cylinder banks of a V-8 engine. A tank-type unit can fully heat only one side of the engine, the side it is piped to. The other side is warmed only by spillover and radiant heat from the heated side. Either way, the engine starts; but equal heat on both sides is better for long engine life.

A new type of engine warmer—the *lower-hose preheater*—has an element that is mounted in line with the lower radiator hose. Heated coolant finds its way up the hose, through the water pump, and into the water jacket. Installation is the easiest of any engine heater. Diameters are made to fit just about any car's lower radiator hose.

Other heaters. You can also get effective engine heaters in the form of *headbolt units* for L-head engines or *water pump bolt units* for old Ford products. Ease of installation is the big benefit of many bolt-type heaters, but their heating capacity is somewhat limited. Headbolt heaters warm the liquid in the water jacket. Some headbolt and water pump bolt installations call for drilling through the water jacket; that makes installation tougher.

Easiest of all to use are the *dipstick* (or *crankcase*) *heaters.* They simply install in place of the oil dipstick to heat the oil and air inside an engine's crankcase. However, dipstick heaters are not very effective—in fact, they can cook the oil to a point where the lubricant is damaged.

A heated *battery mat,* which sells for about $8, may be a good investment—a warm battery provides as much as six times the cranking power of a cold one. Such a mat, with an output of 50 to 65 watts, is superb when teamed with an en-gine preheater, according to Canadian fleet operators, who should know.

Air-cooled engines are not left out in the cold—if you own a VW, a Corvair or a Porsche, you can get an electric heater that fits under the oil sump.

Installing a Preheater

Putting a preheater into a car with a water-cooled engine hinges on the type of warmer unit—tank, core-plug or lower-hose. When you buy a kit, all parts and fittings should be furnished. Just remember that to install a coolant heater, you must first drain the cooling system.

Installing a Tank-Type Preheater

1. Remove an engine block coolant drain plug and substitute the nipple that comes with the kit.

2. Slip a length of the hose that comes with the kit onto the nipple and install a clamp.

3. Install a tee fitting into the existing heater hose. Then, connect the new hose to the fitting.

4. Mount the preheater firmly to the car, and route the power cord out through the grille.

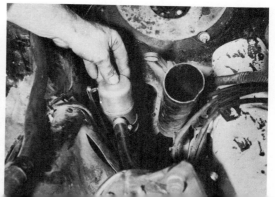

Tank heater installation. Thread a nipple (furnished) into the engine block drain opening and connect it with a hose to the bottom of the heater. For proper circulation, the preheater should be located as close to the block as possible and at least 6 inches below the top of the cylinder head. A mounting bracket is provided.

Install a tee fitting (also furnished) in the hose leading from the top of the engine block to your car's heater. Cut the hose at a convenient spot and insert the tee. See that there is no shut-off valve between the tee and the engine block; such a valve might cut off coolant circulation. Heating element burn-out could result. All hose runs must be below radiator water level. Avoid hose loops that could trap pockets of air inside.

Refill the cooling system using the required amount of antifreeze. Start the engine and loosen the hose at the tee fitting until all trapped air bleeds off. Put the hose back on and reinstall all clamps.

Run the heater's power cord away from hot or moving parts of the engine. Let four inches of cord and plug hang through the front of the grille so you can plug in without lifting the hood. Wrap electrical tape around any points on the cord that pass unprotected through metal. The cord should be anchored all along so it cannot flap into the fan blade. Anchor it behind the grille, too, so that if children pull on the cord, it will not be strained at the heater connection.

Test the unit's operation by plugging it into a 120-volt outlet. Make sure the element is fully immersed, or you may burn out the element. Feel the hoses and block at intervals. The top hose should get warm, while the bottom hose should stay comparatively cool. If the lower hose warms before the whole system does, suspect improper installation, an air leak, a preheater that is mounted too high or is tilted too far, or blockage in the system. Do not worry about the "cooking" sound the preheater makes when operating. It is caused by the vaporization of coolant in contact with the heating element.

Core-plug heater installation. Getting the old core plug out is the toughest part. Be sure you have the correct size heating unit for your engine's core opening. Some makes vary from one engine to another. The surest way to tell is by measuring the opening. Be sure to check clearance for the heater—power accessories as well as exhaust manifolds may affect clearance.

Remove a convenient core plug—the center one usually gives the best circulation. On 289-cubic-inch Ford engines, use the left front opening in the cylinder head. Core-plug heaters cannot be used easily in old Chrysler V-8 models with distributors in the rear. Those have counterbored core openings that must be drilled out.

Core-plug preheater mounts into an opening at the bottom of the engine block. Its heating element extends into the water jacket.

To remove a core plug, drill a hole in the plug and pry it out with a punch inserted through the hole. Never chisel on the edge of the core opening. That mars the sealing surface. Clean corrosion and dirt from the hole by scraping and wiping with a gasoline-dampened cloth. Wipe dry.

Loosen the nut on the back of the preheater and insert the unit into the core opening, terminal side out. You may have to rotate the heating coil to keep it clear of the cylinder wall. Push the sealing gasket tightly against the outer block wall and tighten the nut. That expands the rubber gasket, making it seal against the core opening. Tighten $1\frac{1}{2}$ to $2\frac{1}{2}$ full turns after the gasket begins to seat. Run the power cord out through the grille with enough slack to allow for engine vibration without strain on the cord. Refill the cooling system and test the heater.

Installing a lower-hose preheater is a snap: simply splice the device into the lower radiator hose and clamp it firmly.

Lower-hose preheater installation. Cut the lower radiator hose as close to the water pump as possible, but so that there is a three-inch straight portion. Remove a one-inch section of hose from the center of the straight portion. (If the hose is long and flexible enough, you need not remove any of the hose; simply cut it.) Position a hose clamp (furnished) on one side of the hose and slip the preheater into that side until the edge of the hose is almost touching the plastic terminal housing. Tighten the hose clamp. Do the same with the other side of the hose. You may leave a 750-watt lower-hose engine preheater plugged in overnight if the temperature is 25° F, or lower.

A *final word of caution:* Do not drive off some morning without unplugging your preheater. If necessary, put a tape reminder on your instrument panel.

12

Troubleshooting the Charging System

The charging system has two jobs:

To furnish electrical power for the ignition system and all the car's electrical accessories.

To maintain the battery's state of charge.

Besides the battery, the charging system includes an alternator or generator charging unit, a regulator, an indicator light or ammeter, and electrical wiring.

The charging unit, operated by the engine crankshaft through a drive belt, converts mechanical energy into electrical energy. When electrical current flows into the battery, the battery is said to be charging. When current flows out, the battery is said to be discharging.

In an alternator charging system, the regulator assembly contains either vibrating contacts or a transistorized voltage limiter. These keep the charging output in line with the battery's needs. The regulator also may include a field relay or an indicator lamp relay.

In a generator charging system, the regulator contains a vibrating-type voltage limiter. In addition, it has a cutout relay — an electrically operated switch that connects the generator to the battery when generator voltage is greater than battery voltage. It also prevents the battery from discharging through the generator when the generator is not charging. (An alternator system does not need a cutout because its solid-state diode components act as one-way valves for the flow of electricity. No significant backflow can take place through them.) A generator system also includes a current regulator to limit output of current, thus protecting the generator from overloads.

At idle, the battery may discharge, especially when lots of accessories are on. Do not idle the engine too long while more power is being consumed than is being generated by the charging system. The excess power comes out of the storage capacity of the battery. When that is used up, the battery will go dead.

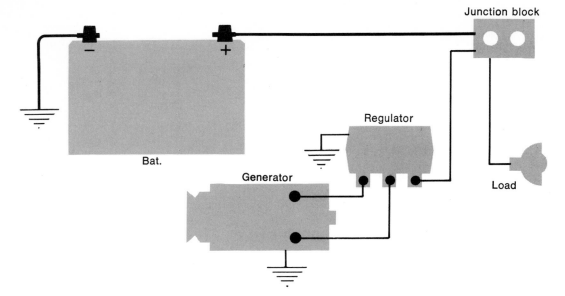

The Generator Charging System

A properly adjusted charging system will not charge a low battery, except on a long trip, but it will maintain the state of charge that is already in the battery. Thus, once it is brought up to full charge, the battery should stay that way. If you find the battery in a low state of charge, have it charged.

Generally, the charging system does not require much attention unless the red charge indicator light comes on when it should not. Unfortunately, by that time some damage may already have been done to part or all of the charging system and to

The Alternator Charging System

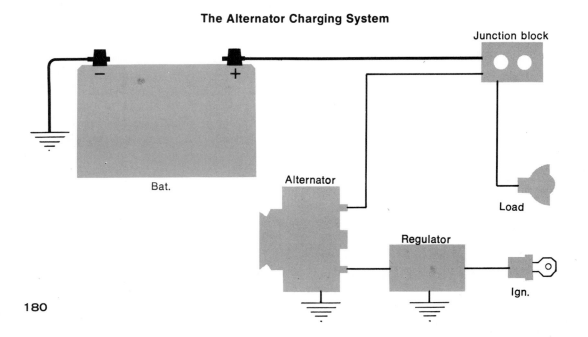

the battery. If you want to have advance warning of problems in your charging system, install an ammeter gauge as described later in this chapter.

Preliminary Troubleshooting

Even without an ammeter, you can spot trouble in a charging system before a no-charge condition occurs.

In normal operation, a car battery needs water only four or five times a year. If your battery needs filling more often, it probably is being overcharged.

A battery that frequently needs charging is another sign that the charging system is not providing enough current. Test your car battery with a hydrometer (see the chapter on the starting system). If it does not show full charge, the charging system may be failing to replace all of the current the battery needs to stay in top shape; probably, the regulator is out of adjustment. The hydrometer test is important whether or not the vehicle is equipped with an ammeter.

Bulbs burning out is another warning of

overcharging and time for a charging system checkup.

When you pull into the garage at night, see if the headlights brighten and dim considerably as the engine speeds and slows. If so, the charging system is malfunctioning.

Failure of the car to start or hard starting could be a charging system problem, although ignition system, fuel system, or battery-starting system troubles also can be to blame.

Checks of Charging System

Low charging rate, fully charged battery	Normal operation
High charging rate, fully charged battery	Wrong regulator voltage setting, defective regulator, grounded field circuit (generator only), defective regulator ground (some systems), high battery temperature
High charging rate, low battery	Normal operation
Low charging rate, low battery	Defective battery, high voltage drop in insulated circuit, too-low voltage regulator setting, dirty regulator points, defective alternator or generator
No charge	Dirty voltage regulator contacts, burned-out fusible wires in regulator, broken drive belt, locked shaft, defective charging unit

First place to look for causes of charging problems is in the system's wiring. All connections should be clean and tight.

When the red indicator light does come on, do not start with electrical tests until you have made a visual inspection of the system.

First, you need to know whether your car has an alternator or generator system. An alternator is short and squat, like a large can of tuna fish. A generator is longer and cylindrical in shape, like a can of vegetable juice. The charge indicator light in an alternator system often spells out "ALT" when it is lit; if so, you can be sure your car has an alternator.

Now, look at the drive belt. If it is broken, loose, or glazed, replace it.

Check the battery cables. If their terminals are loose or corroded, high resistance may be keeping the charging system from pushing current into the battery. Check both ends of both cables. The connections should be clean and tight.

Inspect alternator and regulator wires for loose or broken connections. They can impede the flow of charging current; worse, they can let the charging system run wild and ruin its components.

Check the battery itself. Unscrew the caps and check the electrolyte level. If you can get home and you have the necessary testers there, perform a battery load test and take hydrometer readings of each cell. Check the voltage across the battery terminals while the battery is at normal temperature. Perform a cranking voltage test. The battery may have reached the point where it simply will not accept electricity from the charging system. If it has, replace it.

Sometimes, but not often, mechanical problems develop in the alternator or generator. Uncorrected, they eventually lead to damage and electrical failure of the system.

If the alternator or generator is noisy, check for loose mountings. Look for a

Bent fan blades on a generator or an alternator could cause charging unit noises. With the engine off, see if the blades hit the end frame.

damaged fan, loose pulley, or worn belt. Other noise-makers are worn bearings that need lubrication, a damaged armature or rotor, or a worn commutator. Sometimes, a burned-out diode makes the system whine. If leads from the diodes to the field stator windings contact the rotor at any point, reroute the leads to prevent contact.

TESTS

Charging test. If you have a voltmeter or VOM, you can find out whether the charging system is charging.

Connect the meter's red lead to the battery positive post and its black lead to the battery negative post. The meter will read battery voltage at about 12½ volts. Start the engine and run it at 1800 rpm (about three times the idling speed). If the system is charging normally, the voltmeter reading should increase above battery voltage to specified charging voltage—usually between 13.8 and 14.2 volts on a 12-volt system. No voltage increase indicates that the system is not charging. The cause is most likely either the charging unit or the regulator.

Charging unit test. A functional test of the charging system can tell you whether the alternator or generator is working. The test calls for a voltmeter (not necessarily a sensitive one) or a VOM. It also calls for knowledge of what kind of charging system the car uses.

Generator charging systems come in A-circuit and B-circuit. The B-circuit system is found on all Fords, and 1960 through 1962 Studebakers and Ramblers with Autolite generators. All other cars use the A-circuit system.

As for single- or double-contact regulators, the double-contact ones are for heavy-duty charging systems. However, they are widely used on standard passenger cars. Nearly all double-contact generator regulators have the following wording stamped on the cover: "Double-contact regulator. Caution: do not ground

F terminal. To check generator, detach field lead and ground it."

You can tell whether yours is single- or double-contact unit by removing the cover and examining the voltage limiter's contacts. (Remove the negative battery cable first, to prevent accidental shorts.) If there are contacts above and below the movable arm, it is a double-contact unit. If you still are not sure whether the regulator is single- or double-contact, play it safe and follow the instructions for the double-contact regulator.

The output terminal of a generator is the one labeled "ARM" or "A" for "armature." The output terminal of an alternator may be labeled "BAT" or "B" for "battery." If the field terminal is not labeled "FLD" or "F," you can identify it by the large fiber washer around it. If a radio-frequency suppression condenser is attached to the generator, the field terminal is *not* the one it fastens to.

Charging Unit Tests

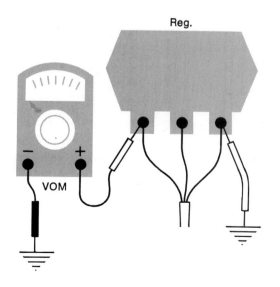

Reg.

VOM

A-circuit generator with single-contact regulator. Attach the red voltmeter lead to the battery terminal of the regulator. Attach the black lead to a good ground on the engine, and hook a jumper wire from the regulator's field terminal to ground. Accelerate the engine until the voltage reaches 15.4 volts for a 12-volt system or 7.8 volts for a 6-volt system; do not exceed those figures by more than one volt.

If grounding the field terminal increases the charging rate to as high a level as it should be, the regulator is at fault. If grounding the field does not help much, the generator is at fault.

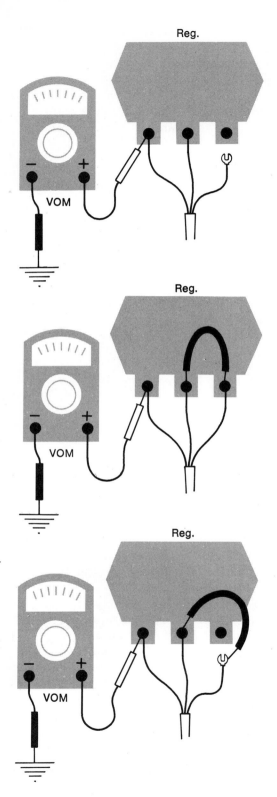

A-circuit generator with double-contact regulator. Connect the voltmeter the same way. But instead of grounding the field terminal, disconnect the field lead from either the regulator or the generator, whichever is easiest, and connect a jumper from the field terminal of the generator (not the regulator) to a good ground. Check charging voltage, diagnose as described on the previous page.

B-circuit generator with single-contact regulator. Attach the volt-meter as before. Connect a jumper wire between the output and field terminals of either generator or regulator. Test charging voltage and diagnose as before.

B-circuit generator with dual-contact regulator. Attach the volt-meter as before. Disconnect the field wire from the regulator terminal, and fasten a jumper wire from the armature terminal of the regulator to the field lead you just disconnected. Test and diagnose as before.

184

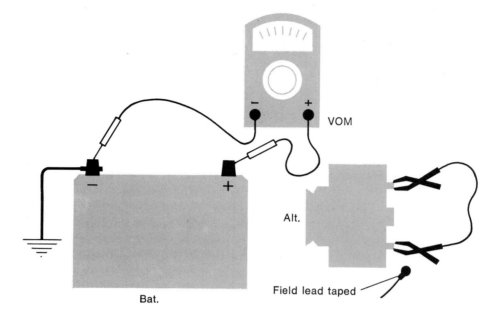

VOM

Alt.

Field lead taped

Bat.

Alternator with separately mounted regulator. First disconnect the battery negative cable. (Never ground or short the terminals on *any* alternator charging system. That can blow the diodes.) Unfasten the field wire from the alternator and tape its end to prevent accidental grounding. Connect a jumper wire between the field terminal on the alternator and the alternator's output terminal (BAT, B or +). With cars that have a protected wiring harness connector at the regulator, test the output by unplugging the connector from the regulator, and sliding in a jumper wire from the "F" receptable in the connector to either the "3" receptable (Delcotron) or the "A" receptacle (Autolite).

In any case, reconnect the battery cable, and connect the voltmeter's red lead to the positive battery terminal and the black lead to the negative terminal. Start the engine and test at or slightly above idle.

Do not run the engine fast; the alternator is running without control and can easily be damaged. The diagnosis is the same as in the generator hookups, except that the alternator's diodes should be checked too, as described later in this chapter. Alternator voltage may come up to specifications even with a bad diode, but the unit cannot charge the battery properly.

Test an *alternator with regulator in back* the same way, but unfasten all wires from the alternator and tape them to prevent grounding. If the specified charging voltage is reached, the alternator or generator is good. Look to the regulator for the trouble.

Voltage drop test. Charging circuit wiring can be checked out with a low-reading voltmeter. A good VOM also does the job. The tests are for voltage drop in the loaded circuit; they are conducted much like those for voltage drop in ignition circuits (see the chapter on the ignition system).

First, visually inspect the system as outlined earlier in this chapter.

Turn on the headlights and enough accessories to bring the charging rate to half that specified for the system—about 15 to 20 amps for an average late-model charging system. Run the engine at about 1800 rpm, set the VOM selector to its lowest volt setting, and make the following tests. (The voltage drops given are maximums for 12-volt systems; halve those amounts for 6-volt systems. Reverse the hookups for positive-grounded electrical systems.) Be careful to keep the test leads—and your hands—out of moving parts.

Insulated charging circuit. Test by attaching the red lead to the output terminal of the alternator or generator and the black lead to the battery positive post. Maximum voltage drop should be 0.8 volt unless otherwise specified.

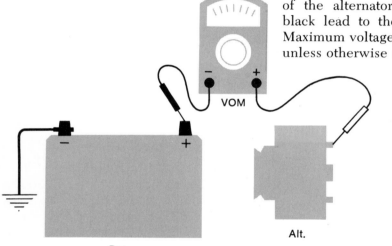

Bat.

Alt.

VOM

Ground charging circuit. Test by attaching the red lead to the battery negative post and the black lead to a clean bare spot on the alternator or generator frame. Maximum voltage drop should be 0.4 volt unless otherwise specified.

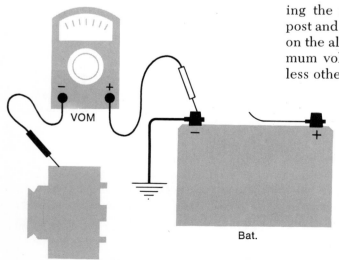

VOM

Bat.

Alt. or Gen.

Entire ground circuit. Test by stopping the engine and leaving the accessories on as a load. Attach the red lead to the regulator base and the black lead to the alternator or generator frame. Maximum voltage drop should be 0.1 volt.

Excessive voltage drop in the above circuits should be located by careful visual inspection of connections. If the fault is at a connection, remove and clean the terminals, reinstall them, and test again.

Wires should be checked for partial breaks. Install new, larger wires if no other cause of excessive voltage drop can be found. New terminals should be either soldered or crimped on with a crimping tool to minimize resistance between wire and terminal.

Too much resistance between the ground circuits of some types of generators and their regulators can make the system charge an already fully charged battery so heavily that the battery is damaged. Too much resistance in the insulated charging circuit and battery prevents sufficient charging in most systems.

If voltage drop is excessive in the ground circuit between the alternator or generator frame and the base of the regulator, install a grounding wire between the two to correct it. The wire should be the same size as the wire from the output terminal of the charging unit; a No. 10 wire should do it on most systems.

Full output tests. If you have an alternator-generator-regulator tester consisting of a voltmeter and ammeter, you can conduct full output tests that tell the complete story of what is happening in the charging system. The best setup is a combination voltmeter-ammeter unit and a separate loading device. They come with

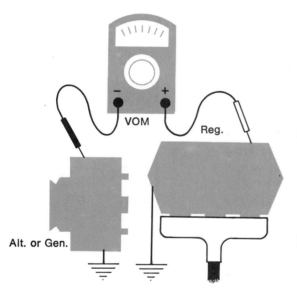

Alternator-generator-regulator tester (*left*) lets you make rapid charging system tests. The load unit (*right*) is a handy accessory.

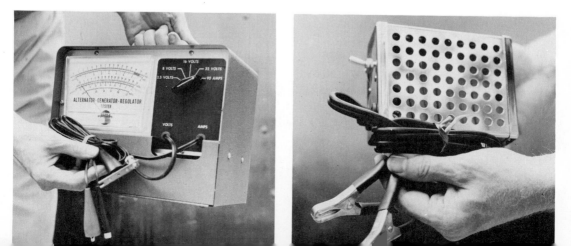

full instructions on charging system tests that you can make with them. The load unit is not vital—you can switch on accessories to load the charging system—but it is useful in putting a maximum load on the system while testing for maximum charging rate.

The alternator-generator-regulator tester shown in the photo has two pairs of leads, as do other volt-ammeters for charging system testing and adjustment. The voltmeter leads are used in all tests. The ammeter shunt leads are only for making current measurements.

Manufacturers publish temperature/voltage figures for their regulators, and regulator voltage settings are specified at operating temperature, usually something like 124° F. A regulator properly adjusted to 14.6 volts at that temperature will provide 16.0 volts at 45°, but only 14.2 volts at 165°.

Run the engine for 15 minutes before testing the charging system. All regulators have some provision for temperature compensation, and thus must be adjusted at operating temperature. If they are not, you must compensate in the adjustment for the temperature of the surrounding air.

The most common charging system problem is too-high or too-low a setting of the voltage limiter—the unit that controls maximum voltage of the charging unit, be it a generator or an alternator. Test the limiter first.

The tester can be hooked up as shown on the next page or in another way to get the same effect. The tester is nothing more than a voltmeter and an ammeter. The voltage leads should always connect from positive to negative, the red one positive. The ammeter shunt bar (or leads on testers without a shunt bar) should always be hooked in line with the current flow, from charging unit to battery. On negative-grounded systems, that would be connected in the positive side of the circuit, somewhere between the output terminal of the charging unit and the battery's positive post.

Various hookups are illustrated in the instructions that come with the tester. Some may be difficult because the terminals on the rear of most alternators are not easy to reach.

An easy hookup on any car calls for a battery post adapter (about $12). The adapter simplifies the attachments by allowing all hookups to be made right at the battery. Otherwise, you must look long and hard for the proper attachment points for the ammeter leads. The battery post adapter fits over the positive battery post, and the positive battery cable attaches to it. A knife switch can be closed for heavy current draw while starting the engine. Opening the knife switch lets all charging current flow through the ammeter for measurement. The voltmeter leads are attached across the battery posts. The ammeter shunt, or leads, are attached in series across the adapter, as at right.

To make a voltage test, set the voltage selector to the 16-volt position (or the closest position on your tester). Set the parking brake, start the engine, and run it up to about 1800 rpm. If you have no tachometer, guess. That speed is about three times as fast as normal idle speed.

The voltage, with all lights and accessories off, should read in the green bar of the meter's voltage scale. Ideally, it should match the specified voltage (14 to 15 volts at operating temperature for most cars).

Remember that battery condition affects the charging voltage reading somewhat. A low battery gives a low reading, a high battery gives a high reading. But the reading still should be within specifications if the battery is not discharged.

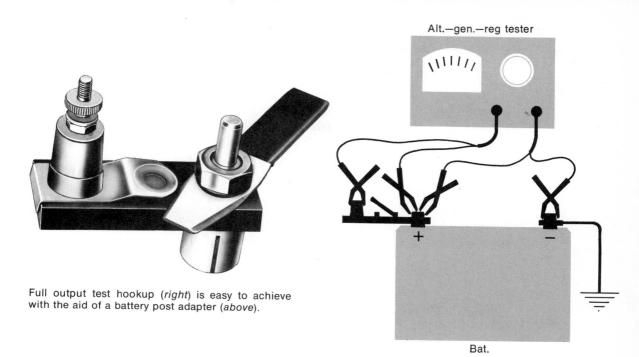

Alt.—gen.—reg tester

Bat.

Full output test hookup (*right*) is easy to achieve with the aid of a battery post adapter (*above*).

Then, switch to the 90-amps scale (or look at a separate ammeter) to see how much current your charging system is putting out. When you first start the engine, the reading should be higher than after the system has replaced some of the electricity used in starting.

If you have a load unit, hook its clips across the battery posts and switch it on. That puts a 50-ampere load on the battery, making the generator or alternator work at maximum capacity. Compare the maximum charging rate with the manufacturer's specification, but add 5 amps to your reading. This takes into account the ignition and field current that is being used before it reaches the battery. The specification depends on the capacity of the charging system installed on your car; normally, though, it is not more than about 40 amperes.

If charging voltage and amperage are normal, the charging system is probably good.

Too high a charging rate into a fully charged battery indicates too high a regulator setting, a poorly grounded regulator, an open circuit inside the voltage regulator, or a fused contact in the regulator.

Too low a charging rate, or an unsteady rate, indicates a loose drive belt, dirty regulator contacts, worn or sticking brushes, high resistance in the charging system, or problems inside the charging unit.

To tell whether charging trouble is in the regulator or in the charging unit, eliminate the regulator from the system, following the directions for full output tests given earlier in this chapter. The results should match the maximum specified for the charging unit. If they do, the charging unit is good and the trouble is elsewhere. If not, look for a very loose drive belt; locked shaft; worn brushes, commutator or slip rings; blown diodes; or an open circuit within the charging unit.

GENERATOR

If a direct-current generator is not charging, remove the cover strap, if there is one. If the copper commutator in the rear looks worn, burned, dirty, or oily, it could be the problem. If, when the engine

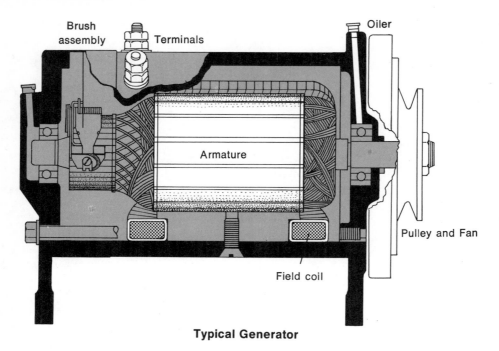

Brush assembly   Terminals   Oiler   Armature   Pulley and Fan   Field coil

Typical Generator

runs, there is much arcing around the commutator, the generator's problem may be internal. Bits of solder thrown off inside, or other signs of generator overheating, call for removal and bench-testing of the generator.

You can remove the generator, but most testing should be left to an auto electrical shop.

Removal. To take out the generator, first remove all leads from their terminals. Identify them with pieces of tape so you can replace them properly. The smallest lead is always attached to the field terminal of the generator. If there is a radio suppression condenser mounted on the generator, its lead is always attached to the output terminal, never to the field terminal.

Loosen the screw or nut that holds the generator tightly against its drive belt. Then, pry the generator away from the belt and remove the belt. (Some engines have idler pulleys that must be slackened

before the generator belt can be removed.) Next, take off the two nuts and bolts that hold the generator frame to the mounting bracket on the engine, and lift out the generator. If the power steering pump is driven from the rear of the generator, it must be removed first. Generator pulley removal is often a shop job.

If the generator obviously is damaged, replace it with a rebuilt one. Replace the regulator at the same time; it probably made the generator go bad.

Tests. If you have an ohmmeter or simple powered test light continuity tester, you can check your generator if it is off the car and disassembled.

The only tests possible are continuity tests of the brush holders and a grounding test of the armature. The rest require professional equipment.

Some *brush holders* should be grounded to the generator frame, while others should be insulated from it. You can tell them apart by looking closely at the mounting. A fiber mounting indicates an insulated brush. But if the brush fastens directly to the end plate or field frame, it is grounded.

Test with the ohmmeter or continuity tester leads, with one lead on the brush holder and the other on the frame. The ohmmeter should be set on high ohms for insulated brushes and low ohms for grounded brushes.

For insulated brushes the reading should be infinite ohms; the continuity tester should not light.

For a grounded brush, the reading should be zero ohms; the continuity tester should light.

The most common problem is an insulated brush that is grounded because of broken insulation or carbon tracking across the insulation. If cleaning does not cure the trouble, have the generator serviced professionally.

All *commutators* should be fully insulated from the rest of the armature. Touch the test leads between the commutator and a ground on the armature. A VOM should be set on high ohms position. The continuity tester should not light, and the ohm reading should be infinity if the armature is not short-circuited. Move the prod all around the commutator. The indication should be the same for all commutator bars.

Service. Check the *brushes* in a generator that does not charge. If they can be serviced, you may be able to save the generator. To get at the brushes, remove the generator's commutator end frame by unscrewing the long through-bolts; some have hex heads, others have slotted screw heads. When the bolts are out, tap the end frame gently to remove it from the center field frame. Remove the pulley end frame

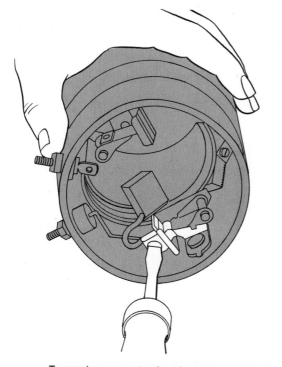 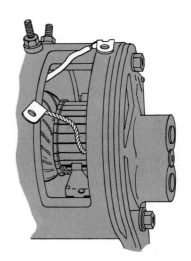

To service generator brushes, take out the brush leads. On some units, you must remove the end frame and unscrew the brushes (*left*). On units with a cover band, remove the band for access to the brushes (*right*).

and armature assembly in the same way, by tapping.

Remove the brushes. Some are mounted in the field frame, others are mounted in the end frame. Remove any corrosion on the inside of the brush holders that might restrict their free movement within the holders. Take out the tiny screws that let the brushes come all the way out.

If the generator has a cover band, its brushes can be worked on through the access openings, without generator disassembly. First, remove the brush leads. Then pull the brush tension arms up so that the brushes can be lifted out. If the brushes are not worn beyond half their original length, they can be cleaned and replaced. Otherwise, install a new set. Get the brush leads on properly, so they do not rub on the armature or commutator. Make sure that the new brushes can slide in and out in their holders. Brushes can be seated perfectly by slipping sandpaper, face out, over the commutator, and working it back and forth under the brush. Blow out residue after brush-seating.

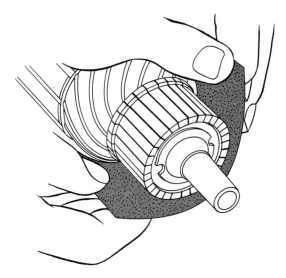

Clean the commutator with fine sandpaper if it is dirty or slightly corroded. If the commutator is pitted or scored, take it to a shop.

Look closely at the *commutator* for high bars, high mica, pitting, or excessive wear. If any of these are present, get them fixed by a professional or buy a rebuilt genera-

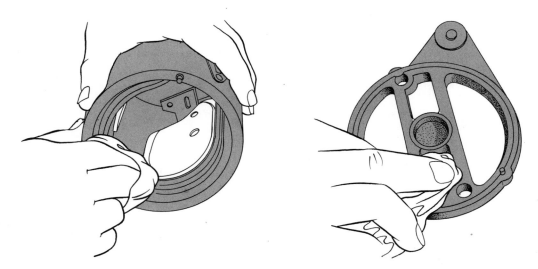

Thoroughly clean the generator with a solvent-soaked cloth. When you wipe the field frame (*left*), be careful not to wet or damage the field coils. If the commutator end frame bushing does not have a bearing (*right*), place two drops of light oil in the recess.

tor. If the commutator is good but dirty, clean it with a strip of fine sandpaper—not emery cloth. Remove sandpaper dust by blowing.

While the generator is apart, remove dirt inside the *field frame* with a clean, dry cloth. Do not use solvents on the field coils. And do not puncture the field coils while cleaning them. Clean the commutator end frame with a solvent-dipped cloth. Put two drops of engine oil on the rear bearing bushing. Clean the armature and drive assembly with a clean, dry cloth or compressed air, not with solvents.

When reassembling the brushes over the commutator, hold them apart with your fingers while sliding in the armature. Make sure they are seated on the commutator before replacing the through-bolts and installing the generator in the car. If the generator has oil cups, put eight to ten drops of light engine oil into each one.

Polarizing

Every new, rebuilt, or overhauled generator should be polarized. That gives it the same polarity as the battery, and helps it charge properly. How you polarize the generator depends on which type of circuit it has.

If the generator does not charge immediately, stop the engine and repeat the polarizing procedure. If it still does not charge, try grounding the field terminal. Still no charge means the generator may have more serious problems. If a check of the charging system wiring and ground do not turn up anything, take the generator or the car to a shop.

ALTERNATOR

Alternating-current generators, or alternators, have been used in most cars since 1965. They are more compact, more powerful, and more troublefree than the direct-current generators they replaced.

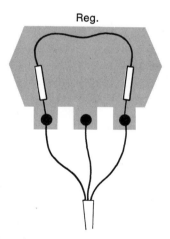

Polarize *A-circuit generators* by momentarily touching a jumper wire across the battery (BAT or B) and armature (ARM or A) terminals of the generator regulator before starting the engine. Sparking is normal.

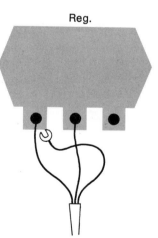

Polarize *B-circuit generators* by disconnecting the field (FLD or F) wire from the regulator terminal, and momentarily touching it to the battery terminal of the regulator before starting the engine. Again, sparking is normal. Do not touch the battery lead to the field terminal; that would damage the regulator.

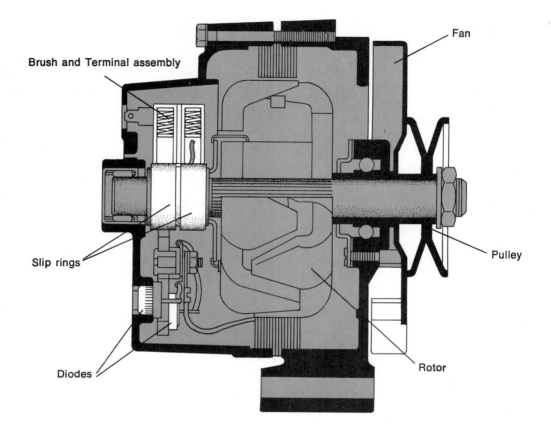

Brush and Terminal assembly

Fan

Slip rings

Pulley

Diodes

Rotor

Typical Alternator

Alternators are equipped with solid-state electronic devices called diodes, which transform alternating current to the direct current that is required by the battery and the rest of the car's electrical system. By a six-diode arrangement called a bridge circuit, alternating electrical impulses are converted to a steady current that flows in one direction.

Although the two types of charging systems are similar, the tests and service they need are different.

Six makes of alternators are found in U.S. cars: Chrysler; Delco; Ford; Autolite; Leece Neville; and Motorola. Construction depends on make. To find out which make your car has, look at the alter-nator's rear end frame. A single Ford model may have either a Ford, Autolite, or Leece Neville alternator. GM uses Delco. Chrysler products have Chrysler alternators. American Motors uses Motorola.

Removal. If the alternator must be removed, the technique is about the same as for taking out a generator. Be sure to first disconnect the ground cable from the battery terminal. This prevents an accidental short circuit from blowing the alternator diodes.

Tests. With an ohmmeter or VOM, you can test an alternator's entire *field circuit*, including the brush-to-slip-ring connections.

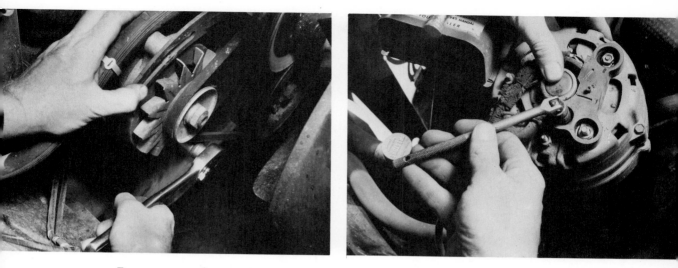

To remove an alternator from the car, disconnect the ground cable and unfasten the mounting bolts (*left*). On some units, you must also undo the recessed terminal nuts that secure an access cap (*right*).

An alternator with high resistance in its field circuit operates at reduced maximum output and may even show no output at all. To test, disconnect the field lead from the alternator or regulator field terminal, whichever is easiest, set the VOM selector to the Rx1 ohms position, and zero the needle by touching the test prods together.

Test with one prod on the field terminal of the alternator (or field wire end, if disconnected at the regulator) and the other prod on a ground on the alternator. The ohm reading should be between 5 and 100 ohms if alternator resistance is normal. Expect some variation in the reading when the alternator is rotated during the test.

If the ohmmeter reads zero, the alternator has a grounded field circuit. If the ohmmeter reads above 100 ohms, the alternator's rotor field circuit is open, or the brushes are making poor contact with the slip rings. In either case, remove and disassemble the alternator to test the field coil resistance against the manufacturer's specifications. Note that the initial reading, with the alternator on the car,

cannot be compared with the manufacturer's resistance specifications for field (rotor) coils because it includes brush, slip ring, and field coils.

With an ohmmeter or continuity tester, you can make many more tests if you disassemble the alternator.

Taking apart this unit is much like disassembling a generator. Follow the instructions given in the service manual. Some units should have their brushes removed before disassembly. Pulley pulling is usually a shop job.

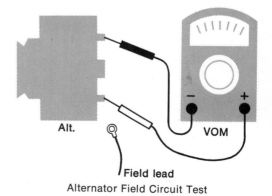

Alternator Field Circuit Test

Alternator Service

1. With the alternator out of the car and on a work-bench, unscrew the assembly bolts.

2. Before dismantling, mark the stator frame, stator and end frame for easy reassembly.

3. Inspect the brushes. If they are shorter than ¼ inch, install new ones.

4. Clean discolored slip rings with fine sandpaper. If the rings are burned, replace them.

5. With a VOM, check the slip rings for continuity. Resistance should match specifications.

6. Set on high ohms, the meter should read infinity.

If you take apart your alternator, first check the *stator*—the part that does not rotate. Disconnect the stator leads, and test between all pairs of leads. If the continuity tester does not light or the ohmmeter (set on low ohms) shows infinity, the stator winding is open. Trade in the alternator parts on a rebuilt one. Also test the stator winding for bad grounds by touching between the leads and the stator frame. The readings should be infinity on the ohmmeter; the continuity tester should not light. Otherwise, replace the alternator.

Check the *rotor* for opens and grounds. Touch the test prods of the ohmmeter (set on low ohms) or continuity tester, one to each slip ring. If the reading shows infinite ohms or the lamp does not light, the rotor windings are open. If the ohmmeter reading shows zero ohms or the lamp lights with full brilliance, the windings are shorted. In either case, get a rebuilt alternator. Test for grounds by placing one test prod on either slip ring and the other on the rotor shaft. The lamp should not

light and the ohmmeter (set on high ohms) should read infinity. If the alternator fails that test, replace it.

Check *alternator diodes* with either the ohmmeter or the continuity tester, provided their batteries are not more than 1.5-volt—a higher voltage can ruin the diodes.

The diodes are pressed into heat sinks in the rear end plate of the alternator. Disconnect them from the stator leads. When unsoldering and resoldering diode leads, clamp a pair of pliers on the lead between the soldering iron and the diode. That way, the pliers act as a heat sink; if much soldering heat gets through to the diode, it can be ruined.

To test a diode, touch one test prod to the diode body, the other to its lead. Note what happens. Then, reverse the test leads.

A good diode gives one low-ohm reading of about four to ten ohms and one higher reading; or, it will make the continuity tester light once but not light the other time.

If you get the same ohmmeter reading

both times, or if the continuity tester either lights both times or fails to light both times, the diode is defective.

Repeat the test with each diode. Some diodes cannot be replaced without special tools, so take the alternator end plate to a shop for that job.

Service. Because of its solid-state components, every alternator charging system needs special care in servicing, or it may suffer expensive damage.

Battery condition is vital to an alternator. A low battery makes the alternator work to its limit, and a defective battery can actually work the alternator to death if its diodes are weak.

Keep *battery polarity* straight. In a negative grounded system (as in most U.S. cars), the positive battery cable should be connected only to the positive battery terminal. Similarly, always connect the ground cable to the negative battery terminal. In using jumper cables to start a car with a problem battery, keep the polarity of the jumper cable hook-up correct or the charging systems in both cars may be damaged.

Do not short out or ground any terminals of the alternator or its regulator. Do not run the alternator with an open circuit at the alternator, regulator, or battery. The high voltages produced can wreck the alternator and shock you. Furthermore, never polarize an alternator. That would damage the diodes.

Belt tension is critical with an alternator. When tightening the alternator to tension the belt, pry only on the center of the unit's body, never on either end frame. Use a belt tension gauge (see the chapter on wiring).

Alternator *brushes* last much longer than generator brushes because they slide on smooth slip rings instead of a rough commutator. Also, only two amps of current flow through them, while generator

When tightening the alternator drive belt, pry against the unit's body, not its end frame.

brushes carry the full flow. The brushes in Chrysler alternators and in some high-output Delco and Ford units can be removed without taking the alternator off the car. An alternator's two brushes are located in the rear, and are reached through the alternator's rear end frame. On the Chrysler alternator, remove the field lead from its terminal and take out the Phillips screws. The brushes then slip out.

Brushes worn to less than ¼ inch or so should be replaced. See that the new ones are not stuck in their holders. No sanding or fitting of new alternator brushes is necessary, as with a generator. Do not clean the brushes in solvent; keep them dry. Grease on the brushes or slip rings can affect alternator performance, too.

Clean the *slip rings* in solvent and brighten them with 3/0 sandpaper. If the slip rings are badly worn or pitted, the alternator should be taken in for replacement of the slip-ring assembly.

ment of the slip-ring assembly.

When reassembling a Ford alternator, push a short length of 1/8-inch rod through a hole in the housing. This holds the brushes off the slip rings. After assembly, pull out the pin.

CHARGING UNIT MAINTENANCE

Generators and alternators without oiler holes are packed for about 50,000 miles of attention-free service. After 50,000 miles, disassemble the unit and clean the bearings with solvent. Dry thoroughly. Repack the bearings a quarter-full with ball-bearing lubricant. Then, fill the rear reservoir, if there is one, half-full of the same lubricant.

If a lubricated-for-life charging unit has a sleeve bearing at the rear end, fill the oil reservoir with 20-weight motor oil, removing the felt seal if necessary. Replace the seal when you have finished oiling.

Check alternator or generator bearings without disassembly by removing the drive belt from the pulley and trying to wiggle the pulley from side to side in the direction of belt tension. Turn the pulley slowly and feel for roughness in the bearings. If you feel side play or roughness, remove the unit and replace its bearings.

If trouble does develop, either the bearing can be replaced or the unit can be exchanged for a rebuilt one. Generally, with ball bearings it is best to replace just the bearing. With bushings, replace the whole unit.

Generators with bushings rather than ball bearings need periodic oiling of front and rear bushings. At every chassis lubrication, put about 50 drops of 20-weight engine oil into each bearing oiler.

If the generator has oiler holes, it needs much less oil; give them eight to ten drops at every chassis lube. Over-oiling can wash out the grease that is packed around many such bearings.

Inspect generator brushes occasionally through the vent openings in the rear end. Watch for wear and freeness of movement in the brush holders. When you replace brushes, inspect the commutator closely.

REGULATOR

Once the generator or the alternator has been ruled out as the cause of a charging problem, look to the regulator. Over- or under-charging makes it suspect, anyway, as do fluctuating charging voltages, which are indicated by headlights that brighten and dim noticeably.

Tests. With a VOM or ohmmeter, you can make several easy checks on a regulator. For each test, the regulator should be out of the car.

To test for a *shorted cutout* on a generator regulator, set the ohm selector to its low-ohm position. Touch the test prods across the battery and armature terminals. If the reading shows zero ohms, buy a new regulator.

To test for *burned out resistors* at the bottom of a regulator, turn the regulator on its cover, and touch the ohmmeter or prods across the ends of each resistor in turn. All readings should be zero. A reading of infinity indicates a burned-out resistor. The cure is replacement.

With a VOM, test each resistor at the bottom of the regulator for continuity.

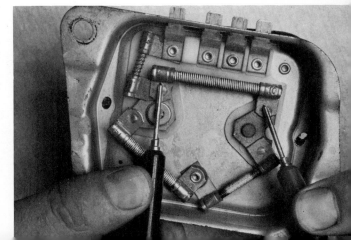

Regulator Service

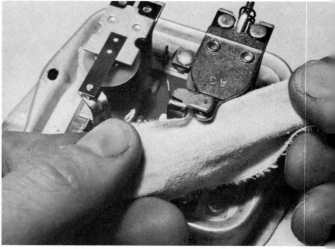

1. Many regulators have a connector block instead of individual leads. Release the unit's locking tabs and pull the block out.

2. Regulators with riveted covers can still be serviced. Drill out the rivets to remove the cover. Reassemble with sheet metal screws.

3. Clean contacts with sandpaper, a fingernail file or, better yet, a regulator-point file.

4. After cleaning the contacts, polish them with a solvent-soaked cloth.

The *diodes* in a transistorized regulator, like those on an alternator, can also be checked with an ohmmeter. Remove the unit's cover and unsolder the diode leads. Then, test across each diode and its lead in both directions with the test prods. One way should produce a high resistance reading, the other way a low one. Test each diode separately. Get a new regulator if any diode tests out faulty.

Service. Professional mechanics seldom service regulators; they replace them. A new regulator costs from $8 to $12.

Without special equipment, you have perhaps a fifty-fifty chance of restoring a regulator to life by cleaning it.

First, unscrew the cover.

Some regulators have riveted covers. These are not designed to be serviced; however, you can still try to fix them. Drill out the rivets. When you replace the cover later, install sheet metal screws in place of the rivets.

Most regulators have sheet metal screws to begin with, and are designed to be cleaned and adjusted rather than replaced.

After you get the regulator cover off, you will see one, two, or three units inside. One- and two-unit regulators have slip-connection terminals; three-unit regulators have screw terminals. Most generator systems have three-unit regulators, while most alternator systems have one- or two-unit regulators.

One of the units is a voltage limiter that has two or more electrical contacts at the end of a movable arm. Dirt, corrosion, or burning of these electrical contacts can cause the entire regulator to malfunction.

After removing the wires from the regulator (tag them for identification later), burnish the contact points. The most effective tool for that is a regulator point file; such files are finely cut. Alternatively,

use a fingernail file. Some manufacturers specify crocus cloth or number-400 silicon carbide paper instead of a file. Fold the sanding strip double for cleaning both upper and lower contacts at the same time. Delco regulator specifications call for cleaning with a curved "riffler" file worked into pitted points. We prefer the fine file to sandpaper. Repeat the cleaning if charging does not improve.

Polish the cleaned contacts with a lint-free cloth dipped in alcohol, trichloroethylene, or carbon tetrachloride. Work carefully so that the point settings are not disturbed.

Pitted or badly burned points must be dressed with an ignition point file. If much filing is necessary, the gap of the points will be changed. While the gap can be readjusted, it is better to replace the unit.

Cleaning is the only service you can perform on the regulator.

Some regulators have a tiny fuse assembly attached to the battery terminal. Test the fuse for continuity. and replace it during reassembly.

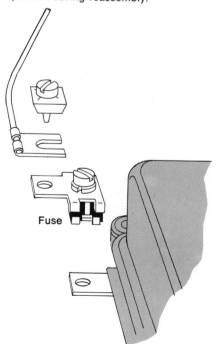

Fuse

Replace the regulator in the car and watch for further signs of overcharging or undercharging. If you notice problems, replace the regulator. That costs less than having professional adjustments made.

The final step in regulator service or replacement should be reconnecting the ground cable to the battery. If the charging system uses a generator, the generator should be polarized as described earlier in this chapter. Do not polarize an alternator system.

Ground the base of the regulator to the frame of the car. If a grounding wire is used, make sure the connections at both ends are clean and tight. If grounding is through the mount, make sure the metal beneath the mounting screws is bright and clean. See that all wires and connections in the charging circuit, including those between the engine and car frame or body, are clean and tight. Bad connections shorten regulator life. Perform the voltage-drop tests described earlier.

Chrysler regulators for alternator systems use two fusible wires that come up through the regulator base and wrap around their terminals inside the regulator. If either of those is burned through because of shorts, overloads, or overcharging, the system will not charge. Replace the regulator.

Generator Regulator Adjustments

These can be made on the car, with the unit at operating temperature.

Hookups are the same as for the output test described earlier. Readings must be taken with the regulator cover on. Of course, the cover must then be removed to make an adjustment.

U.S. cars use five makes of regulators: Delco-Remy, Ford, Autolite, Bosch, and Chrysler. A variety of adjustment methods is used. Although a special bending tool may be called for, you can usually do the job with long nose pliers.

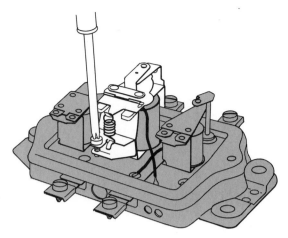

On Delco regulators, turn the voltage limiter screw clockwise to increase charging voltage.

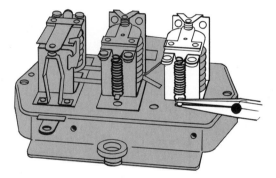

On an Autolite unit, bend the spring hanger down to increase voltage, up to decrease it.

On Ford and Bosch regulators, bend the voltage limiter's tang upwards to increase voltage.

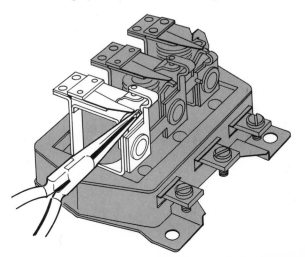

The regulator's contact points should be cleaned first. The battery must be charged to at least 1.230 specific gravity.

Voltage limiter. First, find the voltage limiter unit. It is usually on one end of the regulator, and it is often the largest and most complex-looking of the units. To be sure, hook a volt-ammeter to the battery. Press in the movable arms of each unit inside the regulator while the engine is running at a fast idle. The one you are pressing when the voltage reading moves up is the limiter. That test also shows about how far the limiter is out of adjustment. The harder you have to press for a good voltage reading, the further the adjustment is out.

To *increase* charging voltage, turn a Delco voltage-limiter adjustment screw clockwise; bend an Autolite spring hanger down; and bend a Ford or Bosch tang up. To *decrease* charging voltage, do the opposite. On a Delco limiter, finish any adjustment by turning the screw slightly clockwise.

Make the adjustment to bring the charging voltage at specified speed to the specified amount. Average regulator setting—14.4 volts at a normal 125° operating temperature—is thought to be best for battery use and life. That setting brings the battery to only about half charge. But with temperature compensation, it will keep the battery at full charge once it is there.

If a voltage range is given, adjust to your type of driving within the range. For cold weather and short trips, adjust toward the higher tolerance. For warm weather and long trips, adjust toward the lower tolerance.

After each adjustment, the regulator must be cycled. To do it, switch off the engine and restart it. Then, check your adjustment, doing it again if necessary. If adjusting will not bring the charging voltage within specifications, the regulator

air gaps and point gaps must be corrected. Unless you want to try the job, following directions in the car's service manual, get a new regulator.

Current regulator. If the maximum charging rate is not up to specifications in a generator system, find the current regulator. It will be indicated in the service manual coverage of regulator service. Adjust it in the same way as the voltage limiter, replace the cover, cycle, and check.

Cutout relay. The cutout relay closes when the charging voltage climbs about half a volt over the battery voltage. To test it, switch the voltage leads of your tester over to the generator, putting the red lead to the output terminal and the black one to ground.

Increase engine speed slowly from idle while watching the ammeter needle. The needle will swing up from zero when the cutout points close. Charging current is now flowing in the circuit. The voltage reading the instant before the points close is the cut-in voltage. Compare it with the car specifications.

Now, slowly drop engine speed toward idle while watching the ammeter needle. It will deflect below zero; then, it should pop back up to zero. The lowest reading it reaches is the reverse current needed to open the cutout contacts. That varies from about two to nine amps. Compare the reverse current with specifications.

To *increase* closing voltage, turn a Delco-Remy cutout adjusting screw clockwise, bend an Autolite spring tab downward, and bend a Ford or Bosch tang upward. To *decrease* closing voltage, do the opposite.

If the cutout's opening amperage is incorrect, the air gap between the movable cutout arm and the coil must be adjusted. Either look up the manufacturer-recommended method or replace the regulator.

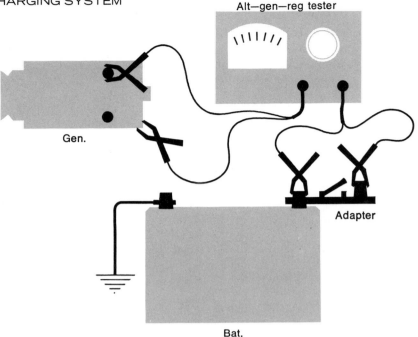

Cutout Relay Test

Alternator Regulator Adjustments

Adjusting the double-contact regulators used with alternator charging systems is seldom necessary unless, for some reason, you wish to tailor the setting. Because of the complex hookups necessary, that should be handled by a professional mechanic. The same is true of the newer solid-state regulators that have no relays or contact points. Voltage is adjusted by means of an external screw, but do not try to do the job yourself.

Tailored Voltage Setting

The desired voltage limiter setting is one that keeps the battery at full charge (1.230 to 1.310 specific gravity) without causing excessive water consumption (more than an ounce of water in each cell every 1000 miles).

Professional mechanics rarely have the time to routinely tailor voltage limiter adjustments to the driving requirements of car owners. Yet, if climate or amount of driving is unusual, tailoring may be required for proper battery charging.

If you have a sensitive voltmeter, tailoring the voltage limiter of a generator regulator is easy.

The regulator must be warmed to operating temperature by running the engine at medium speed for 15 minutes with the hood closed. The battery must be at 1.230 specific gravity or higher; check it with a hydrometer.

Connect the voltmeter's red lead to the battery positive terminal and its black lead to the negative battery terminal. No ammeter connection is required.

The normal range of regulated voltage is at a specified regulator operating temperature. In most systems, the regulator will change voltage, increasing it as its temperature drops and lowering it as temperature rises. This matches the charging requirements of the car battery.

Tailoring Charging Voltage

Battery condition	Setting of voltage limiter
Excessive water consumption, regulated voltage above specified range	Lower the setting to within the upper portion of the normal voltage range and check for an improvement over a reasonable period of driving, perhaps several months
Excessive water consumption, regulated voltage within normal range	Lower the setting 0.2 or 0.3 volt and check for an improvement over several months. An old battery with its plates becoming thin charges and discharges more than a newer one and uses more water. Take that into account when deciding how much water consumption is excessive
Battery consistently undercharged, regulated voltage below normal range	Increase regulator setting to within the lower portion of the normal specified range. Check for an improvement
Battery consistently undercharged, regulated voltage within normal range	Increase voltage limiter setting 0.2 to 0.3 volt and check for improvement. Repeat until the battery stays charged with minimum use of water. Avoid regulated voltage settings above 14.8 volts at 125 degrees. That may damage lights and other voltage-sensitive equipment

With the engine running at about 1800 rpm, refer to the accompanying temperature/voltage range chart. Make the adjustments described in the earlier section on the voltage limiter.

You seldom need to use a setting outside the manufacturer's normal specified range to correct battery problems. A battery that does not respond to voltage adjustments within the normal range usually has been operated consistently at slow speeds or in heavy traffic, or was improperly activated.

When a car is driven only slowly or in heavy traffic, battery charging time may be so short that electrical drains are not offset or replaced. Under such conditions,

Tailored Voltage Ranges

Ambient temperature	Voltage range
65	13.9 to 15.0
85	13.8 to 14.8
105	13.7 to 14.6
125	13.5 to 14.4
145	13.4 to 14.2
165	13.2 to 14.0
185	13.1 to 13.9
205	13.0 to 13.8

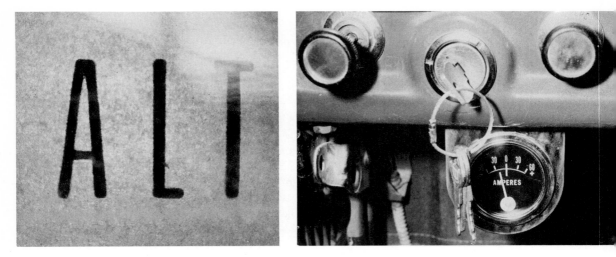

Indicator lights (*left*) have been standard on most American cars since the mid-1950s. For more precise charging system data, though, you can easily install an ammeter (*right*).

a weekly recharge at home may be needed. Installation of an extra-output charging system also will do the job. Any battery that may have been improperly activated should be removed for a complete check (see the chapter on the starting system).

A system that is set for the typical driving you do around home may overcharge on a vacation trip. That is normal. Rather than readjusting the voltage setting for the trip, just check the battery electrolyte often enough to keep the cells from running dry.

INDICATOR LIGHT

Since 1955, most cars have been built with charge indicator lights instead of ammeters. These are connected to the ignition switch in such a way that battery voltage is supplied to the lamp when the switch is turned on. The other end of the light socket is wired to the charging unit output circuit. That grounds the light through the generator when the charging unit is not performing.

As current flows, the bulb lights. But as soon as the generator starts charging, the voltage difference between it and the battery is not enough to light the lamp; the lamp goes out.

Thus wired, the lamp does not come on when more electricity is being used from the battery than is being replaced by the charging system. For that reason, your battery could go dead while you drive, without any warning from the light.

Sometimes when the engine idles, the charge is not enough to keep the light from glowing. With most systems, that is no cause for concern, as long as the light goes out again when the engine is speeded.

If the charge indicator light does not come on when the ignition switch is turned on, the bulb is probably burned out. The wiring also could be defective. In some systems, a defective regulator or loose regulator connections could also be the cause.

AMMETER

With an ammeter to guide you, you can be sure the charging system is working properly.

The ammeter should show a high rate of charge—say 10 to 20 amperes—for several minutes after starting. The rate could go even higher after a cold, hard start. After several minutes of driving, the charging rate should drop back to a few amps, and stay there until you switch off the engine.

Even if you switch on the headlights, radio, heater, air conditioner, tape deck, or other electrical accessory, the ammeter should read above zero all the while the engine runs at street speeds or faster.

When charging current does not equal or exceed the current being used by ignition and accessories, the meter shows a discharge condition, even though the indicator light may not come on.

If you have added heavy-power-drawing accessories since the car was new, its charging system may not have the capacity to handle the extra current draw, and the ammeter may indicate discharging while driving. That is a warning to go easy on the use of accessories, especially at night. If you do not, you will face a dead battery.

Installing an ammeter. You can easily add an ammeter to a car with a charge indicator light. The ammeter comes in kit form. If the number-10 stranded ammeter lead wire is not furnished, you must buy it. You need about 20 feet.

The ammeter circuit is wired between the battery and all electrical equipment except the starter. (Starter load would be too much for the circuit.) Thus, all accessory drain and charging current will flow through the ammeter and register on its scale.

Before beginning the installation, disconnect one battery cable from the battery post to prevent an accidental short circuit.

Install the ammeter bracket and the ammeter.

Install the wiring, locating the connections according to your car's wiring system, as shown in the instructions. Tape all exposed splices carefully to prevent short-circuiting. Solder the connections or use crimped connectors.

Feed the ammeter lead wires through existing openings in the firewall between engine and passenger compartments; or, drill a 3/8-inch hole. If the hole edges are not protected, wrap the wires with tape or insulate them with rubber grommets to prevent fraying. Plug the opening with rope caulk sealant.

Reinstall the removed battery cable. Turn on the headlights, and see whether the ammeter needle moves to "charge" or "discharge." If it shows a charge with the headlights on, switch the two lead wires on the back of the ammeter. It should now properly show a discharge.

If the ammeter is the illuminated type, splice its socket lead wire into any dash light lead behind the instrument panel. Then, your ammeter will operate with the car's light switch and instrument light dimmer.

Readings. In a healthy charging system, the ammeter needle should not swing higher and higher with engine speed. Instead, it should stay slightly above zero regardless of engine speed.

If the needle follows engine speed up and down, the charging system needs attention.

If the ammeter needle jerks back and forth between two spots on the ammeter dial as you drive, charging system trouble is developing.

If the needle stays high and does not drop back to a few amperes of charge after a few minutes, the system is overcharging. That can ruin the battery, especially on a long trip.

If the ammeter needle stays on zero or lower (and the red warning light is on), the battery is not getting any charge. You do not have much time before the battery goes dead.

CHARGING SYSTEM TROUBLESHOOTING

TROUBLE	CAUSE	CURE
No charge	Belt slipping or broken	Tighten or replace
	Loose pulley	Tighten or have replaced
	Locked shaft	Install rebuilt charging unit
	Open-circuited external wiring	Find and repair
	Regulator not working	Repair or replace
	Open circuit or short circuit in charging unit	Install a rebuilt unit
	Brush problems	Clean, fit, or replace brushes
	Alternator diodes blown	Test and replace faulty diodes
	Generator commutator worn or damaged; solder thrown	Install rebuilt generator
Low or unsteady charging rate	Regulator faulty	Clean contacts and adjust or replace regulator
	Loose belt	Tighten belt
	High resistance in insulated charging circuit	Find bad connection or wire and fix
	High resistance in ground circuit	Find bad connection or wire and fix
	Open or shorted alternator stator windings	Install rebuilt alternator
	Shorted alternator diode	Find shorted diode and replace
High charging rate	Regulator defective	Clean regulator contacts and adjust, or replace
	Regulator not well grounded (with generator only)	Clean ground or install grounding wire
	Open diode	Find defective diode and replace

TROUBLE	CAUSE	CURE
Noisy operation	Broken pulley	Have new pulley installed
	Charging unit mounts loose	Tighten
	Worn, loose, misaligned, or glazed drive belt	Tighten, align, or replace belt
	Worn or unlubricated bearings or bushings	Overhaul bearings or bushings. Lubricate if necessary
	Too much end play in generator	Install rebuilt unit
	Pulley fan rubs	Straighten or have new pulley installed
	Generator brush noise	Check commutator and brushes. Have commutator dressed or replace brushes
	Bent armature or rotor shaft	Install rebuilt unit
	Shorted diode	Find shorted diode and replace
Regulator points oxidized	Poor regulator ground	Clean ground connections
	Wrong air gap settings	Check against specifications and replace regulator if defective
	Voltage limiter setting too high	Adjust or replace regulator
	Alternator field shorted	Install rebuilt alternator
Regulator points burned	Voltage or current settings too high	Adjust or replace regulator
	High resistance in insulated circuit	Find bad connections or wire and fix
Regulator points welded together	Faulty regulator ground	Clean ground or install grounding wire

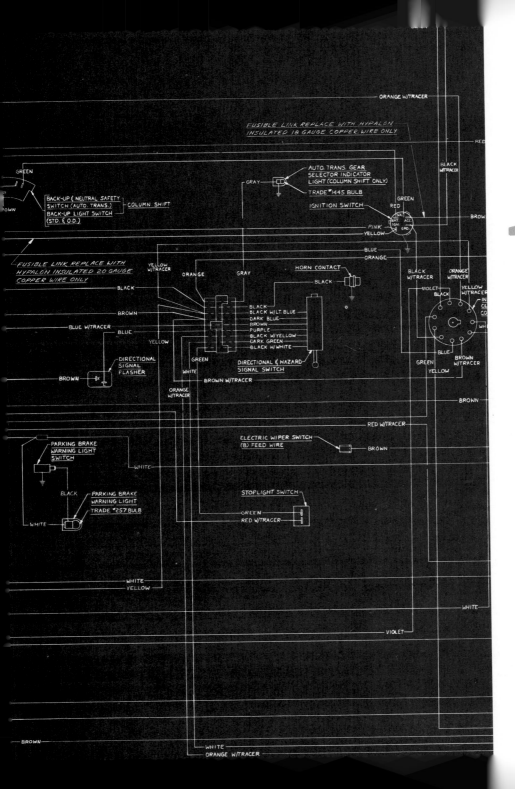

FUSIBLE LINK REPLACE WITH HYPALON
INSULATED 18 GAUGE COPPER WIRE ONLY

ORANGE W/TRACER

RED

BLACK
W/TRACER

GRAY

AUTO. TRANS. GEAR
SELECTOR INDICATOR
LIGHT (COLUMN SHIFT ONLY)

TRADE #1445 BULB

GREEN

IGNITION SWITCH

RED

BROW

GREEN

BACK-UP & NEUTRAL SAFETY
SWITCH (AUTO. TRANS.)
BACK-UP LIGHT SWITCH
(STD. & O.D.)

COLUMN SHIFT

PINK
YELLOW

BLUE
ORANGE

FUSIBLE LINK REPLACE WITH
HYPALON INSULATED 20 GAUGE
COPPER WIRE ONLY

YELLOW
W/TRACER

ORANGE

GRAY

HORN CONTACT

BLACK

BLACK
W/TRACER

ORANGE
W/TRACER

VIOLET

BLACK

YELLOW
W/TRACER

BLACK

BROWN

BLACK
BLACK W/LT. BLUE
DARK BLUE
BROWN
PURPLE
BLACK W/YELLOW
DARK GREEN
BLACK W/WHITE

WHI

BLUE W/TRACER

BLUE

YELLOW

GREEN

BLUE

DIRECTIONAL
SIGNAL
FLASHER

WHITE

DIRECTIONAL & HAZARD
SIGNAL SWITCH

GREEN

BROWN
W/TRACER

BROWN

ORANGE
W/TRACER

BROWN W/TRACER

YELLOW

BROWN

RED W/TRACER

PARKING BRAKE
WARNING LIGHT
SWITCH

ELECTRIC WIPER SWITCH
(B) FEED WIRE

BROWN

WHITE

BLACK

PARKING BRAKE
WARNING LIGHT
TRADE #257 BULB

STOPLIGHT SWITCH

WHITE

GREEN
RED W/TRACER

WHITE
YELLOW

WHITE

VIOLET

BROWN

WHITE
ORANGE W/TRACER

Troubleshooting Car Wiring

If you enjoy solving puzzles, you probably will enjoy curing your car's electrical problems.

A car's electrical wiring system starts at the battery and reaches to all parts of the car. The ignition system, the starting system, and the charging system are parts of it; their repair is covered in previous chapters. Treated in this chapter are the basic wiring harness, test procedures, and horns and buzzers.

With minor variations, all cars are wired the same. Heavy battery cables serve the starting circuit; the charging system wiring and the car's electrical wiring system are attached to these cables. The wires are wrapped together into a harness for neatness and protection. From the harness, wires branch off toward the ignition switch, charging system regulator, and other electrical components. You rarely need to cut into the wiring harness to cure an electrical problem.

Wires are color-coded to help you trace them throughout the car. Sometimes, having the car's wiring diagram is helpful when you work on an electrical problem. Though the diagram usually does not show the actual wire routings, it does indicate wire color-coding.

Lights and accessories branch off this routing. Their supply wires fasten to them through terminals and sockets. Any troubles traced to these components are usually solved by replacing bulbs or repairing or replacing motors.

The ground circuit is the final part of a car's electrical wiring. Unlike house wiring, which comprises a black "hot" wire to feed power and a white neutral wire to complete the circuit, car wiring completes most circuits through the car body, frame, ground cable, and back to the battery. That is called the ground circuit. Nearly every light, relay, motor, and solenoid is grounded to the car's body or frame to complete its circuit.

Poor grounding is a common source of auto electrical troubles. If the ground circuit is incomplete somewhere along the line, the circuit will fail just as though its insulated feed wire had been cut. Ground circuits fail through loosening and corrosion of fastenings. Continuity of the ground circuit must be considered whenever looking for an electrical malfunction. Fortunately, it is an easy check.

TOOLS

Several tools are useful for tackling electrical malfunctions. You can make most of them.

Jumper leads. Two jumper wires are useful for testing. You should have a short one and a long one, each consisting of No. 16 (AWG) stranded insulated wire with an alligator clip at each end. The long lead should be long enough to reach from the front to the back of the car, with some

slack for maneuvering. The short lead should be about three feet long.

A jumper is nothing more than a substitute circuit that tells you whether the circuit being tested is working. Jumpers are used to bridge across doubtful switches, wires, and connections in the insulated circuit, and across parts of the ground circuit. A jumper even can be used to bring electricity directly from the battery's positive terminal to the light or accessory, thereby eliminating everything in between. That tells you immediately whether the trouble is in the wiring or in the accessory itself.

Test light. This is simply a 12-volt automotive bulb—a dome light bulb works fine—with a pair of lead wires soldered

Equipment for testing automotive wiring includes (*top row, left to right*): long and short jumper leads, test light; (*bottom row*) continuity tester and volt-ohm milliammeter (VOM).

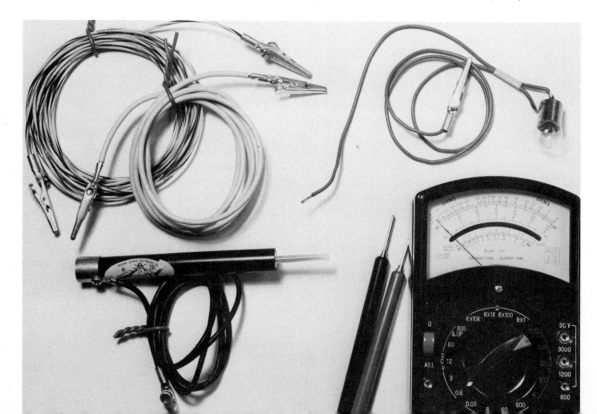

to it. You can buy one, but it is easy to make. It is most useful if you mount alligator clips on the ends of the short lead wires. With one of the leads clipped to an ice pick, you can poke through insulation, corrosion, and the like to get into the circuit.

A test light can find live circuits quickly. If you touch one wire to a terminal or other opening in an insulated circuit, and the other wire to a ground, the bulb will light if the circuit is live. It does not matter which wire is touched to which, as long as the contact is good.

Continuity tester. Also called a powered test light, this tool does not depend on a live circuit to make its reading. Its purpose is to check dead circuits. It has a self-contained battery that lights a lamp whenever the tool's two leads are touched together or into a continuous, though dead, circuit. As its name implies, it checks the continuity (or completeness) of a circuit.

You can easily make your own continuity tester with a flashlight bulb, a pair of flashlight batteries, a mounting board, tape, and wires.

Caution: Never use a continuity tester on a live circuit. 120-volt continuity testers that plug into a receptacle can be dangerous. Do not use them, especially on a car. The two leads in these potential killers come from an ordinary plug in a wall outlet. One of those leads goes directly to a test prod; the other lead is wired to a light bulb, and then to the other test prod. When the prods are touched, the lamp lights. But if the lead without the lamp happens to be plugged into the hot hole of the receptacle, its electrical potential to ground is close to 120 volts. If you touch that test lead to anything that is grounded, to yourself while you are grounded, or to the car while you are touching metal, you could get a serious

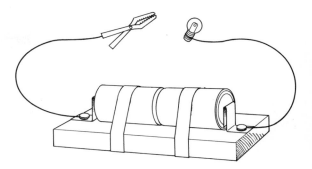

To make your own continuity tester, tape two flashlight batteries to a block of wood. Nail bent-metal clips to each end, then solder wire leads to the clips. Place an alligator clip on one wire and solder a two-cell flashlight bulb to the other.

Standard Electrical Symbols

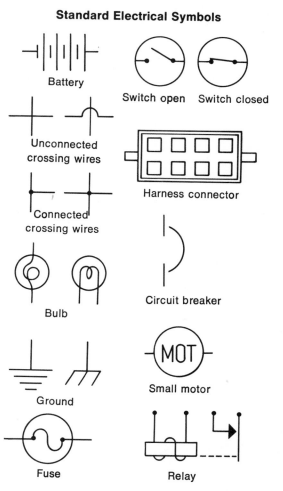

Battery

Switch open   Switch closed

Unconnected crossing wires

Harness connector

Connected crossing wires

Circuit breaker

Bulb

Small motor

Ground

Fuse

Relay

Wire Tapping

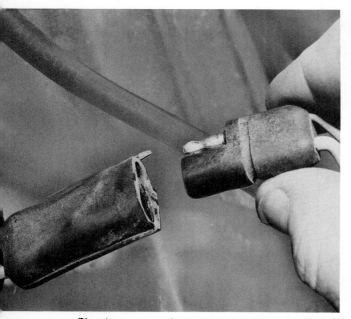

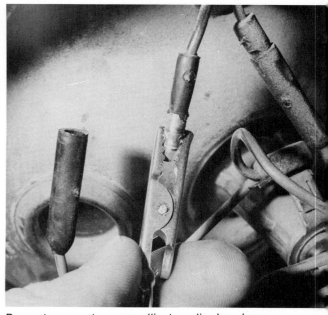

Plug-type connectors are common on cars; pull them apart for access to the circuit.

Bayonet connectors—an alligator clip has been attached to one here—also pull apart.

If the circuit you are testing does not have a handy connector, push a hat pin through the insulation and touch the pin with your tester.

Another way to tap a line is to slice through the insulation with a pocket knife. If you use this method, tape the incision when you are finished.

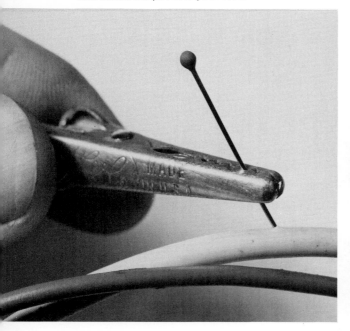

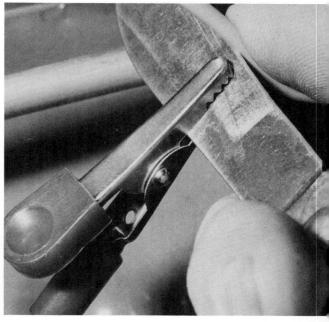

shock. Circuit-testing instructions continue to include that dangerous device. If you have one, get rid of it and buy or make a low-voltage, battery-powered continuity tester.

VOM. Nothing beats a volt-ohm-milliammeter (VOM) for finding short circuits, open circuits, live circuits, and dead circuits. With it, you can check bulbs and fuses in seconds. Voltage drop across parts of a loaded circuit reads out directly. Furthermore, electrical circuits can be tested for resistance when they are not loaded. A VOM also is useful for testing car clocks, gauges, and power accessories.

In automotive electrical testing, there are many possibilities for hookups using the volt and ohm functions of a VOM.

SWITCHES AND RELAYS

The ignition switch is complex because of the many circuits it controls. It has a number of terminals on the back, often hidden inside a terminal block plugged into the rear of the switch. One terminal feeds electricity from the battery's positive post to the ignition switch. Another receives power whenever the ignition switch is turned to the "on" and "start" positions. A third terminal is powered only when the switch is turned to "start." The fourth, an accessory terminal, is powered only when the switch is "on" or in the "accessory" position.

The headlight switch is complex, too. It has a main power terminal that is supplied from the battery. In its half-on position, one terminal comes alive to serve parking lights, taillights, and instrument lights. In its full-on position, the headlights are activated as well. Turning the switch knob left or right brightens and dims the instrument lights in many cars. Sometimes the car's dome light is turned on by turning the switch to the extreme left.

Ignition and headlight switches are fairly trouble-free. If you trace any problem to either of them, it must be replaced. That job is best left to a shop.

Some high-current functions, such as horns, are switched on and off by relays. A relay is simply a magnetic switch. It allows a small current in the relay's secondary circuit to control a heavy current in its primary circuit.

CIRCUIT-PROTECTION DEVICES

Every car, like every house, contains strategically located devices that protect the wiring in case of an overload. A house uses fuses or circuit breakers. A car uses four types of over-current devices: fuse blocks; fusible links; circuit breakers; and in-line fuses.

Fuse block. This is simply a black plastic block with slip-in slots for fuses. Each slot usually is labeled with the purpose, and current-carrying capacity, of that fuse.

Typical fuse block, with proper fuse size stamped next to each opening. Fuses pop out when you pry gently with a screw-driver.

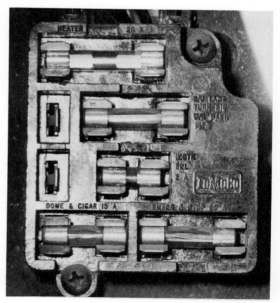

To remove a fuse, insert a small screwdriver behind it and pry it out. To install a fuse, position it over the slot and press it into the gripper terminals.

In nearly all modern cars, the fuse block is located below and behind the instrument panel, just above the brake pedal, or in the engine compartment. Many fuse blocks contain slots for carrying spare fuses.

Automotive *fuses* look different than the household variety. Most are tiny glass tubes that contain slim metal ribbons between metal end caps. If the fuse is good, the metal ribbon is intact all the way across. If the fuse is blown, the metal ribbon may be separated or melted away altogether. Often, the surrounding glass tube also darkens when a fuse blows. Sometimes, however, a fuse can be blown without showing it on the outside. An electrical fuse check described later will tell you the fuse's real condition. Keep spare fuses with you in case you run into a problem on the road. Replace the suspect fuse with a spare and see whether the circuit functions.

Replace a blown fuse only with one of the proper current-carrying capacity. Capacity is stamped on one end of the fuse, along with its type.

Type SFE fuses vary in length from 5/8 to 1 7/16 inches, according to their current-carrying capacity. The longer the fuse, the heavier the current it can carry.

Other fuse types are the same length regardless of their capacity. Type AGA fuses are 5/8-inch long; AGW are 7/8 inch; AGX are 1 inch; and AGC are 1 1/4 inches. (Foreign fuses use completely different designations.)

Do not assume that the fuse you are replacing was of the correct capacity. A wrong-capacity fuse may have been used previously. If you replace with that size again, the protection will be too great or

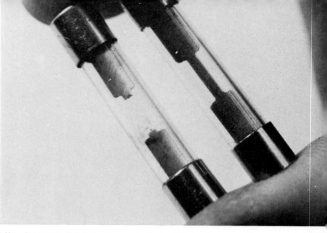

Like household fuses, an automobile's fuse melts (*left*) if a current surge is too great.

SFE fuses come in a variety of sizes for differing current-carrying capacities.

Regardless of fuse type, the capacity is stamped on the metal end cap.

too little; either is bad. Check the correct capacity in your owner's manual.

Sometimes, a fuse succumbs because of vibration and not because of an overload. If you are absolutely sure that this is the case, you can wrap the old fuse in foil from a gum wrapper and replace it in the block. The foil will carry current and get you to a service station where you can buy a new fuse of the right size. But be warned: If the problem is an overloaded circuit, the tinfoil trick could burn out your wiring and even start a fire.

About half the time, a fuse blows because of a normal temporary overload. In such a case, simply replacing the fuse with a new one effects a lasting cure. If the new fuse also blows out, check for the source of the excessive current draw.

Fusible links. Like fuses, these are weak electrical links in circuits. A fusible link is a length of wire several sizes smaller than the wires protected by it. The link melts when too much electricity passes through it. Fusible links are a modern car's main line of circuit protection. They ap-

Though it looks like a normal wire, this cable is a fusible link that melts internally if there is an electrical overload.

peared in cars as early as 1965. Located at the battery, starter solenoid, or main terminal block, they protect all circuits except the heavy-duty starting circuit, which is unprotected.

A fusible link, often colored red, looks much like an ordinary wire. It is never very long. Some cars use more than one for each circuit.

When every circuit in the car goes dead and the trouble cannot be traced to a dead battery, suspect a melted fusible link. To replace a burned-out fusible link, cut it off, bare the ends of the old wire and the new fusible link, and splice and solder them together. Insulate with a double layer of plastic electrical tape. Finally, install the terminal of the new link in place of the old terminal. On some cars, fusible links are part of the positive battery cable. The cable must be replaced to renew them.

Circuit breaker. These serve the same purpose as special appliance circuit breakers or fuses in a house. They are used mainly for electric motor circuit protection because of their ability to handle momentary overloads without breaking the circuit — something a fuse cannot do. Windshield wipers and most motorized power accessories feed through circuit breakers. Headlights and other exterior and interior lights often are on breaker-protected circuits, too. Circuit breakers used in cars, unlike those found in homes, reset automatically when they are tripped.

The automatic-resetting feature makes circuit breakers especially suited for headlight circuit protection. If a short develops in that circuit, the breaker's bimetallic thermostatic arm heats up. When a bimetallic arm heats, it bends. This moves its contact away from the stationary contact and breaks the circuit; the lights go out. With no current flowing, the thermostatic arm cools, bends back to reestab-

A circuit breaker trips when it is overloaded, then resets automatically. This type of protective device rarely needs replacement.

lish contact, and the lights go back on. The effect is to make the headlights flash on and off. The flashing lets you pull off the road safely before turning off the lights and looking for the trouble.

Circuit breakers are metal rectangles, about ¾-by-1 inch, with two terminals. A circuit breaker need not be replaced unless it is defective. A replacement should be of the specified type and amperage. If possible, get it from a dealer who sells your make of car.

Often found on accessory circuits, the in-line fuse is a standard fuse mounted in a socket. To check the fuse, twist the socket open.

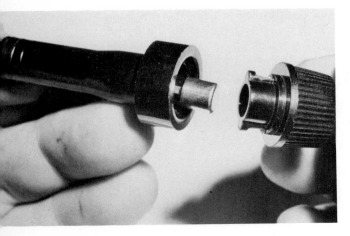

A circuit breaker may be located at the switch controlling the electrical component it monitors, or it may be found elsewhere along the wires between the switch and its component. Sometimes, the breaker is located at the component itself. Some breakers are designed to be inserted into the car's fuse block.

In-line fuse. A fourth type of circuit-protection device, it is like the fuse in the back of your TV set. An in-line fuse consists of a socket that contains an ordinary automotive fuse, with wiring to and from it. One lead goes to a source of electricity and the other goes to the load.

American Motors cars do not use in-line fuses. Chrysler products use them for headlight relays, headlight washer relays, deck-lid solenoids, air conditioner blower motors, tail-gate lock solenoids, console courtesy lights, and spotlights. The actual use varies by make and model. Ford products use in-line fuses for air conditioners, engine compartment lights, and automatic headlight dimmers. GM cars use them for automatic headlight dimmers, automatic speed controls, spotlights, and air conditioners. Other makes use them for tachometers and rear-window defoggers as well.

Remove an in-line fuse to tell whether it is blown. Push the halves of the fuse socket together, and then twist them half a turn as if to unscrew them from each other. Release them and the halves will pop apart, allowing the fuse to drop out of its socket.

ELECTRICAL TESTS

Here are some of the things you can do with a VOM to find car wiring troubles. Which one you should use depends on what portion of the circuit you are testing and what trouble you are looking for.

(Before you make an ohm test with your VOM, be sure that the circuit is not ener-

If the circuit is energized, you can test a fuse without removing it from the block. Either use a voltmeter set at 12 D.C. volts or a test light. Touch the leads across the fuse ends; there should be no reading on the voltmeter nor light on the test light.

gized. To be safe, disconnect the negative battery cable. Your VOM can be damaged by hooking it into a current-carrying circuit when it is set for ohm readings.)

Fuse. Remove the suspect fuse. Switch to the low-ohm scale on your VOM. Zero the meter by touching the test prods together and rotating the zero-adjust knob. Then, touch the test prods across the metal ends of the fuse. If the fuse is good, the needle will indicate zero resistance.

To test a double-filament bulb with an ohmmeter or a continuity tester, touch the leads across the bulb contacts. There should be a low-ohm reading or a continuity light-up.

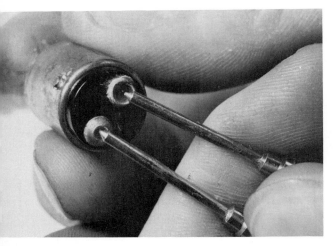

In this test and the next two, the VOM is used as a continuity tester. The VOM's own battery energizes the circuit being tested. If you have a powered test light, it also can be used.

Bulb. Test a bulb that has been removed the same way you would a fuse. With the selector on low-ohms and zeroed, touch one prod to the bulb's base, the other to its contact. The meter should drop to a reading of about 1 to 2 ohms, depending on the lamp's candlepower. If a filament has burned out, the meter will show infinite resistance. If the bulb has two filaments, touch across the two contacts on the bottom of the bulb. If either filament is burned out, infinite resistance will be indicated. When replacing a bulb, check the auto manufacturer's specification. Do not use the old bulb as a guide; someone may have installed the wrong type.

Short circuit. Set the selector for the high-ohm setting and zero it. Touch one test prod to the insulated circuit. Use the pin or knife tricks illustrated or find a ter-

Short Circuit Test

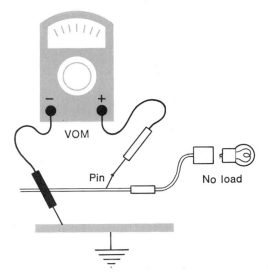

minal. Ground the other prod by touching it to part of the car body. Remove the load on the circuit, be it a bulb or motor. The meter reading now should stay on infinity. If there is a short, the needle will move toward the zero side. Disconnect portions of the circuit at terminals and connections until you have isolated the shorted part. Locate the short by visual inspection and fix it.

Open circuit. Energize the circuit by turning on the proper switch. Set the VOM selector to DC volts, on the 12-volt scale.

Open Circuit Test

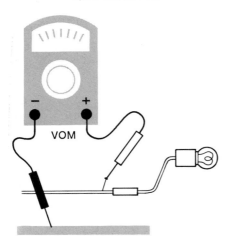

Touch the red prod to the circuit and the black prod to a ground. If the circuit is live, the meter should read somewhere near battery voltage. If open, it will read zero. Find the portion of the circuit nearest the battery that is live. Just beyond that point lies the opening. Visual inspection should pick it out. A test light also may be used for that test.

Excessive resistance. Set the VOM selector on low-ohms and zero the needle.

Excessive Resistance Test

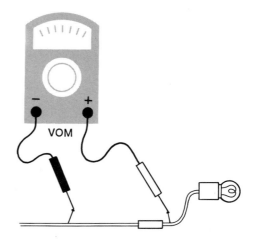

Touch the test prods so they bridge across that circuit part which you suspect of having high resistance. If it is good, the meter should show zero ohms. You can test the ground circuit for continuity, too; touch one prod to the part that is supposed to be grounded, the other to one that definitely is. The reading should be zero.

Voltage drop. This is one of the most useful tests for finding otherwise hidden sources of circuit-damaging resistance. Even though volts do not measure resistance, the drop in voltage over parts of a loaded circuit is proportional to the resistance present in it. Voltage drop will pinpoint resistances so small that you cannot measure them with an ohmmeter. For example, in a 10-ampere current flow, an immeasurable resistance of only 0.01 ohm will cause a 0.1-volt drop. The 0.1-volt drop is easily measured on the 0.6-volt VOM scale, however.

To measure voltage drop, energize the test circuit by turning on the light or accessory. Set the VOM selector to its lowest DC volt setting. Touch the red prod to the beginning of the circuit—usually the positive battery post. Touch the black prod to the end of the circuit—the load's terminal. The lower the reading, the better. When checking voltage drop on a ground circuit, touch the red prod to the load and the black to ground. The meter should read zero.

To isolate the portion of a circuit causing the excessive voltage drop, start at one end and test across each part of the loaded circuit in turn. The faulty part will show a high voltage-drop reading. Then, you can do whatever is needed to correct the high resistance.

Voltage Drop Test

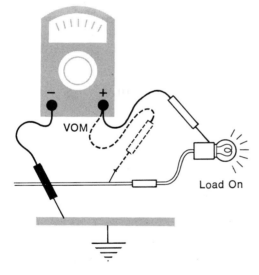

Always keep the red VOM prod toward the battery side of the circuit for a positive reading on a negative-grounded electrical system. If the needle tries to sink below a zero reading, the prods are reversed.

Never connect your VOM test prods across a live circuit unless its volt selector is set for the correct voltage. If too much voltage crosses the meter when it is set for low voltages, it can be damaged.

TROUBLESHOOTING

Look for common troubles first—loose connections, burned out bulbs, and blown fuses. Wires themselves rarely give out.

• There are four good ways of dealing with a broken or frayed wire:

You can replace the wire.

You can, with a crimping tool, cut the wire, strip off a little insulation from the ends and install a crimp-on connector.

You can install one of the new connectors made specifically for automotive electrical repairs—a pair of pliers is the only tool needed for the installation.

You can splice by soldering and taping— just twisting the wires together and taping them is not good enough, for corrosion and vibration will soon destroy electrical continuity through this type of temporary splice.

• A discharged battery is not a common cause of chassis electrical troubles, but checking it is simple. (See the chapter on the starting system.) Switches are readily accessible for testing. You can do it with a jumper, test light, continuity tester, or VOM.

• Suspect faulty mechanical parts before you suspect your car's wiring; motors fail far more often than wiring. Also, moving parts may wear through wiring insulation, causing problems.

• If common and easy tests do not uncover the cause of a problem, begin at the load and work toward the battery, following the circuit. If something should happen and does not (for example, a bulb does not light), check, with a test light or voltmeter, whether electricity is being supplied to that component.

If it is, you have saved the trouble of checking many feet of wiring and various switches and connections. Concentrate instead on the socket and ground circuit.

(text continued on page 224)

Connecting Wire

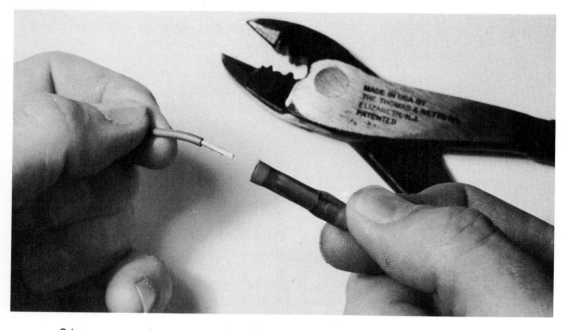

Crimp-on connectors are a good, solderless way to fasten replacement wiring. Simply insert the stripped wire end into the right-sized connector and squeeze.

New connectors such as the *Scotchlok* make splicing easy. Position the wires (*left*) and push the splicing teeth down with pliers. The teeth bite through the insulation, making stripping unneccessary. Snap the cover closed (*right*) to complete the job.

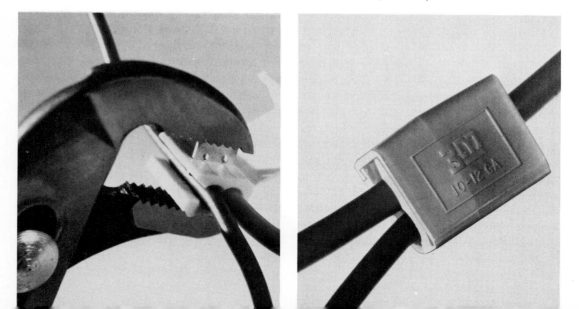

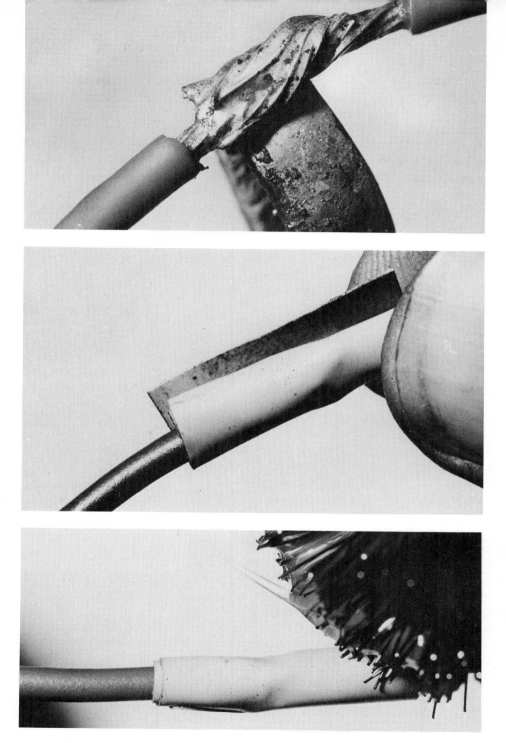

For a traditional splice, use solder. Flow it over the joint (*top*) and let it cool until the gloss disappears before moving the connection. Then, wrap the joint with several layers of plastic electrical tape (*middle*). Finally, cover the tape with a film of weatherstrip cement.

On the other hand, if no voltage is present, forget the ground and socket, and concentrate on the wiring that leads to it. (Be sure the necessary switches are turned on; for example, a "safe" power window will not work with the ignition switch off.)

• If something happens that should not (for example, fuses blow), start at the far end of the circuit protected by that fuse. For instance, if it is a courtesy light fuse, remove the courtesy light cover from the ceiling and test for short circuiting there. Then, check at the door courtesy light switches; then, at the fuse block. The short circuit has to be somewhere between the light and the fuse.

• If an elusive short circuit or a faulty switch somewhere in the car's wiring keeps draining the battery, you may have trouble finding it. Conduct a battery drain test, using an ammeter, voltmeter, or VOM. Set a VOM for its lowest DC milliampere setting, or for 12 DC volts.

Disconnect the negative battery cable and hold it away from metal car parts. All switches should be off and all doors should be closed. Touch the meter's red prod to the negative battery cable and contact its black prod to the negative battery terminal. The reading should be zero on an ammeter or milliammeter. Voltmeters may show about 0.2 volt on cars with alternator charging systems. Such leakage, inherent in the alternator diodes, is minor and will not discharge a battery noticeably.

If battery drain is found, isolate the circuit causing it by removing fuses from the fuse block, one at a time. Note the meter reading each time. When it drops to zero, the circuit protected by the fuse you just removed contains the problem.

• When looking for a short circuit, never jumper across the fuse or replace the fuse with a bolt—you could destroy many feet of wiring and even start a fire.

• Check power-operated windows, seats, or convertible tops systems thoroughly. They may be powered through more than one fuse or circuit breaker. For instance, the power-window circuit may have one main fuse while each motor in the circuit has its own separate overcurrent protector. If you find the main device good but fail to check the individual protector, you will not solve the puzzle.

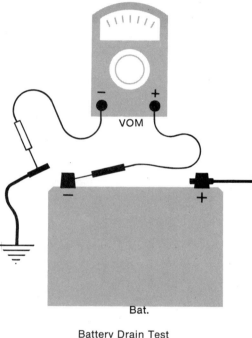

Battery Drain Test

If you come to a deadlock and can think of no more logical way to proceed, take your car to a shop and explain what you have checked. Then, the mechanic can direct himself to other possibilities. He has the advantage of having worked on many electrical problems to learn the weaknesses of each auto electrical system—he may know just where to look. At other times, he can only try various tests the same as you did.

TROUBLESHOOTING GENERAL LIGHTS AND APPLIANCES

SYMPTOM	CAUSE	CURE
Light does not light	Burned-out bulb	Remove and test bulb. Install new one if burned out
	Fuse blown	Test fuse even if it looks good. Install new fuse if blown
	Open circuit, electricity not reaching bulb	Start at battery and test circuit for battery voltage with VOM or test light at every point of access
	Open ground circuit	Connect jumper wire from bulb socket to a good ground and see if bulb lights; if it does, isolate faulty ground by jumping individual parts of the ground circuit starting at the socket
	Short circuit, blows fuses	Make a visual inspection of circuit's terminals, connections, wires, switches; to isolate the short circuit, disconnect and test between insulated and ground circuit for continuity with VOM on high ohms or with a continuity tester—there should be no continuity
	Open switch	Connect jumper wire across the switch; if that energizes the circuit, replace the switch
Motor does not run	See causes above	See cures above
	Internal motor damage	Disconnect motor leads and test with ohmmeter across leads for open (should be infinite ohms) or shorted internal circuit (should be zero ohms); remove motor and repair or replace
	Locked shaft (draws power but does not run)	Try to turn shaft; if locked, remove motor and repair or replace

HORNS AND BUZZERS

Most horns are controlled through relays. When the horn button or ring is depressed, electricity flows from the battery through a horn lead inside the steering column, then through an electromagnetic coil in the horn relay to ground. A small flow of current through the coil energizes the electromagnet, pulling down a movable arm. Electrical contacts on the arm touch, closing the primary circuit and making the horns sound.

Horn buttons. Most horn troubles are mechanical, not electrical, and occur in the horn button area. You can remove the horn button or ring from the steering wheel by pushing it in as far as you can and turning it counterclockwise about 30°. It should pop out. To keep the horn from blowing while you remove its button, disconnect the negative battery cable. Reconnect it later for circuit testing.

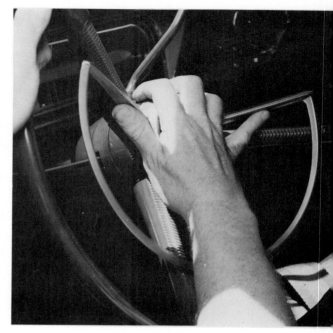

To remove the horn ring, disconnect the negative battery cable. Then, push the ring in and turn it to the left; it should now pull off.

Horn Circuit

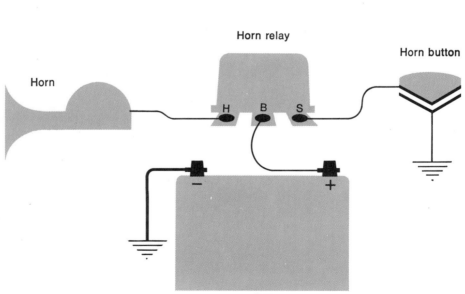

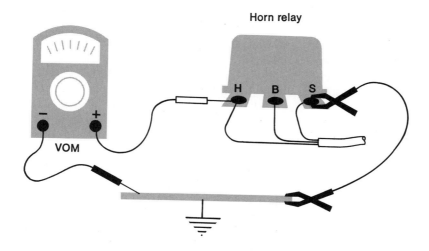

Horn relay

H   B   S

VOM

Horn Relay Check

Some horn buttons are held by screws under a center medallion or through the hub of the steering wheel. The former can be reached by prying off the clip-on medallion with a knife.

Horn circuit. Locate the horn's "hot" and ground contact points in the center of the steering wheel. Try jumping across them with a key or jumper wire. (Some car horns will not blow unless the ignition is on.) If the horn now works, the trouble is with the contacts. Try brightening them with sandpaper. Inspect for mechanical problems such as broken parts within the horn button. Sometimes, the retainers break. The cure is to buy and install a new retainer.

If the horn still does not blow, check the horn relay, which is located under the hood either near the horns or between the horns and battery. Most horn relays have three terminals: one bringing in current from the battery (labeled "B"); one leading to the horns (labeled "H"); and one switching lead to the horn button (labeled "S"). Some horn relays have a fourth terminal marked "IGN." It is connected to the ignition switch so the horn will not blow unless the switch is on.

Some horn relays also have a fuse in a cartridge on the relay's battery terminal. If the horn does not blow, remove the fuse and check it for continuity.

To check the relay with a VOM, connect the red lead of the VOM—set on or near 12 DC volts—to the "H" terminal, the black lead to ground. Ground the relay's "S" terminal with a jumper. If the relay is working, the meter will read battery voltage. If it is not working, the meter will read zero. Relays sometimes can be repaired by removing the cover and sanding the contacts. If that does not help, get a new relay.

Horn-buzzer unit. Some cars incorporate the horn relay and ignition-key reminder buzzer into the same unit. On Delco units, the "1" terminal is connected to the battery, the "2" terminal leads to the horns, the "3" terminal leads to the horn button and the "4" terminal leads to the ignition switch and door switch. The horn relay-buzzer unit must be removed from its mounting before you can identify the terminals.

To check buzzer operation, first be sure that the ignition key is all the way into the ignition switch. Open the driver's door and watch the dome light. If neither the dome light nor the buzzer operates, check the door switch for defects. If the dome light comes on but the buzzer fails to operate, connect a jumper from the "4" terminal to ground. If the buzzer sounds, the trouble is in the ignition wiring or switch.

If the buzzer still does not operate, hook a voltmeter, set on or near 12 DC volts, from the "1" terminal to ground. If the terminals are of the slip-on type, slide a prod made from a paper clip up into the wiring harness connector. If the reading is zero, there is an open circuit from the battery to the unit. If you get a voltage reading, replace the buzzer.

To check horn operation on this type of combination unit, attach a jumper from the "2" terminal to ground. If the horns operate, check the "2" terminal lead and horn button contacts for defects. If the horns do not operate, leave the jumper connected and hook up a voltmeter, set on or near 12 DC volts, from the "3" terminal to ground. If you get a reading, the trouble is in the horns or horn wiring. A zero read-

ing means you should replace the horn relay-buzzer unit.

The horn. To tell whether horn trouble is in the switching circuit or in the horns themselves, connect a jumper from the battery positive terminal to the horn terminal. If the horn blows, it is good.

The ground circuit may be at fault. Run a jumper from a good ground on the horn to the battery's negative terminal and try to honk the horn. If it now blows but did not in the previous test, remove, clean and brighten the horn's mounting connection and test again.

Most cars have two horns. Sometimes one fails, leaving the car with a flat, unpleasant sound when you honk. Feel the horns while someone honks. The one that does not vibrate is at fault.

An inoperative horn or one with a poor, gravelly tone sometimes can be fixed by turning the adjusting screw. Usually, the horn must be removed from the car and its cap taken off for such an adjustment. Sometimes, the adjusting screw is on the outside and covered with wax, which must be removed to make the adjustment.

With the horn out and hooked to a battery with "hot" and ground jumpers, turn the adjusting screw counterclockwise until no vibrating sound comes from the horn. Then, adjust the screw clockwise until the sound is full and rich. Make your adjustments a little at a time to keep from overadjusting. A horn that does not respond to such adjustment should be replaced.

Low voltage can affect horns without relays (found in many foreign cars). If the horns sound weakly while other accessories are operating, that is the likely cause. Installing a horn relay with a primary circuit of heavy, number-10 wire will solve the problem.

TROUBLESHOOTING HORNS

SYMPTOM	CAUSE	CURE
Horn will not blow	Mechanical problem in horn button or ring	Remove horn button or ring, inspect and clean contacts; test horn by shorting across contacts; replace lead to horn button if necessary
	Defective horn relay	Test relay as described in text; repair or replace if defective
	Defective horn	Adjust screw on horn or replace horn
Horn blows weakly	Inadequate voltage to horn	Install horn relay or heavier wire in horn circuit
	Horn out of adjustment	Adjust as described in text
Horn will not stop blowing	Grounded wire or contact in steering wheel	Remove horn button or ring and repair grounded contact or replace grounded wire
	Weak or broken horn button return spring or broken retainer	Remove horn button and replace defective part
	Horn relay contacts welded together	Replace horn relay

14

Troubleshooting Lights and Gauges

HEADLIGHTS

Most headlight troubles are caused by burned-out filaments in one of the sealed-beam units. Short circuits are a much rarer problem. A serious short in a circuit-breaker-protected headlight system will make the breaker cycle so rapidly that it vibrates. The lights may not work at all.

To narrow down the possible causes of the problem, work the headlight switch from "off" to "parking lights" to "headlights" positions.

If the breaker cycles in all positions, the short is in one of the lighting circuits common to all positions; namely, the circuit for the taillights, license light, or instrument lights.

If the breaker cycles only in the "parking lights" position, the parking light circuit contains the short.

If the breaker cycles only when the headlights are on, the headlight circuit is faulty. Narrow down the possibilities to either the high-beam or low-beam circuit by switching the dimmer switch. If the cycling stops on high beam, the short is in the low beam circuit, and vice-versa.

Also see whether the dimmer switch is making both filaments of a headlight burn at once; that, too, can cause the breaker to cycle. Such a dimmer switch should be replaced.

Most headlight dimmer switches last the life of the car without giving trouble. When one does act up, it can be dangerous. If you experience a headlight dimming problem that is not caused by burned-out filaments in the headlamps, go right to the dimmer switch. Sometimes dirt builds up inside the switch button and jams it. Tap the button to see whether dirt falls out. Remove the switch leads and clean them. With the headlights on, connect a jumper wire between the center dimmer switch lead and each of the other leads in turn. If the lights work on both dim and bright beams, replace the dimmer switch.

To do that, roll back the floor mat from the switch area, exposing the switch mounting screws and leads. Then, remove the screws and leads and take out the switch. Modern cars use terminal-block dimmer switch connectors. Simply pull such a unit off. Installation is the reverse of removal.

If the old switch is dirty, try cleaning it, blowing the dirt out of the switch button, and oiling it. If that does not help, you need a new switch.

One problem with headlights is that when your lights are bright enough for you to see as well as you should, they blind oncoming drivers. Another problem comes when a trailer hook-up or passengers in the back seat cause the rear of the car sag. That makes the lights shine upwards so they blind drivers of oncoming cars, even if they are on low beam.

When headlights are too high, other motorists suffer; when your headlights are too low, you suffer. State motor vehicle laws make the driver responsible for correctly adjusted, properly used headlights.

Jarring from rough roads, spring settling, adjustment slippage, and other factors account for changes in headlight alignment. Otherwise, alignment could be set at the factory once and for all.

By law, U.S. automotive headlights are sealed-beam units—standardized, all-glass, lamp-reflector-lens units that are used by all auto makers. The lens is fused to the reflector; sealed inside is an inert gas, the same as in the 60-watt bulb in your reading lamp. The filaments, which glow white-hot to produce the light, are in the reflector. No separate bulb is needed; the unit acts as a sealed glass bulb.

On low beams, properly aimed headlights should enable you to see a man walking along the shoulder of the road 100 feet ahead. High beams should pick him out at 300 feet.

In the two-lamp system, compromises in light distribution must be made because the same lenses are used to focus both beams. Each of the 7-inch-diameter lamps contains two filaments, one for the high beam and one for the low beam. Sometimes, a number "2" appears on the lens.

In a four-light system, each lamp is only 5¾ inches in diameter. The two outer (or upper, in a stacked arrangement) sealed-beam lamps are of the double-filament type; they sometimes are marked by a number "2" molded into the lens. The two inner (or lower) lamps have only one filament and are sometimes marked with a number "1". On high beam, the "1" bulbs shoot light far down the highway, while the off-focus filaments in the "2" lamps provide "body" light to illuminate the roadside. On low beam, only the in-focus filaments of the "2" lamps are lighted; they are aimed considerably to the right side of the road. .

Headlamp alignment should be checked twice a year or whenever the light beam appears too high or too low when you drive with a normal load. When other drivers flash their lights at you, and your

Typical Headlight Parts

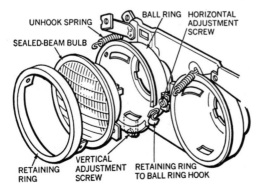

UNHOOK SPRING
SEALED-BEAM BULB
BALL RING HORIZONTAL ADJUSTMENT SCREW
RETAINING RING
VERTICAL ADJUSTMENT SCREW
RETAINING RING TO BALL RING HOOK

lights are on low beam, your lights need adjustment. And unless you have some means of leveling the car (booster springs or an equalizing hitch), you should reset the headlights when you pull a heavy trailer or carry a heavy load. A misalignment of only one degree can put the beams five feet higher than they should be 300 feed down the road. One degree too low reduces illumination to one-fifth normal 300 feet ahead.

Aligning Headlights

You need only two tools: a No. 2 Phillips screwdriver and a regular screwdriver. Sometimes, only the Phillips is needed.

Choose a reasonably level spot to set up a screen. The parking apron in front of your garage door may be a good location. Park the car so that its headlights are 25 feet from the door. With chalk, make four marks on the driveway below the axle lines—two for the front axle and two for the rear axle.

There are several ways to make a screen. One of the easiest is to make a pair of 2 x 4 sighting stands. Their tops should exactly match the center of the highest headlamps. If the headlights are all the same height, any lamp will do as a guide. If the headlights are stacked, put nails into the sighting stands to match the center of the lower lights. The idea is to draw horizontal and vertical center lines on the screen that are even with your car's headlights when the car is parked.

Now, back the car away and put your sighting stands over the front and rear axle lines on the left side. Sight over the tops of stands and chalk or tape an "x" on the garage door where they line up. You can remove the mark later. Repeat the procedure on the right side.

Then, chalk a line between the two

marks on the garage door. That represents the horizontal centerline of the headlamps. If you have driven nails into your sighting stands, sight across them to make a second, lower set of marks. Make another horizontal centerline for the lower headlights.

Measure half-way between the original "x" marks; this represents the center of the car. Then, make vertical marks representing the vertical centerlines of each headlamp.

Pull the car back into its original position. Sight from the rear to make sure the car is aimed for the center line. The chalk lines create a test grid at which you can aim your headlights, and on which you can check their alignment.

Wait until dusk or after dark before making the actual adjustments. If possible, get two helpers to sit in the front seats to provide normal weight. Now, bounce the front and rear bumpers to normalize the suspension. Then, turn on the headlights.

With a four-headlight system, adjust the high-beam number "1" lamps first. Work on one lamp at a time, covering the others with a newspaper or cloth. If a light hits the grid in the wrong position, turn the adjustment screws to correct the alignment.

To move the headlights on most cars, you first must remove the headlamp bezels, or bright trim, to expose the adjustment screws. On some late-model cars the screws are accessible without removing anything.

Two screws position each light. One is for up-and-down adjustment and the other is for side-to-side adjustment. A coil spring behind each adjustment screw holds the lamp housing tightly in position. Turning the screw in (clockwise) pushes that side

(text continued on page 236)

Making a Headlight Alignment Screen

1. Position the car on a fairly level site that is 25 feet from a vertical surface such as your garage door. Mark the tire positions.

3. With one stand at the front-wheel mark and the other at the rear-wheel mark, sight. Have a helper fix the point on the screen. Repeat the sightings on both sides, and, if applicable, for both the upper and the lower headlights.

2. Cut off the tops of the headlight stands at the height of the headlight centers. If your car has stacked headlights, drive nails into the stand at the height of the lower headlight centers.

4. Carefully make a horizontal line between the marks on the screen. Then, make three vertical lines: one to represent the center of the car, and one through the center of each of the headlights.

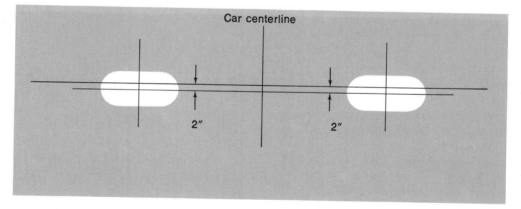

Car centerline

2"   2"

5. When it is dark enough, reposition the car on the tire marks and switch on the lights. First, adjust the high-beams (*above*). Each light should center on the vertical lines; they should also center 2 inches below the horizontal line. Then, adjust the low-beams (*below*). Each light should center 2 inches to the right of the vertical lines; in addition, their tops should touch the horizontal line.

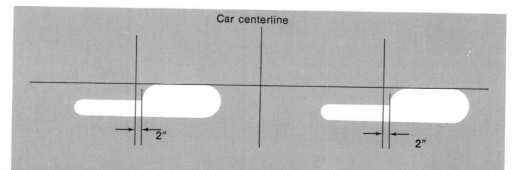

Car centerline

2"   2"

Turn adjustment screws in or out to adjust each light. Always finish an adjustment with a clockwise turn of the screw; this sets the lamp socket in tension.

of the housing in, moving the beam in the same direction. Turning the screw out (counter-clockwise) moves that side of the housing unit out, aiming the beam in the opposite direction. On an outward adjustment, make sure that the spring pushes the housing out. If it does not, pull the housing out with your finger so that it is solidly against the shoulder of the adjustment screw.

Adjust the bright beams first, then the dims.

Aim the number "1" lamp high beam so its hot spot is aimed directly ahead, and focused two inches below the horizontal line on the screen (the lower line, if there are two). When you have completed the adjustment, turn the screw slightly clockwise to hold the lamp in tension against its spring. That way, you make certain that the housing and screw are in contact and that the adjustment is firm.

Adjust the number "2" lamps on a four-lamp system—and both lamps of a two-

lamp system—when they are on low beam. Again, cover the lamp or lamps not being worked on. Adjust to the lamp's own horizontal centerline. Aim the top of the high-intensity zone flush below the aiming line. (That places the hot spot completely below the headlight's horizontal centerline.) Adjust side to side so that the main part of the pattern is two inches to the right of the the light's vertical centerline.

Lamp replacement. For a sealed beam unit, this is a snap. With the bezel off, loosen, but do not remove, the three small screws that are placed about 120° apart around the unit. A metal retainer ring around the lamp unit has slotted tabs under the three screws. Turn the retainer counter-clockwise until the enlarged portions of the slots come under the screws; then, lift off the retainer. Be careful. The old sealed beam unit can fall out and break, leaving you a cleanup job.

A different type of headlight retaining ring is held by a hook on one end and a spring on the other. To remove it, free the spring with pliers and bring the loosened side of the retaining ring out until it can be unhooked.

Slip the old sealed beam unit out and unplug it at the back. Plug the new unit into the socket, installing it right-side-up, with its three glass locaters in place in the lamp housing. Slip on the retaining ring, turn it clockwise to lock. Tighten the three screws or hook the ring back into place and reinstall the spring.

Check the alignment of the new lamp—just in case—before replacing the bezel, even though it seldom is necessary to re-aim the new light. If possible, replace the unit with the same brand as the others on the car; the patterns are usually more compatible that way. Only the burned-out unit need be replaced.

Lamp Replacement

To change a sealed beam unit, loosen the three screws around the retainer ring, turn the unit slightly counterclockwise and lift it off.

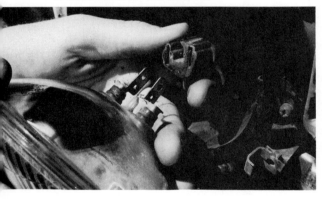

Unplug the sealed beam unit from its socket. No. 1 lamps have two terminals, while No. 2 lamps have three terminals.

When installing new sealed beam lamps, position the glass nibs into the locater holes in the housing; new lamps should not need re-aiming.

BRAKE LIGHTS

Brake lighting systems are so important to driving safety that you should make a habit of checking yours whenever you can. When you pull into the garage or back up to the house at night, push the brake pedal to see whether the wall lights up red. When you back into a parking spot next to the curb, look for red spots reflected in the bumper of the car behind you. Driving on a dusty road at night, apply the brakes lightly. If the brake lights work, the dust behind the car will light up.

If just one brake light fails, suspect the bulb or the wiring to it. The turn light in that direction will not work properly, either. Taillight and parking light bulbs are double-filament. They have two contacts, plus grounding through the metal shell.

When both brake lights fail, the cause may be a defective brake light switch. Some switches are hydraulic, others are mechanical. Hydraulic switches are threaded into the brake master cylinder. To test it, pull off the leads and touch the metal parts together. If the brake lights then go on, replace the switch.

As you unscrew the old hydraulic switch, have the new one ready to thread in quickly before any air can enter the master cylinder. If the brake pedal does

Mounted so it touches the brake pedal arm, the mechanical brake light switch should engage when the pedal is depressed 1/2 inch.

TROUBLESHOOTING LIGHTS

SYMPTOM	CAUSE	CURE
Headlights flash (high beam, usually)	Overloaded circuit; circuit breaker is cycling	Check to see if both filaments are burning in sealed-beam units, replace dimmer switch if they are (common on Fords—see a professional mechanic)
	Short circuit in insulated headlight circuit makes circuit breaker cycle	Switch to other beam and drive carefully to a safe spot to park; inspect for shorts in headlight circuit wiring and at switch; if low beam works, drive carefully to where you can get service
One brake light does not light	Burned-out bulb	Replace bulb if burned out; make general lighting circuit checks if bulb is not burned out
Both brake lights do not light	Burned-out bulbs	See above
	Defective switch	Short across switch leads to test; if lights work, repair or replace switch
Brake lights stay on	Defective switch or switch adjustment	Remove leads from switch; if lights go off, adjust or replace switch
	Insufficient brake pedal clearance	Correct if necessary
	Dragging brakes	Jack up wheel and try to spin it (see chapter on brake service)
Portion of instrument panel dark	Burned-out bulb	Remove bulb from behind instrument panel, install new bulb
Courtesy light does not work	Burned-out bulb	Remove and test; replace if burned out
Courtesy light does not operate from both sides	Defective switch on door that fails to light it	Jump across leads in back of switch with jumper wire; if light goes on, replace switch

SYMPTOM	CAUSE	CURE
Frequent bulb burnout	Charging voltage set too high	See chapter on charging system service
Headlamp does not light	Burned-out bulb	Replace headlamp sealed-beam unit
Backup lights do not work	Switch defective or out of adjustment	Jump across terminals of backup light switch with ignition on; if backup lights work, adjust switch position or replace switch
Battery consistently goes dead overnight	Defective battery	See chapter on battery-starter systems
	Slow drain in electrical system	Test by removing positive battery cable; touch cable terminal to wind electric clock, then connect an ammeter or voltmeter—a reading indicates leakage
All lights get bright and go out; engine may die and not restart	Poor ground cable connection	Remove and clean battery negative terminal; high voltage from alternator probably burned out every bulb that was on; check and replace bulbs as necessary, and check distributor points for burning, too
Lights do not work	Short circuit somewhere in lighting circuit; circuit breaker cycles rapidly	Zero in on short circuit with test light or VOM; repair

not feel normal after switch replacement, bleed the hydraulic system as described in the chapter on brake servicing.

Mechanical brake light switches normally are operated from the brake pedal arm by a lever or linkage. Sometimes, an old-style mechanical brake switch can be removed, cleaned, oiled and made operative again. If not, replace it. The new plastic-bodied switches can only be replaced. If the switch is simply loose on its mounts, tighten or reposition it so that the brake lights come on as the brake pedal is depressed about a half inch.

BACKUP LIGHTS

Most problems with backup lights are caused by a backup light switch that needs repositioning—if the lights can be made to work by moving the shift lever in and out of reverse, positioning is the problem. Otherwise, it may be a blown fuse, a bad wire, a poor contact, burned-out bulbs, or a faulty ground.

First, try shorting across the backup light switch terminals with a jumper. The switch usually is on the transmission or the steering column, where the shift lever can contact it as it is moved into reverse gear. Cars with floor shifts generally have the switch on the side of the transmission. You can reach such a switch from underneath the car.

The neutral safety switch on Fords with automatic transmissions is also the backup light switch. Beginning with 1972 models, a third circuit was added to that switch: the seat belt warning buzzer. When checking Ford circuits, remember that the one switch controls two or three functions.

TURN SIGNAL INDICATORS

Turn signal lighting systems consist of a directional switch on the steering column; the turn filaments of the double-filament parking lights in front; the stop/turn filaments of the double-filament taillights; the panel indicator lights; and a flasher relay. The turn signal switch has many terminals. These are needed for the complex action that takes the brake light filaments out of their normal circuit and puts them into the flasher-controlled turn-light circuit.

The brake light opposite the direction of turn must function normally during a combined stop-and-turn movement. A problem may be traced to any of the lamps or to the wiring serving them. Often, the symptoms are the tipoff to the problem (see the accompanying troubleshooting chart on page 242).

Turn indicator flashers operate thermally. When current flows, it heats a fine wire that makes or breaks the signal light circuit through a relay. The more current

To test a backup light switch—which should engage when the transmission is in reverse—insert two nails into the naked connector openings. Then, short across the nails; the lights should go on.

To adjust a backup light switch, loosen the clamp that holds it to the steering column. Rotate the bracket on which the switch is mounted until the lights go on with shift in reverse; tighten clamp.

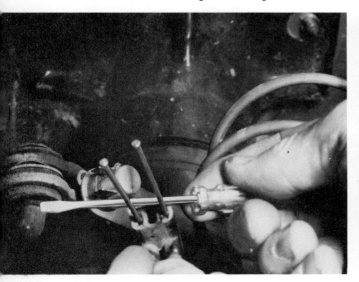

Lighting Tips

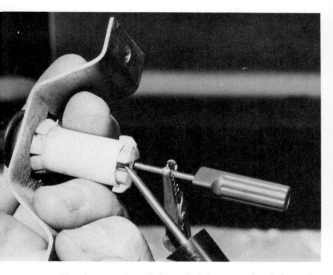

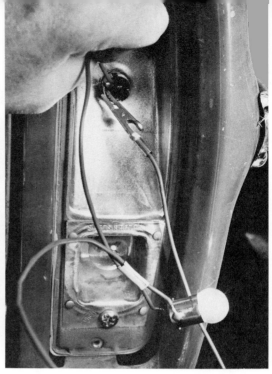

Check a courtesy light switch by removing it from the door and inserting a small screwdriver into one terminal. Then, connect a continuity tester between the screwdriver and the other terminal. Work the switch; the test light should go on.

Test for a live circuit by energizing the circuit but removing the load—in this case, a bulb. Hook a test light between the socket terminal and the socket base. If the test light goes on, you know that current is reaching the socket.

Parking lamp problems are often due to corrosion, especially in the area pointed out by the screwdriver blade. Although this unit is untarnished, corrosion here results in poor ground continuity.

Always replace a defective bulb with one of the correct size; each bulb's number appears clearly stamped on its metal base.

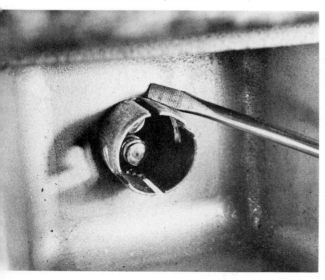

TROUBLESHOOTING TURN SIGNALS

SYMPTOM	CAUSE	CURE
Work in one direction only	Burned-out bulb or sockets not grounded	Remove front and rear bulbs and test, replace if burned out; connect jumper wire from each socket to a good ground and if light works, correct poor ground
Signals do not work at all	Blown fuse	Check; replace if blown
	Defective flasher relay	Install good flasher relay and test
	Defective switch	Replace if defective
Signals flash too slowly	One bulb burned out or socket not well grounded	Check visually to see which one; fix as above
	Heavy-duty flasher relay used	Replace with regular-duty unit
	Wrong-sized bulb, too small	Replace with specified bulb
Signals come on but do not flash	Both sides: fused flasher relay contacts	Replace flasher relay unit
	One side only: burned-out bulb or poorly grounded socket	See cure at top of chart
Signals flash too rapidly	Too large a bulb	Replace with right-sized bulb
	One side only: short circuit in side affected	Check for short; repair
	Both sides: short circuit in wiring common to both sides	Check wires leading to turn signal switch on steering column
	Add-on lights placed in circuit (trailer)	Install heavy-duty flasher relay unit
Directional signals do not cancel	Mechanical problem in switch	Have switch removed and checked for broken or worn parts; have switch mechanism replaced if defective

that flows, the faster the contact is made and broken. Knowing this helps in trouble-shooting. A burned-out bulb decreases the current flow and thus slows or stops the flashing. So does an open circuit in the insulated wiring or ground circuit. A poor ground will reduce the flow of current and stop the flashing. A short circuit increases the speed of the flashing.

A defective flasher relay can cause problems, too. This is a small metal can, with two terminals, that is plugged into a connector underneath the dash. The can usually is clipped to the rear of the instrument panel or to the steering column, where its operating sounds will be transmitted to the driver. Replace if defective.

Since the park/turn lamps in front and the stop/turn lamps in the rear use double-filament bulbs, one filament can burn out while the other still works. Do not assume that because one functions correctly, the other does too.

FOUR-WAY WARNING FLASHER

The hazard warning flasher, used on all cars since 1968, flashes both front turn light filaments, both rear stop/turn light filaments, turn signal indicator lamps and pilot lamp, if any. It has a control switch and a flasher relay all its own. The switch may be located on the steering column, in the glove compartment, or elsewhere. When the flasher is on, all the lights flash in unison. If you apply the brakes, the lights normally stop flashing and burn continuously. The lights will continue flashing for as long as 15 hours, depending on the battery.

Burned-out bulbs are the most common four-way flasher problem. A blown stop/taillight fuse also is a possible culprit, as is a blown fuse to the warning light system itself.

If some lights work and others do not, try the turn signals in each direction with

Turn signal flasher plugs into a socket either under the instrument panel or on the steering column. It is often the cause of turn indicator problems; replacement of this unit is an easy job.

the flasher off. If those work, suspect a faulty flasher switch. If some turn signal bulbs do not work, the trouble must be in those bulbs, their sockets, or their grounds.

The best way to check an inoperative flasher relay is to install a new one. Then try the system. If there is no change, put the old one back and return the new flasher relay to your dealer for credit.

In most cars, when a turn signal bulb fails, the rest of the lights on that side of the car will stay on without flashing. But if the four-way warning lights are switched on, they will override the turn signal's flasher and flash all good bulbs with sound circuits.

You can install a four-way flasher system on any pre-1968 car; complete directions should come with the kit.

GAUGES

Most auto gauges are electrically operated. Exceptions are the speedometer and, occasionally, the oil pressure gauge. They consist of a sending unit, which reads the condition; a recording unit on the instrument panel; and the wiring between.

The *sending unit* is simply a variable resistor, or rheostat, that passes varying amounts of current. Resistance depends on the level of the gas in the tank, oil pressure, or temperature of the engine, whichever is being measured.

If only one gauge acts up, suspect it or its sending unit. If all gauges act up at the same time, suspect the voltage limiter serving them.

Most cars use a *voltage limiter* to feed the gauges about 5 volts. That prevents variations in battery voltage from affecting the instrument readings. Sometimes, each gauge has its own voltage limiter. More often, one limiter serves all gauges, even though it may be attached to the fuel gauge.

If there is only one limiter (check the car's wiring diagram in the service manual), it will affect all gauge readings. Readings may be high, low, or erratic. If the gauges move from one spot to another on the dials, the voltage limiter surely is the cause. To test it, set a voltmeter to read 12 volts DC. Attach its red lead to the terminal of the temperature sending unit (in the engine block) and its black lead to ground. The ignition switch should be on for the test and the sending unit's lead left attached. In a car with a 12-volt electrical system, the voltage reading should jump between 0 and 7 volts (some specifications call for 11 volts) if the voltage limiter is good. The same test can be made with a test light connected in the same way as the voltmeter. If the light flashes on and off, the limiter is good.

If you have to replace the voltage limiter or one of the gauges, and it cannot be reached from below the instrument panel, the entire instrument cluster must be taken out. And to do that on most cars, the steering column housing must be removed. Consider that a shop job.

A *poor ground* makes any gauge read too high (except a tachometer, which reads too low). Attach a jumper from a known good ground to the back of the gauge. If it then reads okay, install a permanent grounding lead from the gauge's mounting screw. Sometimes, merely grounding part of the instrument cluster fixes the problem.

Modern instruments are thermally operated. They read voltage by the heat that it produces. That makes them immune to rapid fluctuations in the sending unit data. The thermal nature of the gauges also smooths out oscillations in voltage limiter output. They are thus better indicators of average fuel level, temperature, etc. You need not delve into how gauges work. The best cure for a faulty instrument is to replace it.

When ground continuity to a thermally-operated electrical instrument is lost, the instrument can be permanently distorted by the needle moving to an extreme reading. A few instruments can be readjusted,

Voltage Limiter Test

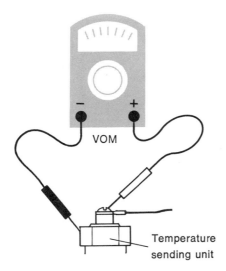

VOM

Temperature
sending unit

but most must be replaced once a good ground has been restored.

Fuel gauge. The most common trouble in a fuel gauge is a poor ground in the instrument or its sending unit. Since the test for grounding is easy to make at the instrument, it should be performed first.

If you must, look for fuel gauge trouble at the sending unit; but be warned that it is quite inaccessible. Most fuel tank sending units are atop the gas tank. Often, the tank must be removed to get at them. If a fuel gauge problem is traced to the sending unit, take the car to a mechanic. Fuel tank removal is difficult and dangerous.

Temperature gauge. Temperature sending units are easy to get at. To test one, eliminate it from the circuit by removing its lead. With the ignition key on, prop the lead in the air and read the temperature instrument. Its needle should move to the extreme hot side and stay there. Next, ground the lead. The needle should move quickly to the extreme cold side and stay there. If it does those two things, the gauge and connecting wiring are all right. Replace the sending unit with a new one. Most often, a defective sending unit shows too low a reading.

Indicator lights. If an indicator—or "idiot"—light for engine temperature, oil pressure, or charging system does not work, see whether its bulb will burn when the ignition key is switched to "on" or to "start." If not, replace the bulb by unsnapping it and its socket from behind the instrument panel.

If the bulb is good but the temperature light shows a cold reading even though the engine is warm, replace the sending unit. Do the same if you get a hot reading too soon after the engine is started.

If the oil pressure light ever comes on, stop the engine *immediately.* Even then, the engine, may have been dam-

To test the temperature sending unit, remove the lead and keep it aloft. Turn on the ignition switch and watch the temperature gauge—the needle should move to the hot side and stay there. Now, ground the lead—the needle should move to the cold side and stay there.

aged, because the light does not signal a lowering oil pressure. Check the oil level. Drive on only if you are absolutely sure that the problem is in the indicator system rather than in the lubrication system.

A sending unit that does not activate the oil indicator light might be the problem. If the bulb is good, remove the wire from the sending unit and ground it. The light should go on. If it does, clean the sender's terminal and tighten it a little in the oil pressure opening. Reconnect the lead and try again. If the indicator lamp still does not light, replace the sending unit.

If you have the right tools along, you can remove the sending unit to check for a clogged passage. That unit is often located on top or below the oil filter, next to the engine block. Like a temperature sending unit, it has one wire leading from it. If its pressure opening is clogged with sludge, clean it out and reinstall it. Start the engine carefully. If the oil pressure light does not go out immediately, switch off the engine. The lubrication system must be checked with a pressure gauge, a shop job unless you have the right gauge.

If the oil level is all right, check oil pres-

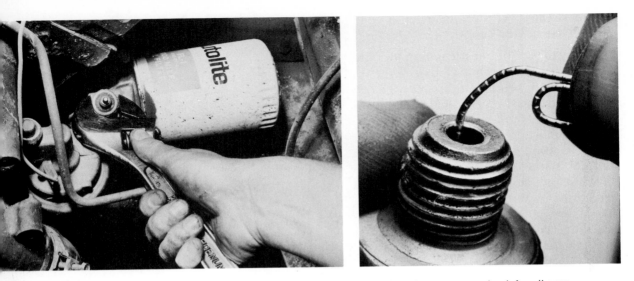

If you know your car has oil, but the oil pressure idiot light comes on, check for oil pressure before continuing. With the engine idling, loosen the oil pressure sending unit (*left*) just enough to let oil leak past the threads. No leakage means no pressure. The orifice in the unit may be clogged; if you can remove the sending unit, clean the hole with a bent paper clip (*right*). Never drive when your car has no oil pressure.

sure by loosening the oil pressure sending unit. Start the engine and idle it. Oil seepage around the sending unit threads indicates pressure; it is safe to drive to a service station.

If there is no oil pressure, have your car towed to a shop for checking and repairs.

When testing, consider engine oil temperature. With hot oil, the sending unit should be moderately loose. With cold, stiff-flowing oil the unit should be looser still.

Ammeter. The ammeter is independent of the other instruments. It is wired directly to the car's battery lead. When current flows in or out of the battery, the ammeter registers the amount of flow. Any ammeter problem must be corrected by replacing the instrument. Fortunately, ammeter trouble is rare.

Speedometer. This is not an electric instrument. Most speedometer problems center around the flexible drive cable, located inside the transmission housing, which connects to a gear at the transmission and turns with the rear wheels and drivetrain. Lack of lubrication may make the cable catch with every revolution and then jump free. That makes the speedometer needle surge. To lubricate the cable, remove the screw-on collar at the end that fastens to the speedometer and pull the cable just out of the speedometer head behind the instrument panel. Squirt special graphite speedometer lubricant into the housing. Reconnect the cable, fitting the square cable end into the recess in the speedometer driveshaft before fastening the housing and collar. Then, draw the housing tight again.

Speedometers and tachometers are delicate instruments. We do not recommend that you do any more than remove them from the car and take them to a specialist when they need repairs.

TROUBLESHOOTING GAUGES

SYMPTOM	CAUSE	CURE
One or all gauges read too high	Faulty ground on gauge or instrument cluster (tachometer will read too low)	Repair ground or install grounding wire
	Defective voltage limiter	Check limiter as described in text; replace if defective
	Poorly grounded sending unit	Remove sending unit, clean mount, and replace with good ground
	Defective sending unit	Test as described in text; replace if defective
	Defective gauge	Replace if no other cause is found
One or all gauges read too low	Defective voltage limiter	Test; replace if defective
	Defective sending unit	Common for temperature sending units; test as described in text, replace if defective
	Defective gauge	Replace if no other cause is found
Indicator light out	Burned-out bulb	Replace bulb
	Defective sending unit	Test as described in text; replace if defective
Indicator light will not go out	Defective sending unit	Test as described in text; replace if defective
	Charging system not charging	See chapter on charging system

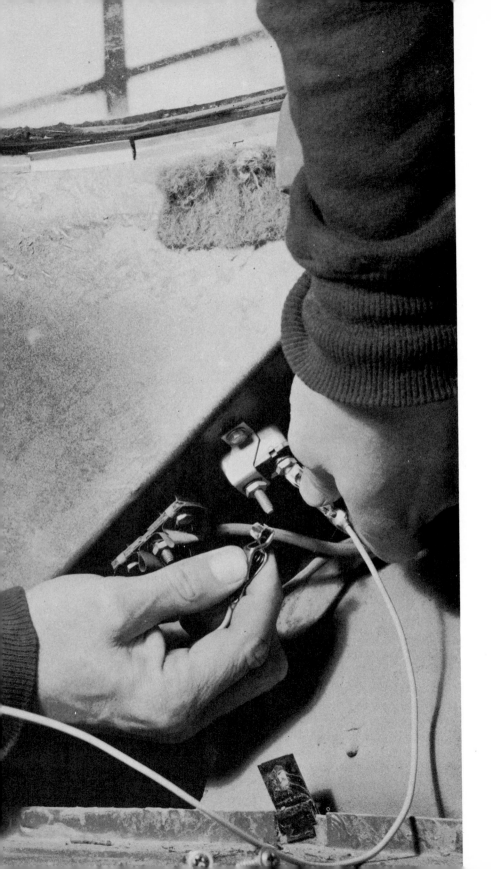

15

Servicing Power Accessories

Power steering, power brakes, power windows, power tops, and all those other seemingly complicated options have been around a long time. Most of us leave their service to professionals, probably because of their apparent complexity. Yet, you can do much of the maintenance and servicing of those systems. You also can diagnose many of the troubles that you cannot fix yourself. How much you can do may be limited by your lack of specialized tools. For example, it hardly would pay to spend $30 for a pressure-tester to check out a malfunctioning power steering pump when a shop may find and fix the trouble for about that much.

Do not try to overhaul the power components themselves. That is a job for professional mechanics, because some formerly simple jobs have become tougher as cars have become more complex. For instance, power steering belts that squeal on turns need tightening. Years ago, you could adjust such a belt with about a half

inch of play. Today, the specifications call for certain strand tensions, and you need a belt tension tester to do the job right.

Caution: Avoid working on a power accessory in a car that is still under warranty. The warranty on that power system would be voided by your work.

POWER STEERING

Most large cars now have this helpful feature. Power steering consists of a hydraulic power-booster arrangement in the steering system that uses oil to help you steer the car. Since straight-ahead driving is a series of shallow turns, the power is taking over many times a minute while you drive. Power steering also resists whatever the road tries to do to the car's wheels. For that reason, some say it takes away the "feel of the road."

The system is powered by a hydraulic pump driven by a belt from a pulley on the engine crankshaft. Oil under as much as 1200 psi pressure is routed from the pump

249

to the power steering unit. If the power steering fails, the car can be steered mechanically, but with considerably more effort.

The power steering pump runs whenever the engine does. A few pumps are driven from the back of the generator, though most are driven from the crankshaft pulley. The pump contains a reservoir of hydraulic oil. A built-in filter on some cars keeps the oil clean.

The system also incorporates a pressure relief valve, which limits power assist to what the steering and power components can handle.

Two types of power steering units are used today: the linkage-type and the integral-type.

In the *linkage-type* unit, hydraulic pressure extends or retracts a hydraulic power piston. The piston is attached to the steering linkage and gives it a push or a pull to help make the turn. Control is through a valve that is part of the linkage. When you turn the steering wheel in one direction, the valve is pushed off center. As soon as the steering linkage catches up with the turn, the valve comes back to its centered position again, and power assist ceases.

Integral-type power steering does the same thing, but it is contained within the steering gear at the base of the steering column.

Both types require a certain amount of manual steering effort before power assist takes over. That manual effort is specified for each car. If the system is outside specifications, steering can be troublesome. Adjusting the effort is not a do-it-yourself job.

Occasionally, power steering problems affect handling. For example, when the steering wheel pulls steadily to one side, you normally would suspect out-of-line

TROUBLESHOOTING POWER STEERING		
SYMPTOM	**CAUSE**	**CURE**
Oil leak	Hoses, hose connections, or reservoir gasket	Fix as described in text
	Aging oil seals	Try chemical transmission sealer; or, see a mechanic
Squeal when turning wheels	Loose or glazed belt	Tighten loose belt. Replace cracked or glazed belt
Gear-growling when turning wheels sharply	Low on hydraulic fluid	Fill reservoir to proper level. Bleed system, if necessary
All other functional complaints	System components out of adjustment or worn out	Take car to a shop

wheels, a front tire with low pressure, or a dragging brake. But a faulty power steering system can make a car pull to one side too. Moreover, some power steering abnormalities are created by front tires that are running on too low air pressure. Correct that condition before blaming the power steering.

With all its workings, power steering gives very little trouble. That is fortunate for us do-it-yourself mechanics, for there is little we can do to repair a faulty power steering system. Following is a checklist of common power steering symptoms that require immediate attention by a mechanic — not by the do-it-yourselfer:

- Pulling to one side;
- Play in the steering wheel;
- Hard or erratic steering;
- Disappearance of all steering effort;
- No power assist in one or both directions;
- Jerking action when turning;
- Steering does not return to center after a turn;
- Increase in turning effort on fast turns;
- Squeals or growls from the pump (a mild hissing sound is normal).

Here are some measures you can take short of tearing into the components.

Fluid level. Check the fluid level while the system is warm by removing the cap on the power steering pump. Unlike checking engine oil, the engine may be running while you do this. Some caps contain a dipstick with "empty" and "full" marks. Other systems simply specify that the level reach a certain point on the reservoir. Make this check each time you check engine oil level so that the level of hydraulic fluid never falls below the prescribed point.

If the fluid level is low, add Type A or Type F automatic transmission fluid — except for Chrysler products, which require a special fluid.

On some power steering systems, the reservoir cap has a built-in dipstick for easy fluid level checks. Perform this check when the engine is hot.

If the level should get low, the power steering pump could run out of fluid and pump air. Then you would hear a gear-growling sound from the pump and steering would become hard. Running dry is tough on a pump's oil seals and may bring on leaking. Add oil at the first opportunity. Meanwhile, avoid sharp turns, which produce the sound.

After refilling a power steering system that has run dry, you may have to bleed air out of it. To do that, drive each front wheel onto a newspaper — that prevents tire scrub against the pavement. With the engine running, turn the steering wheel all the way to one side, then all the way to the other. After the first two turns, inspect the fluid level. If there had been much air in the system, you will have to add fluid before making more turns.

Leaks. This is the most common problem with old power steering systems. Such leaks are small to start with; perhaps the fluid level shows a drop only over a period of months. But the leaks eventually get worse. They are caused by rubber oil seals that become brittle and worn, and thus give under pressure. Seals are located at the oil pump drive shaft, in the control valve (in linkage-type units), and in the power unit.

Fixing a leaking seal is a job for a professional mechanic, but you can first try a temporary chemical repair of your own. Pour a can of automatic transmission sealer into the power steering reservoir, as directed on the can. Drive the car for two weeks and see whether the leak disappears. Such sealers sometimes soften the rubber seals to give them new life. But even if they work, the improvement is temporary. Eventually the seals will have to be replaced.

Other sources of leaks are the hydraulic hoses. Leaks at connections usually can be fixed by tightening. Leaks through the walls require replacement of the hose.

Another easily-fixed source of fluid leakage is the gasket around the top of the oil pump reservoir. Simply remove the cover and install a new gasket.

Locate power steering fluid leaks by spreading newspaper under the front of the car. Idle the engine and turn the steering wheel several times over a 15-minute span. Spots on the paper mean leaks.

Locating a more hidden power steering leak can be exasperating. First, get underneath the car and wipe up all signs of oil leakage on the power steering system and engine. Lay clean newspaper underneath the front of the car. Start the engine and run it for 15 minutes, turning the steering in both directions every few minutes. Watch the newspaper for signs of drips. When you find an oil drip, look above it on the car for its source. That is not as easy as it sounds. Oil can run for some distance along parts before falling onto the newspaper. Look especially around the base of the steering column, on the oil pump, and along all hydraulic hoses. If the system has an external control valve and power piston, look there too.

Leaks in control valves may require only a simple, inexpensive adjustment. Sometimes, though, the control valve needs a complete overhaul, which can be more costly.

Sometimes leaks in external-type power steering units are caused by scoring of the piston shaft. Examine the shaft from underneath the car. Its finish should be bright and smooth. If it is rough or scored, you have found the problem; the entire power unit will have to be replaced by a professional mechanic at considerable cost.

Belt tension. Tension on the power steering pump can make the belt squeal every time heavy power assist is needed. When the steering wheel is turned until the wheels are in their locked position, you are bound to hear stress sounds from the system. But if you hear them at other times, the belt needs attention. Have it adjusted or adjust it yourself to the specified tension.

Adjustment is normally made by loosening several bolts on the power steering pump, levering the pump back, and hold-

Inspect the power steering drive belt twice a year for proper tension and for wear. Replace the belt if it is glazed or cracked.

POWER BRAKES

Power brakes generally need little service. All use engine vacuum to boost foot braking power. The vacuum is created by the engine's intake manifold. In late-model cars, enough vacuum for three or four dead-engine stops is stored in a small vacuum reservoir. Should stored-up vacuum be depleted, you still can stop, but the pedal effort required is far higher.

Power brakes employ a little vacuum to do a lot of work by means of a large vacuum-operated diaphragm. When the brake pedal is pushed, a vacuum line between intake manifold and booster unit comes into play. A valve arrangement inside the power booster unit (located on the engine side of the firewall, opposite the brake pedal) lets engine vacuum draw some of the air out of a chamber on one side of the internal diaphragm. Atmospheric pressure pushing on the other side of the diaphragm gives the master brake cylinder piston a strong nudge, building up hydraulic pressure in the braking system. This pressure

ing it at correct tension while you tighten the bolts. Pry against the pump body, not the pulley or shaft. If the pump is made of stamped steel rather than cast iron, use a wood pry bar to spread the load.

A glazed or cracked power steering drive belt should be replaced with a new one. The job may require removal of all of the engine's belts. If any of them are glazed or cracked too, replace them.

TROUBLESHOOTING POWER BRAKES

SYMPTOM	CAUSE	CURE
Lack of power assist	Vacuum leak in lines or check valve	Find leak and repair or replace defective part
	Vacuum leak inside power booster	Have power booster repaired or replaced; not a do-it-yourself job
	Low engine vacuum	Check engine with vacuum gauge; if below 14 inches, tune engine
All other braking symptoms	Hydraulic or wheel brake system malfunctions are likely causes	Check brakes as described in the chapter on brake service

is added to that furnished directly by your foot. Bellows- and piston-operated power brakes are also in use, but the diaphragm type is by far the most common.

Except for the power booster unit, the rest of the system is conventional; a power brake assembly has a master cylinder just like the one used with manual brakes.

Two types of units are found on U.S.-built cars: pedal-assisted and self-contained hydraulic-vacuum units.

The *pedal-assisted type* is connected through linkage to the brake pedal arm and acts like an extra foot that helps you push on the brake pedal.

Most modern units are the *self-contained type*. They permit lowering the brake pedal and reducing its travel—one of the biggest advantages of power brakes. With the level of the brake pedal close to that of the accelerator pedal, you can get your foot on the brakes quicker in an emergency.

Power brakes suffer the same problems that ordinary foot-powered hydraulic brakes do. If the brakes are not working properly, the trouble is usually with the standard portion of the braking system. Only after you have checked the standard portion should you look to the power portion.

If the power is not working, the brake pedal will feel hard, and stopping will seem difficult. Other problems include failure to release, grabbing, and slowness in releasing. Repairs depend on what type of unit your car has.

Testing the system. To test the operation of power brakes with an outside-mounted check valve, start with the engine off. Apply the brake a few times to use up any stored vacuum. Then apply the brakes. Hold them down while you start the engine. Notice whether the brake pedal stays in place or sinks farther toward the floor

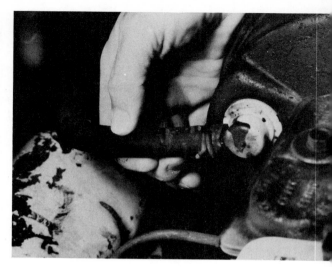

Vacuum leaks due to loose clamps or worn hoses often crop up at the point where the power booster vacuum hose is attached to the booster.

when the vacuum reaches it. If the power is working, the pedal should sink somewhat and then remain firm. A brake pedal that does not sink when the engine is started indicates a power booster problem. Check the vacuum hose from end to end, including its connections with the intake manifold and the power booster.

Next, let up on the brake pedal and idle the engine for about a minute before switching it off. Wait 90 seconds. Then step on the brake pedal three times. If the pedal pressure does not increase each time you step on the pedal, suspect a vacuum leak in the vacuum reservoir or in the check valve.

You can test the check valve on a separately mounted power booster; it probably will be located somewhere near the intake manifold. Remove the vacuum hose from the power brake unit, place your finger over the end of the hose, and have a helper start the engine and run it at idle. You should feel vacuum sucking your finger against the hose. Have your helper switch the engine off while you leave your finger on the hose to see whether the vacuum holds. If it does, the vacuum reservoir and check valve are okay. If it does not, the check valve should be replaced. A shop probably should do that.

Power boosters with *integral check valves* cannot be tested this way. You can, though, inspect all of the vacuum hoses and hose connections for tightness. Tighten hose clamps, if there are any. Replace hoses that are soft and collapsed. Such hoses could stop vacuum short of your brake booster. Remove the hose from the vacuum fitting on the engine's intake

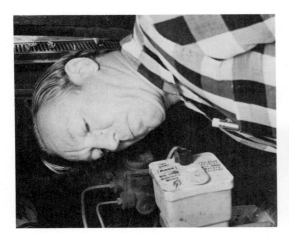

You can hear a leak in the vacuum booster. With the engine idling, lean over until your ear is near the unit. Beware of moving engine parts.

manifold and push a wire into it to be sure it is open.

Ask your helper to start the engine again and hold down on the brake pedal lightly while you listen for a vacuum leak in the hose or around the power booster. If you hear a steady, tell-tale hiss from inside the power booster, take the car directly to the shop for repair or replacement of the booster. A leaking vacuum hose or connection is something you can fix yourself either by tightening or replacing the hose.

Improper release. Occasionally, a power brake will not release completely after the brakes have been applied. That could be caused by a restricted line in the hydraulic system, a misaligned connection between the power booster and the master cylinder and brake pedal, or some other internal trouble. All are shop jobs.

Hard pedal. A power brake with a hard pedal can be caused by conventional brake problems. If the brake shoes become glazed and fail to grab the brake drums or discs with sufficient friction, the car will stop reluctantly, power brakes or not. (See the chapter on servicing brakes for the repair.) On the other hand, low engine vacuum can weaken power-brake assist. Test for it with a vacuum gauge hooked to the intake manifold. If the vacuum at idle does not come up to 14 inches, the engine needs a good tune-up, maybe more. That should cure the hard pedal, too.

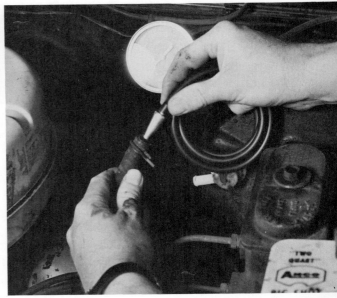

If power brakes work erratically, test the amount of vacuum reaching the booster. Remove the hose from the booster, attach a vacuum gauge and idle the engine. Minimum vacuum should be 14 inches.

Grabbing. An oft-heard power braking complaint is over-eager power assist. Barely lay your foot on the pedal and the car screeches to a halt. That can be caused by a grabbing brake lining. If so, one wheel will slide and leave a black skid mark while the others roll. If the normal braking system is not the cause, let a shop work on the power booster.

Power brake maintenance. Keep the master cylinder topped off with brake fluid. If the power booster has an accessible air cleaner, keep it clean. Check brake pedal free play; it should be the same as specified in the service manual for your car, generally 1/16 to 1/4 inch. Some power brakes should have no free play. At least 1½ inches of travel should remain under the brake pedal when you apply the brakes with the parking brake off. If you have to pump the brakes to get that much pedal clearance, the wheel brakes need adjusting. That is rare with self-adjusting brakes, however. (For information on adjusting brakes, see the chapter on brake service.)

Cars without power brakes can have them with the addition of a power booster unit from an inexpensive kit. The installation is covered in the chapter on servicing brakes.

ELECTRICALLY OPERATED ACCESSORIES

Many automotive power accessories are either electrically operated or electrically controlled. Those include clocks, power windows, power seats, power tops, power door locks, and more. Many of these malfunctions are caused by failures in the electrical systems or operating motors. Before you service any of the small power accessories, be sure that you understand the basic electrical testing procedures covered in the chapter on car wiring and lighting.

In brief, the basic electrical tools are: a pair of jumper leads; test light; continuity tester; and a volt-ohm-milliammeter (or VOM, which can also serve as a continuity tester).

The basic electrical tests are for live circuit, open circuit, short circuit, and ground circuit. You also may need to make a continuity test of the fuse, bulb, and motor, and a voltage-drop test for resistance under load.

One of the first tests is to see whether the fuses or circuit breakers that are supposed to protect power accessory units are stopping the electricity before it reaches the power accessory.

Switches serving power accessories also can become short-circuited to ground or open-circuited. If so, they are "off" even though switched "on." The simplest switch check is to jumper across the switch terminals. If that cures the trouble, the switch is at fault.

Fuses should be the first check when you search for the cause of a malfunction in electrically operated accessories. The fuse at left has blown.

If all else fails, you can connect your long jumper lead to the positive post of the battery and touch the other end to the power terminal of the electrical accessory, thus bridging all switches, fuses, circuit breakers, and wiring in between. Then, if nothing happens, the trouble is in the accessory itself.

Sluggish operation of accessories can be caused by too much voltage drop in the insulated or ground circuits to them, by some mechanical problem in the units themselves or by a partially discharged battery.

Intermittent operation is hardest to solve — it can be either electrical or mechanical. Visual inspections are probably the most productive. Look especially for loose connections, faulty switches, poor grounds, and mechanical binding.

Car Clock

Like other timepieces, car clocks need regular cleaning. If you neglect to clean and lubricate the clock every two years, as manufacturers specify, sooner or later the clock will stop — usually on a cold night. The clock's lubricating oil congeals and in the morning you find the piece dead. When the car warms, the clock may run again, but it is no longer dependable.

Electrical trouble may also keep a car clock from running. Car clocks are electrically-wound and spring-driven. Winding is done by a tiny motor or solenoid. Instead of rotating fast like a regular motor, a winding motor makes only a partial revolution with each wind-up. It winds the clock against a small spring, stretching it. As the spring relaxes, a pair of electrical contacts come together. When these touch, the winding motor snaps on momentarily and rewinds the spring. The contacts again separate and the winding motor stops.

If the tiny fuse that protects the clock's electrical circuit should blow, the clock cannot be wound. Burned or dirty electrical contacts also prevent the winding of the clock. In these cases, even though the clock may not be dirty or in need of lubrication, it cannot run.

Check the fuse first. Sometimes it is an in-line fuse in electrical lead to the back of the clock. In other models, the fuse is in the fuse block. It is usually a 2- or 3-amp fuse. A new one costs about a dime. Remove and check or replace the fuse with one known to be good. If you hear the clock winding mechanism go into action with a "ping" as you insert the new fuse, you have found the trouble.

If the winding mechanism is stiff from lack of attention, it may soon blow the new fuse and the clock will stop again. Winding motors seldom give trouble. But if one does, a new clock is the best fix.

Routine car clock service involves taking the clock out and disassembling the works from the case. You need not know anything about the innards. Just give the works a simple cleaning and a careful oiling — or have the job done by an auto speedometer-clock service shop.

To find the authorized repair shop for your car's clock, you must know what make it is. Only two manufacturers — Borg Instruments and General Time Corporation — make clocks for U.S. cars. Look for the clock manufacturer's code letters stamped on the back of the clock case. Borg clocks are stamped "Borg Instruments"; General Time clocks are stamped "GT."

Getting the clock out is the hardest part of the job. Some come out from the front of the instrument panel, while others come out from the rear. Before you begin to take out the clock, remove the fuse. Otherwise, if the lead should contact a metal part of the car, the fuse will blow out.

Generally, removing two screws or nuts

Cleaning a Car Clock

1. Remove the clock from the dashboard and un-bend the tabs that secure the cover.

2. Wind the clock manually to see if it runs.

3. Clean the contacts with No. 400 sandpaper.

4. Pour solvent over the works. Keep the hands, clockface and winding motor coils dry.

5. With a toothpick, lightly oil bearings, levers and pins, but not the winding clutch or motor.

from the rear of the clock allows it to be taken out. Do that while lying on the floor of the car with your feet up over the front seat. You will need a trouble light propped on the floor to see with. Be careful that the mounting screws or nuts do not fall behind the instrument panel, where you cannot reach them. Sometimes the car radio or speedometer must come out before the clock.

Cleaning and lubrication. Removing the case from the face gives access to the clock's innards. Some clocks are put together with screws, but most have bent-metal locking tabs like those in metal toys. Those can be straightened with pliers and rebent after assembly. Disassembly of the clock's working parts is not necessary for cleaning and lubrication.

Locate the wind-up mechanism and wind it by pushing on the movable spring arm with a small screwdriver. Be careful not to touch the delicate balance wheel. Look at the contacts carefully as they separate. If they are not clean and bright, sand them gently with folded, fine sandpaper. Degrease the contacts with a cloth dipped in solvent. Do not break them off or you will need a new clock.

Now try the clock by connecting it to a car battery with jumper wires. Hook one jumper from the clock's power terminal to the battery's positive terminal. Hook the other jumper from the clock frame to the battery's negative terminal. As soon as you touch the second lead, the clock should wind and run, indicating that the points are making good contact.

Place the clock on newspapers. Blow out dust by puffing at the works. Then, pour naphtha, carburetor cleaner, or other grease solvent into a small bowl, and use a small brush to flush solvent over the clock's works. Keep solvent off the motor windings as much as possible, and off

the contacts, which have already been degreased. Do not get any on the clock face, hands, or crystal. When everything is clean, shake out excess solvent and allow the works to dry.

Next, put a few drops of fine machine oil (not motor oil) into a spoon. Dip a wooden toothpick into the oil and carefully touch the oil-wetted end of the toothpick to the moving parts of the clock that need lubrication. Over-oiling can be as bad as under-oiling—too much oil collects dust.

Oil every metal-to-metal bearing and gear. That includes the bearings on the escapement lever. Lightly oil the escapement wheel pins that contact the lever. Oil the moving parts of the winding mechanism but do not get oil on the electrical contacts, the support plates, or the balance wheel spring. Also, do not oil the wind-up clutch mechanism—the one-way ratcheting clutch that lets the clock wind freely and yet applies spring pressure to the main drive gear. If you oil the clutch, it may slip and lose its winding action. Do oil the tiny clutch ratchet-lever and bearings, though.

If the clock is four years old or more, bend the stationary coil spring mount ever so slightly away from the spring. That stretches the spring and restores its original tension. One, or at most two, coils of stretch is enough. Too much stretch will cause the clock to have trouble winding fully.

Finally, reassemble the clock case. Make sure that the power terminal in back of the clock is centered in the insulating rubber grommet and not shorting against the clock shell. To check cold weather operation, put the clock in the freezer, bring it out cold, and connect it to a car battery. The clock should wind and run, unless frost forms to prevent it.

Mount the clock back in the instrument panel in reverse of the way it came out. If it helps to connect the lead to the clock's power terminal before mounting the clock, do so. But do not install the fuse until the clock is mounted. You should hear that encouraging "ping" when the fuse is finally installed, telling you that the clock is winding.

Most car clocks have automatic speed-up and slow-down linkages. Your clock may run too fast after service. Each time you set the clock back, it adjusts to run more slowly. Thus within a week it should be keeping good time.

Old clocks have a speed adjustment that is accessible from outside the shell. Move the adjusting lever toward "S" to slow the clock down, and toward "F" to speed it up.

TROUBLESHOOTING ELECTRIC POWER WINDOWS

SYMPTOM	CAUSE	CURE
Sluggish operation	Binding window glass or lift mechanism	Lubricate window channels with silicone spray; have lift mechanism adjusted to lift window squarely with channels
All windows do not operate	Open circuit to switches	Check fuse or circuit breaker for power window circuit; check for loose connections between ignition switch and fuse block, circuit breaker and main window control switch; repair or replace defective component
	Dead battery	Charge or replace battery and check charging system
One window does not operate	Binding or locked glass or lift mechanism	Remove door trim panel and inspect mechanism; if tight or locked, lubricate, or have glass adjusted or lift mechanism replaced to correct binding
	Open circuit to switch	Check for voltage at switch battery terminal; repair open circuit
	Open circuit from switch to lift motor	Check for voltage at lift motor when switch is moved to "up" or "down" position; check for open individual circuit breaker; repair

Power Windows

Power windows are continual problems to keep operating. Most power windows today are operated by electric motors, one for each window. The motors are inside the door, at the bottom. To get at them you must remove the door trim panel. (See various ways to do this in the chapter on adjusting doors, hoods, and decklids.)

If only one window acts up, the trouble probably is behind the door trim panel. If all windows are acting up, suspect the circuit breaker, fuse, ignition switch, or wiring circuit between the battery and the main window switch on the driver's door or console.

Power windows have one main insulated circuit supplying each switch with

SYMPTOM	CAUSE	CURE
	Defective lift motor	Connect jumper from battery to lift motor lead; if motor does not run, remove and check further; replace defective motor
	Lift motor or car door not grounded	Ground lift motor to car frame with jumper; if window operates, correct poor ground
Fuse blows or circuit breaker cycles when just one window is operated	Motor armature shorted or grounded	Remove motor and have armature tested; replace defective motor
	Short circuit in wiring to lift motor	Install new wires
	Shorted control switch	Replace switch
Fuse blows or circuit breaker cycles when any window is operated	Shorted wiring in portion of circuit common to all windows	Replace shorted wiring
Tailgate window does not operate	Any of causes above	See above
	Interlock switch not closing	Check continuity of interlock switch with its arm held in closed position; adjust or replace switch

battery power. For safety reasons, that circuit should be routed through the ignition switch so that the windows can operate only when the ignition is on. Each window also has two switched circuits, one for running the window up, another for running it down. If the window goes up when it should go down, reversing the switch leads will fix it.

Each single switch thus has three terminals: "battery," "up," and "down." Whenever the ignition is on, the "battery" terminal should be live and should show battery voltage to ground. If it does, any trouble probably is in the switch or the motor. When the switch is moved up, the "up" terminal should come alive and register battery voltage on a grounded voltmeter or test light. When the switch is moved down, the "down" terminal should come alive. If that happens, everything is all right up to the switch. Concentrate your attention on the motor and mechanical raising-lowering mechanism.

A power window can fail because of a poor ground at the motor switch. Connect a jumper lead from a good ground directly to the lift motor. If the window then works, find the poor ground and fix it.

In cars that have seen much use, the biggest power window problem is the lift motor. Motors are noted for developing internal electrical problems caused by overloading and long-term use. Bring battery and ground jumpers directly to the motor leads to see whether the motor runs. In lift motors with three leads, the third lead is an external ground. On some circuits the door or master switch is grounded to reverse the motor. Before bringing a "hot" jumper to a lead, make sure it is not a ground lead by checking with an ohmmeter or continuity tester for ground continuity. If there is some resistance to ground, it is safe to attach the "hot" jumper to that lead. If the motor does not

A spray of silicone lubricant into the window channels will cure many a binding power window.

run, replace it. When you reverse the two leads, the lift motor should run in the opposite direction.

Lubrication. Window lift mechanisms need lubrication. Do it while you have access to them. Because of the complex levers connecting the lift mechanism to the window, it is easier to do all lubricating with the lift in the door. (Removal may prove to be a job for a professional mechanic.) If any lift motors or mechanisms are worn out, replace them with new ones.

If you remove the lift motor yourself, be careful. As you pull out the motor, the spring-loaded lift arm can come down on your hands like a mousetrap. To avoid that, drill a small hole through both the inside door panel and lift arm or crank, and insert a nail. Or, position the lift arm by turning the motor shaft coupling until you can pinch the arm to the door panel with a pair of locking pliers.

Window binding may be in the glass rather than in the lift mechanism. If it is, the window probably will move, but it will stop part way up. You can help it along by pulling on the glass. Eliminate the binding before the lift mechanism or lift motor is damaged by overwork.

Spray silicone aerosol dry lube on the window channels. If that does not cure the binding, have a shop adjust the lift mechanism.

In some early-model power windows, an electric motor pumps fluid to hydraulic cylinders at each window. Solenoid valves at the cylinder control up and down operation. Servicing such a system is much like servicing electric door locks (described later in this chapter).

Power Tailgate Windows

Station wagons with electric tailgate window lifts operate like other power windows, except that they have an interlock switch that prevents window operation when the tailgate is open. If the interlock switch fails or does not close fully, the tailgate window will not move in either direction. If the window jams while it is up, lean hard against the tailgate to close it fully while trying to lower the window. If the window then works, the interlock

To check the tailgate lift-motor circuit, place a test light across the motor leads. When the accessory's switch is on, the bulb should light.

switch needs attention. If you can open the tailgate, look for the interlock switch along the bottom or side. Operate it manually with the gate open while a helper tries to raise the window. If the window works (do not force it out very far) the switch needs adjusting or replacing.

The way you adjust an interlock switch depends on its location. Some are buried inside the latch mechanism. The main point to keep in mind is that the switch's contacts probably are not being moved sufficiently when the tailgate closes. If adjusting for more movement does not work, the cure is switch replacement. With access into the tailgate limited, even with the trim panel removed, replacement may be a shop job.

Power Seat

In most cases, electric motors and switch controls, as in power windows, activate power seats. Six-way power seats—the most common type—may have one motor or three. The six positions are achieved in the three-motor types by forward and reverse rotation of each motor: one motor controls forward and backward positioning, another controls up-and-down positioning, and the third controls forward and rearward tilt. Troubles here are rare.

In a single-motor, six-way power seat, a transmission with solenoid-controlled shifting engages the motor through flexible drive cables for all six seat movements. The motor runs forward or in reverse, as necessary.

The mechanical linkage in a power seat is simply a worm drive through a system of jacks underneath the seat. It is almost trouble-free. Most problems involve the switch, the motor, or the transmission. Switch repair involves simple replacement. Motor repair also involves replacement, but with the seat removed. Re-

TROUBLESHOOTING ELECTRIC POWER SEAT

SYMPTOM	CAUSE	CURE
Seat does not move, but lights dim when switch is on	Transmission locked	Remove seat; examine transmismission and replace if defective
	Short circuit in wiring	Check wiring to seat and beneath seat for short; repair short circuit; remove seat, replace defective motor
Seat does not move, no power draw	Open circuit	Check fuse, circuit breaker, ignition switch and its wiring, seat control switch, underseat wiring, and motor for open circuit; repair or replace defective component
	Defective motor relay	Replace relay
Motor runs, but seat does not move	Motor coupling slipping	Remove seat and tighten or replace coupling
	Transmission solenoids not working	Remove seat and check solenoid electrical circuit; try shifting solenoid manually; repair circuit or replace defective solenoid
Seat operates in all but one direction	Defective seat control switch	Jump across switch terminals to activate vertical movement; replace defective switch
	Vertical motor solenoid or circuit faulty	Remove seat and test motor, solenoid, and circuit; replace defective component
	Defective control relay	Remove seat and jumper across relay to activate vertical operation; replace defective relay

placing a solenoid is easy too, once you find the faulty one.

The control switch operates through a 20- or 30-ampere circuit breaker. If switch, breaker, or motor drop out, the seat will not operate. Nor will it operate if the drive mechanism locks up. Since checking for locked gears is easy, do that first. While trying to operate the power seat at night with the headlights on, watch for the lights to dim. The engine should not be running, but the ignition key may have to be on to make the seat work. If the lights do not dim, the problem is electrical. If the lights do dim, the problem most likely is mechanical.

The proper way to work on the power seat mechanism is with the seat out of the car and inverted on a newspaper-covered workbench. Label each wire with tape as you remove it from the control switch so you can get it back right.

Make electrical checks of the fuse, circuit breaker, and wiring that lead to the power seat before you remove the seat and make electrical checks beneath it.

Convertible Top

The mechanism that lowers and raises a convertible top is part electrical and part hydraulic. An electric motor drives a hydraulic pump. This then operates hydraulic pistons on either side of the top to move the hardware up or down. The direction of pump rotation controls the direction of motion.

The top's electrical system is similar to that of a power window. When a problem arises, check the battery, wiring, circuit breaker, switch, and motor. The hydraulic

TROUBLESHOOTING POWER TOPS

SYMPTOM	CAUSE	CURE
Top does not operate, no power draw	Open circuit	Check wiring to switch, circuit breaker, and motor for open circuits; repair or replace faulty component
Top does not operate, but lights dim when switch is on and motor does not run	Locked or binding top mechanism	Examine top hardware for free movement; see that luggage is not in way of top movement; may be a shop job
Above condition, but motor runs	Low on fluid	Fill hydraulic fluid reservoir, check for leaks
Top operates one way but not the other	Defective control switch or wiring	Replace defective part

system is similar to power steering hydraulics. Service you can do yourself consists of keeping the fluid level up to the mark. Add Type A or Type F transmission fluid to the reservoir behind the rear seat. If you need to add much fluid, look for leaks in the hydraulic lines, connections, and cylinders. Also, carefully oil the top's hardware joints.

Speed Control

Increasingly popular on modern cars, these complex power accessories hold the car at a preselected speed without driver control.

Making the numerous adjustments called for by a malfunctioning speed control is a shop job. To keep a wayward unit from acting up while driving, remove the control's fuse from the fuse block.

Level Control

Some top-of-the-line cars are equipped with air-operated automatic level controls. A vacuum-powered compressor pumps air into the tops of air-sealed rear shock absorbers to raise the car. To lower it, the air is bled away. A height-sensing switch linked to the rear suspension controls the action.

You can test a level-control system easily. With the car parked, measure the rear bumper height. Start the engine and have several people get in the back seat. The car's rear end should sink with the weight and then slowly come back up as the automatic leveler goes into action. In most systems the rear should be within half an inch of its initial height within anywhere from four to 15 seconds.

Next have the people get out. The car should lift quickly and then slowly sink to within half an inch of the initial height. If the system does not perform properly, take the car to a shop. The repairs require specialized equipment.

Electric Door Locks

For safety reasons, more and more cars are being equipped with doors that automatically lock as soon as the engine is started. Some work electrically, others work by vacuum. In the typical electrical system, relay-controlled solenoids lock and unlock all front and rear doors.

Switches on the front lock buttons lock or unlock the rear buttons on a four-door car. The outside front door key locks are in the circuit, too. The rear door lock buttons can be operated manually from the rear as well as electrically from the front.

A solenoid in each door provides the electromagnetic push or pull needed to work the lock buttons, If a solenoid gets out of adjustment, it cannot push or pull to the right position and the door will not lock or unlock automatically. To reach the solenoid, remove the door trim panel.

Adjust the solenoid by loosening its mounting screws. Move the door lock button to its full down position, and move the solenoid to its full down position on the mounting bracket. Next, raise the door lock button to its full up position. That makes the solenoid actuating rod extend fully upward. Finally, tighten the solenoid mounts and try the lock electrically. It should work.

Electrical checks of the system do not help much unless the solenoids are properly adjusted first. See that the battery is fully charged (1.230 to 1.310 specific gravity).

Find the relays that control the solenoids. On Chrysler cars they usually are behind the right cowl trim panel. Connect a voltmeter's red lead to the bus bar connecting the two relays. Connect the black lead to a good ground. The reading should be about 12½ volts. Then, load the circuit by having a helper turn and hold the door lock switch. The voltage reading should drop to 9.4 volts, showing

TROUBLESHOOTING AUTOMATIC DOOR LOCKS

SYMPTOM	CAUSE	CURE
Electrical system doors do not function	Circuit breaker or wiring open	Replace defective component
	Defective relays	Use jumper lead across relays; replace defective relays
Electrical system doors work only from one side	Defective front door switch	Replace defective switch
One electrical door lock fails to work	Solenoid mounting out of adjustment	Adjust as described in text
	Defective solenoid	Be sure solenoids are correctly adjusted, then check voltage; replace defective solenoid
Vacuum system doors do not work	Low or no vacuum in system	Test vacuum at all points to isolate leak or stoppage; replace or reroute kinked hose or replace defective check valve or control switch
	Vacuum leaks	Listen for hiss along hoses and at valves; repair or replace leaking parts
Vacuum system door lock does not work	Binding lock mechanism	Remove door trim panel and inspect mechanism; lubricate, align, or replace door lock
	No vacuum at actuator when door lock is actuated	Look for kinked or leaking vacuum line between control switch and door lock actuator unit

that the circuit is heavily loaded. No voltage reading at the relay indicates an open circuit breaker. Find it and check for continuity. On Chrysler cars, that breaker often is behind the left cowl trim panel. You should get a battery-voltage reading between both breaker terminals and ground.

A shorted solenoid produces a relay bus bar reading of less than battery voltage when no load is on the system and a reading of about 11½ volts with the system activated. A battery-voltage reading when the system is activated is caused by an open circuit.

To find the defective solenoid, disconnect one solenoid at a time from the circuit while operating the system. Once the defective solenoid is disconnected, the rest of the system should operate normally.

If a sticking switch causes one solenoid to burn out, replace the other solenoids as well; they will be near failure, too.

Vacuum Door Locks

A vacuum-operated automatic door locking system, as in Ford products, is composed of a vacuum reservoir, a check valve, a control switch, locking actuators, and vacuum lines connecting those components. Engine vacuum is routed from the engine intake manifold through the check valve to the reservoir. The reservoir is large enough for one complete door lock cycle after the engine has been shut off. The vacuum supply hose goes directly from the check valve to a tee under the instrument panel. There, it connects to the control valve assembly and to the door lock control switch.

Actuating valves in each door are linked to the door lock button levers. In Fords, a white hose leads from the control switch to the locking side of the actuator, and a green hose is routed to the unlocking side at each door. From the driver's door, other hoses are routed to the other doors.

Leaks can affect vacuum system operation. Run the engine at idle and listen for leaks at each connection and along every hose. All other vacuum checks also must be made with the engine running. At least 10—and preferably 14—inches of vacuum should register at every location. Use an ordinary vacuum gauge plugged into the end of a removed hose.

Start vacuum checks at the reservoir's green hose and work toward the last actuator in the vacuum circuit. Where no vacuum is found, inspect the check valve or control switch immediately before that location, and inspect the hose for kinks

If a vacuum-operated accessory gives trouble, inspect the hoses for leaks and for pinching (*left*). To measure the vacuum in these hoses, use a vacuum gauge (*right*).

TROUBLESHOOTING POWER ANTENNAS

SYMPTOM	CAUSE	CURE
Motor does not operate	Blown fuse	Replace blown fuse
	Defective switch or wiring	Test wiring and switch continuity; repair or replace defective parts
	Poor ground	Test ground continuity; clean ground strap connection if necessary
	Defective motor	Replace antenna
Motor operates in only one direction	Defective switch or wiring	Repair or replace defective parts
	Defective motor	Replace antenna
Motor runs but antenna wands do not move	Bent or corroded wands	Straighten and lubricate wands; replace antenna if necessary
	Defective drive assembly	Replace antenna

and bends. Replace the faulty part, if necessary. Correct those kinks by rerouting the hose, if possible.

Binding of the latch mechanism can be found by removing the door trim panel and inspecting the latch parts. Repair or replace the latch mechanism, as necessary.

If the car has a vacuum-operated luggage compartment door release, it operates similarly, using a vacuum actuator on the decklid.

Power Antenna

Little can go wrong with a motorized radio antenna. To remove the antenna, disconnect its power leads and coaxial cable. Remove the retaining bolt, antenna-to-fender nut, ground strap and spacer. Then remove the antenna from above. Replace it by reversing that procedure.

Concealed Headlights

Either of two systems is used for swinging concealed headlights to their on and off positions: electrical or vacuum. Both have overrides that permit manual operation if the actuating mechanism should fail. Because of the high amperage involved, the electrical systems are relay-operated. Concealed headlights are adjusted the same as normal headlights.

Most GM and Chrysler cars use electrical systems. Ford products and the Oldsmobile Toronado use vacuum systems. Electrical systems are repaired much like

electric power windows. The vacuum systems are repaired much like vacuum-operated door locks.

To quick-check electric concealed headlights that are inoperative, connect a jumper lead from the positive terminal of the battery to the headlight motor power lead. If the motor operates, the trouble is in the switch or wiring. If jumping does not help, the trouble is in the motor.

To repair a vacuum system, first inspect the hoses for leaks and kinks, and check vacuum at the actuators. If the vacuum is 11 inches or more, the trouble is in the actuator or linkage; if less than 11 inches, suspect the check valve, control switch, reservoir, or vacuum lines.

Vacuum actuators (*above right*) control the operation of concealed headlights. An override switch on the master control valve (*right*) lets you manually open such headlights in an emergency.

TROUBLESHOOTING CONCEALED HEADLAMPS

SYMPTOM	CAUSE	CURE
Electrical system lights on, but do not open	Defective control relay	Replace defective relay
	Open circuit breaker	Replace open circuit breaker
Only one electrical-system headlight opens	Faulty motor	Replace defective motor
Electrical-system warning light stays on when headlights are open	Adjusting screw misaligned with limit switch	Realign motor mounting bracket
	Defective lower limit switch	Replace defective switch

SYMPTOM	CAUSE	CURE
Electrical-system headlight does not close	Manual override switch in override position	Switch to automatic position (see owner's manual)
	Defective upper limit switch, override switch, control relay, closing relay, or circuit breaker	Replace defective component
Vacuum-system lights not smooth-operating	Actuator linkage binding	Correct binding condition
	Actuator out of adjustment	Adjust according to service manual instructions
Vacuum-system headlights shake while on	Actuator out of adjustment	Adjust
	Linkage bent	Replace linkage
	Leaking vacuum-tank check valve	Replace valve
Both vacuum-system headlamp housings do not open	Vacuum not reaching control	Find leak, restriction, or defective vacuum switch; replace defective part
	Incorrect vacuum hose routing	Take car to shop
One vacuum-system housing does not open	Broken or binding linkage	Repair or replace linkage
Both vacuum-system headlamp housings do not close	Leaking or restricted vacuum hose	Repair or replace hose
	Incorrect vacuum hose routing	Take to shop for rerouting
One vacuum-system headlamp housing does not close	Broken or binding linkage	Repair or replace linkage
	Broken or leaking control assembly	Replace control assembly

In this microphotograph, antifreeze particles coagulate to stop a leak.

16

Servicing the Cooling System

When an engine runs, it creates heat. The cooling system must prevent the engine from overheating—even if the outdoor temperature is 110° in the shade. Without proper cooling, the engine would eventually burn and score its pistons, and warp or burn its valves. Without its cooling system, the engine block would become a red-hot mass of molten metal. And excessive heat also can break down engine oil to the point where it fails to lubricate.

Paradoxically, the cooling system also keeps your engine warm. On a cold day, some engine parts might never warm to operating temperature without the cooling system, and a cold engine is inefficient. Moreover, combustion gases leaking past the piston rings condense in the crankcase, where they form acids and sludge that can be harmful to vital engine parts. Heat from the cooling system helps vaporize and eliminate those blow-by gases.

Here is how a typical liquid cooling system works: A belt-driven centrifugal water pump circulates coolant—water plus antifreeze—through a water jacket that surrounds the engine's combustion chambers. The coolant absorbs heat from the engine and then is pumped through the radiator.

When the car is moving, outside air rushes through the grille and past the radiator cooling tubes and fins, drawing heat from the coolant. When the engine is idling or the car is moving slowly, a fan, powered by the engine through the fan belt, provides a sufficient flow of air. Sometimes, the fan has a shroud to draw air through the radiator.

A thermostat between engine block and radiator acts as a valve, shutting off the flow of coolant when the engine is cold, opening when the engine is hot.

Even when the thermostat is closed, the engine still needs swift circulation of coolant through its water jacket to prevent hot spots—small areas that get hotter than

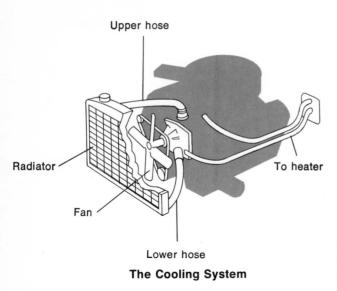

Upper hose

Radiator

Fan

Lower hose

To heater

The Cooling System

the surrounding metal. Coolant circulation is then through a bypass, usually a short length of hose from the thermostat housing to the water pump intake.

When the car heater is turned on, it also works as a bypass circuit, tapping hot coolant from the top of the water jacket and feeding it back to the intake side of the water pump. The heater uses engine heat to warm the incoming air; that is why it does not work well until the engine warms up.

Pressurized system. Almost all modern cars use pressurized cooling systems, with the radiator pressure cap controlling the pressure. A radiator pressure cap keeps the system under higher than atmospheric pressure (in some cases, 15 psi or more higher). That increases the boiling point of the coolant by up to 55° and improves the efficiency of the cooling system.

Two types of pressure caps are used. One maintains a closed system until pressure reaches the maximum; then, a relief valve opens and releases excess pressure out an overflow tube. The second type maintains an open system, except that when the coolant boils, rapidly escaping vapors close the valve and pressurize the

system. Once pressurized, the open type works like the closed type.

Both these kinds of pressure caps have vacuum valves that allow air into the system under $\frac{1}{2}$ to $2\frac{1}{2}$ psi of vacuum. The valve is the small, spring-loaded disk within the large pressure-relief disk. Its purpose is to keep radiator hoses from collapsing.

A new, improved pressurized cooling system remains closed at all times. A reservoir catches any coolant that escapes past the radiator pressure cap. Later, when the engine cools, trapped coolant in the reservoir is drawn by vacuum back into the radiator. Cadillac pioneered the system among U.S. cars in 1969. For less than $10, you can get a coolant recovery system kit to convert your cooling system to the closed type. It takes only about 20 minutes to install, using simple tools. Most auto parts stores sell it. I recommend such a kit if you have, or expect to have, problems with overheating. Besides preventing loss of coolant, the closed system maintains a full radiator at all times. No air can get in.

Coolant recovery system—here, being filled—catches radiator overflow in pressurized systems.

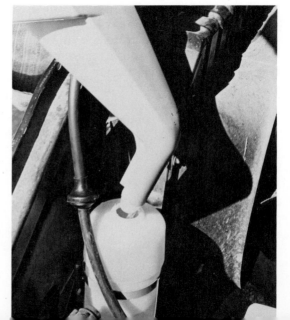

Air is harmful in a cooling system because the water pump churns it into non-cooling bubbles. Lack of sufficient cooling soon lets the temperature inside your engine build to the point where steam is produced. When the water pump passes steam, still less cooling is obtained. Soon, you have to pull off the road, raise the hood and wait for help. With a coolant recovery system, however, all the flow is liquid, making the system work as it is supposed to. Having no air in the cooling system cuts oxidation and increases the life of rubber parts, too.

A coolant-recovery system is filled simply by adding a water-plus-antifreeze mixture to the reservoir, keeping it about half full. The radiator cap need not be removed. Coolant level inside the system is checked by means of a clear section of plastic fitted into the upper radiator hose. A "Do not open radiator" tag keeps service station attendants from unscrewing the pressure cap.

Air-cooled systems. Air-cooled engines have their own problems. Naturally, no antifreeze is required. Boiling is never a problem—but overheating is, as is overcooling. Hot weather stop-and-go driving and overloading will overheat an air-cooled engine just as easily as a liquid-cooled one. And an overheating air-cooled engine has no cloud of steam to warn you. When the engine locks up tight and will not run any more, you will need a new engine.

The cooling fins around the cylinders must be kept clean and the air passages unobstructed. The fan belt should be kept properly tensioned. Air flow dampers, if any, must be in working order too. The difference between overheating and overcooling can be touchy. Follow the manufacturer's recommendations.

ANTIFREEZE

Cooling is no longer a job that water alone can handle—even in above-freezing weather. It takes water plus an antifreeze coolant. One reason is that such coolants contain rust inhibitors.

More than that, *glycol-type antifreeze* raises the boiling point of water. Modern auto engines are designed to run at much higher temperatures than older ones. On some cars, the cooling system warning light is set to come on at as high as 248° F. Plain water at sea-level pressure boils at 212°. Its boiling point rises to 250° with a

How Pressure Affects Coolants (at Sea Level)

Coolant concentration (antifreeze:water)	Boiling point					Freezing point
	Atmospheric pressure	11 PSI	13 PSI	15 PSI	17 PSI	
0:1 (plain water)	212°	242°	246°	250°	254°	+32°
1:2	220°	250°	254°	258°	262°	0°
1:1	227°	257°	261°	265°	269°	−34°

15 psi pressurization of the cooling system —but even that is not enough. An engine with plain water in its cooling system would still boil before the warning light came on.

Adding one-third permanent antifreeze to the coolant, with 15 psi pressurization, boosts the boiling point to 258°, giving a small margin of safety against boil-over as long as the radiator pressure cap holds its rated pressure. The recommended 50 percent concentration of glycol-type antifreeze-coolant gives another 15° or so of protection. A high concentration of glycol-type antifreeze is especially needed in cars with air conditioning.

A 68 percent concentration of glycol may be used to protect an engine against freezing in temperatures down to 90° below zero. But surprisingly, from then on, still higher concentrations raise the freezing point rather than lower it. Pure glycol-type antifreeze freezes at about 5° below zero. A 75% concentration can be used safely.

Incidentally, a popular misconception is that ethylene glycol, sometimes misnamed "permanent" antifreeze, can slip by a small leak that would hold back water or alcohol antifreeze. Actually, the opposite is true. Antileak glycol-type antifreezes contain particles that lodge in openings and seal them in seconds. The particles, however, are not large enough to stop up the cooling system passages.

Plain water leaks faster than ethylene glycol. The reason ethylene glycol is sometimes thought of as the "leaky antifreeze" is its slow evaporation, which means that you can sometimes detect it. In addition, many glycol-type antifreezes also contain blue-green dyes that clearly show up external leaks. If leakage is a problem, try an antileak product.

Methanol antifreeze is not recommended for modern cars. It lowers, rather than raises, the boiling point of a coolant. A typical mixture of methanol and water boils at only 180°. Even when pressurized, such a mixture will boil long before the temperature warning light comes on.

If plain water is used in pre-1962 cars (in above-freezing weather, naturally), antirust and water pump lubricant should be added. That solution must be drained and completely flushed from the system before use of antifreeze-coolant in the fall.

Whenever you add coolant to raise the level in your radiator to specification, add a mixture of water and antifreeze-coolant. The simplest procedure is to pour in a half-and-half mixture.

Testing Antifreeze

If you leave your antifreeze-coolant in for more than one year, you will need to test it for freeze protection. Several types of testers are available.

One is simply a *hydrometer,* in which a glass float measures the specific gravity of the liquid to tell the concentration of antifreeze. (Specific gravity is the density of a liquid compared to the density of water.) Samples of coolant are drawn into the

If for some reason you do not use antifreeze, add rust inhibitor to your car's cooling system.

Versatile antifreeze tester is the floating-ball hydrometer. This instrument uses tester balls to gauge the level of antifreeze in the coolant (*left*) and a chemical sensor tip (*right*) to measure the effectiveness of coolant's anti-corrosion additives.

syringe. A scale on the float tells you the freeze protection for each density reading. With such a tester, a correction must be made for temperature of the coolant when you test it. Temperature correction factors are incorporated into the tester's scale of some antifreeze hydrometers.

Another type of hydrometer tester contains floating/sinking balls of varying densities. With such a tester, you need not warm the cooling system before you check it (not all floating-ball antifreeze testers offer this benefit). To use this type of tester, remove the radiator pressure cap and draw in some solution. Count the number of tester balls that float in the solution. Then, look on the tester's chart and read your freeze protection.

Some hydrometer models also have a *chemical sensor* on their tips to indicate corrosion protection. It does so by reacting to a coolant's pH (a measure of acidity or alkalinity). A fresh half-and-half anti-

freeze-water mixture has a pH of between 8.0 and 9.5. As the coolant ages, its rust inhibitors become depleted. As long as the pH level is above 7.0, it can be used, perhaps with the addition of a compatible rust inhibitor. But if the pH drops below 7.0, you should drain and flush the radiator and pour in fresh coolant.

The tester's sensor changes color to indicate coolant condition. The tip has a brownish reference section and a longer indicator section that changes color. A brown indicator means normal protection; slightly purple is marginal. Purple means drain, flush, and replace. Tip color takes about 10 seconds to change at a 65° coolant temperature, less when hot. Do not rinse or wipe off the indicator tip.

Another type of antifreeze instrument, the *refractive tester,* gauges coolant strength by measuring the amount that a beam of light is bent by a sample of coolant. The read-out is direct; no correction for coolant temperature is needed. Refractive testers generally are used only by professionals.

Whatever tester you buy, use it to check coolant in warm months as well as cold ones.

Summer Coolants

What about summer coolants—those panther potions that are supposed to keep your radiator from boiling?

I know of no auto manufacturer that recommends the use of such additives. Most plainly advise against them in service literature. And instrumented tests performed by the auto industry have yet to turn up such an additive that really improves cooling.

MAINTENANCE

A practical program for cooling system care shapes up as follows:

Check the coolant level once a month, when the engine is cool.

In the fall, inspect for leaks. Look at hoses. Check the thermostat if the engine runs too cool. Drain the old coolant and, if necessary, flush the system thoroughly. Put in a half-and-half mixture of water and a reputable brand ethylene-glycol antifreeze. Clean the radiator front and test the pressure cap. Check belt and belt tension, too.

In the spring, inspect the coolant for signs of corrosion, check for grease inside the radiator, look for leaks, and clean bugs from the front of the radiator.

Routine checks of the coolant level should be made when the engine is cold—preferably by you, not by a gas station attendant. Removing the radiator cap when the engine is hot releases the pressure in the cooling system. The coolant boils, and some of it spills out over the filler neck. Refilling the radiator to overflowing with water then unnecessarily dilutes your antifreeze protection and weakens the rust inhibitors. Checking a properly maintained cooling system is needed only about once a month or every 4000 miles.

When you check the radiator with the engine cold, the coolant level should at least cover the radiator tubes.

If you have to check the level of coolant in a hot system, turn the radiator cap slowly to the left and only as far as the stop. That loosens the seal without removing the cap, and permits pressure to escape out the overflow tube. If coolant or steam tries to escape, tighten the cap quickly and let the system cool off before you check it. With a warm engine, a level of 1 to 1½ inches below the filler neck often is common.

When the level is low, fill to the correct level with antifreeze or with a mixture of antifreeze and water, not with water alone. Overfilling causes some coolant to escape later because of coolant expansion.

Draining

One draining method involves opening hard-to-reach engine block drains.

An easier method—which does not involve scalding your hands or crawling under the car—is to open the radiator drain cock with the radiator cap off and with the car's heater temperature set to "high." If your car has a vacuum-operated heater control valve, have the engine running later as you flush, to make sure that the heater core also is drained and flushed.

Remove the heater hose from its fitting on top of the engine and let the end hang down below the engine. Place the end of a garden hose over the heater fitting, sealing off leakage by squeezing with your hand.

Better yet, a garden hose female fitting, attached to a 6-inch piece of heater hose,

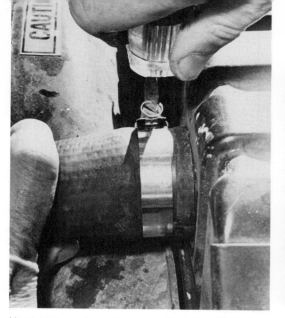

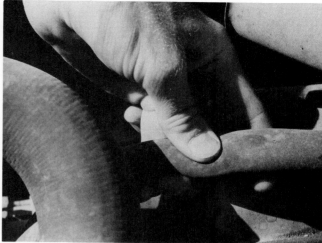

Head off leaks by making sure that all radiator hose clamps are tightly fastened.

At least once a year, squeeze cooling system hoses. Replace brittle, soft or cracked lines.

Check to see that the radiator cap gasket is pliable and that the spring retains tension.

Inspect the water pump belt regularly. Cracked and glazed belts should be replaced immediately.

Every spring, hose down the radiator to remove any insects that might have become lodged there.

makes a fine connector. Water will soon begin running out over the radiator filler neck and out the dangling heater hose, as well as out of the radiator drain cock. Continue flushing until the water comes out clear. Turn off the water (and turn off the engine, if it was running). Remove the garden hose and replace the heater hose on its fitting. Close the radiator drain. The system is now ready for fresh antifreeze-coolant and water in the proper proportions.

Flushing

Water. A flush-and-fill kit is helpful for flushing the system with fresh water, since it saves the trouble of removing a heater hose every time you flush.

The kit is mounted permanently, and installation is simple. Cut through the heater hose (the one leading from the top of the engine block), insert the flushing tee, and install the hose clamps on both sides of the tee.

To use the device, remove the cap from the flushing tee, screw on the hose

Flush-and-fill kit, which features a permanently-mounted tee fitting, makes periodic cooling system flushing an easy task.

adapter, and attach your garden hose. Remove the radiator cap and tighten the plastic deflector in the radiator filler neck. Turn on the hose—water flows through the engine block and out the radiator filler to flush out old coolant. Squeeze the upper radiator hose several times to get out trapped coolant. Continue flushing until water flows clear.

When installing antifreeze-coolant, you can make room for all of it by bleeding water from the flushing tee. To do it, remove the cap. Only water will come out, not antifreeze. Replace the cap afterward.

After flushing, as you refill your cooling system, you will have trouble getting all the drained coolant back in without having it overflow. That is because air in the top of the engine water jacket cannot get by the closed thermostat. To get a complete fill, run the engine until it reaches operating temperature. The thermostat will open and release the trapped air, allowing you to fill the system to capacity.

Cooling system center. You can head off cooling problems in your car by a thorough systems check using professional equipment. The saving over having it done will go a long way toward buying you the necessary professional equipment. And you will be making tests that professional mechanics often are too busy or lazy to perform. You will thus be able to solve many problems of overheating, overcooling, corrosion, leakage and freeze protection.

A complete cooling system center costs about $60 and includes: an antifreeze tester; a water can; a drain pan; a pressure tester; hose clamp pliers; a thermometer; a belt tension gauge; a coolant recovery kit; and a flushing kit. With proper care, the equipment should last a lifetime.

The toughest item to find is a belt tension gauge. Ask your auto parts dealer to

A complete cooling system center lets you check out the system thoroughly.

order one for you if he does not stock them. Low-cost tension testers give spot readings. More expensive models can give continuous tension readings as you tighten and lock the belt adjustment.

Hoses and Belts

The rubber parts of the cooling system, especially the hoses, need periodic attention. Large rubberized hoses lead between the engine and the radiator; thinner but longer ones serve the car's heater with hot circulating coolant. Heat and age can cause seriously restricted flow or even leaks in the hoses. To head off emergency roadside service, replace any hardened, cracked, swollen, or restricted hoses. Tiny cracks in the outside rubber are nothing to worry about. The deep ones, which usually start near an end and encircle the hose at least part way, are the ones to worry about.

If your car heater puts out too little heat, restricted hoses could be the cause. Inspect the heater hoses for pinched portions. Blow through one end of each hose to test for restrictions.

The radiator overflow tube can become clogged, too, particularly on old cars. If it does, cooling system venting will be impaired, with serious damage to the radiator. Check by blowing through the tube. If it is clogged, pass a piece of mechanic's wire through it to clear the deposits. If a

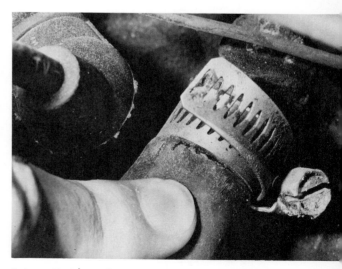

A hose that is as badly cracked as the one above should be replaced.

rubber overflow tube becomes clogged, hardened, or cracked, replace it with a new one.

Water pump and fan drive belts eventually become glazed, cracked, brittle, or worn. Replace such belts. See that all belts are at specified tension.

Belt tension. A sluggish water pump lets the engine overheat and lets hot spots develop in the engine block. A loose, slipping drive belt can be the cause. To prevent belt slippage, check the belt tension with a belt tension gauge. Checking by feel is not accurate enough for most of today's cars. A belt tension gauge can be used on all automotive belts, not just the water pump belt.

To use your belt tension gauge, fold out the feeler bar to its perpendicular test position. Pull it down below the gauge line before each test. Adjust the spring sleeve to the required tension by turning it. Then, place the feeler bar on the belt at the center of the span. Press down harder and harder until you feel the touch-

With the aid of a belt tension gauge, keep the water pump belt at its specified tension.

button at the top of the tester cap. This contacts your finger when the spring sleeve reaches zero. Remove the gauge to a good light without hitting it on anything and note where the bottom of the feeler bar rests. If it is above the gauge line, the belt is too loose. If it is below the gauge line, the belt is too tight.

You can also use the tester to pinpoint a belt's tension. Set and position the tester on the belt. Watch the feeler bar and gauge line while you press down until the bottom of the bar and gauge mark are aligned; at that point, read the tension scale.

To adjust tension, loosen the holding bolt and move the adjustable component, usually the generator or power steering pump. Tighten the lockbolt and recheck tension.

Water Pump

A water pump that is about to fail usually shows signs of leakage at the drain hole underneath. Also, you can test the smoothness of rotation and the tightness of the bearings by removing the belt and wiggling the shaft. It should not feel loose. Turn the shaft to make sure it moves smoothly and silently. If it binds or is noisy, remove the entire pump and trade it in for a rebuilt unit.

To remove the pump, drain the radiator and remove the belts and fan blade if necessary. Thermostatic fan clutches that vary fan speed with temperature must be kept in an "in-car" position. The clutch disk must remain vertical to avoid leakage of the silicone actuating fluid. Remove the lower radiator hose and small bypass hose, if it is attached. Remove the bolts around the pump and pull out the old pump.

Scrape off the old gasket. Apply contact adhesive gasket cement to the engine, pump, and gasket surfaces; or, use a sealer-coated gasket. Install the rebuilt pump and all the parts that were removed, and refill the system with coolant.

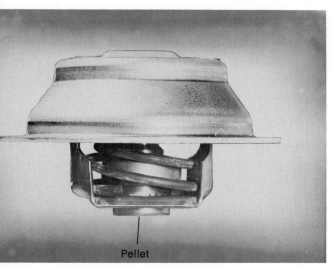

Pellet

Typical cooling system thermostat.

Thermostat

To maintain engine temperature at the desired level, an automobile engine relies on a thermostatically operated restriction valve, or thermostat, in the cooling system passage between the engine block and the top or hot side of the radiator. When a cold engine is started, the thermostat is closed to hold back the flow of coolant and help the engine warm up quickly. After a few minutes, when the coolant reaches a sufficiently high temperature, the thermostat opens, and the coolant in the engine is allowed to flow to the radiator.

Most thermostats use a copper-impregnated wax pellet to actuate the valve. If your car is not an old one and the radiator has a pressure cap, use such a pellet-type thermostat. Install the pellet end of a thermostat toward the engine, not toward the radiator—installed backwards, a thermostat will make your cooling system boil over. (Old-model cars used a bellows, rather than a pellet, type.)

Thermostats come in different temperature settings. That is, they are designed to begin opening at a specified temperature —often 180°, 195°, or 205°. A thermostat is fully open at 15° to 20° above its start-to-open temperature. Check your shop manual for the proper opening temperature for your car.

Years ago, car owners were instructed to use a hot thermostat in winter and a cooler one in summer. Recent-model cars have high-temperature thermostats that are designed for year-round use. For better heater performance, you can use a thermostat that is hotter than specified in an old car, too.

A thermostat may last for years, but overheating and corrosion finally may do it in. When a thermostat goes bad, it usually sticks in the open position, preventing the engine from warming up as quickly as it should. Lack of enough heat from the heater is a common symptom. A thermostat also may fail in the closed position, causing immediate overheating. Do not try to fix a defective thermostat. Replace it.

On the other hand, never take out a good thermostat to prevent engine overheating —find the real cause of the overheating and correct it.

Testing accuracy. A dashboard temperature gauge or indicator light is not reliable enough to show thermostat action. To check the thermostat accurately, immerse a thermometer in the radiator water. If there is a baffle plate beneath the radiator

Easy-to-use radiator thermometer inserts into the filler neck of the radiator.

opening, the thermometer should poke down through the hole that is usually in it.

Start the engine and run it on fast idle (with a worn dime between the carburetor idle screw and its stop). If the thermostat is working properly, the top of the radiator should stay cool until the engine itself has warmed to specified temperature. As the thermostat opens, hot coolant begins to flow into the radiator, raising the thermometer reading rapidly. When the reading stops climbing, that is your thermostat's opening temperature.

A still more accurate test is made with the thermostat out. To remove it, take out the cap screws holding the thermostat housing. Pry the housing free from its gasket and pull out the thermostat. Insert a 0.003-inch thickness gauge between the valve and seat, and put the thermostat in a pan of water with a thermometer. (See that the actuating pill at the bottom does not touch the sides or bottom of the pan.)

Heat the water and tap on the thermostat lightly with a screwdriver to agitate it. When the valve opens 0.003 inch, and the gauge is held but loosely, take a temperature reading. The water should be within 3° of the temperature stamped on the thermostat.

Let the temperature climb another 20°, if possible, to see whether the thermostat is open all the way at that point. Most will open about a quarter inch. Turn off the heat and watch while the water cools. The valve should close fully at about 10° below its specified opening temperature. If the valve fails to open or close properly, buy a new thermostat—and test it before you install it, just in case.

When you replace a thermostat, be careful. Its outer flange usually fits in a recess on either the coolant manifold or coolant outlet. If the flange slips out of its recess during installation, it can crack the outlet when you tighten the housing's cap screw.

To avoid that problem, first scrape both mating surfaces clean. Then, smear the surfaces with a contact adhesive gasket cement. Insert the unit into its recess and stick a new gasket over the thermostat to hold it in place. Do not try to reuse the old gasket. Finally, install the thermostat housing.

Heat indicators. The thermostat test also is a double-check of your car's heat indicator, whether it is a light or a gauge. Incorrect heat indicator action with a working thermostat usually means that the temperature sending unit needs replacing. The sending unit is threaded into the top of the engine block with tapered pipe threads, and has one or two wires leading to it. When you replace the sending unit, you will lose little coolant if there is no pressure in the system and the radiator cap is on.

A temperature gauge rarely breaks down. Indicator lights are easily checked for burn-out. See your owner's manual.

LEAKS

If the system is to do its job properly, it cannot be allowed to lose its coolant. But if there is even a slight opening anywhere in the system, the pressurized coolant will find it and leak out. An average car loses about a pint of coolant per thousand miles, according to one fleet test. Your goal should be no coolant loss at all.

External Leaks

Leaks can develop when corrosion eats holes in thin metal of the radiator parts. Most radiator leaks, however, are caused by mechanical failure of soldered joints. Repeated expansion and contraction of cooling system parts, during engine warm-up and after shut-down, are important factors. But engine vibration and road shock are the major causes. For instance, a stiff radiator hose connected to a rocking

Thermostat Service

1. Remove the thermostat without draining the coolant by loosening the radiator cap, then squeezing the upper radiator hose as you tighten the cap (*left*). When you release the hose, vacuum keeps the coolant from running out when you remove the unit (*right*).

2. Hold the removed thermostat to a bright light. If you can see a slit of light through the valve, replace this temperature-controlling unit.

3. To test the unit's opening temperature, suspend it with a thermometer in a container of water. Heat the water until the valve opens.

4. To replace the thermostat, first coat its flange with gasket cement (*left*). Then, position the unit, pellet toward engine block. Fit a new gasket (*right*) and bolt on the housing.

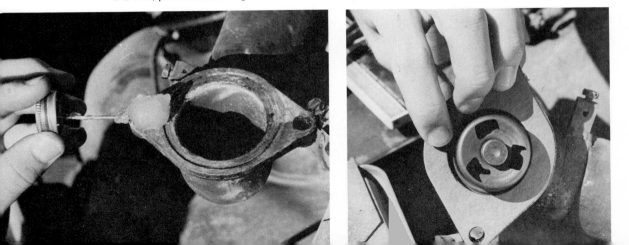

This radiator hose outlet was soldered in an attempt to stop a leak. But the job was poorly done—expansion and contraction reopened the leak.

engine can rupture the seam between the radiator inlet pipe and tank.

If you have to add water to your radiator periodically, first examine the radiator carefully for leaks. White or rust-colored stains indicate old leaks. If plain water or alcohol antifreeze is in the radiator, a leak may not even be damp; those coolants evaporate quickly. If ethylene glycol antifreeze-coolant is used, the leaks probably will be damp, since that chemical evaporates slowly.

Pressure tester. The best way to look for leaks is with the cooling system under its designed pressure. A pressure tester lets you do just that. Some models even let you pressure-test the cooling system and radiator pressure cap at the same time, by duplicating actual operating conditions (except for heat). If your cooling system does not have a pressure cap, you can still check the cooling system by substituting the analyzer cap furnished with the kit.

To use the kit, first remove the radiator pressure cap and check it for defects in the rubber seal and for corrosion deposits. Fill the radiator with a half-and-half mixture of antifreeze-coolant and water. Then, fasten the pressure cap securely to the top of the analyzer neck, which is shaped like the radiator filler neck. Attach the bottom of the analyzer neck to the radiator filler neck.

Note the pressure rating of the cooling system in your owner's or shop manual. Do not rely on the pressure stated on the radiator cap; it may be a replacement with the wrong rating.

Pump the analyzer handle like a tire pump until the needle on the gauge reaches the specified pressure. (Caution: Overpressurizing can blow the solder seams in the radiator.) If the pressure needle holds steady within the proper range, the system and cap are in good working order.

If, however, the pressure will not reach the specified point and you can find no leaks, the pressure cap is releasing at too low a pressure and should be replaced. A pressure cap with a relief setting too low or too high keeps the cooling system from functioning properly, and may even cause the system to blow.

To find what is causing the leak, replace the pressure cap with the kit's analyzer cap and retest the system. If there is still a leak, it is in the system, not in the cap. If there is no leak during the retest, the cap should be replaced with a new one of the proper pressure rating. Do not try to adjust or repair a defective pressure cap.

Hunting for leaks. Leaks commonly show up at *hose connections*: around the water pump shaft, in the gasketed joint between the water pump and engine block, and in the gasketed joint between the engine block and water outlet (the thermostat housing). To correct such

Making a Pressure Test

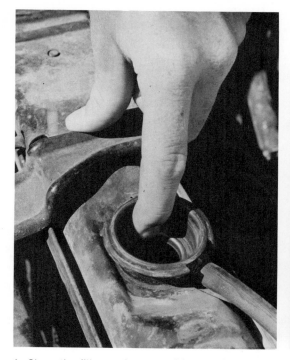

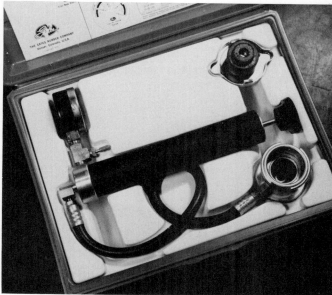

1. Clean the filler neck seat and inspect it carefully for corrosion and cracks.

2. Connect the tester's analyzer neck (*lower right*) to the radiator filler.

3. With your car's pressure cap atop the analyzer neck, pump the tester to the specified pressure.

4. Needle should hold firm. If it drops, there is a leak in the pressure cap or the cooling system.

Check water pump shaft seal for leakage after the engine has been shut off.

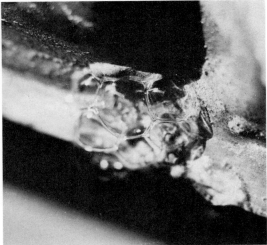

Bubbles signify a pressure leak above the water line of your car's cooling system.

leaks, tighten the hose clamps or bolts, or replace leaky gaskets with new ones, using gasket cement. A leaking water pump shaft calls for the installation of a new or a rebuilt water pump. Check for leaks around the intake manifold if the manifold has water passages running through it.

If you have recurring problems with a hose clamp, replace it with a stainless steel worm-drive clamp. One size will fit many sizes of hose. Worm-drive hose clamps beat all others in pulling an even pressure around a hose. For heater hoses, spring-wire clamps are adequate. Use hose-clamp pliers to remove and install this type of clamp. It is wise to run a second pressure test with the system hot; some leaks do not show up when the system is cold.

Look for leaks around *core plugs*, which are located on the sides of an engine block and are often miscalled "freeze plugs." Replacing such a plug is no fun, and there is the danger of mutilating the engine block. Let your shop handle that job. Replacement may be with a new metal plug or an expandable rubber plug.

Leaks around *cylinder heads* call for tightening of the head bolts. But on some cars, that may destroy the gasket seal. Do not try it unless the manufacturer okays it for your car—ask your dealer, or look in the manual. Tighten the head bolts with a torque wrench to the specified amount. The car maker also specifies in what order the head bolts should be tightened. Follow those instructions precisely if you do the job yourself. If tightening does not stop the leak, the cylinder head gasket must be replaced. Perhaps the mating surfaces of the head and block are uneven and must be machined flat. Take your car to a shop for that.

Leakage at *water jacket joints* is worsened by cooling system pressure. Expansion and contraction of the engine parts only aggravate the problem. Inspect the block both hot and cold with the engine running. Leaks that show up one way may not show up the other way.

Some minor leaks can be sealed with a stop-leak added to the coolant. Use a reputable brand; some can gum up radia-

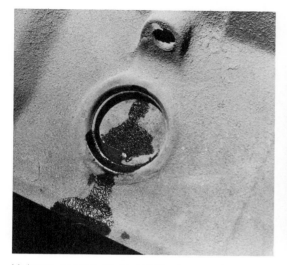

Moisture around an engine block core plug means the plug should be punched out and replaced.

Whitish deposits are caused by coolant leaking out of tiny cracks and evaporating.

tor tubes if not used properly. Make sure the label says that the product is compatible with your antifreeze-coolant. If the stop-leak does not work, remove the radiator and take it to a radiator shop.

Internal Leaks

A stop-leak is ineffective against internal engine leaks, which let coolant into the cylinder and combustion chamber, and gases into the water jacket. Such leaks are hard to detect. Coolant that foams or runs over the top of the radiator is a tip-off. Signs of moisture on the oil dipstick may be, too.

The "no-equipment" way to test for combustion chamber leaks is to start with a cold engine. Drain the radiator down to the thermostat level, and remove the coolant outlet and the thermostat. Remove the belt from the water pump. Refill the radiator until coolant comes to the top of the engine block at the thermostat opening. If the opening is vertical, you will need a short length of hose coming off the coolant

You may be able to stop minor radiator leaks with a commercial preparation.

Cream-colored globules on your car's oil dipstick point to an internal leak.

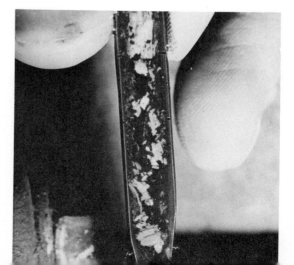

outlet. The coolant outlet must be replaced temporarily without the thermostat.

Block up both of the car's rear wheels and set the emergency brake. Have a helper start the engine, then load it by shifting to "drive" and running up the engine speed. Never load an automatic transmission for more than a minute. Follow by running the engine at a fast idle in neutral for cooling. Watch that you do not overheat the engine, which temporarily is functioning without a complete system.

To load the engine in a manual shift car, shift into top gear, release the emergency brake, run up the engine with the clutch pedal out, and apply the service brakes moderately.

While your helper loads the engine, watch the thermostat opening for bubbles caused by combustion gas, which would indicate an engine combustion chamber leak. You may be able to isolate the problem by removing and replacing one spark plug wire at a time. When you pull the wire on a leaky cylinder, the bubbling will decrease or stop. The procedure must be done quickly, before boiling occurs.

Combustion chamber leaks allow acids that are harmful to form in the engine and cooling system. If the leak is in a head gasket, torquing the head to specifications may fix it. If not, take the car to a shop. The head gasket may have to be replaced, or the cylinder head or engine block will have to be machined to correct for warpage. A crack in the engine block or head can permit leaks, too. A replacement block or head is the usual repair.

Coolant that leaks into a combustion chamber also can leak past the piston rings and into the engine oil. Diluted oil is a poor lubricant that can cause engine failure.

Another way air can get into the cooling system is by being drawn into the suction side of the water pump. The circulating air sometimes can be heard bubbling through the heater. A leaky pump shaft seal or a leaking lower hose or hose connection allow this. It also can cause loss of coolant.

Air induction, as the problem is termed, is easy to check. Run the engine at a fast idle while you submerge the end of the overflow tube in water. The radiator pressure cap should be on, but its lower pressurizing gasket should be made to leak by inserting a wooden toothpick or match between it and the gasket seat. If a steady stream of air bubbles from the tube, shut off the engine and try tightening the clamps on the lower hose and heater hoses. If that does not stop the bubbling, look around the water pump housing for a gasket leak. Tighten the water pump bolts. If you still have no luck, suspect a leaking water pump shaft seal. Some seals can be replaced. Others require replacement of the entire pump.

Test for combustion chamber leakage by running up hose from the thermostat housing. Run the engine under load. Bubbles indicate a leak.

To test for air induction, break the pressure cap seal with a match (*left*) and submerge the overflow tube in water (*right*). If bubbles appear as the engine idles, there is a leak.

CORROSION

Sooner or later, the metals in the cooling system may begin to rust. Air in the system from loss of coolant, combustion chamber leakage, and air induction hasten the process. Corrosion gives a rusty or muddy look to the coolant. Such coolant should be completely drained as soon as practical.

Corrosion buildup causes 90 percent of radiator clogging. In advanced stages of neglect, nothing short of dismantling the radiator and mechanically rodding it out will remove all the accumulated rust.

With proper use of antifreeze-coolant and proper maintenance, a clean, corrosion-free cooling system (as in a new car) probably can go for two years of normal driving without signs of corrosion. Avoid using hard water in your radiator. It contains minerals that may deposit on the engine water jacket walls, forming heat-insulating scale. Softened hard water is better; its minerals are less harmful. Better yet, use pure, naturally soft water.

Good antifreeze-coolant contains effective rust inhibitors. When you add at least 33 percent ethylene glycol antifreeze-coolant to your cooling system, (some auto manufacturers specify higher concentrations) the antirust compounds in it will prevent corrosion for a long time. For that reason and others, the use of antifreeze is advisable both summer and winter. Better yet, for freeze protection to 34° below, use equal parts of antifreeze and water.

The rust inhibitors in antifreeze eventually become depleted. For that reason, you should drain, flush, and refill with fresh antifreeze-coolant at least every other year—and preferably every year.

Check for corrosion with the engine cold. Remove the radiator cap and run your finger around the inside of the radiator top tank. A greasy scum there indicates that the whole cooling system—radiator, engine block, hoses, water pump, thermostat—is covered with the same heat-insulating deposit.

Open the drain valve at the bottom of the radiator and run off a sample of coolant into a jar. A muddy appearance or a rust color is a bad sign. In aluminum block systems, corrosion has a milky, whitish appearance. If you find evidence of corrosion, drain the coolant completely.

Chemical Flushing

1. If the filler neck is coated with a greasy deposit, the radiator needs a chemical flush.

2. Remove the upper heater hose and couple on a common garden hose.

3. If you use a fast-flushing solvent, add it to the radiator, idle the engine, then drain and flush. With a heavy-duty flush, first add the cleaner (*above*). Then, after draining and rinsing, add the all-important neutralizer (*below*).

4. Finally, fill the clean cooling system with a fresh mixture of antifreeze and water.

Chemical Flushing

If your car's cooling system gets proper care from the time it is new, chemical flushing may never be needed. Some auto manufacturers make no mention of it in service literature. But if corrosion or grease deposits are allowed to develop, ordinary water flushing will not be sufficient. Then, you will need a chemical cleaner.

There are two types of chemical cleaners: solvent-type and acid-type.

A solvent cleaner is often called a fast flush. If you can wipe a finger around the inside of the radiator below the filler neck opening and bring out an oily scum, a fast flush is needed.

To use this pleasant-smelling liquid, pour it into the radiator and allow it to circulate for a time with the engine running. Then, drain and flush with water. After flushing, put fresh antifreeze-coolant into the system. Fast flushes are mild-mannered, and if a little is left in the system or if you spill some on yourself, no damage results.

Acid-type cleaners are practically pure oxalic acid crystals. These are often called heavy-duty radiator cleaners. If the old coolant comes out muddy or rusty, a heavy-duty cooling system cleaner is called for.

They come in dry powder form in two-part containers. One side of the container holds the acid, the other an acid-inhibiting neutralizer.

To use a heavy-duty cleaner, first drain the system and water-flush out all old coolant. Fill the system with water and run the engine to warm it. Pour in the cleaner while the engine runs at a fast idle. Allow the cleaner to circulate for the specified length of time, then drain it and thoroughly water-flush again. Flush until well after the water comes out clear. Refill the system with water and repeat the whole process with the neutralizer powder. After

a final, thorough flushing with water, install antifreeze-coolant to the proper level.

Flushing is vital. Unless all traces of acid cleaner are neutralized or flushed away, the antifreeze-coolant's corrosion-protection reserve will be rapidly depleted. Then, corrosion will soon begin all over again.

Professional Service

A cooling system that is too badly corroded to be helped by a heavy-duty cleaner will need professional service. For this, go to an auto radiator specialist. Ideally, the owner should be a member of the National Automotive Radiator Service Association, the national trade organization of such shops. His service will most likely comprise removal of the car's radiator, disassembly and rodding out of the coolant passages. It should make the system perform virtually as good as new.

A sure sign of serious corrosion deposits is a cool spot in the radiator. Feel the entire front surface of the radiator after the engine has been running for some time. In a downflow radiator (one in which

With the engine running, feel the radiator core. There should be a smooth transition from hot to warm areas, but no cold spots.

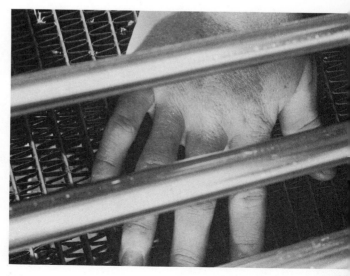

coolant from the engine flows in at the top and out at the bottom) the top should be hot. In a crossflow radiator (one in which coolant flows in at one side and out the other) one side should be hot and the opposite side should be just warm; the radiator should feel progressively less warm, with no cool spots, as you move your hand from hot end to warm end.

A radiator core with a cool spot must be either pressure-flushed or removed from the car, taken apart, and mechanically rodded out. Either method is one for a professional radiator repairman. Pressure-flushing should also include reverse-flushing of the engine block and heater core. Corrosion deposits will have been at work on them, too. Reverse-flushing is air/water purging in the opposite direction to normal coolant flow.

PREVENTING OVERHEATING

Even a new car can suffer from overheating, especially in hot weather. Turning on the air conditioner can raise coolant temperature 10° to 20° at idle. The problem can be worse with a hang-on air conditioner than with an original-equipment one, because the car's cooling system may not be designed to handle the added load of the hang-on unit. Idling the engine with the transmission in drive also raises coolant temperature.

To make things worse, new low-emission engines are built to run at higher temperatures. Emission controls incorporate leaner air/fuel mixtures, retarded spark timing, and auxiliary combustion devices, all of which produce more engine heat. And lowered compression ratios, which permit engines to burn lower octane fuels, increase the heat rejection from engine to cooling system. Filling your car with passengers, hitching a boat trailer to the rear, and running your car in bumper-to-bumper traffic or up a long, steep grade on a hot day also can easily boil the cooling system.

You can forestall boiling by installing a

Keep an eye on the temperature gauge, especially in the summer.

75-percent concentration of glycol-type antifreeze-coolant. That, plus 14-psi cooling system pressurization, raises the coolant's boiling point to 280°, providing an extra 17° or so of boiling protection over a normal mixture.

If your cooling system is sound and if you use the 75-percent concentration, remember that the temperature warning light will show red long before the system boils. Ignore the light and watch carefully for signs of boiling.

Turning on the heater and heater fan full blast will not make the car comfortable on a hot day, but it will lower the cooling system temperature by a few degrees. If you are stopped in traffic, shift into neutral and race the engine; the increased radiator fan speed will help cool things down. If the radiator does boil, stop, shut off the engine, and wait until things cool down. Do not undo the radiator pressure cap; that will let more coolant escape.

Really tough cases of overheating, caused by extremely hot climates or other hard driving conditions, may have to be cured with heavy-duty accessories such as a larger radiator and a transmission cooler. Many such items are optional on a new car as part of a trailer-towing package. They add little to the purchase price of the new car. If you add them later, they will cost more.

Any time you must repair or replace a radiator, consider buying an oversized one. It will greatly minimize overheating. A transmission cooler for an automatic transmission is available for cars with and without built-in transmission cooling. It works by air-cooling the transmission fluid. A transmission cooler is fairly easy to install from under the car, and it helps prevent overheating of the transmission when the car pulls heavy loads such as a large trailer.

Cooling tips. Finally, there are a number of other factors that can lead to overheating. Be aware of them:

• Bugs lodged in the radiator air passages block the flow of cooling air. Blow them out with compressed air shot through from the back of the radiator, or brush them off.

• Ignition and valve timing have an effect on engine heat. Late timing adds to the heat a cooling system must handle. (See the chapter on ignition.) Have a mechanic check valve timing if you are in doubt about it. A worn, loose timing chain could conceivably slip a notch. It would be accompanied by a loss in power and an increase in fuel consumption—and perhaps oil-burning.

• A restriction in the exhaust system can cause overheating. Make the vacuum-gauge test shown in the chapter on engine breathing.

• Using regular-grade gasoline in engines that should have premium can cause overheating, as well as serious engine damage. Do not slavishly follow the car manufacturer's fuel recommendations. Some engines require higher-octane fuel than other supposedly identical ones. If your engine knocks—that is, makes a metallic tapping noise—during acceleration, switch to a higher-octane fuel regardless of what the manufacturer recommends. As some engines age and build up internal deposits, their octane requirements go up.

• In a stubborn case of overheating, check for dragging brakes. Self-adjusters on the brakes may have done their job too well —not common, but a possibility. Wheel cylinders rusted by moisture in the brake fluid can have the same effect. Jack up each wheel and turn it to see whether the brakes are dragging. Front wheels should spin freely. Rear wheels should turn easily. (Brake servicing is described in a later chapter.)

1Z

Servicing the Exhaust System

The series of gas explosions that makes your car's engine run cannonades out of the firing chambers up to 15,000 times a minute. Each explosion generates a sound wave at least 50 feet long; each sound wave pulsates 20 to 250 times a second. The exhaust system must quiet these explosions and discharge all exhaust vapors.

To do its job, the automotive exhaust system relies on a number of passages.

An *exhaust manifold* (or manifolds) collects the discharges from the cylinders and routes them into a tube called an *exhaust pipe*. In-line engines have one exhaust manifold and one exhaust pipe. The V-8 and opposed-cylinder engines have two manifolds. Unless the car has dual exhausts, the two small exhaust pipes join beneath or behind the engine into one large exhaust pipe.

Because a constricted exhaust system that does not let gases escape smoothly and quickly robs power from the engine, the exhaust system passages must do their job without greatly increasing back-pressure. To handle large volumes of exhaust gases in big V-8s and other high-performance engines, dual exhaust systems are used. Each system handles the exhaust from only half of the cylinders.

The exhaust pipe feeds either into an *exhaust extension pipe* or directly into a *muffler*. The muffler's job is to silence the noise. On some cars, it is located underneath the passenger compartment on one side. On other cars, it is beneath the rear of the car on one side or centered parallel with the rear bumper.

For even better sound control, some cars use additional devices called *resonators*. They may be located before or after the muffler.

A *tailpipe* conducts exhaust gases from the muffler out beneath the rear bumper.

Rear-engine cars, naturally, have very small exhaust systems, because of the short distances involved.

The auto exhaust system is made of

steel or aluminized steel tubing bent to fit the under-chassis area. At joints, one pipe slips inside another. A metal clamp fits around each joint, squeezing down on the outer pipe for a gas-tight connection. Rubberized strap hangers support the piping without transmitting exhaust-system vibrations to the car body.

EXHAUST PROBLEMS

The major cause of exhaust system deterioration is corrosion. For each gallon of gasoline burned, about a gallon of acid-bearing water is created by the engine. If your driving consists mostly of short trips, the exhaust system will not have a chance to heat up much, and those corrosive liquids will condense inside the muffler and pipes. There, they will eat away at the metal. Mufflers are especially susceptible to corrosion because of their complex innards. Most contain drain holes to let condensed acidic water out. Top-quality mufflers are designed to combat acidic corrosion in other ways as well.

Exhaust service is needed when the system develops hisses, throbs, and other unusual noises that denote leaks. The mileage you can expect from an exhaust system varies widely depending on use. Dual exhausts rust out faster because they warm up slower.

Other signs of the need for exhaust system service are rattles from underneath the car. Nine times out of ten, under-car rattles are caused by loose joints or broken hangers that let a tailpipe or muffler bang against some other part of the car. Broken hangers put a great strain on the flanking hangers, often breaking them too. Eventually, the whole exhaust system may drop off.

The Exhaust System

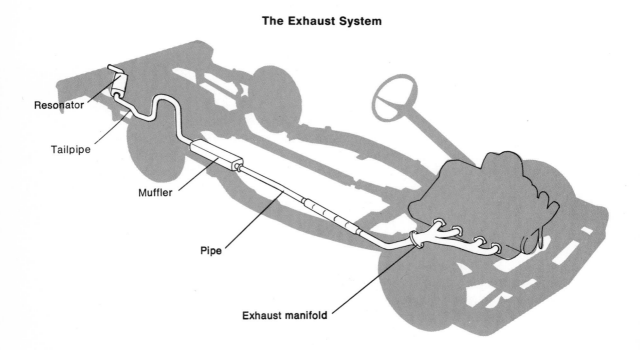

Resonator

Tailpipe

Muffler

Pipe

Exhaust manifold

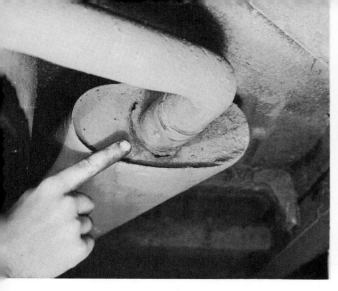

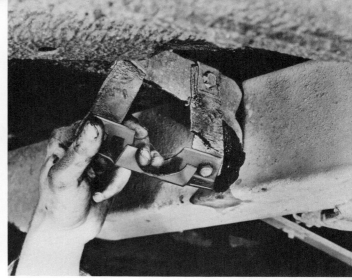

When you hear hissing from under the car as it idles, look for this; such a muffler should be replaced.

Deteriorating muffler hangers should be replaced promptly, or the entire exhaust system may fall off.

Testing the system. Whenever your car is up on a hoist for other work, inspect the exhaust system. To make a special check of your car's exhaust parts, raise the rear or one side of the car sufficiently for you to roll underneath on a creeper. Instead of jacking up the car, you can buy a pair of raised ramps and back the car onto them. Such ramps are available at most auto parts stores. Before you slide underneath, make sure the ramps are firm.

Begin your inspection by jabbing at rusted areas of the exhaust with a screwdriver. If you can jab through the metal at any point, that part needs replacing. Tap on parts of the exhaust system with the handle of the screwdriver. A ringing sound means that the metal is good. A badly corroded part gives out a dull thud.

Next, grab each part firmly and try to wiggle it. It should move on its rubber hangers, but not enough to hit another part of the car. When it does move, there should be no flex at any joint—the entire system should move as one piece. Loose joints often can be cured by tightening the clamp at that point. Otherwise, the joint must be taken apart and repaired or replaced.

Test all joints for leaks—*outdoors.*

Start the engine. Make sure the car is well supported, then slide underneath. While a helper stuffs rags into the end of the tailpipe as the engine is idling, feel around every exhaust-system joint for gas leaks. If you find any, try tightening the clamp. If that does not work, the joint will have to be removed and repaired.

Any patched parts should be replaced; patching is only a short-term emergency repair.

One place often neglected in a leak-check is the connection at the engine's exhaust manifold. That connection is sealed by a clamp that holds the pipe to the manifold, with a thick asbestos gasket between. If tightening does not fix a leak there, replace the gasket.

The manifold heat-control valve is another part of the exhaust system that may give trouble. That valve, found on the exhaust manifold, routes hot exhaust gases through the engine's intake manifold while the engine is still cold, thereby giving faster warmups. When hot, the valve is supposed to open and let the exhaust go out directly through the exhaust pipe. It may have a counterweighted arm attached

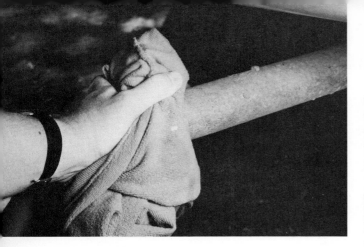

To test your car's exhaust system, stuff a rag into the end of the tailpipe. As the engine idles, listen for hisses, which indicate leaks.

to it. The arm and shaft should rotate against a spring without binding.

Servicing the manifold heat control valve is easy. Coat the valve with silicone or graphite lubricant whenever you have the hood open and the lubricant is handy. If the valve is stuck, tap inward lightly on the shaft with a hammer. This should free it. Then, lubricate the shaft and rotate it back and forth until it moves freely through about 90°. Do not use engine oil on the manifold valve, for exhaust heat will carbonize the oil and jam the valve. Accelerate the engine when it is cold. The valve should open and then close momentarily.

If the valve cannot be freed, or if its coil spring is broken, it should be replaced— a job for a professional.

EXHAUST SYSTEM SERVICE

Exhaust system service is the least productive work you can do on a car. Without a garage hoist, you have to work lying on your back. Corroded parts resist removal. Dirt and rusted metal falls in your face; you will need goggles to keep it out of your eyes. Often, the pipes must be cut apart to remove them.

A muffler specialty shop will quickly install new exhaust system parts, some-times guaranteed for as long as you own the car. Installation takes just a matter of minutes, and the cost is often comparable to what you would pay for undiscounted new parts alone.

On the other hand, some mechanics take the "start-at-the-engine" approach to exhaust work. They remove all parts: exhaust pipe, muffler, extensions and tailpipe. Whether the parts are good or bad, you get back all new equipment. That is easier for them—and more expensive for you. And yet, the average exhaust pipe will outlast two mufflers and two tailpipes because, being closer to the engine, it runs hotter. So if you do the job yourself, you can replace only the parts that are needed. Furthermore, the only way you can ensure getting top-grade, name-brand parts is to purchase and install them yourself.

Tools. If you plan to do your own work, you should get three tools: a slitter, a tailpipe cutter, and a pipe expander. Together, they cost about $25.

The *slitter* is used to undo joints where the inner pipe is to be saved. It peels back the outer pipe, leaving the inside one relatively undamaged.

The *tailpipe cutter* removes corroded parts easily when the parts are to be replaced. It lets you cut the system into sections small enough to remove and discard.

The *pipe expander* lets you salvage old parts, whether off the car or on, by forcing a shrunken or out-of-round pipe back to its original size and shape.

Other necessary tools include a ball peen hammer, wrenches, and perhaps a pair of locking pliers.

Loose joint. To repair a loose joint whose clamp cannot be tightened, install a new clamp. If that does not work, take the joint apart so you can make a new one.

Pipe Removal

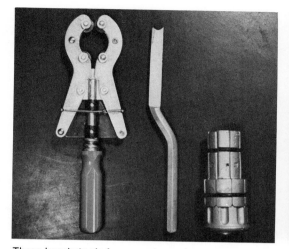

Three handy tools for removing exhaust parts: (*from left*) tailpipe cutter, muffler slitter and pipe expander.

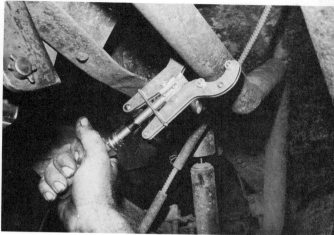

Tailpipe cutter is used for severing a badly corroded pipe that is to be replaced.

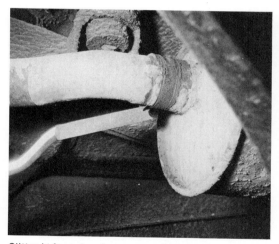

Slitter is for salvaging a reuseable pipe; it peels away pipe or flange end to allow easy removal.

Check all exhaust system clamps for reusability; this muffler clamp, with cleaning, can be reinstalled.

Pipe expander is designed for restoring reusable pipe to its original configuration.

Sandpaper a 1½-inch strip at the ends of all pipes that are to be reused.

First, loosen the clamp, along with any hanger clamps that keep the two parts together. Usually, you can get enough movement in the exhaust hangers to take apart a joint without loosening more than one hanger clamp.

A joint that is loose and leaking gas will not necessarily come apart without binding. If it catches, try persuading it with a hammer. Make sure the car is well blocked before you do any pounding. Hammer all around the joint to loosen corrosion; then, try to separate the pipes. If they still resist, squirt penetrating oil into the joint and wait several minutes. If still no success, try heating with a propane torch.

As a last resort, cut off the outer pipe about 1½ inches back from its forward end, using a tailpipe cutter or a hacksaw. To work the cutter, open it up by unscrewing the handle. Then tighten its blade onto the pipe where you want the cut and swing the handle around to slice a circle into the pipe. The tool is arranged so that only a third of a turn makes a complete cut around the pipe. After a few swings, retighten the cutter handle and make several more swings. Keep tightening and cutting until the pipe parts.

Then, remove the 1½-inch stub of outer pipe that remains on the inner pipe. It may come right off with pounding or prying; if not, cut through it with a hacksaw and twist it open and off.

Sandpaper the corroded end of the inner pipe. Loosen all hangers behind the joint to let the entire exhaust system be moved forward 1½ inches. That makes up for the piece you cut out. Most systems have enough extra length to permit one such adjustment without affecting the clearances appreciably. Check the tail-pipe-to-axle clearance to be certain the pipe is not dangerously close to the brake line, which is routed along the rear of the axle housing.

Spread muffler cement around the outside of the smaller pipe and slip it about 1½ inches into the larger pipe. Muffler cement not only seals the joints, but it makes them easier to get apart the next time. Use it on every joint before assembly. Install a new clamp and tighten it to the specified torque. Start the engine and listen for the tell-tale popping or hissing of an exhaust leak. There should be none.

Parts Replacement

If your inspection shows that an exhaust system component needed replacement, first list the replacement parts you will need. When you order the new parts, be sure to give all the information on your car's make, model, body style and whether it has a single or dual exhaust system. Figure on scrapping all of the old clamps. If you replace the exhaust pipe, you will need a new flange gasket and a pair of flange nuts—the old nuts are likely to be destroyed by the time you get them off.

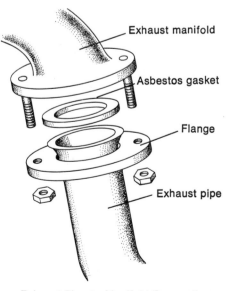

Exhaust manifold

Asbestos gasket

Flange

Exhaust pipe

Exhaust Pipe-to-Manifold Connection

Normally, the muffler is the first component to go, followed shortly by the tailpipe. If one or the other shows signs of leaking, it is best to replace everything from the end of the exhaust pipe extension rearward. If the exhaust pipe extension and exhaust pipe will not pass the screwdriver test, they should be replaced, too.

Removal. Take off all clamps holding the joints and hangers. The clamp and hanger nuts are generally ½-inch or ⁹⁄₁₆-inch. Besides a ratchet wrench, short extension, and the two sockets, you also may need a ½ x ⁹⁄₁₆-inch box-end wrench. The U-bolt clamps can be loosened best with a deep socket that reaches over the long bolt ends onto the nut. If you do not have a deep socket, use a box wrench to loosen the nuts. Then, use a regular socket wrench.

Often, the clamp and hanger nuts are so corroded that the U-bolts or through-bolts break before the threads loosen. That is a blessing, for then you do not have to fight tight, corroded threads. For that reason I recommend *not* using penetrating oil on clamp threads.

Using your tailpipe cutter, cut the old pipes into pieces that can be snaked out without much trouble. Generally, a single cut immediately behind the muffler is sufficient. Before removing the old tailpipe, note its routing so you can mount the new pipe properly.

Salvage. If the exhaust pipe and extension are to be saved, do not remove them. Instead, cut the muffler's hub, or other outer pipe, at the exhaust pipe with your slitter. Start the slitter's point in the joint between the two pipes to be separated. With a hammer, drive it onto the outer pipe to remove a 1½-inch curl of metal from that pipe. If the outer pipe is the one to be saved, you may be able to square off its end with the tailpipe cutter and assemble the new pipes 1½ inches shorter, as

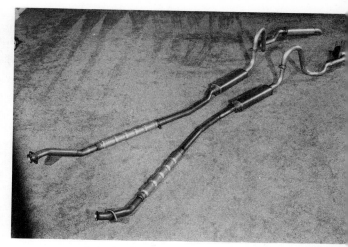
A dual exhaust system.

explained previously. Sometimes, limited undercar clearances will not permit that kind of salvage, but it is worth a try.

Broken or badly damaged hangers should be replaced. New ones are readily available. They usually fasten to the car with small bolts and nuts, and to the exhaust system with tabs and clamps.

Use the pipe expander on outer portions of mufflers and pipes that are to be salvaged. Each usually is ringed by a clamp groove that makes it too small to slide over other pipes, as it is supposed to. The pipe expander removes the clamp groove and restores the pipe to its original size. An expander that can accommodate pipes and flanges from 1 to 2½ inches in diameter is adequate for most cars. Use the small end for 1- to 2-inch pipes, the large end for 2-inch and larger pipes.

The largest part of the expander, next to the nut, is the handgrip. Hold the tool by its handgrip and insert it into the pipe or flange. Be sure that the expander's rubber O-ring is not located under a clamp groove in the pipe; then, it would not be able to remove the groove. Turn the expander nut clockwise with a ⅝-inch wrench to expand the tool; a socket wrench with a

Pipe Installation

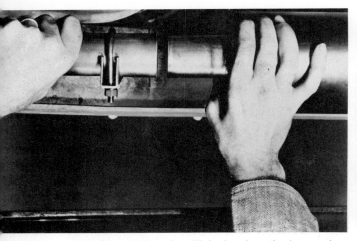

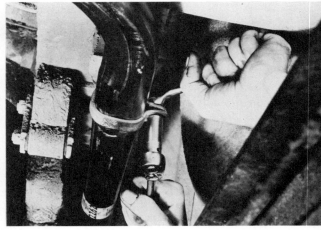

1. Slip smaller pipe 1½ inches into the larger pipe. Clamp firmly.

2. Clamp all of the system's hangers firmly, but do not overtighten them.

3. Check all exhaust parts-to-chassis clearances; use a crowbar, if necessary, to bend the pipes enough to thwart rattles.

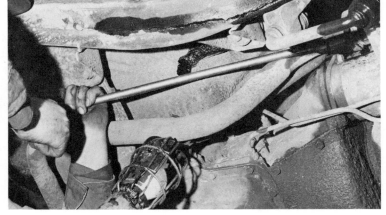

4. With the system properly positioned, double-check all clamps and hangers.

5. Finally, wiggle the system. If play or thumps remain, recheck clamps, hangers and clearances.

ratchet handle works the fastest. The expander does not rotate inside the pipe. Instead, its segments are forced apart against the pipe to smoothly and easily round it out to its original size.

Then, loosen the expander by turning the nut counterclockwise until you can pull the tool out. You have just saved a part.

Installation. In assembling parts, start at the front and work toward the rear. Use muffler cement on all joints except at the exhaust manifold; use a new asbestos gasket there. Lap the joints about 1½ inches. Drive them on with a hammer, if necessary, using a 2 x 4 block of wood to protect the end that you drive against. Do not lap too much at the muffler or you may create an exhaust restriction. Install all clamps and hangers loosely, ½ to ¾ inch in from the pipe or flange end.

Jiggle the new tailpipe into the same position the old one occupied. To get sufficient body-axle clearance to get in a new tailpipe, you may have to jack the body up off the axle. You can use a bumper jack, but be sure that you block the car securely after jacking and before getting underneath. Some tailpipes go in best from the rear. With others, it is easiest to start from under the center of the car, threading the pipe backwards.

Make a final check of the alignment and routing of all pipes. Check for clearance between the tailpipe and rear frame, shock absorbers, rear axle, springs, fuel tank, and bumper. Make sure clearance between the muffler and the car frame is ample. See that no exhaust system parts are too close to a fuel line, brake line, or brake hose. Lower the body onto the axle and check the clearances again. Sometimes merely rotating one pipe in another will improve clearance over the rear suspension parts.

When everything fits properly, tighten the clamps and hangers. Make them reasonably tight, but do not force them or they may break. A torque of about 100 inch-pounds does it on U-bolt clamps. Before you slide out, grab each pipe and try to shake it. If any part contacts another part, loosen the clamps and realign the system. Tighten and check again.

To test the new system for leaks, start the engine, let it idle, and crawl under the car. Listen for gas leaks. There should be none.

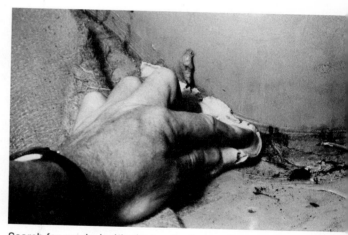

Search for cracks inside the trunk; plug small cracks with nonhardening rope caulk, but leave large, rusted-out spots to a body shop.

Added safety. Because exhaust systems may leak slightly without showing any symptoms, you should seal any cracks in the car's underbody that could let exhaust gases into the passenger compartment. Corrosion from road salt often eats through the metal, leaving openings for fumes. Get a roll of polybutene rope chalk—the kind that never hardens. It is sold in hardware stores for caulking around home storm windows. Use wads of it to plug any opening in the floor pan, body, and firewall not intended for drainage. Lift the carpet or mat from the trunk floor and force caulk into any openings in the trunk floor.

If you find large rusted-out openings, have a body shop make permanent repairs. Those not only will seal out exhaust gases, but they will keep dust and water out of the car, too.

Final test. Use a vacuum gauge to make one last check. Attach the gauge to the intake manifold (see page 62 for the correct hook-up), then simply accelerate the engine to about half speed, and then close the throttle quickly. (You can do that from the engine compartment by pulling or pushing the throttle rod or carburetor throttle arm.) The vacuum gauge should read at least 24 inches of vacuum when the throttle is closed. A lower reading indicates a restriction in the exhaust system, a faulty manifold heat control valve, or blocked or kinked exhaust passages. Such an exhaust restriction affects gasoline economy, performance, and engine life.

With a vacuum gauge, you can test for restrictions in the exhaust system.

Carbon Monoxide: Killer

A faulty exhaust system is not only loud, it can leak deadly carbon monoxide gas from the engine into the passenger compartment. Carbon monoxide is a colorless, odorless, tasteless gas. In sufficiently high concentrations, it can cause headache or a throbbing head, nausea, impaired heartbeat, confusion, impaired vision, drowsiness, unconsciousness, and, eventually, death.

If you or any of your passengers begin to experience any symptoms of carbon monoxide poisoning, stop the car immediately, switch off the engine, and open the windows. Once the symptoms subside, drive *with all of the windows open* to a shop and have the exhaust system checked. If symptoms do not disappear after you breathe fresh air for a few minutes, go directly to a doctor. Breathing carbon monoxide for a long time can cause permanent injury to both the body and the brain.

TROUBLESHOOTING THE EXHAUST SYSTEM

SYMPTOM	CAUSE	CURE
Excessive noise	Leaking joints	Tighten clamps or reassemble joint with muffler cement
	Rusted-through muffler or pipe	Replace corroded parts
	Manifold flange leak	Install new gasket
Poor performance and economy	Pinched pipe	Repair or replace damaged part
	Restriction inside muffler	Replace muffler (after testing for exhaust restriction with vacuum gauge)
	Inoperative manifold heat control valve	Free up and lubricate valve or have it replaced
Engine hard to warm up or will not return to idle	Heat control valve frozen in open position	Free up and lubricate valve or have it replaced
Undercar rattles	Exhaust system parts loose or with insufficient clearance	Tighten, realign, or replace parts

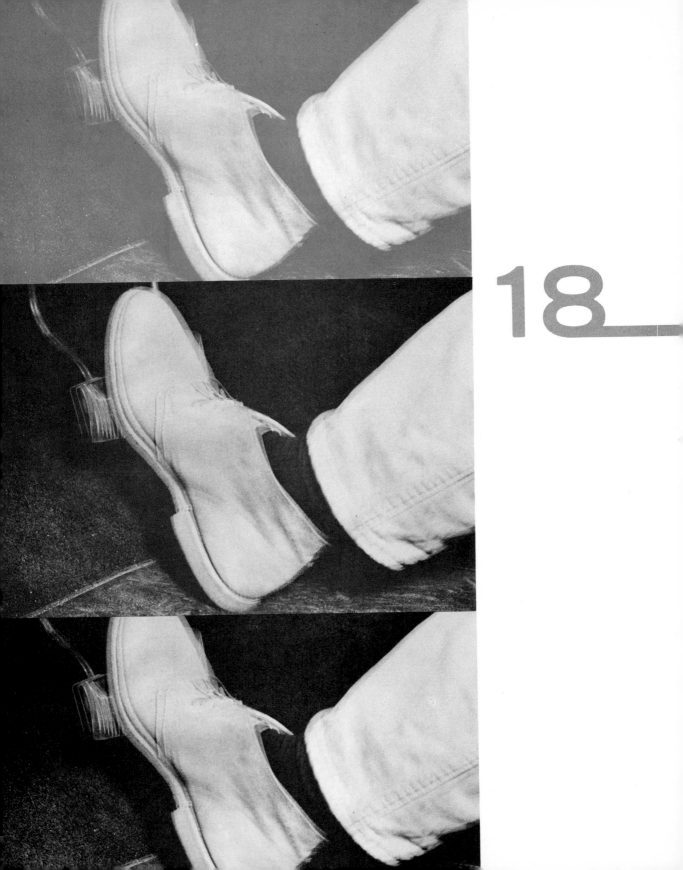

18

Servicing the Brake System

Some auto experts feel that brakes are a part of the car that do-it-yourselfers should leave alone, since the results of a mistake could be tragic. After reading this chapter, you yourself must decide whether you can safely perform brake servicing and repairs. Even if you decide against tackling such work, at least you should be able to detect brake problems sooner than the average motorist.

A brake is simply a heat machine that transforms energy stored up in a moving vehicle into heat. The amount of heat varies according to the square of the vehicle's speed. Double the speed and you get four times the heat.

A single stop from 70 mph by a 4,000-pound car produces 840 BTU (British Thermal Units, a standard measure of heat quantity). You would have to burn almost 1,000 wooden kitchen matches to generate that much heat. During one such stop, the temperature of wheel brake parts can rise by 200°. Make several stops in quick succession, without allowing time for cooling, and your brakes may not be able to cope with the heat that is generated.

Hydraulic brakes. For years, cars have used effective, dependable hydraulic brakes. These are built around a *master cylinder* with a pressure piston that is worked by a foot brake pedal. As you step down on the pedal, the piston in the master cylinder forces brake fluid through a system of thin steel brake lines and tough rubber hoses to each wheel. The hydraulic brake system works well because the brake fluid pressure is transmitted equally to all wheels.

In power brakes, master-cylinder hydraulic pressure is boosted by engine vacuum.

Since 1967, all U.S.-built cars have had dual hydraulic systems. In such systems, the master cylinder contains two pistons and two sets of brake lines. One set of hydraulic lines goes to the front wheels, the

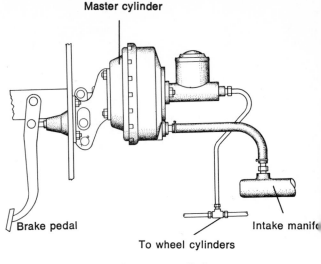

Hydraulic brake master cylinder.

other set to the rear wheels. If one system should suffer a hydraulic failure, the other system could still stop the car—though, of course, not as quickly.

At the wheels, hydraulic *wheel cylinders* react to the pressure by pushing lined "shoes" outward against a rotating brake drum, or by pinching a rotating disc between lined pads or shoes. The friction of the brake linings on the drums or discs slows the wheels. Friction of the tires against the road brings the car to a stop.

Drum brakes. This type expands from within. Lined brake shoes inside the drum are pushed outward and into contact with the drum. The most popular feature of the drum brake, called duo-servo, is that once applied, the brake shoes themselves supply some of the force necessary to hold them in contact with the drums. Such brakes are known as self-energizing.

The advantages of drum brakes are that they can easily be made self-energizing, and they require lower hydraulic pressures.

Disc brakes. These work like your fingers do when you pinch a rolling quarter between them.

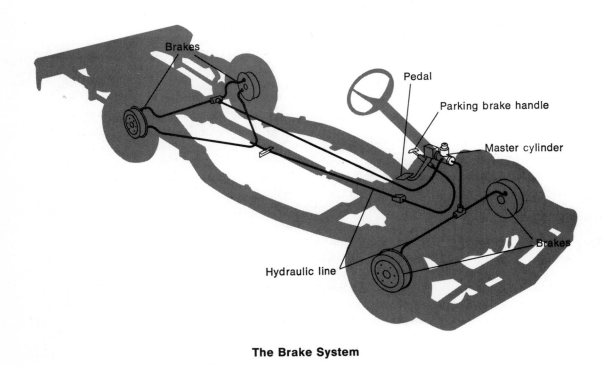

The Brake System

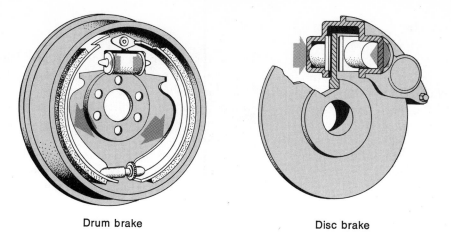

Drum brake   Disc brake

In a drum brake, a cylinder pushes outward on the lined shoes, which in turn slow the wheel. In a disc brake, a caliper squeezes the lined pistons against the rotating disc.

The advantages of disc brakes are that they are more open to the stream of passing air than are drum brakes, whose linings are enclosed in the drum. Disc brakes therefore tend to dissipate heat faster, and thus tend to be less subject to swerving and "fade"—a condition in which brakes lose some or all of their stopping ability.

Disc brakes also tend to be affected less by water. (After going through a large puddle, some drum brakes lose most of their stopping ability until they dry.) Many disc brakes also are easier to reline.

One problem with discs on all four wheels, as in the Chevrolet Corvette, is that installing a parking brake in such a system is difficult and expensive. Front discs with rear drums make an excellent braking compromise, since the front brakes do up to 75 percent of the work. Such a system is optional on most U.S. cars and standard on some U.S., and many foreign, models.

Antiskid braking. The newest development in braking is the antiskid system. Some manufacturers call it "skid-control braking," others call it "adaptive braking," still others call it "antilock braking."

The system uses speed sensors at the wheels, an electronic control module, and an actuator. Normal braking is used until wheel lockup is approached. If the brakes begin to lock when you apply the brakes on a slippery pavement, the system releases and reapplies the brakes in pulsations of about five per second. This provides braking action without locking the wheels. Braking thus feels pleasantly sure-footed.

Antiskid braking is claimed to cut dry-pavement stopping distance by five to 15 percent. Wet-pavement stopping distance improvements of two to 23 percent have been claimed for one system. Of course, tire condition has a lot to do with the degree of improvement.

Normal braking defects are serviced the same as on cars without the antiskid system. Only if the antiskid system fails does it need service. Then, it is a job that only a highly trained mechanic should tackle.

Brake break-in. New brakes need breaking in, as do the engine, tires, and other auto parts.

Fast, hard stops can ruin new brake linings. Try to avoid hard braking for the first 300 miles, if possible. Breaking-in the brakes is important both on a new car and on an older car with newly relined brakes.

After the break-in period, work your

brakes hard once in a while, especially if most of your driving is done in town at slower speeds. Cars driven without much hard braking often balk and swerve when braked hard on a freeway. Some linings take on a slick glaze that covers their friction surfaces. Making several moderate stops from 50 mph should remove the "city" glaze. (Be sure you make those stops in a safe area, away from traffic.)

Do not set the parking brake after using your brakes hard, if you can avoid it. You may make the rear drums oval and end up with a pulsating brake pedal.

CHECKING YOUR CAR'S BRAKES

Brakes rarely fail suddenly; they usually give some warning of impending trouble.

Fluid level. The first thing to check is the fluid level in the brake master cylinder. In most modern cars, this cylinder is found under the hood, immediately in front of the brake pedal. It is usually high on the firewall, where it is easy to service.

With the lid removed, check the level of brake fluid inside. It should be a half inch from the top of the reservoir. If not, add clean brake fluid.

Dual hydraulic systems have two reservoirs. Both should be brought to proper level.

Always use a name-brand brake fluid, preferably the type recommended by the car manufacturer. Cars with drum brakes require one type; cars with front disc brakes or four-wheel discs require another. Do not mix the two.

Brake fluid for drum brakes, usually called "super heavy-duty," should say on the can: "Meets or surpasses SAE specs J-1703 and 70R3." Amber in color, this is absolutely the lowest grade brake fluid that should be used in any hydraulic system, even though older specifications permitted a lesser fluid.

Disc-braked cars need a brake fluid with a high boiling point to be safe. The only suitable one is blue-green-colored, 550° boiling-point fluid. Sometimes, the auto manufacturer recommends a different fluid for disc-braked cars—notably Chrysler. The "550" fluid may be used in drum-

Keep the fluid level in the master cylinder ½ inch from the top. Always use a top-quality fluid.

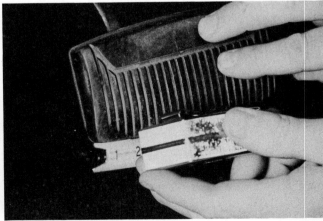

Check pedal play: When it is fully depressed, there should be 1½ inches between pedal and floor.

braked cars too, if the master cylinder has a rubber diaphragm underneath its cover. But all of the old amber fluid should be flushed out (see page 341) so that the two fluids do not mix. Most new cars come with disc brake fluid in them, whether or not they have discs.

Check fluid level at least twice a year.

Pedal play. Now for the next self-check: With your car stopped, press hard on the brake pedal with about 50 pounds of pressure, and hold it for half a minute. The pedal should remain firm, showing no tendency to fall away from your foot.

Pump the brake pedal. A soft, springy feeling indicates air in the hydraulic system. "Bleeding" the air out of the system is covered later in this chapter.

Check brake pedal free play—the distance it must be depressed before it activates. There should be ¼- to ⅜-inch of play in a manual system. The adjustment is often made by turning an eccentric nut on the brake pedal linkage under the dash. Adjusting the play in power brakes is a shop job.

With the parking brake released, measure the amount of brake pedal travel left between the fully-depressed pedal and the floorboard. Self-adjusting brakes should have about 3 inches; power brakes tested with the engine running should have about 1½ inches.

Leaks. Look underneath the car, especially at the insides of the wheels and tires, for signs of hydraulic fluid leakage. See that wheels, tires, shock absorbers, axle, fender aprons, and exhaust system and suspension parts do not rub or knock against any of the brake lines and hoses.

The brake lines are easy to spot. They are about ³/₁₆-inch in diameter, and are routed along the frame from the master

Periodically inspect all brake lines for deterioration and damage. Flex them to check for cracks. Replacing worn lines is a shop job.

cylinder on the engine firewall to each wheel.

At each front wheel, the brake lines connect to flexible rubber hoses that absorb the body-to-wheel flexing. A flexible brake hose is also located between the body and the center of the rear axle.

Road behavior. Drive the car at 45 mph. When no traffic is near, apply the brakes moderately hard and watch for pulling to one side. Then, try a hard stop on dry pavement from about 20 mph. All four wheels should lock and slide under reasonable brake pedal efforts.

Brakes that pull can be dangerous. A light brake pull can be caused by either a front or rear brake problem. A strong pull is always caused by the front brakes or by faulty front wheel alignment.

Road noises. With the car window open, make a slow, gentle stop and listen for a scraping or grinding sound from the brakes. Such noises indicate the linings have worn through. A light wire-brush sound, however, is characteristic of some brake linings.

Stop gently, going both forward and

backward in the garage, and listen for repeated clicks. Clicks indicate burred brake shoes — the metal parts in drum brakes that hold the linings — and burred backing plates — the stamped metal plates the brake parts mount to.

Some brake noises indicate major problems; others are simply a nuisance. If you can find no cause and the sound is mild, live with it. If it bothers you, try relining both brakes on the axle the sound is coming from. Disc brakes especially tend to squeal. Often, no cure is possible.

Other checks. Apply the parking brake fully. Is the reserve ample? Release the brake. Does it release fully or do the brakes drag?

Periodically, when starting the car, be sure that your car's brake system warning light (if it has one) is working. It tells you if one of the dual hydraulic systems has failed.

Beware of any change in normal brake operation. The characteristic smell of brake fluid, or any other unusual odor such as the smell of hot brake linings, is a tip-off to brake trouble.

A "complete" job. Brake experts do not agree on just what items should be included in a complete brake relining. One thing is certain: No shop can perform a complete, safe brake job for $19.95. A cheap brake job is like a cheap parachute.

The brakes should always be relined on both sides of the axle or, better yet, on all four wheels.

A good job, according to most experts, should also include turning all brake drums, whether or not they are badly worn. If little wear or out-of-round is found in a drum, only a light clean-up cut need be taken. Some reputable shops, however, do not normally turn drums unless they are badly worn or out-of-round.

Grease-soaked linings cannot be cleaned; they must be replaced. Before relining, though, find and fix the source of the leak.

LININGS

Every time you stop, particles of the brake linings are ground away by the discs or drums. A set of linings may last from about 10,000 to 40,000 miles. Stop-and-go driving wears linings much sooner than highway driving with long distances between stops.

In addition to normal wear, brake linings are subject to other forms of attrition. Correcting these conditions, which lead to premature failure, usually involves service to, or replacement of, the brake linings.

Grease or *brake fluid* on linings or drums always calls for replacement of the linings. Grease and brake fluids soak into the linings, and cleaning cannot remove them. A fluid-soaked lining, contrary to what you might expect, tends to grab and lock. If one wheel slides when you apply the brakes, its lining is probably greasy or soaked with brake fluid.

Each wheel has a grease seal to keep

bearing lubricant out of its brake, and road dust out of its bearing. Grease gets on linings by slipping past a worn grease seal. Brake fluid gets on linings from leaking wheel cylinders.

The opposite wheel across the axle also should get new linings at the same time, since new and old linings have different frictional characteristics. If only one wheel were relined, the brakes would probably pull to one side. The only exception is if the brakes were recently relined. Both drums should be turned, too.

Glazed linings slip when they contact the drum, and make the brakes require too much pedal effort. They also cause brake noises. If several high-speed stops do not cure the glazing, sanding the linings with coarse sandpaper may break up the glaze. (To do that, you must remove the drums.) If sanding does not help, new linings are called for.

Lining Facts

The performance of your car's braking system depends almost wholly on the lining material used on the shoes. The surest way to end up with poor brakes is to reline with poor linings.

All organic brake linings—good and bad—are made of some combination of asbestos, resin, and filler. Some also contain small wires or metal chips. Do not confuse those with metallic linings, which are different.

The fade and friction characteristics of a brake lining should match the requirements of your car's brakes. The only way to tell is to follow the recommendations of a reliable lining manufacturer. The best manufacturers do lots of testing, and you pay for such testing when you buy the linings. With cheap, off-brand linings, you do your own testing—out on the highway.

Some brake linings fade seriously (lose their effectiveness) when hot. A different composition of lining may grab harder when hot. That is also undesirable, since it makes for rough, hard-to-modulate braking. Grabby linings can get so bad that they self-destruct. Good linings are designed to fade just a little. Recovery from fade should be rapid.

Grades. Aftermarket linings come in three principle grades: low-cost, standard, and premium. (They are not always called by those names.)

The best advice on buying brake linings is: Use original-equipment linings designed for your car; or use the best quality premium linings made by a reputable brake lining manufacturer.

Never use *low-cost linings*, even those made by a reputable manufacturer. Often, they give you only single-friction linings,

Linings for a drum brake often come already bonded or riveted to a replacement shoe.

the same grade for the primary and secondary shoes. With single-friction linings, the lining on the secondary shoes will wear out first. That costs you in wasted lining life.

Dual-friction linings give you one grade for the primary and a harder grade for the secondary shoes.

Finding original-equipment *standard linings* is not easy. Some original-equipment linings come mounted on brake shoes; those often are sold in boxes bearing the name of the relining firm, rather than the lining manufacturer. Dealers selling those shoes do not always know what brand of lining is used.

To complicate the situation, some new-car dealers carry factory-furnished "com-

Linings for a disc brake fit into the caliper on both sides of the disc.

petitive-grade" linings made to meet the cheap-lining competition. Because these second-rate materials come in boxes with the auto manufacturer's name on them does not mean they are original-equipment linings. Furthermore, some new-car dealers may sell an inferior private brand instead of factory-supplied linings.

If you go to a new-car dealer's parts department, insist on original-equipment linings.

If they suit your driving style, use standard linings.

Some car enthusiasts prefer *premium linings*. They feel that original-equipment linings are all right for average driving conditions, but not for really hard driving. With premium linings, you have a choice of hard and soft lining material—either type is good.

The premium linings of every firm are not necessarily equal in quality. Do not consider price alone; some brake linings carry huge markups.

Next comes the question of bonded versus riveted linings. Both are good. Most experts recommend relining with the same type that came with your car when new.

Metallic linings. Made of sintered iron or a mixture of powdered iron and graphite, metallic linings are used chiefly because they can take terrific punishment without fading or burning. In fact, they work better when they are hot—which is why you may not want them for your car. Until they warm up, they work poorly. Thus, the first few stops in the morning may scare you.

Squeaking and rapid drum wear are additional drawbacks of metallic brake linings. Some require drum pretreatment. Unless your car has power brakes, expect a hard pedal.

Metallic linings are used on police cars, taxis, and other hard-use vehicles.

Severe service is their bag. You should consider them only if premium linings cannot handle your car's braking requirements. Trailering in mountain country or pulling a heavy boat or travel trailer might qualify you. Hot-rodding should.

Lining standards. While new-car brake linings undergo all kinds of on-the-car testing before being approved by the auto's manufacturer, some aftermarket linings do not meet such rigid standards. In fact, until a few years ago, no standards existed.

Now some states, including New York, require laboratory friction testing of brake linings sold within their borders. Those tests, nicknamed the New York tests, require the lining manufacturer to affix brand and friction codes to every lining.

For passenger cars, those codes run from "D" to "F"; "D" signifies low friction, "F" signifies high. The codes come in pairs, such as "EF." The first letter represents cold friction; the second, hot friction. Whether or not you live in a state with such a standard, you may well find the codes printed on your new linings.

Such codes do not guarantee good linings. The coefficient of friction of linings can drop as low as 0.15 at 600° F., and the linings could pass. That temperature often is reached in mountain driving. You would take a long, long time to stop at a friction coefficient of only 0.15.

The New York tests basically screen out the really bad linings, but do not establish the capabilities of really good linings on the car.

Lining size. This depends on the finished size of your car's brake drums after turning. Linings come in standard sizes and varying degrees of oversize (thicker than standard).

Standard-sized linings should be used only with drums that have not been turned out more than .030 inch. The general rule is that extra thickness of linings should equal the metal removed from one side of the drum. If the drum has been turned out the maximum .060 inch, the linings should be .030-inch thicker than new-car linings for that car. Most suppliers stock that size.

For drums turned out less than the maximum, a good solution is to buy the thicker linings and have them ground down to fit the drum. Linings should be fitted by grinding for optimum results. Your machine shop should have a brake shoe grinder.

On the grinder, each shoe should be surfaced slightly smaller than the drum so that the center of the shoe touches the drum, and the heel and toe have .005- to .008-inch clearance. The heel-toe clearance keeps the shoes from grabbing. Check clearances with a thickness gauge.

If the shoes are for duo-servo brakes (most are, today), the shoes should be ground to an anchor pin. Your machinist

Self-adjusting mechanism of a drum brake.

Shoe-retracting springs

Adjuster spring

Adjuster wheel   Adjuster lever

Self adjuster cable

knows what that is. If your local auto-motive machine shop does not have the proper shoe-grinding equipment, go to a reputable dealer who specializes in brake service.

DRUM BRAKES

A duo-servo drum brake consists of a pair of lined brake shoes that are separated at the lower end by the star wheel adjust-ment screw, and at the upper end by the wheel cylinder and its two slotted push-rods.

A spring at the lower end holds the shoes against the adjustment screw. A pair of shoe-retracting springs at the upper end holds the shoes together there. Those springs also force the pistons back into the cylinder. Each shoe also has one or more

hold-down springs that secure it against the metal backing plate.

An adjustment lever, adjustment spring, and self-adjuster cable make up the self-adjusting mechanism.

Hydraulic fluid enters through a hose threaded into the rear of the wheel cyl-inder, behind the backing plate. Rubber dust boots cover both ends of the wheel cylinder.

Rear brakes also contain a parking brake arm, link, and cable that force the shoes apart mechanically when the parking brake is applied.

As you make various brake inspections, always handle the drums—and for that matter, the discs—with care. Never block the car under the drums, and never let the car fall on the drums or discs.

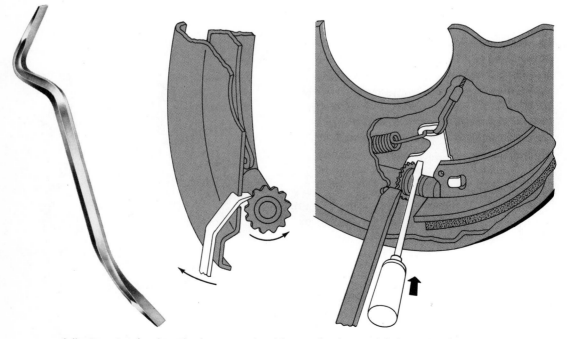

Adjustments of a drum brake are made with an adjusting tool (*left*), which fits into the slot on the backing plate. On a manual adjustment brake (*center*), ratchet up to tighten and down to back off the brake. On a self-adjusting brake (*right*), push the adjusting lever back with a screwdriver. Then, ratchet down to back off the brake and up to tighten it.

Adjustment

Good drum brakes rely on close proximity of the shoes and drums. Adjustment for shoe-drum clearance is always provided.

Duo-servo drum brakes adjust with the serrated star wheel at the lower end of the wheel brake assembly. They also feature an anchor pin—adjustable or fixed—at the upper end. Immediately below the anchor pin is the two-way hydraulic wheel cylinder. If your car does not have duo-servo drum brakes, the adjusting procedures will be very different from those described here. Look them up in your service manual.

Self-adjusters. For ten years and more, most cars have had self-adjusting brakes. Every time the car is stopped while it is moving backwards, the brake shoes take up play, should there be any.

When brake shoe clearance is excessive, the self-adjuster cocks an arm against the star wheel during a backup stop. Then, when the brakes are released, the adjustment wheel is turned toward a closer shoe clearance, accompanied by a click.

Problems are rare.

If a *stuck self-adjuster* is the problem, the clearance between the brake shoes and the drum will increase as the lining wears away. The result will be that the brake pedal has to travel farther toward the floor to move the shoe into contact with its drum. Thus, if you notice increased brake pedal movement, either you have not been making enough backward stops, or a self-adjusting mechanism is defective. A stuck adjuster usually can be loosened by one hard back-up stop.

If a *low brake pedal* is your problem, make one fast backup stop in your driveway. Then, make about ten more alternate forward and backward stops, driving about 20 feet in each direction. That should bring the brake pedal back where it should be.

If it does not, make ten more stops. If the pedal still has too much travel, the brakes need attention.

Never replace the self-adjusters with manual adjusters. Fix them instead.

Manual adjustment. Older brake shoes that are not self-adjusting need regular adjustments, an easy job. The same method also works on self-adjusting brakes if backup stops fail to raise the pedal.

Jack up the wheel, block it safely, and roll under on a creeper. Pry the rubber dust cap out of its slot at the bottom of the brake backing plate. Insert a brake adjusting tool—a screwdriver will do—through the slot and feel for the star wheel behind the slot. The front wheels may have to be turned to one side for access to the star wheel.

Stick the tool into one of the serrations, and move the tool's handle down for self-adjusting brakes, up for manual-adjusting brakes. That moves the shoes closer to the drum. Spin the car's wheel as you adjust. Keep going until the brake shoes get tight enough to prevent easy turning of the wheel.

Then, ratchet the star wheel in the opposite direction to back off the adjustment. (With self-adjusting brakes, hold a small

To maintain existing balance when you remove a wheel, mark one stud and its hole with chalk.

screwdriver in the slot behind the adjusting tool; this releases the adjusting lever so the star wheel can turn backwards.) Back off until the wheel spins with little brake drag. If you must back off the adjustment more than 20 clicks to make the shoes stop dragging, the anchor pin may need repositioning—a shop job.

Install the rubber dust cap and proceed to the next wheel.

Because of rear-end gearing, rear wheels never spin freely. Adjust them so they move without much brake drag.

Checking Linings

To tell whether drum brakes need relining, remove a front and a rear drum and inspect the linings. Make a lining check at least every 10,000 miles, or once a year.

If you intend to have a mechanic handle your brake service, let him do the lining check, too. Most shops make no charge for the check because they hope to pick up a reline job.

Drum removal. To remove a *front drum*, pry off the hub cap or wheel cover to expose the hub. Use a screwdriver to pry off the hub dust cover in the center of the wheel. That exposes the large spindle nut that holds the drum on the front spindle.

After removing the brake drum, inspect the linings for grease and fluid stains and check lining thickness —there should be at least $1/32$-inch remaining.

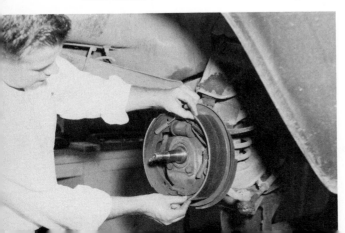

Jack up the wheel and block the car securely. Then, unbend, pull out, and discard the large cotter pin that goes through the spindle and castellations of the spindle nut or nut lock.

With a large open-end wrench or slip-joint pliers, remove the nut lock, if present, and spindle nut. As with all wheel bearing parts, put those nuts on a clean piece of newspaper. Do not let dust or dirt get into the bearing parts.

Once the spindle nut is off, wiggle the wheel until the outer tapered roller bearing works its way to the end of the spindle. Remove the bearing and its large washer.

Now the whole wheel, drum and tire assembly can be lifted off. Lean the wheel against a wall to keep dirt out of the bearing.

The front wheel brake is now exposed. It may be dusty, but no grease or brake fluid should be on any of the parts.

Note whether your car uses bonded or riveted brake linings. Bonded linings are glued to the shoes, with no recesses. Bonded linings that are worn to $1/32$-inch at the thinnest spot are ready for replacement. Riveted linings are held to the shoe with brass rivets, about eight per shoe. The shoes have recesses for the rivet heads. Riveted linings that are worn to within $1/64$-inch of the rivet heads also should be replaced.

Front brakes usually wear faster than rear brakes, since they do most of the braking. But the rears should be checked, too.

To get at a *rear drum*, jack up, and remove, a rear wheel as though you were going to put on the spare tire. That exposes the rear brake drum. On three of the wheel studs, look for tiny flat metal clips, called linnerman nuts, which must be removed. They help hold the drum solidly on the shoulders of the lug bolts. A drum that is not properly seated will allow the lug bolts to loosen, and may even let the wheel work loose. For that reason, save the linnerman nuts and replace them when you put the drum back on.

With the parking brake off, pull the drum toward you. If it does not come off, tap the axle with a hammer, wiggle the drum or turn it.

Once the drum is off, inspect the rear linings for wear. They, too, should be free of grease and brake fluid.

If the parking brake cable sticks, a rear shoe will be held out from the anchor pin. Moreover, the self-adjuster on this wheel will not work. The shoe will show heavy wear at the top. Remove and lubricate the parking brake cable when you reline.

Checking wear. The wear pattern on all front and rear linings should be about the same. Normal brake lining wear leaves little or no lining in the center of the shoe. The shoe ends should show nearly equal thickness — shoes very rarely show great differences in wear from one end of the lining to the other. If they do, the problem is a misplaced anchor pin (if the pin is adjustable) or a worn or distorted brake shoe. Correction is a job for a professional mechanic.

All worn brake linings require installation of relined brake shoes. Those are bought with linings already riveted or bonded to the metal portion of the shoe.

Other checks. While you have the drums off, look for signs of *heat damage* to the brakes. Examine the brake drums. Too much heat causes blue spots or cracks on the braking surface of the drum.

Heat also cooks brake linings — making them either glazed, cracked and shiny, or soft and unglazed, with the resins burned out. Replace such linings whether or not they are worn thin.

Signs of heat damage on drums and linings means that heat also may have stretched the shoe-retracting springs. When you reline, install new retracting springs.

And while you have the drums off, check for *leaks*. Peel back the rubber dust boots on both ends of the wheel cylinders at the top of the brake plate. You should see no trace of brake fluid leakage past the wheel cylinder pistons.

Installation. If the brakes are to be relined, do it while you already have two of the drums off. If a reline is not needed, you can put the drums back on. First, wipe the front spindle to keep dust out of the wheel bearing. Slip the wheel on and install the outer bearing, washer, and nut.

Adjust the bearing nut according to the directions and photos on pages 434 and 435. When it is properly adjusted, install a new cotter pin, and bend it around the castellations.

Put on the hub dust cap and the wheel cover, and you are done.

Relining

You can reline your own brakes if you want to.

A self-adjusting brake may look complicated, but there is no need to be frightened. If the service manual covering your car gives specific step-by-step instructions for brake disassembly and assembly, you can do the job yourself. Take special note of the drawings that show the arrangement of front- and rear-wheel brake parts.

Tools. A pair of *brake spring pliers* or a *brake spring tool* helps get the shoe-retracting springs off and on without damage. You can handle the retracting springs with regular *slip-joint pliers* — but be careful not to hurt your hand if the pliers slip off.

Never handle brake springs with side-cutting pliers. Nicks left by the pliers set the stage for future spring breakage. Broken shoe-retracting springs can cause

BRAKE RELINING CHECKLIST

ITEM	MINIMUM	RECOMMENDED
Drums, discs	Inspect, turn if faulty	Turn all
Linings	Original equipment or reputable premium lining	Original equipment or reputable premium lining
Shoes (drum brake)	Fitted to drum	Oversize linings fixed-anchor-ground to fit drum
Hydraulic fluid	Flush new fluid through system	Flush new fluid through system
Wheel or caliper cylinders	Rebuild or replace all	Rebuild or replace all
Master cylinder	Check for leaks, rebuild or replace if needed	Rebuild or replace
Shoe-retracting and hold-down springs (drum brake)	Inspect, replace if damaged	Replace
Backing plate (drum brake)	Clean and lubricate	Clean and lubricate
Front wheel bearings	Repack	Repack
Grease seals	Replace front; inspect rear for leaks, replace if necessary	Replace front; inspect rear for leaks, replace if necessary
Front wheel cotter pins	Replace	Replace
Brake lines, hoses	Inspect, replace if aged, cracked, damaged, or leaking	Inspect, replace if aged, cracked, damaged, or leaking

brake pull, noises, dragging brakes, and rapid lining wear.

Besides tools, you need a good working arrangement with an automotive machine shop or parts house to take care of your machine work on brake drums and shoes.

Preparation. Unless you are familiar with the wheel brake assembly, work on one wheel at a time. That way, you can look at the opposite brake as a reference.

Jack up and block all the wheels to be relined. Remove the wheel covers and lug nuts. Take off the wheels and set them aside.

Mark each brake drum with chalk or crayon to show which wheel it belongs to. See the chapter on lubrication for front wheel bearing care, from repacking through clean-up of the bearings and hub.

Brake parts are typically dusty. But if there is a film of grease or brake fluid, you will have to locate the source of contamination.

Remove the rear drums, as previously described for inspecting the rear brake linings. Rear drums come off without affecting the axle bearings or grease seals. If any grease is present in the rear brake parts, the axle should be removed, and a new grease seal installed. You can do it according to the directions in your car's service manual.

If you have a paint-spray compressor, use it to blow out dust from the drum and wheel brake assembly. Otherwise, brush out what you can.

Examine the brakes as described earlier.

Brake removal. Next, get the brake shoes off. To pull off a shoe-retracting spring with a brake spring tool, slip the large end of the tool over the end of the anchor post, and rotate the tool. It picks up the retracting spring, and lifts it off the anchor pin onto the tool. There, it can slide easily into a relaxed position. In a pinch, slip-joint pliers can be substituted.

Unhook the self-adjuster cable eye from the anchor pin and remove the anchor pin shoe guide, if there is one.

Remove the two or four shoe hold-down springs. To do that, hold the pin against the backing plate from behind, and grasp the hold-down washer with pliers. Push the washer in as far as it will go, and twist 90°. The washer should then pop off over the deformation in the pin. Remove the inner washer and spring. Push the pin out behind the backing plate and catch it.

Take off the brake shoes by pulling them apart at the top. This frees them from the slotted pushrods. Cross them to free their lower ends from the adjusting nut, spring, and self-adjuster parts.

On rear brakes, take off the parking brake link and spring from between the shoes. To get the secondary shoe free from the parking brake lever, spread the jaws of the horseshoe retaining clip with a

(*text continued on page 326*)

Brake Shoe Removal

1. Begin by removing all shoe-retracting springs. The brake spring tool (*above left*), when turned over an anchor pin, lifts the spring (*above right*). Equally handy is the brake spring pliers (*below left*). Lacking these tools, you can undo springs with a pair of slip-joint pliers (*below right*).

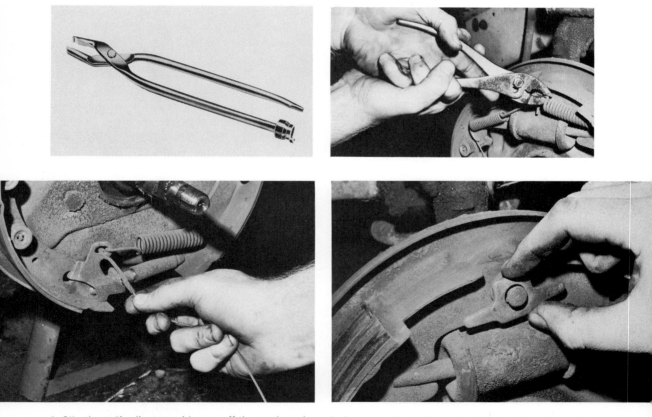

2. Slip the self-adjuster cable eye off the anchor pin and unhook the cable from the adjuster lever.

3. Remove the anchor pin plate, located above the cylinder, from the anchor pin.

4. Remove all the shoe hold-down springs. Hold each pin from behind while you push and twist the outer washer 90°.

5. Free the shoes from the wheel cylinder pushrods by expanding them at the top.

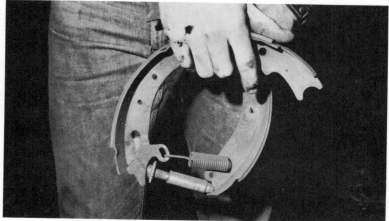

6. Lift the plates out and over-lap the tops of the shoes. This will allow the adjuster parts to drop out. The job is done.

screwdriver and, using pliers, slide the clip off, along with its spring washer. In some cases, the job is easier if you first disconnect the parking brake lever from the parking brake cable.

Put all the small brake parts—but not wheel bearings—in the overturned hub cap inside the wheel, so nothing will be lost. In some models, retracting springs for front and rear shoes are different colors to signify different strengths. Note which color goes where.

Test each brake spring by dropping it onto a concrete surface. A good spring hits the floor with a dull thud. A weakened or heat-stretched spring bounces like a rubber ball.

Resurfacing. Brush remaining dust from the brake backing plate. Look closely at the ledges—the flat spots that hold the shoes out from the rest of the backing plate. If they are deeply scored, they should be filed flat to keep the shoes from catching as they move.

When the wheel brake parts have been disassembled, take the drums to an automotive machine shop and have the drums inspected for hard spots and wear, and measured for size.

Minimal drum wear may require only a light machining cut. But if the linings wore through to the shoes, and metal-to-metal contact took place, wear may be beyond the permissible tolerances. If machining would make any one of the inside diameters more than .060 inch oversize, buy new drums. The machinist can make the measurements with a brake drum micrometer. Blue marks in the drum are also cause for drum replacement.

As a brake drum is turned in the brake lathe—the machine used to resurface it—the cutting tool may run into hard spots in the cast iron surface. Those are caused when excess braking heat and pressure

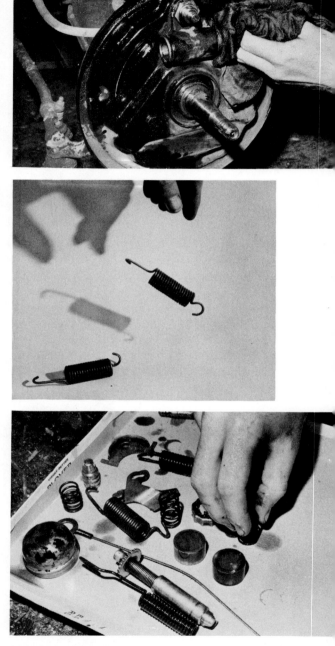

After the brake shoes are off, swab the backing plate with a solvent-soaked cloth (*top*). Be sure to keep the cylinder dry. Test all springs by dropping them on a concrete floor (*center*). Replace any that bounce. Thoroughly clean all parts to be reused—except the shoes—in solvent (*bottom*).

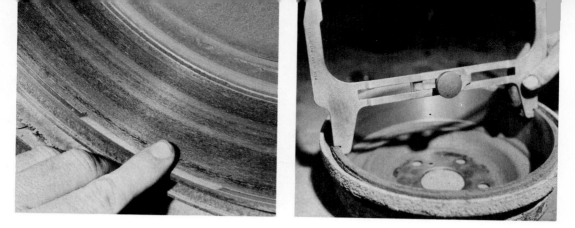

Brake drum should be inspected for wear, scoring and signs of heat damage; the one at left is in good condition. The drum should also be checked for size by a machinist (*right*).

harden the cast iron. The cutting tool rides over each hard spot, leaving a lump. If the spots do not go too deep, such a drum may be saved by grinding instead of turning. The grinder eats right through the hard spots and removes them.

Ask the machinist to inspect the front drum bearing races. If abnormal wear is found, a new race can be pressed in after the old one is pressed out. Crystallization on any of the wheel bearing surfaces means that the bearing should be re-placed, and at the same time, a new race installed in the hub.

Wheel Cylinder Service

While your car's brake drums and shoes are being serviced, start rebuilding the wheel cylinders. You will need a rebuilding kit for each wheel. A kit consists of two rubber cups, a spring, and two rubber boots.

Also buy a wheel cylinder hone, a pair of new front-wheel grease seals, and a quart of brake fluid.

Wheel Cylinder Parts

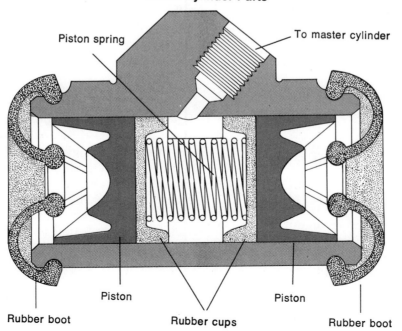

Piston spring

To master cylinder

Piston

Piston

Rubber boot

Rubber cups

Rubber boot

Removal. Take off the old rubber dust boots from the cylinder ends and discard them. Poke your finger through from one end and push out the old rubber cups, metal pistons, and piston spring, catching the parts. Discard the rubber cups and spring, but save the pistons.

Many brakes have piston stops molded into the backing plate, or attached to it. These prevent the pistons from coming out of their bores during a stop. They also prevent you from rebuilding the wheel cylinder without removing it from the backing plate.

To get the cylinder off, open the bleed screw in back with a ⅜-inch box-end wrench. Some fluid will come out and run down the rear of the backing plate.

If the valve is badly corroded, it may break off during opening. If that happens, you will have to buy a new wheel cylinder. Unbolt the wheel cylinder from behind the backing plate, and pull it forward out of the plate opening. It can be disassembled without removing the hydraulic hose.

Cleaning. Check the wheel cylinder pistons as you remove them. Minor corrosion can be scraped from the flat piston head with a putty knife or screwdriver. Major corrosion calls for replacement of the entire wheel cylinder. You can clean parts with alcohol, but never use solvent on any brake cylinder parts.

Chuck your brake cylinder hone in a ¼-inch electric drill and run it through the wheel cylinder. Lubricate with brake fluid from a squirting oil can. The initial honing should consist of several back-and-forth passes. The hone should reach from one end of the cylinder to the other so that the entire inner cylinder surface is cleaned. Flush with fluid, and then pull a clean cloth through from one end of the cylinder to the other.

Look in one end, against a light. If any defects show up in the cylinder walls, try a second honing. If the defect remains, buy a new cylinder.

Remove the bleeder valve completely and poke a wire or pipe cleaner through the bleeder opening to clean it. Then, put the bleeder valve back, and snug it down in its seat. That prevents having a stuck valve break off when you get the wheel back together and try to open the valve to bleed the brakes.

Put clean brake fluid onto the rubber cups and pistons and assemble them, while they are still clean, into the wheel cylinder.

Reassembly. First, install the left dust boot, fitting it tightly into the recess around the outside of the wheel cylinder. That keeps the left piston from being forced out when you put in the right piston.

Next, install all the other parts, sliding them in from the right. Coat each one lightly with brake fluid before installing. Start with a metal piston; its flat surface goes in last. Next, install one of the rubber cups, flat side first. Thus, the two flat sides of the metal piston and rubber cup mate.

Now install the separating spring. No lubrication is necessary. Then, put in the second rubber piston, flat side last. Install the second metal piston, flat side first. Finally, slip the dust boot onto the right end of the wheel cylinder.

Slide in both pushrods, with their slots vertical, through the holes in the boots until they touch the metal pistons. If the wheel cylinder was removed from the backing plate, reinstall in the plate, snugging up the mounting cap screws.

Replacement. If a wheel cylinder must be replaced, remove it from the backing plate as already described. Then, unscrew

Cylinder Servicing

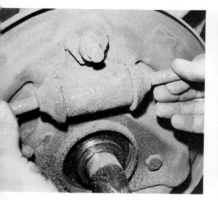

1. Pull out pushrods.

2. Peel off rubber boots.

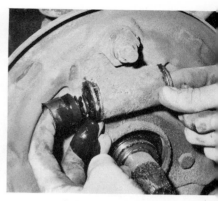

3. Push out inner parts.

4. Squirt alcohol or clean brake fluid into the cylinder as you scour it with a wheel cylinder hone attached to an electric drill. After cleaning, check the cylinder for damage.

5. After cleaning the bleed screw, coat new cylinder parts with fresh brake fluid.

6. Finish by reassembling all the components in the clean wheel cylinder.

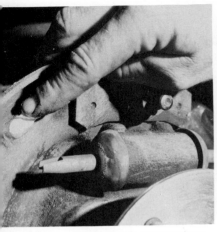

1. Dab high-temperature grease on shoe ledges.

2. Install relined shoes with spring washers.

3. Grease the adjusting wheel's threads.

6. With self-adjuster cable properly routed, hook on secondary shoe-retracting spring.

7. Reconnect the self-adjusting lever to its cable and spring, and push the lever into place.

it from the brake hose, holding the hose fitting with an open-end wrench. Save and reuse the metal washer, if there is one, between the hose and cylinder.

Screw the new cylinder firmly to the brake hose and bolt it onto the backing plate. If the brake hose has even a slight twist in it, remove the hose from its clamp on the car frame and take out the twist. Otherwise, the hose may eventually unscrew itself from the wheel cylinder, causing loss of brakes on two, or all four, wheels.

Installation

With drums and shoes correctly fitted to each other and labeled so they match properly, you are ready to put the wheel brakes back together. Do the fronts first. Since they have no parking brake mechanism, they are easier.

Follow the instructions in your car's service manual. They probably read something like this:

Smear some high-temperature lubricant (white lube or distributor cam lubricant) onto the ledges of all four backing plates.

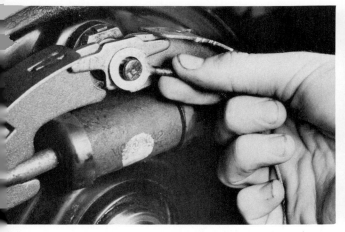

4. Install the anchor pin plate and hook on the eye of the self-adjuster cable.

5. With brake spring tool or screwdriver, hook the primary shoe-retracting spring into place.

8. Test self-adjuster by pulling cable toward rear shoe. Star wheel should gain one notch.

9. Swab the drum braking surface with an alcohol-dipped cloth and install the drum.

Failure to lubricate them will cause brake squeal, and possibly pulling to one side.

Do not interchange the primary and secondary linings. Sometimes they are labeled, sometimes they are not. The primary lining is always the lighter-colored one. It may also be thinner or shorter than the secondary lining. All primary brake linings should be installed in front of the axle. Secondary linings should be installed in back of the axle. Get them wrong and not only will your brakes not work properly, but they will wear out quickly.

Assemble the rear secondary shoes to their respective parking brake levers, and secure them with the spring washers and horseshoe retaining clips. Pinch the ends of the horseshoe clips together with pliers.

See that the parking brake cable is connected to its lever. Test both parking brake cables for freedom of movement. Under severe road salt conditions, they can become so corroded that the parking brakes cannot be applied or released properly.

If the cables are frozen, remove both brake cable housings and replace them with new ones. If the cables are all right, lubricate them with white lube where they reach through the cable housings.

Position the relined brake shoes on the backing plate. Get the wheel cylinder pushrods over the shoe webs, and fasten the shoes with the hold-down spring assemblies.

On rear brakes, install each parking brake link between the shoes. Its small antirattle coil spring should be in front, against the primary shoe. If the parking brake linkage is adjusted too tight, it will hold the shoes off the anchor pin. Loosen the adjustment on the parking brake (more on that later in this chapter).

If there is a shoe guide plate for the anchor pin, slip it on over the anchor pin. Also hook the eye end of the self-adjuster cable over the anchor. The crimped edge of the eye should go toward the backing plate. See that the eye is not cocked or binding on the anchor pin.

Install either the primary or the secondary shoe-retracting spring, whichever your service manual calls for first. Hook the small end of the spring in the proper hole in the brake shoe. Rest the small end of a brake spring tool, or the tip of a large screwdriver, over the anchor pin. Hook on the shoe-retracting spring, and pry backward. The spring slides down and hooks onto the anchor pin.

Install the other shoe-retracting spring in the same way. With proper installation, the springs should clear the wheel cylinder and other parts.

Slip the brake-adjuster cable guide into the hole in the web of the secondary shoe. Then, thread the adjuster cable around the guide—be sure that the cable is positioned in the guide's groove, not between the guide and shoe web.

Put white lube on the threads and socket end of the adjusting screw. Turn the screw all the way into its pivot nut, and then back it out half a turn. Be sure that the self-adjuster mechanism is on the proper side of the car; reversed installation would make the brakes adjust looser rather than tighter.

On some adjusters, the socket end is stamped either "L" or "R." On some cars, the pivot nuts have one groove for left-hand threads (used on the left side), and two grooves for right-hand threads (used on the right side).

Put the adjusting socket on the screw, and install the screw assembly between the lower shoe ends, with the star wheel nearest the secondary (rear) shoe. Put the hook end of the adjuster cable into the hole in the adjusting lever. Adjusting levers are often stamped "L" or "R" to indicate the side they are for.

Next, put the hooked end of the lower adjuster spring into the large hole in the shoe web at the bottom. The last coil of the spring should be even with the edge of the hole. Connect the loop end of the spring to the adjusting lever hole. Pull the adjusting lever, cable, and adjuster spring down and toward the rear. This engages the pivot hook in the large hole in the secondary shoe's web.

The difficult part of the installation is complete.

Check the action of the self-adjuster by pulling the adjuster cable toward the secondary shoe far enough to lift the adjusting lever past a tooth on the star wheel. The lever should snap into position. Releasing the cable should let the adjuster spring pull the lever back to its original position. In the process, the star wheel should turn one notch.

Clean the brake drums with alcohol to remove all traces of metal dust produced by the turning process before you reinstall them. Also remove fingermarks on the brake linings.

The front wheel bearings should now be repacked according to the instructions in the chapter on lubrication, and all four drums should be installed (reverse the removal sequence). Some cars use right-hand-threaded lugs on the right side and left-hand ones on the left side. Do not get them reversed, or the wheels will tend to loosen as you drive.

Newly relined brakes should be adjusted; this process was covered earlier in this chapter.

DISC BRAKES

The brake disc is a metal plate that revolves with the wheel. Straddling the disc is a caliper, which carries the braking cylinders, pistons, and brake linings. Hydraulic pressure presses the linings hard against the disc from both sides. When two pistons operate one brake lining, it's called a shoe. A lining operated by one piston is called a pad. The hydraulic system for disc brakes is practically the same as for drum brakes.

Disc brakes, by their design, are self-adjusting. In most, the brake linings retract from the disc just enough to leave a light drag—not enough to waste fuel, but enough to keep the disc clean and dry, and the brake pedal high. No adjustment is possible or necessary on disc brakes.

Caliper assembly on a disc brake pinches the disc to slow the wheel.

Servicing disc brakes can be summed up as the three Rs—replace, resurface, and recondition. You can do the first and last. An automotive machine shop must do the resurfacing.

Troubleshooting

Disc brakes rarely develop problems. But if yours ever do, a few pointers may save you a trip to the shop.

The most common complaint is the *"creep-groan"*—the actual noise may vary from a grunt to a groan. You hear it when the brakes are applied and the car is rolling very slowly. The same noise, which affects drum brakes, too, is the result of the difference between the static (stopped) friction of the lining and the moving friction. There is no cure, but the sound stops immediately when you increase brake pedal pressure to completely stop the car's movement.

Squeal is the most serious disc brake complaint. If your car is so afflicted, check the caliper mounting bolts for tightness. If a special adapter bracket is used to mount the caliper, check its mounting bolts for tightness. If that fails to cure the problem, try replacing the offending linings and having the disc resurfaced. Also, try the Permatex cure for rattling brakes, as described below.

Finally, check all the clearances between the disc friction surfaces and caliper. If they are not equal, the caliper needs shimming—a professional job.

A *rattling* or *clanking* noise in the caliper on rough roads may be caused by movement of the shoe and lining assembly inside the caliper. The cure is simple: Squeeze a little Permatex No. 2—the non-hardening kind—onto the piston or insulating disc that contacts the shoe or pad. Use just enough for a 1/32-inch layer, and keep the compound off the inner surfaces of the lining, caliper, and disc.

Disc *scoring* can cause noisy brakes. The cure is to have the discs turned.

Light *rust* on discs that have not been used for some time is no problem. But if the car has been idle for a long time, heavy rust may have formed. A bad case of rust will cause noise, rapid lining wear, and scoring of the disc and lining.

Wheel bearing adjustment is especially important, too. Bearings that are too loose

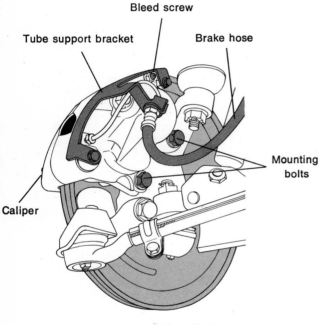

Bleed screw

Tube support bracket

Brake hose

Mounting bolts

Caliper

Caliper Parts

let the disc wobble back and forth. Bearings that are too tight wear out quickly. Follow the bearing adjustment procedure on pages 434 and 435.

Disc brake components you should not try to service yourself are the power-assist unit, the proportioning valve, the residual check valve, and the metering valve. If your car has problems in these areas, leave them to a professional mechanic.

Checking Linings

Disc linings should be visually checked for thickness every 10,000 miles. All you must do is remove a front wheel, and take out the screws (usually two) that hold the caliper's metal splash shield. This exposes the linings to view.

Kelsey-Hayes disc brakes feature telltale tabs, which are small protrusions on the metal pad or shoe. You don't even have to remove the wheel to tell when such a disc brake needs relining—you will hear a metallic scraping sound every time the brakes are applied.

Budd discs should be relined before the thickness gets down to .030 inch.

Replace Bendix pads when they are down to 1/8-inch.

Delco Moraine linings call for a change at about 1/16-inch thickness; they feature a groove in the lining that disappears when the lining reaches that thickness.

Disc removal. If the disc linings need replacing, remove the holding device that retains them.

On Kelsey-Hayes discs, remove the splash shield and antirattle springs. Then, use two pairs of pliers to pull the linings out by their tabs. Mark the location of each shoe or pad on the rear. Disc brake shoes wear thinner at the leading edge than at the trailing edge. If you intend to use them again, you must replace them in the same position.

Budd and Bendix calipers must be removed to get at the linings. The linings can then slip out from the disc side of the caliper. Remove the mounting bolts of the caliper and lift the unit free of the brake disc.

Bendix calipers are mounted with shims to hold them in proper alignment. Be sure to catch those, and replace them exactly as they were.

Removing a Budd caliper calls for a spe-

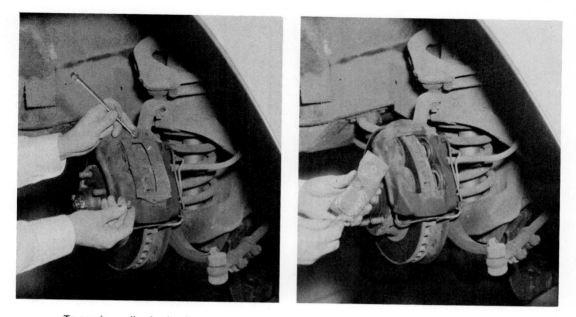

To service a disc brake, first remove the splash shield (*left*) by unfastening the cap screws. Then, carefully mark the location of each brake shoe that is to be reused (*right*). These linings must be reinstalled in the same position.

cial piston compressing tool. A block of wood will do if you are careful to keep dirt and grease off the brake linings.

In Delco Moraine discs, removing a pin allows the linings to be lifted out.

With the linings out, pry each piston back into its bore with a screwdriver. If any is sticky, the caliper must be overhauled. If not, you should overhaul the calipers anyway if you want to do the best possible job—especially if the brakes already have been relined one or more times.

Front disc removal itself is like front drum removal.

Resurfacing. Using a brake lathe, a machine shop can resurface the disc to bring it back within the manufacturer's specified tolerances.

The discs must be flat, with no warpage.

Runout in a disc brake is like eccentricity (out-of-roundness) in a drum brake. It causes loss of brake pedal height be-

cause of extra lining clearances. Moreover, runout wears the caliper pistons and their seats rapidly because of the high-speed pulsations created whenever the brakes are applied. Runout tolerances are critical, usually only about .002 inch.

Thickness variations in a brake disc cause pedal pulsations because the opposing pistons in the caliper work against each other.

Dishing, or distortion, in a brake disc, can be created when a lining is worn so thin that piston travel is restricted on one side. Then, the opposite piston deflects the brake disc against the stuck piston whenever brake pressure is applied.

Usually, as much as .015 inch of metal can be removed from each side of the disc without exceeding specifications. In some cases, even greater removal is permitted. If removing the maximum specified amount will not clean up a disc's problems, get a new disc.

Checking the Disc

Carefully measure the disc with a micrometer for thickness variation and runout.

With the outer caliper half off, remove the disc assembly for resurfacing or replacement.

If the disc is within tolerances, have a machinist turn and grind it.

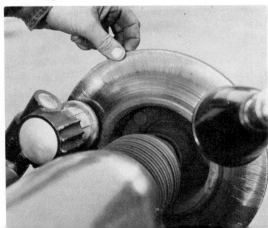

Caliper Service

Most brake manufacturers feel that caliper service should be left to professional mechanics. In light of that advice, if you still want to tackle caliper service, look up the exact procedures for your make of car in the shop manual.

Some calipers will come apart on the car. The outer half of those is removed and serviced in a vise. The inner half is left attached, and is serviced with the rotor removed.

Caliper conditioning, in many ways, is similar to rebuilding a drum-brake wheel cylinder. Here is a general idea of the steps involved:

Removal. The pistons must be removed from their bores; using hydraulic pressure to force them out is the easiest way.

With the shoes or pads removed from the calipers, and the calipers still attached to the hydraulic lines and in place on the car, push on the brake pedal until the pistons on both sides come out and contact the disc. If the disc is thinner than specified, they may pop out. Normally, they will not come entirely out of their bores. Push one side out, then remove the linings on the other side.

To keep brake fluid from squirting out, cover the calipers with a cloth. Sometimes, additional brake fluid must be added to the master cylinder to make the pistons contact the discs.

If the caliper has an external hydraulic transfer tube, remove it by undoing the fittings with an open-end wrench.

Removing the bolts that hold the caliper parts together allows disassembly. Most disc-brake calipers in U.S.-made cars consist of two caliper halves that are held together by two to four bolts. Those may prove hard to loosen because they are tightened to 100 and 150 foot-pounds torque, and may be corroded. The easiest

Caliper Removal

With splash shield off and linings out, pump the brake pedal until the pistons touch the disc.

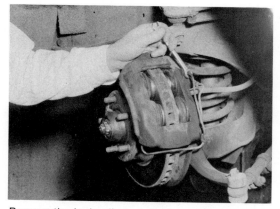

Remove the hydraulic transfer tube. Then, unfasten the bridge bolts.

Carefully slip off the outer caliper half. Mark any damaged bridge bolts for replacement.

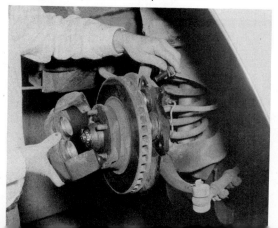

method is to do it on the car.

The Girling disc brake caliper, used on many imports, and the ATE (Teves) caliper, used on Volkswagen and Opel disc brakes, must be removed from the car for service. Calipers on Volkswagen discs should not be taken apart, since that would damage the seal between the caliper halves.

Cleaning. Now, remove the seals, boots, pistons, and springs. Clean them in alcohol, and wipe them dry with a clean, lint-free cloth. Blow out the drilled passages and bores; use a service station air hose if you do not have a compressor. If the rubber dust boots are punctured or torn, replace them.

Inspect the cylinder bores in both sides of the caliper housing for scoring or pitting. Bores that show light corrosion can usually be cleaned with crocus cloth. Caliper bores with deep scratches or scoring should be honed with a brake cylinder hone attached to a ¼-inch electric drill. (The same attachment is used for honing wheel cylinders on drum brakes.)

The caliper cylinder must not be honed out larger than the manufacturer's specifications, generally not more than .002 inch oversize.

Black stains on the bore caused by the piston seals are not harmful and need not be removed.

After honing, take great care in cleaning the caliper parts. Flush them with alcohol, wipe dry, then flush and dry again. Clean mating surfaces with No. 400 wet-or-dry sandpaper, never with a file.

The cleaned caliper should be carefully assembled, using new parts from a caliper rebuilding kit.

Caliper bridge bolts, the ones that hold the halves of the caliper together, should not be replaced with any other type of bolt. Torque the bolts to specifications.

(*text continued on page 340*)

Caliper Rebuilding

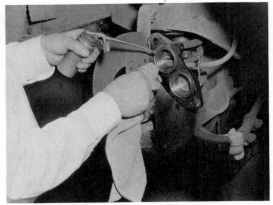

1. Remove the piston boots from their retainers, then the piston seals. Replace non-integral retainers.

2. Thoroughly clean the caliper cylinder bores with an alcohol-soaked cloth.

3. Scour cylinder with a brake cylinder hone and squirts of alcohol or clean brake fluid.

4. If you cannot get the cylinder and piston this clean, you will have to get replacements.

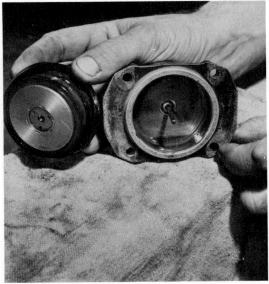

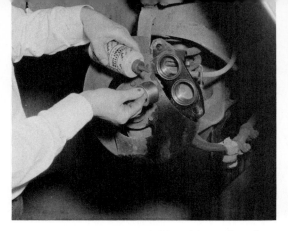

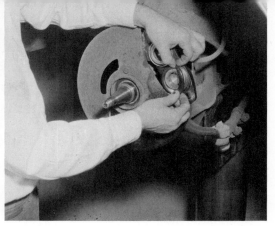

5. Coat piston with brake fluid and insert in caliper bore without dislodging piston seal.

6. Install the new piston boot. On late-model calipers, boot and piston go on together.

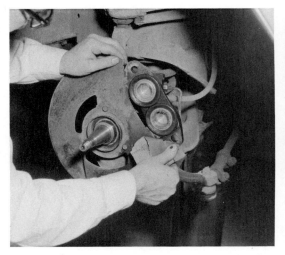

7. Brighten mating surfaces of caliper with fine emery cloth or No. 400 wet-or-dry sandpaper.

8. After the resurfaced disc and the wheel bearings are installed, tighten nut to torque.

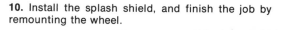

9. Assemble caliper halves. Tighten bridge bolts to proper tension. Connect crossover tube.

10. Install the splash shield, and finish the job by remounting the wheel.

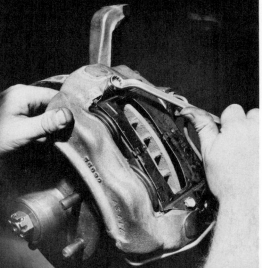

Installation

Once the calipers have been serviced and the discs resurfaced, put them back on. The new linings may now be installed. They go in the reverse of removal. Finally, install the splash shields, making sure you get them on so the wheels cannot rub against them.

Remember to refill the master cylinder and bleed the system. On some disc brakes, the wheels must be removed for access to the caliper bleed screws. Corvettes have two bleed screws, one inboard and one outboard; both must be bled. All calipers should be tapped lightly with a soft-faced hammer while bleeding, to dislodge air bubbles.

If your car has drum brakes on the rear wheels, reline them when you reline the front discs. Use the same brand and quality of lining. If the rear linings are neglected, the balance between front and rear braking may be upset.

Before you road-test the car, be sure the pedal is firm and high.

When road-testing the car, apply the brakes lightly at first, being alert for pulsations in the brake pedal. These indicate faulty resurfacing of the disc. Check too for excessive pedal travel or effort, pulling to one side, excessive squealing or other unusual noises and for brake roughness. If you find any of those, get professional help.

HYDRAULIC SYSTEM

No brake job—disc or drum—is complete without a thorough inspection of all hydraulic system parts. Brake hoses are too often neglected; road salt, road oils, and ozone in the air all take their toll on those critical rubber parts, making them unsafe in as little as a few years.

Inspect brake hoses for tiny rubber cracks, the kind that beset tires after a time. Look, too, for chafing, torn covering at the ferrules, and damage from flying stones. Any of those are cause for hose replacement—probably best left to a shop.

New hoses should meet Federal Safety Standard 106. Check them for a good crimp on the end fittings and for freedom from cuts. The code "40R1" should be stamped on the hose, signifying that it meets that SAE specification.

Bleeding

Any time that the hydraulic system is opened, as when rebuilding a wheel cylinder, air gets in. To remove the air, the system must be bled. Brake bleeding is not difficult, but it calls for a helper to work the brake pedal while you open and close the bleeder valves.

To bleed the hydraulic system, station a helper in the driver's seat. On cars with power brakes, be sure that the engine is off, and that the vacuum reserve has been used up. Push and release the brake pedal five or six times to make sure.

Attach a rubber bleeder hose first to the right rear wheel cylinder bleeder screw. Submerge the end of the hose in a jar partially filled with fresh brake fluid. Ask your assistant to press moderately hard (with about 50 pounds of pressure) on the brake pedal and hold it down. Open the bleed screw.

Notice the color of the brake fluid. Good fluid is clear.

When the brake pedal touches the floorboard, close the bleed screw and have your helper release the brake pedal slowly. Repeat until air bubbles no longer come out of the hose, and the fluid comes out clean.

After every five or fewer repetitions, refill the master cylinder with fresh brake fluid. This keeps the cylinder at least half filled during bleeding. If it runs dry, air will be pumped into the brake lines, and

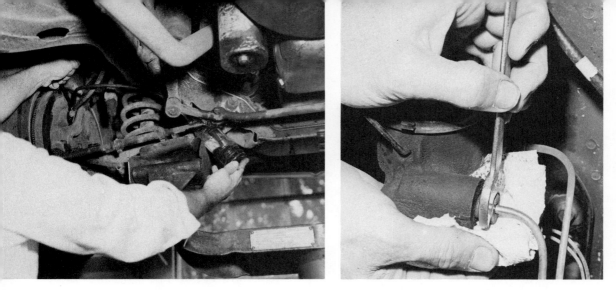

To bleed a hydraulic brake system, fit a rubber hose to the brake bleeder fitting and immerse the other end in brake fluid (*left*). As a helper steps on the pedal, open the bleed screw. Tighten the screw when the pedal is floored. Or, bleed at the master cylinder by loosening the brake line nut (*right*).

you will have to start bleeding all over again.

Repeat the bleeding procedure next at the left rear. Then, bleed the right front, and finally the left front wheel, in that order, until all air has been removed from the hydraulic system. The brake pedal should be firm and at the proper height.

After bleeding, check the fluid level in the reservoir. If necessary, bring it to within a ½-inch of the top.

Flushing. If your brake fluid is dirty, you will have to flush the system. Add special flushing fluid to the reservoir instead of brake fluid, and go through the entire bleeding procedure. When the flushing fluid comes out clean, add brake fluid and go through the entire procedure a second time to replace the flushing fluid with brake fluid. Never leave flushing fluid in the system. Never reuse flushing fluid or brake fluid that comes out of the bleeder openings. Discard it.

PARKING BRAKE

All parking brakes are mechanically operated. Some work on a small driveshaft drum; most work by forcing the rear service brake shoes apart and against their drums.

The brake shoes are actuated by cables from the parking brake pedal or handle. If the rear hydraulic brakes are working properly, often no parking-brake adjustment is necessary. In many cases, adjustments are made from underneath the car, by turning an adjusting nut to take up slack in the parking brake cables. The cables should be lubricated with white lubricant wherever they rub against another part of the car.

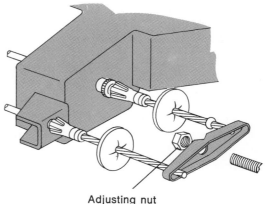

Adjusting nut

Parking Brake Adjustment

Next, test the parking brake. When the pedal or handle reaches about one-third of its total travel, the rear wheels should be locked, or at least both should have the same resistance to turning. Release the parking brake and make sure that the wheels turn freely again.

BRAKE WARNING SWITCH

The brake warning light switch, found on all cars since 1967 with dual hydraulic systems, warns the driver when one of the two hydraulic systems has failed.

To test the operation of the light, first look for a faulty electrical circuit. Disconnect the wire from the switch terminal, and use a jumper to connect the wire to a ground. Turn the ignition key on. The lamp should light.

If it does not, replace the bulb or repair the electrical circuit, whichever is at fault. Once the lamp lights, turn the ignition off, disconnect the jumper, and reconnect the switch's lead to its terminal.

To test the switch's hydraulic operation, attach a rubber bleeder hose to a rear brake bleed screw. Immerse the other end in a container of brake fluid. Open the bleed screw. Now, have a helper turn the ignition switch on and step heavily on the brake pedal. The lamp should light.

Close the valve and repeat the test with a front wheel. If the lamp does not light either time, but does light when grounded, the switch should be replaced.

In some 1967 and 1968 cars with dual hydraulic systems, the brake warning light will be on after bleeding. That is because the piston in the warning light switch is not self-centering. To center it, attach a bleeding hose to a rear brake, again immersing the other end in brake fluid. Have your helper turn on the ignition key.

Open the bleed screw, and have him carefully and slowly press down on the brake pedal until the warning light goes out. That means that the piston has been centered in its bore. Have him hold the pedal steady at that point while you close the bleed screw. Then, he may release the brake pedal and turn off the ignition.

ROAD TEST

First, press on the brake pedal to check its height. It should be within specifications. The pedal should be hard and firm when held.

If the brake pedal does not come up to where it should be, do not drive the car. Instead, recheck your initial brake adjustment to see whether any loose shoes need snugging up.

If the pedal is still low or spongy, the master cylinder probably needs rebuilding. We recommend that a shop do that, or that you buy and install a new or rebuilt master cylinder. Bleed the system after such an installation.

Get the car down off the stands and road test it. If possible, make only gentle stops for the first 300 miles. When the brake pedal is released, the car should coast easily and without drag. There should be no unusual noises and no grabbing. One wheel should not lock up and slide before the other one on the same axle.

BRAKE MODERNIZATION

You can install two brake modernizing kits on a car with manual brakes and a single hydraulic system. One adds *power brakes*. The other adds a *dual hydraulic system* for fail-safe braking. Both are sold through auto parts jobbers, and come with full installation instructions. Those given are for Bendix units.

Power brake. Since the car's existing master cylinder is used, check its operation first. Rebuild or replace it if it is defective. (On an older car, we suggest that you get the dual hydraulic system kit, too. It includes a new dual master cylinder.)

Add-on power brake kit relies on a vacuum booster unit to assist a manual system.

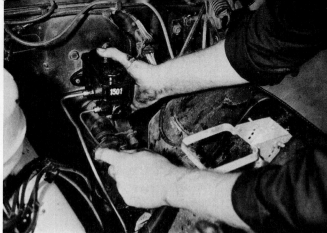

Dual hydraulic kit replaces the single master cylinder. It comes with necessary lines.

Remove the old parts, discarding those being replaced. Install the new vacuum booster unit on the firewall, over the studs left by the old master cylinder. Connect the brake pedal to the booster's pedal link. That lowers it nearer to the floor than originally.

Install the master cylinder on the booster. Install the elbow to the master cylinder, and connect the brake line to it. Check pushrod operation and adjust it as described in the kit's instructions.

Now, connect the brake light, hooking up the new wiring harness to the brake light switch.

The booster's vacuum connections are made to the engine intake manifold. The procedure varies on six-cylinder and V-8 engines. Hoses, angles, fittings, and a tee for the hookup are provided in the kit.

The last step is to fill the master cylinder with brake fluid, bleed the brakes, and check for leaks. Test the brake pedal before you move the car.

Dual hydraulic system. To install, remove the old master cylinder and cylinder-to-frame brake tube. Save the nuts, washers, and gasket.

On cars with power brakes, the oil dipstick tube may have to be bent one or two inches nearer the engine, and the dipstick turned 180°.

Mount the new dual master cylinder to the firewall. On cars with power brakes, the snap-ring and washer on the master cylinder are removed and discarded.

Connect the old hydraulic lines so that front and rear systems are separate. To do this, remove the line to the rear-wheel brakes from the frame tee, and plug the opening in the tee. Use the furnished union, adapter, and brake line to route the line to the "rear" master cylinder port.

Use the adapters and new line to connect the frame tee to the port marked "front." When bending all steel lines furnished with the kit, be careful; they can easily split at the seams.

Check all nuts for tightness, and see that tubing is not kinked, twisted, or rubbing on other parts. Adjust as necessary.

Remove the master cylinder filler cap and fill both reservoirs with clean brake fluid. Bleed the brake system.

On cars with power brakes, check the pushrod length adjustment as described in the kit's instructions and adjust it if necessary. Pushrods on Delco Moraine power brakes are not adjustable.

Check brake light operation with the reservoir covers open. The brake lights should go on when brake fluid erupts from the compensating port. Install the filler cover and seal. Test the brake pedal before you move the car.

TROUBLESHOOTING BRAKES

SYMPTOM	CAUSE	CURE
Low pedal, excessive pressure needed to stop	Self-adjuster not working	Try a harsh backup stop followed by a series of backward and forward stops; replace self-adjuster if pedal still low; lubricate star wheel, replace adjusting lever if bent
	Glazed, cracked, thin linings	Inspect linings and replace if faulty
	Glazed, polished brake drums	Have drums turned
	Half of dual hydraulic system not pressurizing	Check operation of warning light; repair faulty half of hydraulic system
	Power brake booster not working	See chapter on servicing power accessories
	Shoe ledges grooved or rusted	Clean and smooth ledges; lubricate
Low pedal, soft and spongy	Air in hydraulic system	Bleed system
	Low or nearly empty master cylinder	Look for leak in hydraulic system, refill cylinder, bleed brakes
	Defective brake hose	Have brake hose replaced
	Poorly fitted new brake shoes	Have shoes ground to fit drum
	Brake drums turned beyond specifications	Replace drums and have shoes refitted by grinding
	Anchor pin needs adjusting	Have adjustment made
	Ridged disc faces	Have disc surfaced or replace
	Defective check valve in master cylinder	Have master cylinder rebuilt or replace it with a rebuilt unit

SYMPTOM	CAUSE	CURE
High pedal, too hard	Master cylinder pushrod adjusted too long	Have pushrod adjusted to suit master cylinder piston clearance
	Self-adjusting brakes over-eager in adjusting	Back up adjustment with brake tool and screwdriver; if pedal comes back up again, consult a shop
	Hard, glazed linings	Inspect linings; reline if hard or glazed
	Low-friction lining	Reline brakes with proper material
	Piston frozen in disc brake caliper	Remove each lining and inspect piston action by prying with screwdriver. If sticky, replace or rebuild caliper
	Power brake booster faulty	Have unit serviced
Pulsations in brake pedal	Drum or disc not running true	Check rear drums to see that they are properly seated over the axle; also, see that wheels are correctly tightened to avoid distorting drum or disc; have drum or disc turned on a brake lathe
Brakes pull to one side when applied	Sticking piston in wheel cylinder	Rebuild or replace faulty wheel cylinder
	Restriction in brake line or hose	Hard to find: Take car to shop for diagnosis and repair
	Primary and secondary shoes reversed, or both primary shoes installed on one side of axle	Switch shoes
	Brake fluid or grease on a lining	Install new grease seal (to stop grease) or rebuild wheel cylinder (to stop brake fluid) and reline brakes on both sides of axle

SYMPTOM	CAUSE	CURE
	Brake shoe-retracting springs reversed	Clean springs and install according to color-coding and service manual instructions
	Brake-retracting springs overheated or stretched	Test by dropping on concrete floor; replace if they bounce
	Brake shoes not properly fitted	Remove all shoes on affected axle and have them fitted to their drums correctly by grinding
	Front wheel bearing loose	Adjust according to directions in chapter on lubrication
	Misaligned front wheels	Have wheels aligned (see chapter on wheel alignment and suspension)
	Worn steering parts	Perform "look-and-shake" tests as described in chapter on wheel balance and alignment
	Unequal tire pressure	Adjust tire pressure
	Unequal tire size	Install same-sized tires across each axle
Brakes drag	Stuck wheel cylinder piston	Rebuild or replace wheel cylinder
	Stretched or fatigued shoe-retracting springs	Replace retracting springs
	Rear-wheel parking brake cables frozen	Lubricate and free up or replace
	Shoes adjusted too tight	Back off star wheel at least ten notches
	Master cylinder compensating port closed	Have master cylinder pushrod adjusted for proper length
	Master cylinder with check valve in line to disc brakes	Replace with master cylinder without a check valve

SYMPTOM	CAUSE	CURE
Brakes squeal or squeak	Hard, cracked, or glazed linings	Have brake shoes ground or reline brakes
	Glazed, thin, loose, scored, or polished brake drums	Have the drums turned or replace them
	Dirt embedded in linings	Remove drum and blow out all dirt from brake assembly and drum
	Fatigued or overheated shoe-retracting springs	Replace springs
	Shoe ledges need lubrication	Remove drums and lubricate ledges
Brakes chatter when applied	Brake fluid or grease on lining	Replace shoes, turn drums or discs
	Shoes ground improperly or not ground at all	Have shoes reground with .005 to .008 inch clearance at heels and toes
	Backing plate loose	Tighten bolts on backing plate
	Too much end play in rear axle	Have rear axle bearings adjusted to specifications or have bearings replaced
Fading pedal, falls away under pressure	Worn or damaged master cylinder	Check for hydraulic leaks; rebuild or replace master cylinder
	Wheel or caliper cylinders worn or damaged	Check for leaks at wheels; if found, rebuild or replace caliper or wheel cylinders
	Defective brake lines or hoses	Find leak and tighten loose connection or have line or hose replaced
	Cracked or thin brake drums	Replace drums

19

Servicing the Suspension System

Every automotive suspension uses some type of energy-absorbing device — usually either coil or leaf springs or torsion bars — to hold the car up on its wheels. Most U.S. cars today use coil springs in front. Chrysler-built cars use torsion bars, which absorb energy by twisting.

A shock absorber is put close to each spring or torsion bar to control the spring action. Without shock absorbers, a car would bounce up and down like a pogo stick. Not only would the ride be nasty, but the bouncing wheels would be off the pavement so often that the car would be hard to handle during cornering, fast starting, hard braking, and when encountering the slightest road roughness.

In most U.S. cars and some imports, a heavy cast-iron or steel rear-axle housing contains a live axle inside. This keeps the rear wheels aimed straight ahead, and perpendicular to the ground, at all times.

The front suspension is not that simple. To permit steering as well as free up-and-down movement, most late-model cars have ball-and-socket-joint front spindles. The front spindles hold the axles and are mounted through ball joints to the upper and lower suspension arms.

The front suspension works like a human shoulder joint. With your arm outstretched, you can point it right, left, or straight ahead; at the same time, you can raise it above your head or lower it below your waist. In a car's front end, the springs, shocks, and steering linkage, and the car's weight combine to control the motion.

To reduce rattles, many suspension parts are mounted in rubber or plastic. Those that are not — and some that are — require periodic lubrication. For instance, if ball joints are properly lubricated, they usually last for 100,000 miles or more. Without this care, squeaks, which are a sign that rapid wear is taking place, soon develop. Since suspension lubrication should be a regular part of your car care program, it is covered in detail in the lubrication chapter at the end of the book.

Most suspension work is a shop job. The

main work you can perform yourself, besides lubrication, is the care and replacement of shock absorbers.

SHOCK ABSORBERS

A shock works by forcing hydraulic fluid through restricted passages inside its body. A shock with more fluid can absorb more energy. Such a unit can also work at lower pressures for longer life, and dispel heat more efficiently. That makes large shock absorbers best suited for heavy-duty use. There are units sized for every need.

Modern, direct-acting shock absorbers provide what is called a velocity-sensitive two-way control. The faster they are pushed—in either direction—the harder they resist. Most shock absorbers resist more when they are extending than when they are compressing. A few resist equally in both directions. The amount of resistance required in each direction is determined by the engineers who design a car's suspension. Thus, when you replace shocks, you should always get new ones that are suited to your car.

Types. Two shocks may look alike but vary in size of restrictions, fluid capacity, and other internal features. When you replace your shock absorbers, be sure you are buying ones of the correct specifications.

Basically, there are four types of shocks:
• Standard duty shocks, whether regular or premium grade, are for driving at normal speeds on well-paved roads, with infrequent heavy loads. They give a soft ride, but they must be replaced fairly often.
• Heavy duty shocks give better control and longer life. They are recommended if

The Suspension System

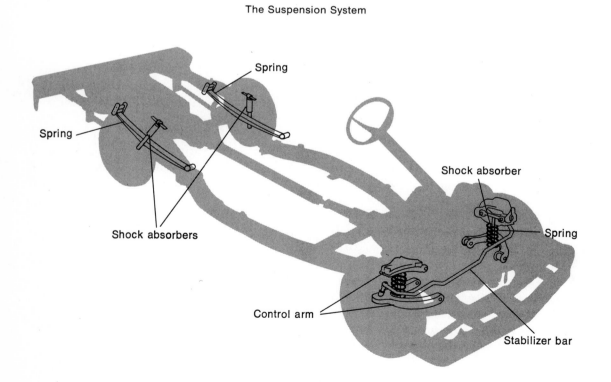

Spring

Spring

Shock absorbers

Shock absorber

Spring

Control arm

Stabilizer bar

you often drive on rough roads at high speeds.

• Spring type (load-leveling) shock-stabilizers are recommended if you often carry heavy loads in the trunk. In addition, they can correct even a permanent suspension sag if the springs are still sound. Sagging in the front can be caused by the post-factory addition of an air conditioner or other heavy power accessory. Sagging in the rear is caused by heavy trunk loads or frequent towing of a trailer.

The best load-leveling shocks use variable-rate springs. Such shocks do not greatly raise the riding height of a car at normal height, but they permit extra loads to be carried without the rear-end dragging. The spring's compressibility increases rapidly as it nears the fully compressed position. You can tell that kind of spring by its coils; they are much closer together at one end than at the other.

Load-leveling shocks must always be installed in pairs. Of course, you may also install a full set of four for maximum handling control.

• Special high-performance or police-type shocks give top cornering and all-around roadability—and a firm, less-comfortable ride.

Service. A set of shock absorbers generally lasts about 25,000 miles. The actual wear depends on how rugged the shocks are, and how and where the car is driven. Nearly all modern shocks are the direct-acting airplane type. While they serve much better than the older kinds, they do wear out in time. The process is so gradual you may not notice it.

To detect defective shock absorbers, look for loose bushings and fluid leaks around the seals. If you find any such problem, repair it. Also, push down hard on each corner of the car. If the car rises and centers itself, the shocks are good. If the car continues bouncing up and down, the shocks should be replaced.

Replace worn shock absorbers in sets of four. If you replace only the front or rear pair, the old shocks will not balance with the new ones, and you may get a pitching ride. In a new set of four, though, the front pair may be different than the rear pair.

Installation. You can save about $8 on labor and even more on parts by replacing your own shock absorbers. Ninety percent of the job is getting the old shocks off. The

Conventional Loop

Loop and Stud

Loop-and-Crosspin

Shaft-mount

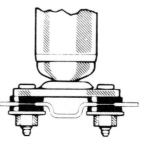
Two-stud Plate

Cup Type

Bad Shocks
vs.
Good Shocks

These sequences show the benefits of firm shock absorbers. The car above—with worn shocks

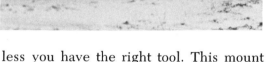

night before, apply penetrating oil to all threaded fasteners, both front and rear.

There are six kinds of shock absorber mounts to deal with. Often, two or three different types are used on the same car.

The *loop* mount, the most conventional kind, has a loop end on the shock with a rubber bushing inside. The bushing fits over a stud that is fastened to the suspension or frame; a nut and washer hold it on. That type of mount usually does not present much of a problem. Remove the nut with a socket wrench, and slip the bushing and shock off the stud. If the bushing sticks, drive it off with a heavy hammer.

The *loop and stud* comes with its own sleeve or stud. With that type, the entire stud is removed from its mounting hole.

The *loop-and-crosspin* is often found on the lower end of a front suspension-arm-mounted shock. Remove the two small cap screws that hold it to the lower suspension arm to free that end. If the screws are so rusted that they break or their threads strip, drill them out. Substitute a bolt in place of the cap screw during replacement.

The *shaft-mount* can be a problem un-

less you have the right tool. This mount is mostly for upper ends of front shocks.

The problem is in holding the stud while you remove the nut that holds it to the car frame. You are working in cramped quarters, often under the front fender (though removing the front wheels may help). Furthermore, when you hold the flattened end of the shaft with a wrench, pliers, or locking pliers, you cannot use a socket wrench to turn the nut. That means making many hard turns with an open-end wrench. And often, the nut gets rounded off so that you must use locking pliers.

If your car has such mounts, get a shock absorber tool for under $10. A socket wrench fits over the $9/16$-inch mounting nut. The shock shaft tool fits through the socket's center, and down over the end of the shock shaft, to hold the nut. A ratcheting box-end wrench turns the socket—and the nut—in either direction as you hold the shaft to keep the tool from turning.

The *two-stud plate* is found on fairly late-model independent front coil-spring suspensions in which the spring is located above the upper control arm. Remove the

nosedives, then bounces, before coming under control. The car below—with new shocks—levels off quickly.

nuts from the studs, and it comes apart.

The *cup* is like the shaft mount for coil-spring front suspensions. However it has a cup near the top of the shaft. Remove it as you would a shaft-mount unit.

Work tips. When you replace shock absorbers, observe a few precautions. Do not allow the rear wheels of cars with coil or air springs to hang. That stretches brake hoses, and may even let the spring slip out of position. Jack up the car just high enough for you to work underneath. Block it, too, before you get underneath.

Note carefully the position of the old shock and the locations of all rubber bushings, washers, and fasteners so you can reassemble everything properly. Some new shocks come with extra parts that fit them to various mounting systems. You may have parts left over; don't use all of them just because they are there.

Never force nuts off studs; you risk breaking off the stud. Use penetrating oil, heat, or a nut-splitter.

Do not hold the polished shaft of a new shock with pliers. Any nick or scratch will cut through the oil seal and make the shock leak.

Sometimes, shaft mountings are supplied with locators—large washers that fit around the end of the shaft and position it in larger holes in the car. If several different sizes are supplied, be sure to use the right size. Tighten the lower end of such a shock first, and then let the car down on its wheels. Make sure the locators are properly positioned before tightening the upper ends.

Do not over- or under-tighten shock shaft mountings. They should be drawn up until the rubber cushions squeeze out to the same size as the metal washers on either side. The cushions should not be so tight that they bulge beyond the washers.

Inspect each shock to see that it will not rub on such underbody parts as brake or fuel lines, or suspension, body, or exhaust system parts when the shock is either compressed or extended. To be sure, move the front and rear of the car up and down before leaving the job.

Finally, take your car for a test ride over a bumpy road.

20

Wheel Balance and Alignment

BALANCE

Nearly every car wheel needs balancing. At high speeds, only four ounces of excess weight in one spot around the tire causes an unwanted force of 35 pounds on the wheel as it turns.

Balanced wheels make for greater driving safety, easier steering, smoother and quieter car operation, greater riding comfort, and longer life from chassis, steering, and suspension components. You can expect up to 30 percent more tire life, too.

An out-of-balance condition leads to cupped tires, worn bearings, loosened ball joints, overworked tie-rod ends and suspension arm pivots, and battered shock absorbers. Though power steering masks some of the effects of unbalance, the power steering components themselves also take a beating.

Two different kinds of balance affect car wheels: static and dynamic. *Static balance* affects the wheel when it is at rest. *Dynamic balance* affects the wheel when it is in motion. A wheel can be perfectly balanced statically but be way out of balance dynamically, and vice-versa.

Front wheels must be balanced both statically and dynamically, and rear wheels must be statically balanced, for your car to be free of vibration.

Static balance. When the weight of a wheel assembly is equally distributed around its axle, it is in static balance. Jacked up off the ground and free to rotate, a statically balanced wheel will not turn, no matter what position it is in.

If there are heavy or light spots, though, the wheel may move. Such static unbalance makes a wheel hop up and down as it rolls along the pavement. Called "tramping," it can be felt most at about 45 to 50 mph. Static unbalance is often harmonic; that is, its effects increase at some speeds and decrease at others.

Static unbalance in the front wheels makes the hood vibrate up and down in

355

time to wheel rotation. On rear wheels, it makes the rear seat vibrate up and down. You can spot rear-wheel static unbalance easily by placing a sheet of paper on the rear seat and having a helper watch it while you drive. At harmonic speed, the paper will bounce in time to the wheels.

Dynamic balance. When the weight of a wheel assembly is equally distributed around the vertical centerline of the wheel, it is dynamically balanced.

Dynamic unbalance shows itself as front-wheel wobble at 60 mph and more. The faster you drive, the worse the side-to-side "shimmy" gets. Although dynamic unbalance occurs in both front and rear wheels, the rear axle (on most rear-wheel-drive cars) is solid, and prevents appreciable wobbling movements.

Auto manufacturers consider wheel balance so important that they factory-balance all rotating components — tires, wheels, brake discs and brake drums. Despite their care, though, most new cars

are delivered with a noticeable amount of wheel unbalance, since all balancing is done with a slight margin for error. Thus, a new car can have unbalanced wheels if:

• A slightly unbalanced tire and wheel assembly is placed on the same side as a slightly unbalanced brake assembly;
• A large-center-hole wheel is mounted on a small-pilot hub, thereby allowing excessive run-out, or side-to-side wobble;
• Bare wheel runout coincides with the maximum allowable unbalance in the brake assembly.

With all of these factors working against it, a factory wheel assembly ends up on the car with an average unbalance equal to a one-ounce balance weight placed randomly on the rim. This is enough to show up at high speeds, but it is far better than no balancing at all.

Even if your new car comes from the factory with its wheels perfectly balanced, normal driving and tire wear will throw this adjustment out after a period of time.

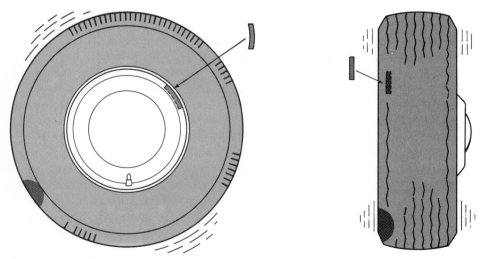

Wheel unbalance is caused by a heavy spot in the tire. Static unbalance (*left*) makes a wheel hop up and down. It is cured by positioning a weight directly across from the heavy spot. Dynamic unbalance (*right*) makes the wheel wobble. It is cured by positioning a weight on the same side of the wheel. Both static and dynamic balance may be obtained with the same weight positioned as shown at right.

The best way to check wheel balance is to jack up the car and spin the wheel. There should be no vibration and no visible wobble.

Other factors, too, contribute to unbalanced wheels.

The *wheel* itself can affect your car and simulate unbalance. An eccentric wheel can be balanced, but the vibrations caused by it will still be present. If eccentricity exceeds ⅛-inch, a new wheel is the only cure.

Heavy, unbalanced wheel covers can cause balance problems. Some weigh as much as six pounds, enough to wreck a good balance job. Ideally, such wheels should be balanced with wheel covers on. Only a few machines can do it. You can, though, with either front-axle or spin-and-try balancing.

A wheel that is incorrectly mounted will run out and cause unbalance. The remedy is to take off the wheel and remount it correctly, bringing alternate lugs to proper torque gradually by making several passes around the circle of bolts.

Tires affect balance, too. Some need balancing more than others. Those that need it least are original-equipment tires. Premium tires with deep, heavy tread rubber need balancing more. Most in need of balancing are retreaded tires.

Tires that contain hard spots in the treads can sound unbalanced as they roll along, even though they are perfectly balanced.

A badly out-of-round tire cannot be corrected by any type of wheel balancing. You can tell whether that is your problem by jacking up the wheel and spinning it. Watch the tread to see if it runs reasonably true while turning. A small imperfection will not be noticeable when driving, but a large amount of runout—⅛-inch or more—will be noticeable, especially on a softly sprung car.

Put your most-out-of-round tires in the rear, where the rigid axle will help hold them steady, and where the steering wheel will not transmit their vibrations.

A tire that is properly mounted on the wheel can be balanced right away. But if the tire bead is not fully seated, it can shift and destroy the balance job. It is best to wait until the tires have been broken in before balancing.

Because tire rotation destroys on-the-car wheel balancing, I recommend that you not rotate your car's tires. Other reasons for not rotating them are given in the chapter on tire tips.

Checking Balance

Twice-a-year balance checks should be made. It's a good practice to make them along with your wheel alignment checks. Regular tires and snow tires should be balanced when they are installed, unless you have separate wheels for them.

Most shops do not charge to check balance; they expect to get the balancing job, if one is needed.

Checking front wheels requires only jacking up the wheel and spinning it with a wheel spinner. No vibration should be

Before you undertake a wheel balance, buy a supply of weights, including at least two different sizes.

felt in the bumper. Checking the balance of rear wheels is even simpler, for the wheel spinner is not needed. You can do it by stepping on the gas with the transmission in top gear.

The only problem is that rear wheel unbalance and an unbalanced driveshaft often feel much the same. To distinguish one from the other, block up the car's rear axle and remove both rear wheels. Replace the lug nuts to hold the drums on. Shift into top gear and run the speed up to 70 mph. If the vibration has gone, wheel unbalance is indicated. If the vibration is still there, driveshaft unbalance is the cause. Correcting the latter is a professional job.

Do-It-Yourself Balancing

To correct unbalance in automotive wheels, you must add weights to proper places on the wheel rim.

To correct *static unbalance*, add weights to the rim 180° from the heavy part of the wheel.

To correct *dynamic unbalance*, add weights to the wheel rim either on the same side of the axle across the centerline from the heavy spot, or opposite the axle on the same side of the centerline. That corrects for dynamic unbalance without affecting static balance.

Various methods are used to position balance weights. Some, though, require costly equipment and can be done only by professionals.

Weights. Before you start balancing, get an assortment of balance weights, which are sold by mail order supply houses and auto jobbers. You will also need a pair of balance-weight pliers, with jaws for removing weights and a hammer head for installing them.

You should have at least two different sizes of weights to make a neat job. To balance four wheels that are not too badly out of balance, you will need about eight 1½-ounce weights and about a dozen ½-ounce weights. You can save by bending in the metal tabs on old balance weights and reusing them when possible.

Special mag-type wheels built for strength and looks may have no place to fasten standard balance weights with rim clips. For those, stick-on weights must be used. Stick-ons can be cut to the length needed with metal snips or diagonal cutters, and attached to the underside of the wheel like tape. They will not scratch the wheel and will not pull loose unless they are being removed. Then, they just peel off. Indianapolis racing cars use them.

The present industry standard is to balance wheels to the nearest ½-ounce. Some experts feel that that is not close enough for high-speed driving. If you want really precise balancing, have some ¼-ounce weights on hand.

Static Balancing

The best home wheel balancer is the front axle of your car. By following a few easy directions, you can do a perfect on-the-car static wheel balancing job and save about $3.50 per wheel. When done on the car, balancing covers the wheel, tire, and brake disc or drum as a single assembly.

If one or both of your front wheels is dynamically as well as statically unbalanced, you will have to take further steps to complete the job. Most wheels can be successfully balanced, though, with the front-axle method alone.

The system takes advantage of wheel bearing friction to help locate wheel weights. With a slight modification, the system also balances rear wheels acceptably.

Start do-it-yourself home balancing by running the car several miles to warm up

the wheel bearing grease. (Thick, cold grease makes the wheels rotate sluggishly on their bearings.) Then, jack up both front wheels. Scrape off any heavy accumulations of mud on the wheel. Stones lodged in the tire tread need not be removed unless the tire is to be spun rapidly. Then, they should be removed for safety, rather than for any effect on balance.

Take off all old balance weights. Remove the hub cap and spin the wheel. If it does not spin completely (and few do), remove the hub dust cover and cotter pin, and loosen the bearing adjustment nut one-quarter turn.

You may also have to back off the wheel brakes to prevent dragging brake shoes from slowing the wheel. Disc-brake linings may have to be freed by loosening the hub bearing nut and rocking the disc. This pushes the linings back. On self-adjusting drum brakes that drag, loosen the brake adjustment (see page 318).

Locating unbalance. With the wheel turning free, let its heavy spot settle to the bottom. Then, mark the bottom with chalk.

Rotate the wheel 180° (half way around), bringing the heavy portion to the top. Then, turn the wheel clockwise, a bit at a time, until unbalance just begins to pull the heavy side down again. That may be only a few degrees, or it may be nearly a quarter of a turn, depending on how badly out-of-balance and how free-running the wheel is. Stop the wheel at that point and chalk-mark the tire at the very bottom.

This is the first of two balance-weight positioning marks.

Put the heavy end topside again and turn the wheel gradually counterclockwise, until unbalance just begins to turn the wheel. Mark the very bottom again.

Half-way between the two chalk marks you have just made is the lightest point of

(*text continued on page 362*)

Static Balancing

1. Perform this job on the front axle. First, loosen the wheel bearing adjusting nut about a quarter turn to free the bearing; then, back off the brake.

2. The wheel should now move freely. The heavy spot will settle to the bottom. Mark the bottom with chalk or a piece of tape.

3. Move the heavy spot to the top and slowly rotate the tire clockwise. When the heavy spot begins to turn the tire, hold it and mark the bottom.

4. Repeat Step 3, but this time rotate the tire in a counterclockwise direction. The weights will be added between the last two marks you made.

5. Position the marks horizontally and, with a balance weight tool (*left*), begin tacking on weights (*right*). To calculate the amount of weight you should add, see the text. After you have added the correct amount, exchange groups of smaller weights for larger ones.

6. The wheel is now balanced. As a test, rotate it to any position and take your hands off. If the wheel does not move, it is in static balance.

7. Finish by dividing the weights in half. Leave one group in place and tack the other group on the inside rim to preserve dynamic balance.

the wheel. All balance weights should be centered between these marks.

Calculating weight. To find how much weight is needed, move the lightest point of the tire to a horizontal position. Start adding weights between the two marks, a ½-ounce at a time. Put on enough weights to *almost* balance the wheel — the weights should rise when you let go of the wheel. Jot down the total amount of weight you have added.

Now, add more weights about the same point until the weighted portion of the wheel just begins to fall when it is released. Tot up the new total weight.

Remove half of the weight you added in the last step. The wheel should be in balance. You can check by stopping it in various positions. If it is balanced, it will not turn.

To get a neater looking job and to save your ½-ounce weights for future use, exchange groups of light weights for fewer heavier weights. Knock half of the weights onto the outside of the rim between marks, and the other half on the inside of the rim, directly opposite. That keeps the weights from affecting the wheel's dynamic balance.

If it takes more than six ounces of weights to balance a wheel, something is radically wrong. First, check runout. If that is less than ⅛-inch, remove the wheel from the drum or disc and remount it properly. Then, try balancing again. If more than six ounces of weight are still needed, have the tire taken off and remounted. Balance again. If the problem is still not cured, you probably need a new tire.

After you finish static balancing and before you let the wheels down off the jacks, readjust the wheel bearing adjustment nut and safety it (see pages 434 and 435); also, snug up both front wheel brake adjustments, as shown and described on pages 318 and 319. Disc brakes need no

readjustment, but you should pump the pedal several times to remove shoe-to-disc play.

To balance the rear wheels using the front-axle method, do them first. Block up all four wheels of the car, remove the front wheels, and install both rear wheels on the front. Mark any three lug-bolt holes "1," "2," and "3." Tighten the lugs in that order; that centers the wheel on the disc or drum. After balancing, the position can then be duplicated on the rear simply by using the same lug-tightening sequence. Balance the rears as described for front wheels and then remount them on the rear.

Bubble Balancing

Front-axle static balancing beats any other type of procedure except for a professional off-the-car static-dynamic balancing job. There is, however, another alternative — bubble balancing. This requires a bubble balancer (about $20), and it is suitable for nearly all rear wheels and for about half of all front wheels.

However, it cannot locate, or correct for, dynamic unbalance.

Start by removing the wheel and cleaning off heavy deposits of mud. Pull off all old balance weights with a balance weight tool. Place the wheel gently over the balancer's center cone, with the outside of the wheel facing up. The bubble balancer must rest on a fairly level surface. Steady the wheel with your fingertips to slow its oscillation.

The bubble will move to the side where balance weights should be added. Add the smallest amount of weight that will center the bubble inside its circle of tolerance. Chalk-mark where the weight should go, remove the wheel from the balancer, and tap the weight onto the rim with the hammer end of the weight tool. Weights should be pounded on with the

Bubble Balancing

1. Heart of the balancer (*left*) is the bubble in the spring-loaded nose cone (*right*). When that bubble is within the circle of tolerance, the wheel is in static balance.

2. Gently set the debris- and mud-free wheel onto the balancer, centering it on the nose cone.

3. Position weights around the rim until the bubble is within the circle of tolerance.

wheel off the balancer to keep from damaging the balancer's delicate support mechanism. If two weights are necessary, put one inside the rim, the other directly opposite it on the outside.

Should your lightest weights be too heavy to center the bubble, move two of your lightest weights in opposite direc-
tions from the point where a single but still-lighter weight is needed. Move them equal distances from that point until the bubble is centered. Take the wheel off the balancer and tap on both weights. With a good assortment of weights, you can usually succeed with just one weight per wheel.

363

Dynamic Balancing

1. Perform dynamic balancing of all wheels—including rear ones—on the front axle. First, remove all stones and debris from the tread.

After you have bubble-balanced a wheel, be careful when you mount it. If you install it off-center, you will negate all the work you have just done. For best results, use an alternate-lug tightening sequence. Go around the circle of bolts several times, gradually bringing each lug to its proper torque.

Dynamic Balancing

With the wheels balanced statically, take the car out on the freeway and run it at the top legal speed. No wheel tramping—a sign of static unbalance—should be noticeable.

But an occasional flutter in the steering wheel means dynamic unbalance. To correct it, you will have to balance the front wheels dynamically. To do so, you need a ½-hp, 3600-rpm electric motor, with an eight-inch pulley, mounted on a board.

The system uses a "spin-and-try" method to locate the proper spots for weights that will achieve both static and

2. With the car jacked, spin the wheel with an electric motor and pulley. Hold a piece of chalk near the wheel to mark the point of maximum wobble.

3. Add weights, a bit at a time, at the center of the chalkline. Add equal weights across the axle and inside the wheel to preserve static balance. Stop when the wobble is gone.

dynamic balance at the same time. The method is based on the principle that most wheel unbalance is caused either by runout, or by a single heavy or light area in the tire-wheel-brake assembly.

Say that a tire is unbalanced because it was built with a thick area in the casing. If the thick spot is in the center of the tire tread, static balancing alone will correct for it. But if the thick spot is on a sidewall, static balancing alone is not enough. When the wheel spins, centrifugal force will make the heavy spot rotate about the centerline of the wheel. That tendency of the heavy spot to move from the side to the center of the wheel causes the wheel to wobble.

In dynamic balancing, all the weights should go on the same side of the rim as the heavy spot. Since you cannot see the heavy spot, you must experiment; hence, the term "spin-and-try." The object is to watch for side-to-side movement in the wheel when it is spun; that wobble signifies dynamic unbalance.

Locating unbalance. First, try moving all of the static balance weights to the outside of the rim, keeping them centered between the chalk marks.

Block up the wheel and spin it by placing the fast-spinning motor's pulley in contact with the tire tread. Cocking the steering wheel to one side puts more play in the steering wheel; play helps show up the wobble. If you notice any wobble, stop the wheel and move all of the weights to the same relative position on the inside of the rim. Spin the wheel again. If the wobble is gone, you have succeeded.

Problem jobs. Static balancing cures five out of ten balance problems. Weight repositioning by the "spin-and-try" method can correct four more. That leaves the one in ten that resists easy balancing.

Try spinning and chalk-marking before you give up. That is similar to what professional dynamic balancers do, but it is not as accurate. While spinning the wheel at top speed, hold a piece of chalk near the tire's sidewall so that the tire touches it on each revolution. Stop the wheel by gentle braking and put a ½-ounce balance weight on the outside of the wheel rim centered on the chalk mark. Also, put another ½-ounce balance weight on the inside of the wheel rim across the axle from the chalk mark. Those weights do not affect static balance, but will change the dynamic balance of the wheel assembly.

Wipe off the old chalk mark and spin-test again. If the wheel still wobbles, make a new chalk mark. If it falls in the same position as the old one, double the amount of dynamic weights. If it comes opposite the old mark, halve the amount of dynamic weights.

If the new mark occurs at right angles to the old one, you have corrected the largest dynamic unbalance, but a smaller one has taken over. Pound in the weights, let down the car, and road-test it again.

If you still have problems, go to a shop with more sensitive static-dynamic balancing equipment. Or, for a more economical solution, mount that problem wheel on the rear axle, and move one of the rear wheels up front and balance it statically.

Professional Balancing

Every shop claims that its method of balancing is the best. Some shops even offer a variety of methods at varying prices. Bear in mind, though, that if you have already tried balancing your own wheels with the front-axle or "spin-and-try" methods, chances are that professional bubble-balancing will not help.

In professional spin balancing, the operator feels for vibrations as he moves test-balance weights (*left*). When vibrations have stopped, the test machine indicates how much weight should be added, and where (*right*).

Spinning balancer. A more effective professional method uses a spinning balancer to correct static unbalance. A unit is clamped onto the jacked-up wheel, and the wheel—and balancer—are both spun at up to about 70 mph.

Through a complex system of gears, the operator can reposition test weights inside the balancer until they are located correctly. The operator may brace a pencil on the fender or bumper to test for vibrations.

When vibration stops, the wheel is stopped.

Indicators on the balancer tell where balance weights are needed and how heavy they should be. Such a system produces what is called a running static balance. On a spinning balancer, dynamic balance can be approached only with some luck.

Strobe balancer. A newer on-the-car balancer achieves something approaching full static and dynamic balancing of rear wheels. It uses a stroboscopic light to help pinpoint unbalance. A vertical pickup held to the suspension arm vibrates up and down with the wheel. On each revolu-

tion, the pickup arm moves enough to trigger a flash of very short duration.

The flash visually "stops" the spinning wheel. The operator can note the position of the "stopped" wheel. He then halts the wheel in that position to locate the heavy spot. Balance weight is added, and the balance rechecked by spinning.

The addition of a horizontal pickup in front-wheel balancing checks dynamic

Stroboscopic balancer relies on sensors to pick up signs of unbalance. Such signs trigger a strobe light that guides the mechanic.

366

balance, too. Such a pickup attaches to the brake backing plate. Wobble, caused by dynamic unbalance, triggers the strobe light with each revolution. Weights can be added to correct dynamic unbalance.

Static-dynamic balancer. The best balancing of all is done off the car on a sensitive static-dynamic balancer. That method is used officially at the Indianapolis 500 auto race. The same type balancing machines are available to balance your car's wheels. Some of those can balance wheels that are mounted on the brake drum or disc, but most balance only the wheel. That method alone can balance a problem wheel successfully, giving a true static and dynamic balance.

Caution: One professional balancing method is thankfully passing out of use. In

Off-the-car static-dynamic balancing is the best professional method. Even problem wheels can be completely balanced on this machine.

it, balance weights are placed under the lug bolts — instead of being clipped to the rim. Because the weights are so near the axis of rotation (the center of the spindle or axle), they have to be quite heavy to have any effect. In fact, the weights used in this method are measured not in ounces but in *pounds*. Although a wheel can be perfectly balanced this way, unsprung weight is increased so much that the car's ride and handling suffer. Avoid shops that still do this kind of balancing.

ALIGNMENT

Proper alignment allows the wheels to roll straight — without scuffing, dragging, or slipping — under many different road conditions. Correct alignment makes driving safer and easier, affords sure steering and long tire wear, and puts less strain on many of the car's parts.

All automotive front wheels get out of line gradually through wear and tear on suspension parts, settling of springs, and slow loosening of rubber bushings and joints. Rear-wheel alignment problems, which are rarer, are brought about by high-powered engines commanded by heavy-footed drivers, by heavily loaded station wagons and by pulling heavy trailers.

In addition, all wheels can be knocked out of line quickly by the hitting of curbs and chuckholes, by jack-rabbit starts, and by panic stops. An accident is another sure way to put a car's wheels out of line.

Wheel alignment experts estimate that at least three-fourths of all cars on the road need front-wheel alignment. The need is costing their owners extra money every mile.

Front-wheel alignment involves five angles: camber, caster, toe-in, steering axis inclination, and toe-out on turns. Those angles are designed into the vehicle to locate the weight of the car's front end on its moving parts, and to aid steering. The first three angles are adjustable in most cars. The last two are built into the design of the steering parts.

Camber. As you look from the front, the camber angle is the outward or inward slant of the top edges of the wheels. Camber helps stabilize the car. It is measured in degrees, positive or negative. Too much positive camber—wheels slanted out too far at the top—makes the tires wear quickly at the outside of the tread. Too much negative camber—wheels in at the top—makes the inside edges of the tread wear too quickly. Practical camber settings for most cars range from $0°$ to $+\frac{1}{2}°$.

Caster. Caster is the slant of the ball joint sockets when viewed from the side. Its purpose is to place the steering axis ahead of, or behind, the center of tire tread contact. Placing it ahead (positive caster) makes your wheels tend to hold a straight line better.

Toe-in. Toe-in means the front wheels are slightly pigeon-toed when the car is at rest. That is, the inner leading edges of the front tires should slant toward each other slightly. Its main purpose is to keep those front edges from being pushed out

excessively by road friction when the car is moving. At speed, the ideal front-wheel position has both wheels dead parallel. This is called zero running toe. Because any deviation when the car is in motion causes tire wear, this setting must be extremely accurate. A serious toe-in error can make front tires wear out four times faster than normal.

Steering axis inclination. In today's cars, this is the most important of the five angles in terms of handling stability. A function of spindle design, its purpose is to center the steering axis of each wheel directly under the center of the tread. In a fortunate accompanying feature, the front spindles are at their highest when the wheels are pointed straight ahead. On a turn, the spindle (and the wheel) tries to go lower, but cannot; instead, the front of the car is raised. As you come out of the turn, the weight of the car helps return the steering wheel to its straight ahead position. Steering axis inclination has largely replaced caster as the force for keeping a car on a straight, stable course.

Toe-out on turns. This alignment angle is required because the front wheels travel different arcs during a turn. The wheel on the inside of the turn covers a

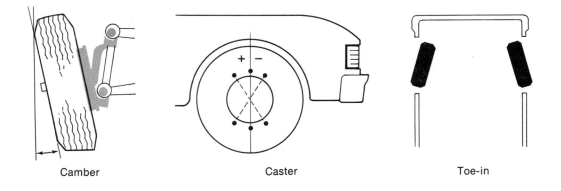

Camber   Caster   Toe-in

smaller circle. Therefore, it must be turned sharper than the outside one.

The five alignment angles have a profound effect on handling and front tire wear. Too much of one and not enough of another can make driving a car about as easy as herding buffalo—and about as safe, too.

Personalized Alignment

Most drivers do not realize that wheel alignment is one of the most personal adjustments on the car. Like front-seat position and rear-view mirror setting, wheel alignment should be tailored to your driving. It can also be used to compensate for normal wear in your car's front end—up to a point.

All wheel alignment specifications contain built-in tolerances. The too-common belief among many a mechanic is that those tolerances are for his benefit—that they give him leeway in the accuracy of his work. The truth is that a good mechanic can set the wheel alignment practically wherever he wants it.

If you drive mostly around town, a good mechanic would set your alignment one way. If you do a lot of highway driving, he would set it a different way. Or, if you are mostly alone when you drive, one setting, and if you usually take the family with

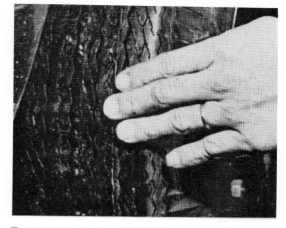

Test a tire for toe wear by feeling the treads. Suspect too much toe-out if the ridges "fight back" as you move your hand in. Suspect too much toe-in if you feel resistance as you draw your hand out.

you, another setting. A traveling salesman who keeps the rear of his car loaded with heavy samples gets still a different setting. All are within manufacturers' specifications.

Old Wive's Tales

If you can tell fact from bunk in wheel alignment, you stand to save money—and have a safer, better handling car to boot.

• It is a common misconception that the only way to know when an auto's wheels need aligning is to test them with aligning equipment. The truth is that you can often tell just from tire wear whether the wheels are out of line, and whether the problem is toe-in, toe-out, or camber wear. To make your own diagnosis, look at the front treads.

Feather-edging of the tread means that toe-in or toe-out is taking miles off the useful life of your front tires. If such a condition exists, pass your hand over the tread, first in toward the center of the car and then out. If the tread seems to fight back on the in stroke, the wheels are toeing out. If it resists on the out stroke, too

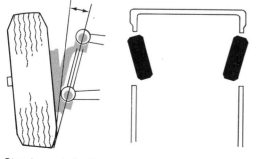

Steering axis inclination   Toe-out

much toe-in is the problem. Because a change in caster, camber, ball joint inclination, and toe-out on turns each would affect wheel toe, this check is a useful clue to all wheel alignment troubles.

One-sided wear of the tire tread is usually a sign of camber problems.

Unfortunately, by the time abnormal tread wear is noticeable, a lot of tread already has been worn off. That condition can easily cost you more than an alignment job. For that reason, it is wise to get regular wheel alignments.

• The play in a modern ball joint front end gives rise to more alignment bunk. On any car over a year old that has its front wheels off the pavement and no weight resting on the ball joints, the wheels can be wiggled in and out at the bottom. Unless the play is more than the ¼-inch that most manufacturers specify, new ball joints are an unnecessary expense.

On the other hand, unless the manufacturer specifies play in the upper ball joint, there should be none.

• Another common misconception is that a little play in the steering wheel is permissible. Modern steering gear adjustments provide for taking up every normal type of wear.

To test your car's steering wheel play, stand alongside it with the front window open. Reach in and turn the steering

Do not be concerned if you can wiggle a front tire in and out (*above*). An unloaded ball joint can let the wheel move as much as a quarter inch. Steering wheel play, though, is unacceptable (*right*). Modern steering should have no play when the front wheels are in the straight-ahead position.

WHEEL ALIGNMENT TROUBLESHOOTING

ANGLES	FUNCTION	TOO MUCH CAUSES	TOO LITTLE CAUSES	UNEQUAL (UNCOMPEN-SATED) CAUSES
Caster, positive	Directional stability; places point of load in front of tire contact; wheel returnability; feel of the road; compensates for road crown	Hard steering, noticeable road shock, low-speed shimmy, poor cornering	Poor stability, insufficient returnability, poor feel of road	Pull to side of least positive caster; if excessive, causes unequal brake action
Caster, negative	Easy steering; places point of load behind tire contact; minimizes road shock; improves parking ease; compensates for road crown	Touchy steering, little feel of road, wander and weave, road shock	Hard steering, poor returnability	Pull to side of most negative caster; if excessive, causes unequal brake action
Camber	Places point of load under tire contact area; easy steering; distributes load on wheel bearings; reduces tire scrub	Tire wear on outside of tread (positive), hard steering, poor handling, wear on ball joints and wheel bearings	Tire wear on inside of tread (negative), hard steering, poor handling, wear on ball joints and wheel bearings	Pull to side of greater camber, hard steering on corners
Toe-in	Keeps wheels parallel when moving by compensating for steering linkage looseness; prevents rapid tire wear	Rapid tire wear, feather-edged tread, scuffing sound, wandering tendency	Rapid tire wear, feather-edged tread, scuffing sound, wandering tendency	Could result in steering wheel off center
Toe-out on turns	Allows inner front tire to roll freely on turns, thus preventing tire wear and wheel fight	Increased tire squeal or wheel fight on turns, tire wear	Increased tire squeal or wheel fight on turns, tire wear	Tire wear
Steering Axis inclination	Directional stability; turning ease at low speed; returnability; reduces tire scrub; reduces need for excessive camber	Hard steering	Wander and weave	Pull to side of least inclination

wheel. The slightest steering wheel movement should move the car's front wheels.
• A popular mistake is that rear wheels need no aligning. Actually, rear-wheel misalignment is common. Rear tires as well as front ones should be inspected for the typical feather-edged toe-wear pattern and the one-sided camber-wear pattern. Rear-wheel toe and camber can be further checked on professional equipment.

Checking Alignment Yourself

Though alignment is a job for professional mechanics who have the right equipment, you may wish to invest in a wheel alignment center. With two pieces of equipment, you will be able to accurately judge if your car needs such a job.

You will need a toe board—a good one costs about $80—and a caster-camber gauge—about $15. These testers represent an appreciable investment, but if they are used correctly and regularly, they could save you money over a period of years.

Actually, you could do your own alignments on the basis of tester readings, but I do not recommend it. The job requires a great deal of knowledge of wheel alignment principles; in addition, you need to know how to make many often-complicated adjustments. Unless you are willing to go to alignment school, restrict yourself to alignment checks only.

Toe board. No knowledge of alignment is required to use an Ammco toe board. If you invest in one, test your car about once a month, or every 1,000 miles, for tire side slip.

During a toe board test, one front tire rolls firmly on a paved surface while the other tire rolls onto the board. The tire on the board can move the free-swinging top plate of the toe gauge in or out, depending on the combined side-slip of both front wheels.

Toed-in wheels push out. Toed-out wheels push in. The amount of push during the roll-on reads out on the scale in feet of side-slip per mile of driving. Thus, if the gauge reads 100, your tires are being dragged sideways 100 feet in every mile of driving.

Place the toe board in your driveway half a car length ahead of either front tire. The driveway should be smooth, fairly level, and hard-surfaced. Aided by a helper, drive the tire to be tested carefully onto the gauge, without moving the steering wheel position during either the approach or the run-on. Stop gently with

Toe board, which measures tire side-slip, tells you whether or not you need an alignment. If used regularly, it can soon pay for itself.

the center of the tire directly over the white line. Now, have your helper read the pointer on the gauge while you remain in the car.

A reading of 0 feet per mile is ideal. Gauge movement beyond the 30-feet-per-mile safe zone indicates a need for wheel alignment service.

Needed service may involve one or more of the following: toe setting; camber setting; caster setting; repair of bent or damaged front end assembly; fixing of sagging springs; or replacement of loose or worn front-end parts. Let a professional mechanic find and fix the trouble. Then, check the repair with another side-slip test after you get your car home. While you are at it, run a rear wheel up onto the board in the same way to check for rear wheel misalignment.

If you keep your toe board dry and hanging on the garage wall, it should last you a lifetime. The board is wide enough to handle wide-tread tires.

Caster-camber gauge. The other piece of alignment equipment you may want to get is much less expensive than a toe board but not as widely useful: a caster-camber gauge.

Before you measure caster and camber, the car must be perfectly level. Check your garage floor with a straight board and a good level. If your floor is not perfectly level, use squares of plywood to shim the wheels. Note the position of each shim, and keep them with your caster-camber gauge. That way, you will not have to make new shims for your next test.

To prepare the car, jack up the front wheels and test for excessive looseness of all moving parts. Remove both front wheel covers and pry off the dust caps from the wheel hubs. Inspect the machined hub surfaces for damage. Any nicks or burrs should be filed off to provide a firm seat for the caster-camber gauge. Keep filings from getting into the wheel bearing by stuffing a small strip of cloth around the hub.

In cars with power steering, the engine should run at idle during the tests. In cars with manual steering, turning the wheels is easier if you put some loose sand on the floor where the tires will rest during the check.

Lower the car. Fasten the gauge's clamp to the first tire's spindle nut, with the spring upward and the screw downward.

Then, bring the gauge up and seat it firmly against the hub's machined surface. Aim the car's wheels straight ahead and read the camber angle on the *left* side of the scale. (All readings should be taken at the center of the bubble.) Jot it down.

Next, turn the wheels toward you until the rear edge of the gauge is at right angles to the car. Record the reading on the caster scale on the *right* side. Turn the wheels away from you until the forward edge of the gauge is at right angles to the car. Record the new reading on the caster scale.

Caster-camber gauge is another handy alignment checker. Compare its readings against specifications to determine if you need professional service.

The difference between the two caster scale readings is the actual amount of caster in that front wheel. If the first reading, with the wheel turned toward you, is larger, the caster angle is positive. If the first reading is smaller, the caster angle is negative.

When you take the camber reading, the top of the gauge should be reasonably level, front-to-rear. It will tip somewhat when you take the caster readings, but do not try to relevel it.

Finally, move the gauge to the opposite front wheel and take the same readings. Then, consult the wheel alignment specifications for your car and compare them with the actual readings. If your figures are outside the tolerances, or if one wheel is near one tolerance and the other wheel is near the other, a wheel alignment is needed.

Professional Alignment

Frequency. Some experts recommend having wheels aligned every 5,000 miles. Others say twice a year, in spring and fall.

If you do much curb-bumping or high-speed driving on rough roads, consider having an alignment every three months.

If you have any of the usual misalignment symptoms, though, it is time for an alignment, regardless of the mileage or length of time since the last one. The symptoms include: pulling to one side; wander at highway speeds; wind-wander; shimmy; road shock transmission to the steering wheel; play in the steering wheel; and rapid, uneven tire wear.

Cost. The average basic front-wheel alignment costs $12 or more, plus another

All professional alignment equipment is built to be accurate. If you need such servicing, choose a shop that features trained alignment specialists and that seems to keep its equipment clean and well calibrated.

$5 or so if the steering gear needs adjusting. Other extras include adjusting the torsion bars and, if necessary, a front wheel bearing repack, new steering linkage parts, new ball joints, new shock absorbers, shimming the springs, or cross-switching the tires. A rear wheel alignment can cost still more.

Shop equipment. From your standpoint, there is no difference in the accuracy of the various makes of equipment. While all makes will do the job, some work differently from others. Each provides a means of measuring angles from the wheel, hub, or tire. There is also a provision for measuring the number of degrees that the front wheels are turned one way or the other, and a means for measuring toe.

There is one unbreakable rule, though: The test racks, stands, rollers, or whatever is used to hold the car during the alignment tests, must be level. A 1/2-inch difference in height between one front wheel and the other throws the camber of each wheel off 1/4°, enough to affect the car's handling noticeably. A 1-inch front-to-rear height difference on the alignment rack throws the caster off 1°.

A car should not be aligned while resting on the garage floor, for only one floor in a thousand is level enough. Even garages with wheel alignment racks must check them for level at frequent intervals. In addition, the alignment instruments should be calibrated regularly.

The mechanic. The man who uses the equipment is the weakest link in the whole wheel alignment chain. Too few mechanics have adequate training in alignment. In fact, by the time you finish this chapter, you may know more about alignment than some mechanics.

Most auto manufacturers and alignment-equipment makers offer training courses for mechanics. But not all dealers and shop owners are willing to foot the expense of sending their mechanics to such courses.

What it boils down to is that nearly all mechanics can manage to set alignment within specifications. But few can interpret the manufacturer's specifications, and then choose the most prudent settings from among broad tolerances. One way to tell whether a mechanic has been thoroughly trained is to ask to see his diploma from a wheel alignment school. If he has one, he should be only too glad to show it.

Preparation. Prepare your car for a wheel alignment by filling the tires to their recommended pressures. Remove all unusual weight from the car and the trunk. Fill the gasoline tank. Have the tires cross-switched, if you want that done. And if you are about ready to buy new tires, get them on the car before the alignment.

Preliminary tests. When you order a wheel alignment, the mechanic first should pay careful attention to your complaints about the car, such as hard steering or pulling to one side.

Then, he should check the car visually for correct curb height and level posture. Spring shims or special shock absorbers may be needed to bring the riding height back to where it should be. (Cars with torsion bar suspension can be adjusted for height.) Sometimes—but rarely—new springs are needed.

Next, he should check the tires for pressure and for abnormal wear, which might indicate wheel unbalance, worn shock absorbers, or misalignment. The mechanic also makes sure that the tires on each axle are of the same size. He checks the car's track (width between tires) and tests the steering system for looseness. He also looks for evidence of collision damage, which could affect alignment.

Parts worn beyond serviceability are replaced.

If he is still not sure of what is wrong, the mechanic will road-test the car. By the time he has finished the road test, he should know what is causing any poor handling or unnecessary tire wear.

Then, the car is run up on the alignment rack.

The front wheels are jacked up and tested for looseness of the ball joints. A maximum of ¼-inch of in-out movement is specified for the lower ball joint. No more than ½-inch of up-down play is allowed in the idler arm. Tie-rod ends on the steering linkage that show any lateral play are replaced. The front wheel bearings are adjusted. Run-out for each front wheel is also determined while the car is still jacked up.

The car then is lowered onto a pair of graduated ball bearing turntables. These let the wheels be turned easily, and they measure the amount, in degrees, that each

Professional caster-camber alignment tester has three fastening arms that help the mechanic gauge wheel angles precisely.

turns. The steering wheel is centered. If the car has power steering, the engine is run at idle. Only then comes the real alignment—the part where all too many shops begin the job.

Alignment. The *caster-camber* gauge is put on each wheel, the alignment readings are recorded, and the necessary corrections are made. Both caster and camber can be adjusted at the same time, since they both relate to the position of the upper ball joint socket.

If your car tends to wander on a flat, fairly level road, or suffers from tire rounding, the mechanic should use the most positive caster tolerance specified. To correct hard steering, wind-wander, and wander on high-crowned roads, the mechanic should use the most negative caster tolerance.

In one common method of alignment toe is found by marking a chalk line around the tire treads and then scribing it with a pointer. The scribed mark represents the true plane of each wheel. By measuring the distance between the scribe marks in front and in back of the wheel and subtracting, the amount of toe-in or toe-out is found.

Toe-in is adjusted to leave the steering wheel centered when the left wheel is pointing straight ahead. Thus, the right tire, in a sense, carries all the toe-in. That is done as an allowance for road crown.

Next, the wheels are turned left and right and the angles of each, as shown on graduated turntables, are compared with the car's requirement for *toe-out* on turns.

Steering axis inclination often is not checked unless there is some reason to suspect a misalignment.

Rear alignment correction, when necessary, is done by bending the axle housing with a powerful jack until the alignment comes back within minimum tolerances.

After a wheel alignment, be sure to drive your car over a scuff gauge. Such an instrument serves as a double-check on the job.

Actually, the mechanic should try for a little rear wheel toe-out to compensate for the toe-in tendencies of wheels that are pushing forward under power.

Post-alignment. Part of a post-alignment road check, some experts agree, should be a run over an instrument that measures tire side-slip. That serves as a check on the accuracy of the toe-in setting, and assures the car owner of long wear from his front tires. An instrument called a scuff gauge, which is like a toe board, employs blades with saw-toothed edges sticking up out of slots. As the front wheels roll over them, the blades are pushed in the direction of the side-slip. In the case of a car with normal toe-in, the blades would be pushed outward, away from the car. A dial on the instrument reads the result in feet per mile of side-slip. The less the better.

21

Tire Tips

Tires are far more important to your car than you may think. To a great extent, they control stopping, starting, turning, and smoothness of ride.

They are more responsible for a quick stop than your brakes. Tires alone can account for a 25 percent difference in stopping distance. After the brakes lock up all four wheels, tire friction against the road surface determines how far the car will slide before it stops.

The development of the automobile has actually hinged on tire progress. The speed, power, and weight of modern cars would not be possible without adequate tires. At one time, a few hundred miles was a long life for a tire. Today, 30,000 miles and more is common.

Modern rubber tires are more than just rubber. They have a tough fabric and stiff steel reinforcement on the inside to give them strength. All of the tire's components are put together on a drum and molded into shape on a heated press. Heat vulcanizes—or toughens—the rubber into a solid mass that can resist pavement wear better than steel.

The four basic parts of a tire—tread, body or casing, bead and cord—are designed for specific purposes.

Tread rubber consists mostly of synthetic rubber and hardeners such as sulfur and carbon black. The tire's tread enables the tire to roll smoothly over the pavement and to resist damage from road hazards—and most important, to grip a variety of road surfaces as firmly as possible. Tread designs vary. For instance, a tire that grips especially well on wet pavement may not be a good tire on a dry pavement. You can choose treads for all-around use, for wet-gripping, or for mud and snow and ice-gripping.

The tire *body* or *casing* flexes as the tire rotates and supports the car's weight. It is also designed to resist abrasion, as from scuffing the curb. Of course, there is a limit to the punishment a tire can take.

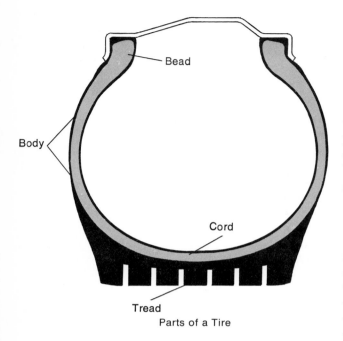

Parts of a Tire

Types of Tires

Bias-ply. A bias-ply tire has a body made of layers, or plies, of cords that run from one wire bead to the other at an angle to the circumference of the tire — hence, the term bias-ply. There are either two or four plies in a typical tire. Alternate plies run at opposite angles to form a criss-cross design. They are laid at cross angles between 30° and 38° to give rigidity to both sidewall and tread.

Belted bias-ply. This type is similar to the bias ply, except that the undertread area is reinforced with relatively stretch-free belts of fiberglass or steel. Two to six of these belts run the circumference of the tire, restricting tread squirm. Thus, the tread of a belted bias-ply tire does not wear away as rapidly as that of a regular bias-ply tire. Belted bias-ply tires generally cost more than conventional bias-ply tires. They should be used in full sets, or at least in pairs across an axle.

Radial-ply. A radial-ply tire is belted, too. But instead of running on the bias, its body plies run from bead to bead at 90° to the tire's circumference, much like the stripes around a zebra. That makes the tread rigid and the sidewall flexible, resulting in superior road-holding qualities.

Constant slamming into deep chuckholes and over curbs will ruin even a new tire; so will driving on a flat.

The *bead* of a tire is a strip around each edge that is shaped to hold the tire tightly to the rim of the wheel, and thus prevent air from leaking out between it and the wheel flange. The bead is made of loops of steel wire, which keep it from stretching from pressure and from the centrifugal force of rapid rotation.

Body *cords* are folded around the beads. They are made of rayon, nylon, polyester, glass-fiber, or other material. Each has its advantages. Rayon-cord tires are noted for their low cost and good ride. Nylon-cord tires usually give a slightly harder ride — especially for the first mile or two after the car has been parked — but offer toughness and resistance to road damage. Polyester and glass-fiber are new tire fabrics that bear consideration. Even steel is coming into use as a tire cord material; you can guess the toughness and impact resistance it offers.

Bead gauge shows that the tire is properly seated; it should be even all around the rim.

Radials also tend to give the longest wear—but they are the most expensive type. Use radials only in sets of four. If you use rear-mounted snow tires in winter along with radials in front, buy radial snow tires. Mixing radials with non-radials is like wearing a tennis shoe on one foot and hiking boot on the other. You get different types of traction, which can be dangerous.

Tire Profiles

A recent addition to tire designation is the "series" designation. Tires are called 60 Series, 70 Series, 78 Series, or 80 Series, depending on their profile, or cross-sectional shape. In a 70 Series tire, the sidewall height, as measured from bead to tread, is 70 percent as much as its tread width. A 60 Series tire is lower and wider, while in a conventional (80 Series) street tire, sidewall height is about 83 percent of tread width. The higher the series number, the higher and narrower the tire profile. Because of differences in handling characteristics and in running radius, use 60 Series and 70 Series tires only in pairs on the same axle.

Tire Sizes

Tire sizes can be confusing because they change with each new development in tire design. The new, wide-profile tires have different size designations even though they fit the same rims. For example, a common pre-1965 original-equipment tire, the 6.70-15, has been replaced by a wider tire, the 7.75-15. The newer bias-ply and belted bias-ply wide-profile designations for that tire are F78-15 in 78 Series, F70-15 in 70 Series, and F60-15 in 60 Series. The radial ply designations for the same size tire are FR78-15 in 78 Series and FR70-15 in 70 Series.

Before switching to different-sized tires, check the auto manufacturer's recommendations. Never use tires smaller than those specified for your car. Usually, though, you can move up one, or sometimes even two, sizes to improve tire life, handling, and load-carrying ability. However, in some cars wheel well clearances or rim sizes do not allow a larger size. Again, check all the dimensions on your car before changing.

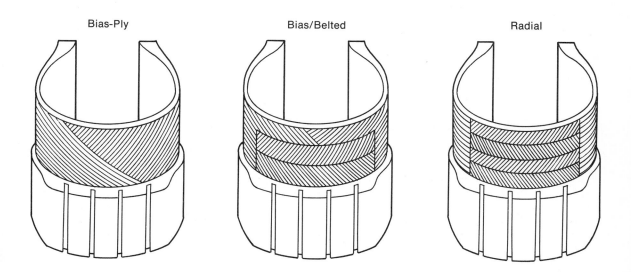

Bias-Ply   Bias/Belted   Radial

Never put two different size tires opposite each other on an axle. In the front, that would affect wheel alignment and could cause the car to drift to one side. In the rear, it would strain the differential gearing because the larger wheel would make fewer revolutions than the smaller one in covering the same distance.

When you replace just one tire, get one the same size as the others. Pair it with the best of the three remaining tires and use both on the rear axle, where the better treads will help traction. When replacing two tires, pair the new ones on the rear axle. Put the next-best tires in front and use one of the poorer ones as a spare.

New tires need to be broken in (even the new spare put on to replace a flat). That means driving at no faster than 60 mph for the first 50 miles. Normal city driving is a good tire break-in. Break-in allows the complex elements of the tire to adjust gradually and function as an integral unit.

Tire Rating

At one time, all passenger car tires were made of four plies of rubber. When two-ply tires were introduced, they carried the designation "four-ply *rating*." That meant that the two-ply tire would do the same job as the four-ply tire. Tests by tire and auto manufacturers and the U.S. government have shown that a two-ply tire with a four-ply rating is in some ways even better than a four-ply. You need have no qualms about using a two-ply.

But because the two-ply/four-ply rating scheme was confusing to most motorists, the load-rating system was instituted in 1969. All tires now conform to it. Combined with tire size, the load range indicates the safe load-carrying capacity of a tire at various inflation pressures. The load rating of tires required for each 1970 and later car is posted on the glove compartment door or other convenient spot.

On the tire itself, the term "Load Range" is molded onto the sidewall, followed by a letter. Tires with the former four-ply rating are now designated "Load Range B." Tires with the old six-ply rating are designated "Load Range C." Tires with the old eight-ply rating are designated "Load Range D."

By federal law, tires also carry designations showing size, maximum load, maximum inflation pressure, manufacturer's name or code, composition of cord mate-

Tire Sidewall Information

rial, actual number of plies, tubeless or tube construction, radial construction (if a radial tire), and DOT (U.S. Department of Transportation) symbol indicating conformation to applicable Federal standards. The tire may also carry a statement that it meets RMA (Rubber Manufacturers Association) standards and SAE (Society of Automotive Engineers) standards J918 and V-1. All such information appears on both sidewalls.

Tire dealers are required to have charts

showing such facts for all of their tires, including load-carrying capacities at various inflation pressures. A brochure containing the same information is supposed to be given to every new-tire buyer.

Tire Rotation

Individual tires may wear unevenly because each one does a different kind of work. Front wheels steer. Rear wheels drive. Tires next to the road edge may wear faster because of the cross-slope of the road.

Auto and tire manufacturers call for switching the positions of car tires about every 5,000 miles to make them all wear evenly.

But tire rotation has drawbacks. For one thing, it is a lot of work. If you have it done, the least it will cost is $2.50. Add the cost of balancing the tires after each rotation, and the job becomes even more expensive.

Perhaps worst of all, tire rotation may mask a misaligned front end, badly worn shock absorbers, or defective brakes. Such mechanical problems cause premature and uneven tire wear—but you may rotate the tires before the uneven wear becomes obvious.

Radial, belted bias-ply and studded winter tires should not be rotated. When they are taken off and stored, label them for remounting in their original wheel positions so they will roll in the same direction as during their first season. (Radial and belted bias tires may be switched from front to rear or rear to front, as long as they rotate in the same direction.)

Tire Storage

When storing any tire, lay it flat on a clean, dry, oil-free floor. Keep it away from electric motors. Sparking motors produce ozone, a form of oxygen that deteriorates rubber rapidly. And store it in the dark; sunshine is hard on tires.

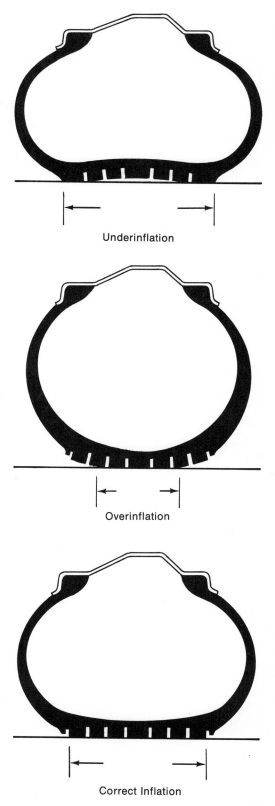

Underinflation

Overinflation

Correct Inflation

CARE OF TIRES

You will get more mileage and better service from your tires if you treat them right.

Pressure. Most important, keep tires properly inflated.

Too little pressure makes the tread scuff off at the shoulders or the outside. It also allows excessive flexing of the sidewall. That heats the tire body from inside and causes faster wear and even tire failure.

Too much air pressure causes severe wear in the center of the tread. It also strains the tire body and makes it prone to damage by impact with road hazards.

Your car owner's manual should show a range of pressures, depending on the type of driving you do.

Keep an accurate tire-pressure gauge in the car, and use it at least once a month to check pressures when the tires are cold. If adjusting pressures properly is a problem because you live more than a few

Keep a tire pressure guage in you car. Pressure should be checked when the tires are cold.

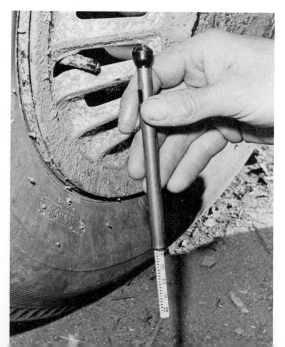

miles from a place where you can get air, try the following: With your gauge, test one tire at home while it is cold, and make a note of its pressure. Then drive to the service station, and with the same pressure gauge, take another reading of the same tire. The difference between the two readings is the amount the pressure was increased by the warmup drive. Simply add that difference to the tire pressure specifications and inflate the tires accordingly.

For instance, say the trip to the station expands the air in the tire two psi. Add this difference to all your cold-pressure specs. If your manual calls for 23 psi in the rear and 26 psi in the front, fill the rear tires to 25 psi and the front tires to 28 psi.

When the weather turns cold, tire pressures fall off, and must be boosted back up to the specified cold pressure to avoid running underinflated. Every 10° temperature drop lowers the pressure about 1 psi.

If you must check tire pressure when the tires are hot, such as after several miles of fast driving, never bleed air from the hot tires to bring their pressures to the cold specifications. Such pressure buildup is normal; bleeding the tires would leave them underinflated.

Tread. Check the tire treads often. Nails, small stones, and pieces of metal or glass embedded in the tread should be pried out. A tire that leaks should be removed and its inside inspected. Permanent repairs should be done only from inside.

Check regularly for tread wear. Tires that are worn below 1/16-inch tread depth are dangerous and should be taken out of service. Tires of recent make have built-in tread-wear indicators—bars of solid rubber that appear across the tread when the tire has only 1/16-inch of tread remaining. When the tread-wear indicators contact

Checking Tread

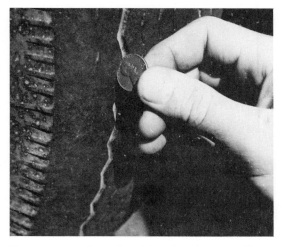

Place a penny head-first into a tread groove; if you can see space above the head, you need a new tire.

Modern tires often have built-in wear indicators. When bars (*arrows*) surface in adjacent grooves in several places around the tire, you need a new one.

Tread wear gauge with $\frac{1}{32}$-inch calibrations is a more exact way of determining wear; tires should be replaced when they are down to $\frac{1}{16}$-inch of tread.

the road in two or more adjacent tread grooves and in three intervals spaced about 120° apart around the tire's circumference, that tire should be replaced.

Tires without tread indicators should be measured in two or more adjacent grooves and at three locations, about 120° apart, around the tire. You can gauge $\frac{1}{16}$-inch easily with a Lincoln-head penny. Place the penny on edge in a groove, with the top of Lincon's head pointing into the tread. If the top of the head is out of the groove in several spots around the tread, the tire needs replacing.

For more precise measurements, buy a tread wear gauge (about $1). Such a device shows you which tires are wearing fastest, and whether the wear is even or spotty. If the front tires are wearing considerably faster than the rear ones, your car probably has a wheel alignment problem.

Valves. Tire valves, valve cores, and extensions should be in good condition. Valve stems should have valve caps that are screwed on fingertight.

You need at least one metal valve cap that is designed for removing and replacing valve cores. If the special cap cannot be on the valve stem, keep it in the glove compartment.

One valve cap on your car should have a notched end that lets you turn valve cores. Then, if you find a leaking core, you can tighten or remove it.

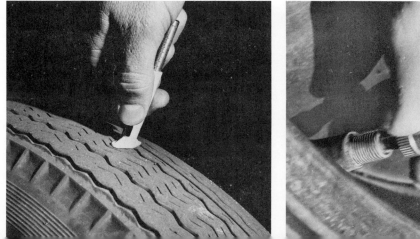

About every other tire change, you should change the valve. Snap-in replacement valves for tubeless tires are carried by tire dealers and are lubricated so that you can pop them into the wheel's valve opening. The replacement should match the original in length and in TR number (molded into the valve base).

Whitewalls. Some whitewalls come from the factory with a colored protective coating on the white portion. That coating should be removed before you use the tires, since it is not as flexible as the rubber and tends to crack, causing the sidewalls to check. In no case should a whitewall be driven more than 50 miles without removing the coating.

To get it off, wet the tire surface thoroughly with warm water, let it soak for a minute, and then wash off the coating with a soft-bristle brush or a sponge. The coating can also be removed in a jet-spray car wash by close jetting. Never use gasoline or other petroleum solvents or a wire brush.

Road dirt that collects on whitewalls should be removed only with soap or a nonabrasive cleaner and, when necessary, a soft-bristle brush. Oil-based cleaning fluids, gasoline and kerosene deteriorate the rubber and may discolor whitewalls.

ABNORMAL WEAR

Tire wear patterns can tell you a lot about your car and the way it is driven. Learn to look at your tires whenever you walk up to your car to use it. This doesn't mean you have to look at all of them, but notice the ones on the side you approach. If they bulge out more than usual, check their pressures.

If the *center* of the tread shows more wear than the edges, overinflation is the cause. Reduce tire pressure to that specified by the manufacturer for the load and type of driving you do. If the tread is cracking, take the wheel to a shop for an internal inspection.

If the *edges* of the tread show more wear than the center, the cause is underinflation. If serious enough, underinflation may cause hidden fabric damage. The only way to be sure is to have the tire removed from the wheel for an internal inspection. The cure for underinflation wear is proper inflation through regular checks of pressure while cold. You can drive a short distance on a slightly underinflated tire, but if the underinflation is great, pump up the tire or remove it and put on the spare.

If the edges of the tread are worn more than the center and the tire has a *smoothly rounded tread profile*, the driver must take the blame. Fast driving around corners is the cause of the problem.

Tiny *feather-edges* on one side of tread blocks are caused by too much or too little toe-in. (See the chapter on wheel alignment.) A slight toe problem (in or out) usually wears rubber from just one tire. A severe toe problem can wear rubber rapidly from both tires or even from all four.

Upon installing a new whitewall, immediately scrub off the protective coating over the white band. The coating, if left on, can damage the sidewall.

Rapid center wear points to overinflation.

Rapid side wear points to underinflation.

Rounded-off tread points to high-speed cornering.

One-sided wear points to incorrect camber.

Saw-toothed wear points to jerky braking.

Spotty, cupped wear points to incorrect alignment.

Tires that *squeal* easily on turns, or make a loud *hissing* noise as they roll, may also be signaling toe troubles. (The hissing is noise reflected from parked cars that you drive by.) Car handling may or may not be affected.

Tread blocks with a *saw-toothed wear* pattern indicate too much or too hard use of brakes. The problem is called heel-and-toe wear. A certain amount of such wear is normal. Rear tires show it less than front tires because they receive a driving force from the engine that wears off the opposite ends of their tread blocks. But only braking forces act on the front wheels of conventional, rear-wheel-drive cars. The remedy is to change driving habits—and to equalize abnormal wear by rotation if the problem becomes serious enough to produce tire noises.

Tread with *one side worn off,* on a front wheel, is caused by driving on highly

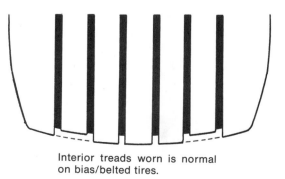

Interior treads worn is normal on bias/belted tires.

cambered roads or by improper camber setting of that wheel. To tell whether the wear is caused by incorrect camber, see the chapter on wheel alignment. One-sided front-tire wear can also be caused by taking turns too fast.

Uneven or spotty tread wear, which sometimes takes the form of cupping, scalloping, or bald spots around the tire, may be caused by alignment irregularities such as unequal caster or camber, bent suspension parts, out-of-balance wheels, out-of-round brake drums, or brakes that are out of adjustment. (See the chapters covering those subjects.) Other mechanical problems also can cause such wear. The remedy may be a case for a professional mechanic. Once an uneven wear pattern is set, correcting the cause alone will not improve the pattern. Tire rotation is called for. When placed on a rear wheel, a front tire that has become cupped will partially true its tread.

A *vibration* or a *whining sound* that is especially noticeable on a smooth road may signal tread abnormalities. Unless it is a wheel tramp that comes once with every revolution of the wheels, it may be tough to tell from differential gear noises.

To tell tire noise from gear or exhaust noise, find a smooth stretch of highway. Drive at various speeds and note the effect of accelerating and decelerating. When it is safe to do so, brake lightly. Axle and exhaust noises change in intensity under these conditions. Tire noises, though, usually stay the same throughout.

If tires seem to be the cause, balance all the wheels temporarily, inflate them to 45 psi, and drive the road again at the same speeds. If the noise is changed or eliminated, deflate one tire at a time to the proper pressure, repeating the road test with each deflation. When the noise returns to what it was, the last tire deflated is probably the offender.

Wheel tramp (also called tire thump) usually occurs between 20 and 40 mph. The bad tire is easy to locate with the tire-at-a-time deflation method. The only cure for a thumper is replacement.

Tire *roughness* from two or more thumping tires, or one tire with more than one thump-spot, most often shows up at speeds between 40 and 70 mph. Tire roughness feels like a low-frequency rumble or vibration. It may be felt in the seat or steering wheel, or both. Front tire thumps are most noticeable in the steering wheel, while rear tire thumps usually show up as seat vibrations. To find the trouble-maker(s), you may have to replace the tires one at a time with the spare. For this, all tires should be at normal pressure.

An *out-of-balance driveshaft* can feel like thumping tires. To tell one from the other, block up the rear axle, remove the wheels, and accelerate the engine with the transmission in gear. Hold the accelerator pedal at the speed where the vibration was most pronounced. If you feel no vibration, the front or rear tires are the cause. If the vibration is still there, the driveshaft is the likely cause.

REPAIR OF TIRES

Tire repairing is not as complex as brake servicing, but it is hard, unpleasant work when it is done at home without the costly equipment that tire dealers and service stations have. Better let them do the repair jobs. However, you should know a few facts to make sure you get a good job.

Discard any tire with tread or sidewall cracks, cuts, or snags deep enough to expose the body cords. Replace any tire that has a fabric break or that has been temporarily patched. Do not accept a tire that has been regrooved below the original tread depth.

Tire injuries often happen long before the tire fails. Impacts that damage a tire

Two easy safeguards against on-the-road tire problems: a spark plug tire pump (*left*) uses the engine's power to force in air; a tire inflator/puncture sealer (*right*) lets you drive to a nearby service station.

beyond repair may not show up on the outside, and the tire may go many miles before it gives up. Such an injury usually appears on the inside of the tire casing as an "X" or straight-line break in the cord body. Constant flexing enlarges the break until the tire finally fails.

In tubeless tires, an impact injury most often produces a slow leak. In tube-type tires, it can cause a serious blowout.

Damage that you can see on the outside of the tire is a sure tipoff that the tire must be replaced. Look too for bulges or knots, which indicate separation of the tread or sidewall from the tire body. Rims that are bent, loose, cracked, or otherwise damaged also should be replaced.

As effective as tubeless tires are in preventing blowouts, they present a problem in repairing. Not many service stations know how to do the job right. The tire must be taken off the rim; on-the-rim repairs are short-lived at best.

However, in an emergency, you can temporarily repair leaks in modern tubeless tires if you have a tubeless tire external patching kit. The purpose of such a repair is to keep you on the road, for no more than 100 miles at speeds no higher than 50 mph. But if the hole in the tire is larger than 1/4-inch or if the plies are separated around the leak, do not try to repair the tire. Replace it immediately.

To try a repair, you will need a spark plug tire pump, a spark plug wrench and a patch kit.

First, locate the leak. Ordinarily, you need not remove the wheel to do that. Just listen. Feel around the tread for escaping air. If necessary, jack up the wheel.

If a tire is too flat to show a leak, fill it with the spark plug tire pump. With one plug removed, insert the adapter into the spark plug opening. The pump threads into the adapter and the hose screws onto the pump. With the engine idling and the dangling high-tension wire grounded through the removed spark plug, the pump will supply air. A bicycle pump is a tedious alternative.

When you find the leak, probe it with the tire-patch tool, feeling for metal or glass. Remove any foreign material. Squirt some rubber cement from your patching kit onto the tip of the needle and run it in and out of the puncture.

Do-It-Yourself Tire Patching

1. If the puncture is ¼ inch or less and the plies are not split, you can make a temporary patch with a tire kit. First, locate the puncture.

2. Probe the puncture thoroughly for metal or glass, and remove any such foreign matter with a handy tire-patch tool.

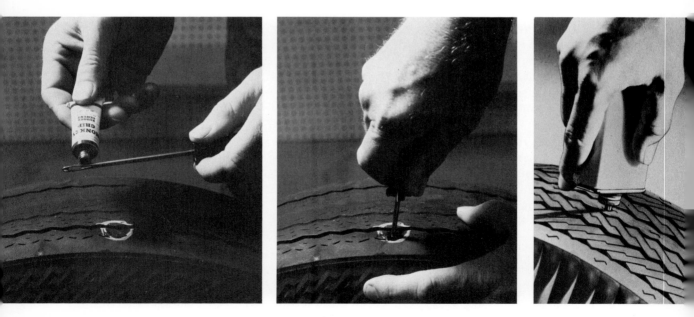

3. If the cement comes in a tube, squirt some onto the tool (*left*) and run the tool in and out of the puncture (*center*). If the cement comes in a spout can, use the spout to smear the adhesive into the puncture (*right*).

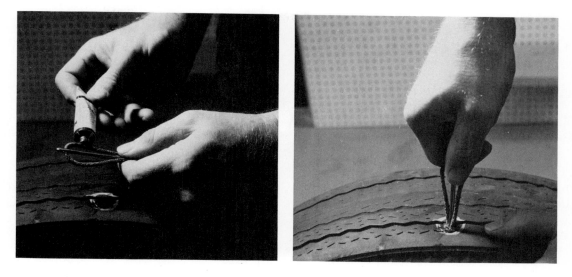

4. Insert a 4-inch length of soft rubber plug into the eye of the patching tool; half of the plug should be on each side. Coat one inch of the plug on each side of the eye with the cement (*left*). Push the tool—and the plug—into the puncture until only a ½ inch of plug sticks out of the tire (*right*).

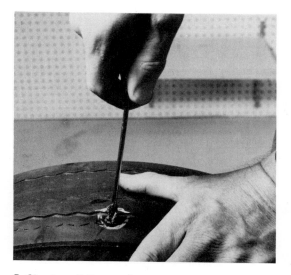

5. Slowly pull the needle out until the eye is ½ inch out of the hole. If the leak has stopped, trim off the excess plug. If the tire still leaks, try a second plug. In either case, have a professional put a permanent patch on that tire.

Thread a length of soft rubber plug into the eye of the needle so that half the plug is on each side. Smear rubber cement on one inch of plug on each side of the needle. Push the plug into the puncture until one-half inch of plug is left sticking out.

Slowly pull the needle out until the eye is half an inch out of the hole. If the leak has been stopped, nip off the excess plug on the outside with a knife, razor blade, or side-cutting pliers. If the plug still leaks, insert a second plug in the same way.

By the time you get the car off the jack, the tire should be ready for driving. At the first opportunity, have a shop remove the tire from the rim, inspect it for internal damage, and make a lasting repair if the tire is salvageable.

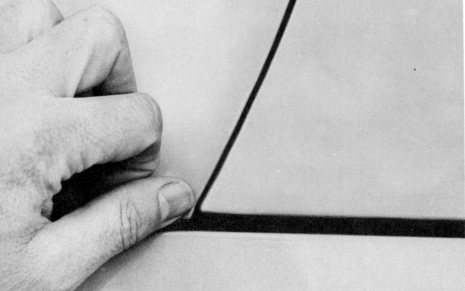

22

Adjusting Doors, Hoods and Decklids

One of the most annoying of all car problems is an out-of-adjustment door, hood, or decklid (the mechanics' term for trunk lid). All of those panels are hinged to the car body at one end and fitted with some kind of latch at the other end. Either the hinge end or the latch end can get out of whack through body settling, collision, or wear.

To put hinged parts back where they belong, some adjustment is provided, usually at both hinge and latch. You can make most of the adjustments yourself.

In some cases, you may have to compromise. Take, for example, a hood's rear edge that is too high on the driver's side and too low on the passenger's side. If you raise the passenger's side and lower the driver's side, which is easily done, you may find that the front of the hood has become twisted out of line; the misalignment has merely been moved from rear to front. Obviously, either the hood or the front of the body is twisted, perhaps both. Getting rid of panel twist is a tough problem, even for a body man—all you can do is decide which condition looks least objectionable, and adjust for that. Often, the best possible adjustment is half-way between the two extremes.

New cars sometimes come from the factory with compromise adjustments already made in the doors, hood, and decklid. Ordinarily, the factory allows about $1/16$- to $3/16$-inch clearance around movable panels. In-out tolerances are closer.

Spaces between hinged panels and other surrounding panels should be nearly even along the sides. Hinged panels look better if they are set in from the surrounding nonmovable body parts than if they stick out. Spaces at the hinged edge should be close, but not so close that the panel rubs the body when it is opened and closed. If a panel looks right, does not leak water or air, and does not squeak, rattle, or whistle as you drive, the setting should be reasonably good.

Most auto manufacturers publish specifications for setting adjustable body panels. It is helpful to have them. Otherwise, go by what looks best to you.

Tools needed to make hinged panel adjustments are a few wrenches, a special screwdriver or wrench for loosening door strikers, and a hammer.

DOOR ADJUSTMENTS

Car doors tend to get out of adjustment because they get lots of use, especially if they are abused by constant slamming. If a car door does not latch fully without slamming, it needs adjustment.

Weatherstripping becomes compressed with age, sometimes to the point where it no longer seals the opening. That also calls for adjustment.

Door rattles caused by a latch that is too loose can be identified by grabbing the door handle with the door closed and shaking it all around. A slight, silent movement is all right. Anything more calls for repairs.

Not all rattling doors, though, call for an adjustment. The cause of the rattle may be loose glass channels or spare parts that have fallen into the door bottom. Open the door and shake it. Slap it at the bottom several times with your open hand. If you hear a rattle, it is caused by something inside the door. To remove the object, you must take off the trim panel.

Striker

A loose or noisy latch means that the striker, which holds the door closed and keeps it from moving up and down, is out too far. A door that must be slammed shut has its striker set in too far.

Considerable striker adjustment is provided by enlarged mounting holes.

To adjust the striker, loosen the mounting screw or screws. You may need an offset Phillips screwdriver with No. 3 and No. 4 heads. Recent Ford products call for a special tool to loosen the post-type striker; pliers will do in a pinch. Late model GM car strikers can be loosened with large-hex set-screw wrenches. Some early-model cars used clutch-head screws; you need a clutch-head screwdriver for those.

Loosen the screws just enough so that you can shift the striker by tapping it with a hammer. Snug up the screws and close the door to check progress. Move and check until you get the striker where you want it. If you are adjusting the striker in

To adjust a post-type striker (*left*), loosen it with pliers or, on GM models, an allen wrench. Then, slide the striker and tighten. To adjust a screw-mounted striker (*right*), loosen with a Phillips angle screwdriver. Tap it into place with a hammer and tighten.

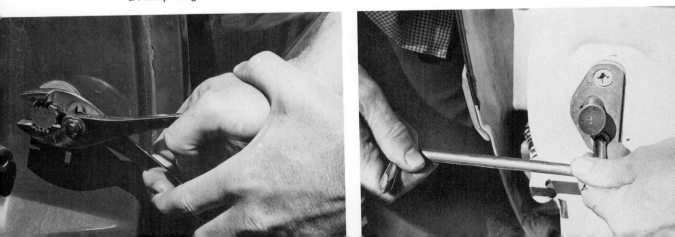

or out, try not to disturb the up-down adjustment, and vice-versa.

Up-down. For this alignment, close the door slowly while you depress the door button or otherwise hold the latch open. The door should close straight in and align correctly, with no binding, as the free-moving latch contacts the striker. Raise or lower the striker as necessary. In a few hardtops and convertibles and some Chrysler cars, the striker is supposed to give a slight lift to the door as it closes; that helps the window glass seal at the top. If you are in doubt, check your car's specifications.

In-out. If the door closure is too loose or too tight, adjust the in-out alignment. Loosen the striker and tap it in or out until you can close the door tightly without slamming.

Fore-aft. Besides the up-down and in-out adjustments, a door striker can be moved fore or aft to align with the latch. To check fore-aft alignment, put a lump of modeling clay or putty in the door latch opening. Close the door on the putty just enough to get an impression of the striker. (If you completely close the door, you will have a mess to clean out.) Open the door and inspect the putty impression. Bolt-type striker shoulders should be centered in the latch opening. Plate-type strikers, as used on Chrysler cars, should be nearly centered on the latch cog.

The putty method does not work with bear-hug latches such as those in recent Ford products. To check their fore-and-aft alignment, coat the latch contacts with dark grease. Close the door and reopen it. Grease marks on the striker should be $3/32$- to $5/32$-inch in from the flange end of the striker bolt.

For all fore-aft adjustments, add or remove shims beneath the striker base; you

If striker does not bind when you close door with button depressed, its up-down setting is correct.

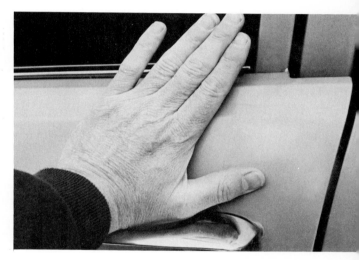

If the striker just latches when you stiff-arm it closed, its in-out setting is correct.

If the post-type striker on a Ford shows a $3/32$-to $5/32$-inch clearance between the shoulder and the circle of contact, its fore-aft setting is correct.

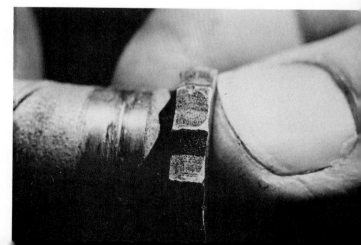

Squirting lock lubricant onto a key, then manipulating the key in its lock, helps keep locks unfrozen — even in the dead of winter.

can buy shims from your car dealer. When the striker is where you want it, tighten the screws. Test again to be sure.

Before you leave the striker-setting job, see that the safety catch is working. That feature stops the door at half-latch, preventing it from flying open if it should be unlatched accidentally. To test, push the door in until it is almost latched. Then, try to open it without using the button. The door should be held by the safety latch. If it opens, suspect either an incorrect striker setting or a worn or sticking latch mechanism. The cure may be a shop job.

A striker should never be set to pull the door into alignment. That adjustment is made to the hinges.

Frozen Locks

If you go out some icy morning, especially after washing the car the night before, and find the door lock frozen, you need not be locked out for long.

The standard emergency cure is to warm the key with a match or cigarette lighter. If you do not have access to a flame, hold the key tightly in your hand to warm it; then, insert it in the lock. Try several warmings and insertions if the first one does not work. Sometimes, cupping your hands around the lock and blowing into them for several seconds is effective.

Most likely the lock will freeze again soon. A more lasting remedy is to squirt alcohol de-icer, windshield washer antifreeze, or rubbing alcohol into the lock cylinder. With pliers, pinch the end of an oil can spout so it will fit into the lock about 1/8-inch. Warm the de-icer to room temperature before spraying it into the lock. Aim the spray up, down, and sideways. Try the key a few times. Spray again to help the de-icer melt and carry away the ice.

Then, pump a couple of squirts of penetrating lubricant into the lock cylinder, and put two drops of light machine oil on your key. Insert and pull out the key, and try the lock — it should be good as new.

Most exterior auto locks have dust shields that spring away when the key is inserted. Dust shields are also supposed to keep water out of the lock cylinder. Sometimes, a dust shield is damaged or loses its spring action and lets in water and dust. Such a lock is especially prone to sticking and freezing; it will need more frequent attention than a fully protected one. You can try saving it by lubricating it with graphite or some other lock lubricant. If that does not help, replace it. Let a car dealer or locksmith do that. He can key the new lock cylinder to match the door keys you already have.

Hinges

The way a door fits into its body opening affects not only the looks of a car but the operation of the door as well. Car manufacturers provide elongated mounting holes for hinge-to-body and hinge-to-door adjustments.

Most hinge adjustments are best left to a bodyman. There is, however, one adjustment you can make yourself. Fortunately, it corrects the most common problem: sagging. Door sagging is most noticeable just below the window—the rear edge of the door is too low in relation to the body.

Each door has two hinges. They are held by screws that fasten to caged, tapped metal plates. The mounting holes are slotted to permit adjustment by sliding. These can often be made at either the door or the pillar, whichever is easier to get at.

Before any adjustment, study the alignment problem and decide which way the hinged edge of the door must go. To make the adjustment, loosen the holding screws sufficiently for the parts to slide when forced. Once the adjustment is right, tighten the screws. If shims are necessary, remove the screws from one hinge at a time and install cardboard or, better yet, metal shims.

To fix a sagging door, remove the striker. If it is left on, it may affect your adjustment.

A tapped plate behind the door pillar holds the striker bolts. The plate itself is held in a pocket and cannot fall away. Do not worry about finding it again when you need it.

Check for door sag once more with the striker off. Lift the closed door up and down by the handle to see whether it is loose. Looseness most often comes from a loose hinge mounting bolt. The bolt must be found and tightened before you try to make any adjustment.

You sometimes need a special wrench, especially with some GM models. In that case, it may pay to have a shop do the repair.

If a hinge-to-door bolt is loose, you usually must remove the door trim panel to get at it. If the hinge-to-body bolt is loose, it may be accessible with the door open. In most cars, at least some of the hinge bolts are accessible. Tighten those that you can, and recheck the door for looseness.

The adjustments you can make depend on which of two types of hinges you are dealing with.

To adjust a door hinge, loosen the screw cluster (*left*) enough to let you slide the member about. On Fords with recessed hinges (*right*), loosen the accessible mounting cap screws.

One type has its members at right angles to each other when closed. It allows in-out, up-down, and fore-aft adjustment without shims.

The other is built so that both members are parallel when the door is closed. This allows in-out and up-down adjustments by sliding. Fore-aft alignment requires shimming between the hinge and the door or pillar.

Not all doors use these two common hinging methods. Early-model Fords have hinge-to-door cap screws behind the door trim panel. To get at them, you must remove the panel (discussed later in this chapter).

● Correct door sag at the latch edge on a right-angled hinged door by loosening the screws of the longitudinal (front-to-rear) member and lifting the latch edge into alignment. Then, tighten the screws. In parallel-member hinges, shims under the lower hinge will correct sagging. Depending on the evenness of the gap running up and down the hinged edge of the door, one or both hinges may need adjustment.

● Another common problem finds the hinged edge of the door out at the top and in at the bottom—a result of straining the door while it is open. To correct such misalignment, loosen the lower hinge screws somewhat at the pillar or cowl. Open the door and lift it at the latch edge. Then, close it and check your progress. When the alignment is right, tighten the screws.

● Up-down door alignment corrections are made by loosening the screws of both hinges and forcing the door in the desired direction.

There is a cruder method of removing door sag that does not involve taking the door apart. Simply slip protective blocks of wood onto the door step plate and under the door bottom. (Get the block on the door's flat bottom surface, not under the lip.) With the door open about a foot, put a four-foot-long 2 x 4 on top of the door

Adjusting Door Sag

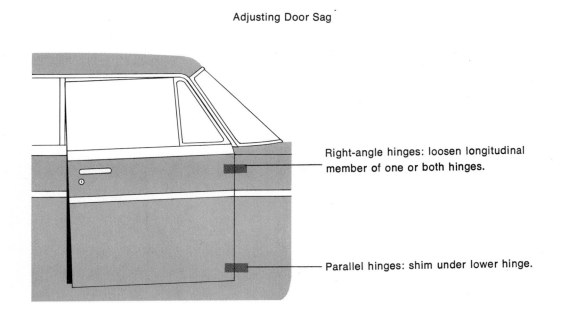

Right-angle hinges: loosen longitudinal member of one or both hinges.

Parallel hinges: shim under lower hinge.

Rough but efficient way of aligning a sagging door calls for muscle. Clamp protective wood blocks to the bottom of the door; then, pry up with a length of 2 x 4 lumber.

plate block and under the door bottom block. Pry up on the end of the 2 x 4 to raise the door at its latch edge. Essentially, that springs the door mounts to a new position—a rough but effective method. Pry and check until all sag is gone. Do not bend too much or you will have to bring your door back down again.

Other hinge adjustments are possible, but not easy. Aligning a door's leading edge, for example, consists of loosening the hinge-to-body bolts, moving the door in the desired direction, and tightening the bolts. In most cases, some of the bolts are hard to reach, and a special wrench is often required. You can get the wrench and try it if you like, but I do not recommend it.

Upper Door

Not all fitting is limited to that portion of the car door below the belt line. The upper door, the narrow frame part around the window, often needs adjustment, too. Never adjust the fit of the lower part of the door because of a poor-fitting upper door.

The most common upper-door problem is loose fit. The weatherstrip does not make contact but gapes open, letting outside air in. If the metal portion of the door does not seem to be too far out or in, restrict your fitting to the weatherstrip. But

To align an upper door that closes too much (*left*), roll down the window and pull the frame towards you. To align an upper door that does not close enough (*right*), keep the door from closing with a wood chock; then, push the frame away from you.

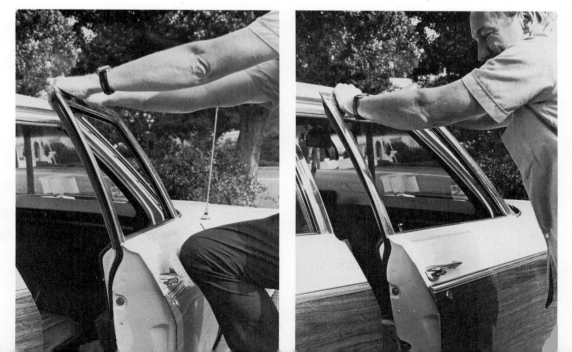

if the culprit is an out-of-position frame, it must be bent into place.

First, roll the window down to get the glass out of the way. Open the door, and grab the frame with one hand and the lower part of the door with your other hand. Bend the frame the way it should go. Close the door and check. Bend more, if necessary, to get a good fit.

If the frame resists fitting this way, block the door open at the latch and push in on the upper door frame with both hands. If the upper door is already too far in and must come out, block with a knee while you pull out on the frame with both hands. If still more force is needed, pull the car close to a tree or building and open the door against it. Pad the door thickly with cloth to protect the finish, and pull or push the upper door frame to bend it. Check after each pull or push so you do not go too far.

Trim Panel Removal

To take off this door part, you often need a special tool to reach the lock rings or clips that are behind the door and window handles.

Use a No. 2 Phillips screwdriver to take the screws out of trim moldings and to remove the armrest.

The door trim panel is held around the edges with spring clips every six inches or so. Stick a screwdriver between the trim panel and the door, and pry each spring clip out of its hole. When the last one is out, the trim panel should come off.

Whenever you have access to the inside of a door, apply white lubricant to the window winding gear. Squirt motor oil on all other moving parts except the window channels. Spray silicone lubricant along window channels to help window movement. Tighten all screws and bolts, too, to forestall future rattles.

Finish the job by replacing the trim panel. Position it over the door handle and window operator spindles. Start the spring clips into their holes. Give a sharp blow with your fist to the panel over each clip to snap it in place. Install the armrest, crank handles and molding. Ford and GM cranks snap into place when you position the lock ring on the handle and slip the handle onto its spindle.

Weatherstripping

Once the door has been fitted to its opening and you are satisfied, check the weatherstripping all around.

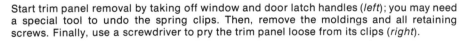

Start trim panel removal by taking off window and door latch handles (*left*); you may need a special tool to undo the spring clips. Then, remove the moldings and all retaining screws. Finally, use a screwdriver to pry the trim panel loose from its clips (*right*).

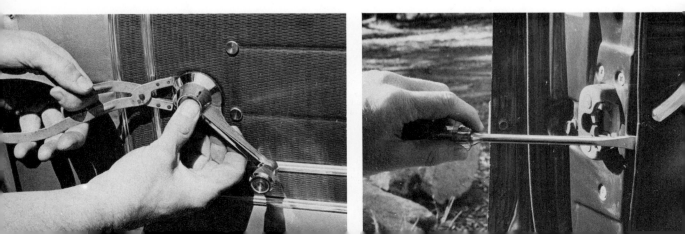

The old refrigerator-door-gasket trick is a good one. Close the door on a two-inch-wide strip of brown paper cut from a grocery bag and try to pull the paper out. If the paper comes out easily, the weatherstripping is not making good contact at that point. If the paper tears when you try to pull it out, chances are the contact is too tight. Repeat the test all around, using chalk to mark the areas that need fitting.

Or, if you have a stethoscope, you can use it to find leaks in door weatherstripping. Close all doors and windows, set the car's heater control on "heat," and turn the blower on its highest setting. This pressurizes the car interior. Put on the stethoscope and move its probe around the door edges. When the probe comes to a spot where air is rushing out, you'll hear a sound like a muted waterfall. Mark the spot with chalk.

If you have no stethoscope, you can watch for leaks instead of listening for them. Pressurize the car interior with the heater and blower and, from outside the vehicle, raise clouds of bath powder around the closed door edges. The clouds will be disturbed where air is rushing out, pinpointing the leaks.

Replacing old weatherstripping is seldom satisfactory. The new stripping usually takes on the shape of its storage bin, and fitting it properly can be a problem.

The best cure for undersized weatherstripping is to shim it up. With a single-edged razor blade or utility knife, slice the weatherstrip from the door in the areas where it needs beefing up. Then, cut off thin slices of sponge-rubber weatherstripping (the kind used for house storm doors and windows). Secure the slices to the frame with automotive trim cement or weatherstrip cement. Cement the old weatherstrip over the slices. Retest.

To cure oversized weatherstripping, pare it, a little at a time, with your razor

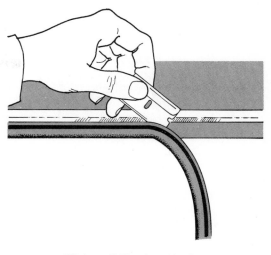

Slicing off Weatherstripping

blade or knife. Be careful, or you may take off too much; then, you will be forced to beef it up with shims.

HOOD ADJUSTMENTS

An automobile hood has three adjustments: hinge, latch, and bumpers. Together, the three let you position the hood to line up closely with surrounding parts and to be tightly closed without slamming.

The first step is a critical examination of hood fit. How does it match up with other parts of the body? Does it rub at any point? Are the gaps between panels even? Is the front-to-rear hood positioning correct? Is the height the same on both sides? When the hood is closed, can you push the latch end down farther?

Hinges

Hood hinge mounting bolts have elongated holes in the body-mounted panel that allow raising or lowering of the hinge.

Up-down. If the hood needs an upward or downward adjustment at its hinged end, lightly scribe a line around the hinge

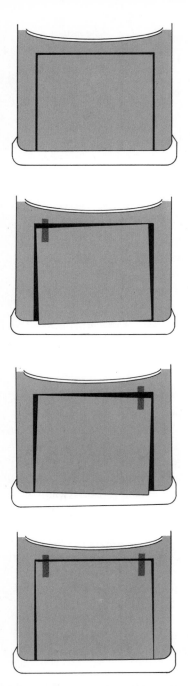

Few hoods are perfectly aligned (*top*). If the skew is obvious (*center two illustrations*), adjust the proper hinge until the front edge is aligned. But if the hood is warped (*bottom*), loosen both hinges to attain a compromise setting.

mount onto the body. Use a pointed instrument such as a nail. That will show where the mount was before you adjusted it. If all else fails, you can at least get the adjustment back where it was initially.

Loosen the bolts that hold the hinge mount to the body just enough to permit the mount to move when it is forced. Hammer or pry the mount in the desired direction. Move it a little, tighten the bolts, and test your adjustment by closing the hood. If further adjustment is required, open the hood, loosen the bolts, and move the mount again. Before you tighten the mounting bolts for good, be certain that no other portion of the hood has been thrown out of alignment by the adjustment you have completed. If both sides of the hood's hinge end need raising or lowering, make both adjustments at the same time.

Fore-aft. Besides an up-down adjustment, you can make a fore-aft adjustment. That is usually made possible by elongated holes in the hinge-to-hood connection. When they are used together, you can get a forward or backward movement of the hood to widen or narrow the hood gap at the hinge end. That also gives a corresponding change in gap at the lock end, but without affecting side-to-side hood alignment.

To make the adjustment, open the hood and loosen both hinge-to-hood sets of bolts. Pull or push the hood into alignment. Sometimes, it helps to close the hood and stiff-arm it with the heel of your hand. Then, open it ever so gently to keep from disturbing the adjustment until you can tighten the adjusting bolts.

Side-to-side. Besides controlling fore-aft hood alignment, the hinge-to-hood slotted mounts allow adjustment of side-to-side fit at the latch end. Take, for example, a hood that is too close to the pas-

Hood Alignment

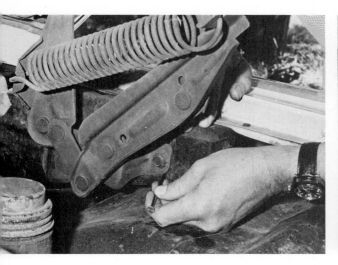

1. Scribe a line around both hinge brackets, in case you must return to the original alignment.

2. Loosen the hinge-to-body bolts just enough so you can move the brackets with a little force.

3. With a 2 x 4, tire tool or large screwdriver, pry the bracket one way or the other. If prying is not practical, use a hammer.

4. To align the hood with the front of the car, loosen the brackets quite a bit. Then, pull (*left*) or push (*right*) on the hood until it is in position.

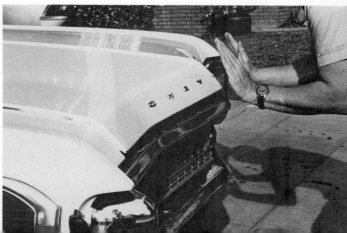

senger's side at the front and that leaves a wide front gap on the driver's side. Rather than loosening both hood-to-hinge mounting bolts, loosen one and push the hood sideways toward the driver's side to narrow the gap.

Which hinge mount you loosen depends on whether the whole hood is too far forward, too far backward, or just right. When you force the latch end of the hood to one side to align it, you move one hinged corner of the hood backward and the other forward. Pushing toward the driver's side, as in photo No. 3, tends to move the driver's side of the hood backward and the passenger's side forward. Conversely, pushing the front of the hood toward the passenger's side tends to force the passenger's side of the hood backward and the driver's side forward.

If the hood is properly positioned front-to-rear, loosen both sides equally. The hood should then move in on one mount and out on the other. That may affect its alignment at the hinge end slightly, but not its front-to-back alignment.

Hood Bumpers

Adjusting the hood bumpers up or down controls the height of the closed hood at

Adjust hood bumper height by loosening the locknut, turning the screw either in or out, then tightening the locknut.

the latch end. On hoods that latch in front, that often controls the hood-to-grille alignment. When the adjustment is off, the car looks as if it has been wrecked.

Hood bumpers are simply large-head screws that are covered by soft rubber cushions to prevent metal-to-metal contact. Once you loosen their locknuts, you can turn the screws in or out with a No. 2 Phillips screwdriver. If necessary, you can lower the hood on one side and raise it on the other. Always set the bumpers high enough to prevent the hood from touching other parts of the car at the latch end. Close the hood periodically to check your progress.

If the bumpers are raised too much, the hood may not latch. A simple latch adjustment later can fix that. After you have the bumpers where you want them, tighten the locknuts.

Once in a while, you may run into a frozen hood bumper, one that will not turn after the locknut has been loosened. Squirt penetrating oil on the threads and wait a few minutes for it to work in. If the bumper still will not turn, peel off the rubber cushion, clamp the metal head with a pair of pliers, and twist.

Latch

Hood latch mounts work on a dowel-and-latch principle in most cars. After a hood alignment, the dowel nearly always needs adjustment—fore-aft to let it be centered in the latch opening, in-out for a tighter or looser closing.

Never use the dowel to force the hood into alignment as it closes. You can move the dowel around somewhat once its locknut has been loosened. Align the dowel with the latch, tighten, and check by trying to close the hood.

When the dowel does not bind or pull as the hood is closed, work on the tight-

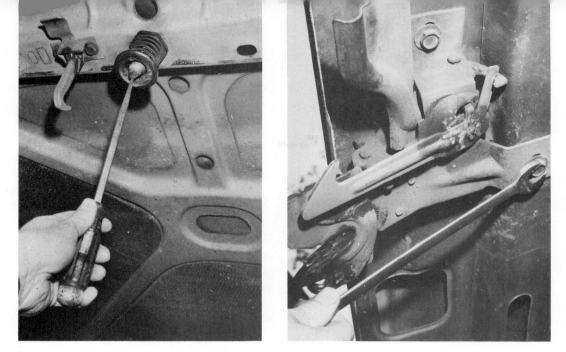

1. With a bayonet-type latch (*left*), loosen the locknut and adjust with a screwdriver. With a more complex latch (*right*), loosen the cap screws for side-to-side adjustments. Never use the hood latch to pull the front of the hood into line.

Hood Latch Adjustment

2. The hood catch bar can be raised or lowered slightly to provide a looser or tighter latch; just loosen the cap screws and, with a hammer, tap the bar into place.

3. Always check to see that the hood safety catch is working. Pull it back and let go; it should snap forward. Then, close the hood, but do not latch it. Pull up; the catch should keep the hood from opening.

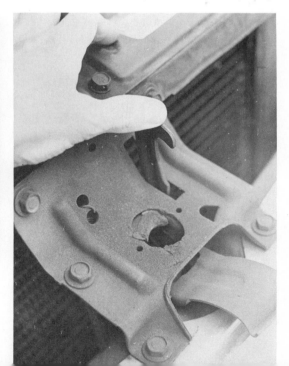

ness of the close. Screwing the dowel in makes the hood latch tighter; screwing it out makes the hood latch looser. Tighten the locknut once you complete the adjustment.

A hood should not have to be slammed hard to latch. Ideally, you should be able to bring the hood within about four inches of closing, then latch it with a quick two-hand downward push. Effort to unlock the hood should be reasonable. In no case should the hood be loose when latched.

A safety catch keeps the hood from flying open if the main lock should fail to hold. Make sure the safety catch has not been affected by the hood adjustment.

DECKLID ADJUSTMENTS

The decklid works somewhat like a door and somewhat like the hood. Like a door, the decklid seats against a rubber weatherstrip, and it has a similar latch and striker. Like a hood, it has elongated bolt holes in the hinge mount that permit up-down and fore-aft adjustments.

Decklid locks and strikers permit a wide range of vertical and horizontal adjustment. As with hoods, make the hinge adjustments, if necessary, first, and the latch adjustments last. The decklid should line up flush with, or slightly below, the sur-

rounding body parts and contact its weatherstripping all around its circumference.

Hinges. To adjust a decklid hinge, follow the directions for making hood hinge adjustments.

Decklid hinges without provision for raising or lowering the lid at the hinged end can be shimmed under the hinge-to-lid mount with pieces of shirt cardboard or light roofing paper. No need to remove the hinge bracket; just loosen it enough to slip shims in front of, and behind, the mounting bolts. You can usually get your shims the right thickness without tedious trial and error by placing them on top of the decklid until they reach the desired level. When they are installed, the lid will close to that level. After an up-down adjustment to the hinged end of a decklid, an adjustment to the lock usually is necessary, even though the lock was correct to begin with.

Latch. A decklid lock is different than a hood lock, though it serves a similar purpose. The decklid lock uses a latch and a striker. Sometimes, the latch is mounted to the decklid and the striker is mounted to the car body; sometimes, the arrangement is reversed. Use the putty tip sug-

To make decklid shimming easier, stack cardboard shims on top of the lid. When the top shim is flush with the fender, you have enough; now, place the stack under the hinge.

A wad of putty in the decklid latch shows whether or not the striker is meeting the latch in a centered position. Lower the decklid gently—if you slam it, you will have a lot of smeared putty to clean.

White lubricant with a handy applicator spout should be used on heavy-duty latch parts.

Stainless stick lubricant is recommended for strikers and latches.

Silicone lubricant should put an end to squeaky weatherstripping.

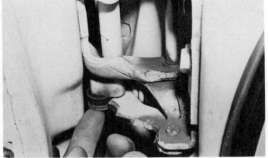

Never lubricate the detent rollers, found beneath the lower door hinges of GM cars.

gested for checking door alignment to see that the latch and striker meet properly. The decklid striker usually adjusts sideways to meet the lock. It also adjusts up and down to close tighter or looser. A decklid should close short of slamming, but without any looseness that could cause rattles or let dust or water into the trunk.

Weatherstripping. If the lid closes in alignment but its weatherstrip is not making proper contact, rub chalk all along the weatherstrip. Then, close the lid and reopen it to see how the chalk has transferred onto the lid's seating surface. Spots where the weatherstrip does not make contact must be raised by shimming, as with a car door.

If the weatherstrip rubber is too thick, it may prevent the lid from closing properly. Remove the offending length of weatherstrip, trim it with a razor blade or sharp knife, and glue it back with weatherstrip cement. New car weatherstripping that is too thick often flattens out within a few months. But if age does not do the slimming job, you will have to.

LUBRICATION

Hinges, locks, and strikers must be lubricated if they are to work smoothly and without squeaks.

Use *white lubricant* for latches, cylinders, and hinges. Spread it on the hood lock and tapered striker bayonet, as well as on the decklid latch and striker. *Engine oil* may also be applied to hinges or lock mechanisms.

Use *stainless stick lube* on door latches and strikers and other areas that may be touched by clothing; white lubricant stains.

Squirt *rubber* or *silicone lubricant* onto weatherstripping to keep it soft, pliable, and squeak-free.

Graphite lube is best for locks. Insert the spout in the lock cylinder and squeeze; then, insert the key and turn it a few times. Wipe the key clean before putting it back into your pocket.

Never, however, lubricate door detent rollers, which hold the door half, or fully, open. The detents should have a rolling, not sliding, action.

23

Cleaning Upholstery and Trim

Automotive trim—upholstery, floormat or carpeting, headliner, and top—has a way of becoming shabby without your noticing it. Or, an accidental stain may blemish it suddenly. Either way, you need not be afraid of doing your own clean-up. With the right cleaner, correctly applied, few stains cannot be removed completely.

A spot on the surface of the material can best be removed by touching it lightly but repeatedly with the sticky side of a piece of masking tape. Afterward, a quick wipe with a sponge dipped in the proper cleaning agent completes the job. Spots caused by fluids that have soaked into the fabric's weave call for enough cleaning agent to completely saturate the fibers and dissolve the foreign substance.

A number of preparations are on the market for cleaning car trim. Because of the variety of materials (and the variety of stains that must be removed), no one cleaner could possibly do it all. Applying the wrong cleaner to the wrong stain or wrong material could "set" a stain so it will not come out, no matter what you do. Or, it could create a ring around the spot; the spot disappears but the ring stays. Furthermore, a cleaner could dull certain trim material or even eat it away. Choose your cleaners with care.

Fabric

Before you clean your trim, determine what material it is made of. Plain and patterned upholstery fabrics in today's cars are made of synthetic materials, mostly rayon and nylon. Coated fabrics—vinyl and mylar—are often used, too.

On coated fabrics, avoid auto body cleaners and polishes, volatile cleaners, furniture polishes, varnishes, oils, and other household cleaning and bleaching products.

Broadcloth upholstery may lose its gloss if cleaned with water-based products; use volatile cleaners instead. On the other hand, if a water-based product is the only one that will remove the stain, you may have no choice.

Much interior trim is backed by sponge rubber, which is dissolved by volatile cleaners. Use such cleaners sparingly.

Genuine leather upholstery is rare in today's cars. But if your vehicle has it, clean it only with saddle soap. Other cleaners can produce stickiness and loss of luster. Apply warm soap suds from a damp—not wet—porous cloth, such as cheesecloth. Whip up the suds on the cloth and scrub. Then, scrub with a cloth that was wetted in water and wrung out. Finally, wipe with a soft, dry cloth. The gloss finish may be removed by the first operation but will be restored by the buffing with the dry cloth. Never use volatile cleaners, polishes, oils or varnishes on leather.

Cleaners

Most cleaning agents are either water-based or volatile.

Water-based cleaners are soaps and detergents, which work well on most stains.

Volatile cleaners are colorless and contain evaporative solvents that dissolve stains not soluble in water. They work well on stains made by grease, oil, and road grime. Volatile cleaners include naphtha, benzine, and carbon tetrachloride. They are often called cleaning fluids.

You can also use household spot-lifter on some fabrics and stains. Ordinarily, however, household cleaners are not suitable for cleaning automotive trim. Besides detergents and volatile cleaners, neutral (nonalkaline) soap has some uses.

Do not use gasoline—other than lead-free white gas—as a cleaning solvent. Tetraethyl lead in many gasolines leaves unsightly deposits on trim cleaned with them. Also avoid using powerful solvents such as lacquer thinner, nail polish remover, acetone, methyl ethyl ketone

Typical collection of trim-cleaning solvents and tools.

(MEK), enamel reducer, or paint thinner on car trim. They can dissolve or discolor the material. Other cleaners to be avoided are laundry soap, household bleach, and reducing agents, which include potassium permanganate, chlorine, hydrogen peroxide, javelle water, and photographers' hypo.

You are safest if you buy cleaners from your new car dealer.

Water-based. To clean a fabric with detergent, dissolve the detergent in warm water and whip it into frothy suds. Apply the suds—not the solution—to the dirty upholstery with a clean polyurethane sponge or a clean cloth. White cheesecloth is excellent. Try to clean only the surface rather than working the suds into the fabric. Apply the suds several times, each time using a clean area of the applicator. Wipe off the excess detergent and loose soil with another cloth dampened in warm water. Finally, polish with a clean, dry cloth. If all the stain has not been removed, go through the cleaning process again after the material has dried somewhat. When the stain is gone, let the fabric dry completely before using it.

Some detergents intended for vinyl come in handy applicator cans; some even come with a brush. Generally, the cleaner is squirted on and brushed onto the vinyl. Wipe off the soiled detergent with a damp cloth, then polish with a dry cloth. Such cleaners should leave vinyl as bright as new and with a soft, pleasant finish.

Volatiles. With volatile cleaners, the solvent does the cleaning—you merely apply it. Use such solvents sparingly, for they can be dangerous.

If possible, use them outdoors and with the car's doors open. If you work in a garage, have the garage doors open. Do not breathe vapors from the cleaner, especially if it contains carbon tetrachloride;

its fumes are heavier than air and can settle in your lungs and poison you. If you can smell carbon tetrachloride, you are not using it carefully enough. Should you get a large dose of fumes, get out of the area to where you can lie with your head lower than your body. That helps empty your lungs of fumes. If you feel ill, see a doctor.

Avoid prolonged or repeated contact of volatile cleaners with your skin. Keep them away from your eyes and mouth. Carbon tetrachloride is not flammable, but the other volatiles are. Never use them near fires or while smoking.

To clean with a volatile, first brush away loose dirt with a whisk broom, or pick it up with a vacuum cleaner. (You should do that regularly anyway.) Use a vacuum, not a whisk broom, on fabrics with raised tapestry patterns; whisking breaks the small threads of the pattern.

Try the volatile cleaner on a hidden portion of the fabric, such as under the seat. If it changes the color or sheen of the fabric, try another cleaner.

To remove the stain, put the cleaner on a piece of clean, porous cloth such as cheesecloth or turkish toweling. Wait for some of the cleaner to evaporate. When the cloth is just slightly damp, rub it over the stained area lightly in a circular motion, lifting the cloth often. Move to a clean area of the cloth after every few circles. Work from the outside of the stain toward the middle.

Blot the cleaner-dampened stain with a fresh white blotter or wad of facial tissue, using a clean area of blotter each time. Blot until no stain is transferred to the blotting material. Wait while the cleaner evaporates completely.

You may have to go through the process a few times to completely eradicate the stain. Use a fresh cloth each time.

If you get a ring, clean the entire panel of fabric. Let it dry before using it.

COMMON TRIM STAINS

Some common stains are almost impossible to get out with ordinary cleaners. Drive your car to a drycleaner and ask whether he can get rid of the spot.

The following stains are problem ones that do not come out easily. But with care you can handle them, though you should expect some discoloration and roughening of the trim finish.

Blood. Avoid hot water and soaps. They set the stain. Instead, rub with a clean cloth wetted with cold water. Continue until no more blood comes off on the cloth. If any is left, pour household ammonia on it and rub with a clean, wet cloth. If the stain still is not gone, make a thick paste with cornstarch and cold water. Put it over the stained area and leave it until it dries. The starch should absorb what remains of the stain. Lift off the dried starch with your fingers. Finally, brush off any remaining starch. If there is still a trace of blood, cross your fingers and try the starch a few more times.

Milk. Get most of the stain out by cleaning with a cloth soaked in cold water. Then, wash gently with mild, neutral soap and warm water. To remove the smell, mix one teaspoon of baking soda in a cup of warm water and soak the stain. Rinse with a cold-water-soaked cloth. If any stain is left, try a volatile cleaner.

Urine. Sponge first with warm soapsuds made with a mild soap. Rinse with a cold-water-soaked cloth. Dip another cloth in a one-to-five mixture of household ammonia and water. Apply and leave it on for a minute; rinse with a wet cloth.

Grease and oil. Carefully scrape off what you can with a table knife. Use a volatile cleaner and blot.

Water spots. Sponge the entire panel with a clean cloth dampened with cold water. Then, sponge the spots with a detergent cleaner.

Battery acid. Act quickly before the acid eats through the trim. Even fabrics that are not eaten by battery acid can be damaged if the acid is left for a few hours. Pour household ammonia directly onto the acid-soaked spot and leave it there for a minute. Rinse with cold water.

MATS AND RUGS

Auto floormats, carpets, and headliners need special care.

Floor mats. Keep rubber floormats clean by vacuuming or by sweeping with a whisk broom. From time to time, you can brighten them by washing with a cloth soaked in household detergent and water. Wring out and sponge up all excess water. Rinse the cloth in water, wring it out, and wipe the mat to remove detergent. Clean the pedal pads and door step-plates, too. Let everything dry before using.

Carpets. Clean carpets with a vacuum or whisk broom. If the carpet is very soiled, remove it, and beat and vacuum thoroughly. Clean with a foam-type carpet shampoo. Work on one square foot at a time—apply foam, work it in, vacuum it off, and rinse with a wrung-out cloth. Dry and fluff the carpet with a dry cloth. Allow it to dry before using. When it is dry, fluff it again by brushing. The foam-cleaning process may be performed in the car if the carpeting is not too dirty. In that case, use foam sparingly.

Grease and oil spots are best removed

Chocolate. Rub the stain with a cloth wetted in warm water. Let the stain dry. Then clean lightly with a volatile cleaner and blot.

Other candy. Rub the stain with a cloth wetted in very hot water. If the stain does not come off, let the trim dry and then use a volatile cleaner. Stains from filled candies respond well to rubbing with a cloth containing warm soapsuds. Scrape the stain with a table knife while it is wet. Rinse with a cold-water-soaked cloth. After the spot dries, use a detergent cleaner on it.

Gum and tar. Apply an ice cube to harden tar and chewing gum. Then, scrape with a table knife. If any is left, use a volatile cleaner to soften the gum. Coax it out of the weave with a table knife.

Fruit and liquor. Avoid soap and water; that sets the stain. Stay away from dry heat too, such as force-drying with an iron or hair dryer. Instead, first apply a cloth wetted in hot water. Then, scrape off any fruit pulp with a table knife. Now, rub hard and fast with the hot cloth. Pour very hot water on the stain as a last resort, and then scrape and rub. That harsh treatment may discolor some fabrics. If the stain remains, try a volatile cleaner.

Ice cream. Use the same methods as for removing fruit stains. Try not to let the ice cream dry. Warm soapsuds may help; use a mild soap after the first hot-water treatment. Rinse away the soap with a cold-water-soaked cloth. Let the trim dry, and finish by using a volatile cleaner.

Lipstick. Pour a little detergent cleaner solution directly onto the spot. Press a clean, white blotter over the stain. Repeat, using a new blotter each time until the stain is removed.

Ballpoint pen ink. Lubricate the stain with vaseline. Flush the lubricant and stain through the fabric with carbon tetrachloride. Repeat until the stain has gone. Scraping gently with a dull knife speeds the removal process.

Catsup. Use a cold-water-soaked cloth Then, try rubbing with detergent. Rinse. Use more detergent if needed and rinse.

Periodic vacuuming helps carpet nap.

with a volatile cleaner. Use the cleaner very sparingly, for it may affect the color of the carpeting.

Some carpeting has its pile set in a rubberized material. Do not use volatile cleaner on that type because it loosens the pile.

Fiberglass headlining. Molded fiberglass headlinings, found in some American Motors cars, require careful cleaning. Do not rub the material; that can cause discoloration. And do not work the soiled spots into the headlining. Instead, pick

With masking tape, you can "pick off" many of the marks and spots that get on fiberglass and plastic headlinings. Do this before you try a solvent.

off the soil with masking tape. Use a clean piece of tape each time you contact the headlining. Keep picking until all surface soil is gone.

Then, apply a volatile cleaner with a polyurethane sponge. Dampen the sponge with cleaner and daub at the soiled area. At the same time, squeeze the sponge to wash out the soil. Blot and dry immediately with another sponge or with a dry end of the same sponge. Keep the cleaner-moistened area as small as possible.

Once the spot is gone, moisten a clean sponge and work around the entire moistened area with long and irregular strokes to avoid formation of a cleaning ring.

Plastic headlining. Headlining made of plastic-coated laminated fiber is easy to clean. First, remove surplus soil with masking tape. Then, wash with mild, lukewarm soapsuds soaked up in a piece of cheesecloth. Rinse with a clean cloth dampened in clean, lukewarm water. Finally, wipe the headliner dry with a soft, clean cloth. Remove grease spots by daubing with a naphtha-type volatile cleaner. Wipe lightly, but do not rub.

VINYL

Vinyl hardtops and convertible tops should be washed with mild soap and warm water. Use a washing mitt or soft brush. Rinse well.

If the top is still soiled, wet it with water and clean it with a foam-type vinyl cleaner. Do the entire top at once. Use a soft hand brush to work up suds all over the top. When soil has been worked loose, wipe off the foam in that area with a damp cloth. Pat on more foam and brush again. If necessary, put a thin plywood support under a convertible top from inside the car.

When you have finished the top, hose it down to remove all cleaner. Hose the car body down too, to avoid leaving streaks on it. Let the convertible top dry before you lower it.

Vinyl is easily harmed by a volatile cleaner. Use one only if you are faced with removing a bit of spilled top sealer— and then use it very carefully. Never use bleach on a top.

Auto manufacturers sell vinyl cleaner/restorer that rejuvenates a weather-beaten, sun-faded vinyl top. Use it according to directions.

Repairing Vinyl

Abrasions, cuts, bubbles, wrinkles, looseness, and split seams can be repaired until your vinyl hardtop is almost as good as new. For most jobs, you need a soldering iron with an adjustable heat range, or one that heats to about 225° Fahrenheit.

If your hardtop is a few years old and dirty, clean it thoroughly before beginning any repair. Use cleaner recommended by the manufacturer.

Scuffs and abrasions. To repair these, clean the soldering iron's tip thoroughly with a 3M abrasive sponge (available at paint and hardware stores). Whenever the

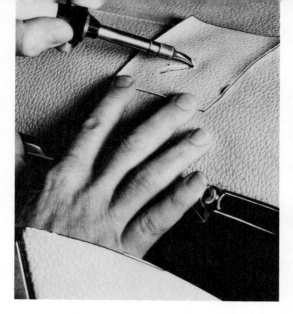

To repair a simple vinyl scuff, first obtain a scrap of the same material. Then, melt the scrap with a soldering iron and transfer it to the scuff.

soldering tip becomes coated with vinyl during any repair procedure, clean it with the sponge. Once the tip is heated to 225°, slide it lightly over the frayed vinyl along the scuff in short, overlapping strokes. That fuses the material into the base.

If the vinyl surface has been scuffed down to the cloth backing, as is often the case, you must fill in the damaged area with new vinyl scavenged from a scrap of the same material. If the seats are upholstered with vinyl of the same color, you can cut a small piece from underneath one of the cushions. Otherwise, remove a small scrap from the edge of the vinyl top — from underneath the chrome trim, where it will not show. Be careful not to slice too near the trim. The vinyl might later lift outside the chrome.

Lay the scrap near the scuffed area and pick up some vinyl from it, a bit at a time, with the hot iron tip. Fill in the scuff carefully with short, overlapping strokes. Then, try to match the textured surface of the surrounding vinyl by etching the texture into your repair with the sharp edge of the hot soldering iron tip.

The glossy look left by a fusion repair can be dulled by rubbing it with a pencil eraser. Or, apply vinyl spray that is the same color as your car's top to the patch. The spray is available from your auto dealer. The last coat of spray should be a fog coat, with the aerosol nozzle held far from the top to minimize gloss.

Scuffs in vinyl seat upholstery and door panels can be repaired in the same way; so can marks made by cigarette lighters.

Cuts. A surface cut that has not gone through the cloth backing can be repaired quickly with a soldering iron. Use quarter-inch, or shorter, strokes until the cut is bridged with fused vinyl. Then, smooth out the surface by running the tip lengthwise over the cut. Texture and degloss the patch as described earlier.

Repairing a cut that penetrates the cloth backing takes a more complex procedure. If the cut is not over a padded area and it is more than one inch long, apply trim cement lightly under it. Do not use so much cement that it oozes out when you press down the edges of the cut.

Let the cement dry for several minutes. Press down the material, butting the cut edges as close together as you can. Then fuse the vinyl across the cut, following the directions for repairing minor cuts.

Smeared automotive trim cement is difficult to remove once it ages. If a new car comes with an adhesive smear on its top, have the dealer remove it immediately. If you make the repair yourself, rub a piece of art gum back and forth over the smear. You can buy art gum in an art supply store.

Bubbles. Air bubbles under the vinyl top material can be removed by puncturing them with a hypodermic needle and working the air out by pressing.

Then, activate the old adhesive under the vinyl by blowing hot air from a hair dryer over the vinyl. To avoid overheat-

(*text continued on page 416*)

Repairing Cut Vinyl

1. A small cut that does not penetrate the fabric backing can be fused with a soldering iron. But if the cut penetrates the fabric and is more than one inch long, you will need cement.

2. Apply trim cement lightly under the cut.

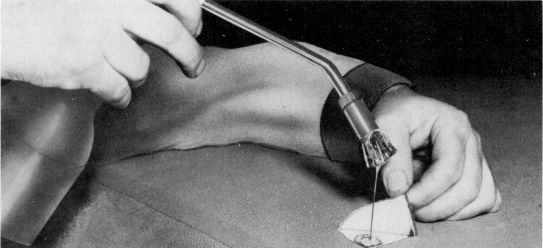

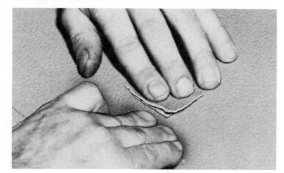

3. Press the cut flap down and lift it immediately— this allows the cement to air-dry. Wait several minutes; then, press down again, mating the edges as closely as possible.

4. Finish by fusing the edges with a soldering iron.

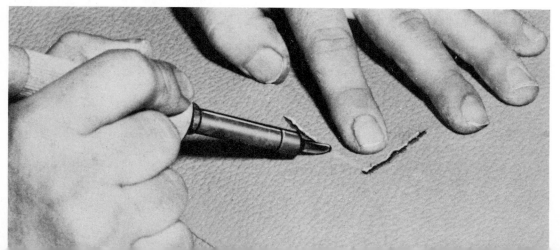

Repairing Bubbled Vinyl

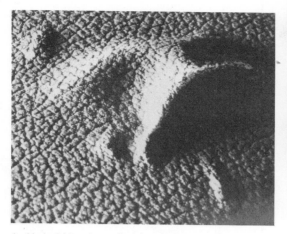

1. Air bubbles in a vinyl hardtop not only look unsightly, but they may also expose the material to other damage.

2. Soften the adhesive beneath the vinyl with a hair dryer or a heat lamp. But be careful that you do not melt the vinyl.

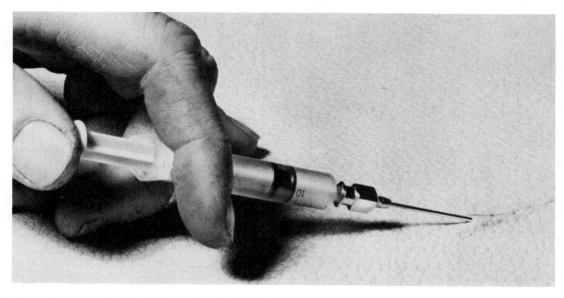

3. Try to pat the vinyl in place. If the old adhesive is too dry to hold the material in place, inject fresh trim cement with a hypodermic needle.

4. If you must inject fresh cement, remove the syringe but leave the needle in place. Then, work excess cement back out through the needle.

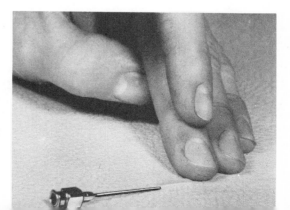

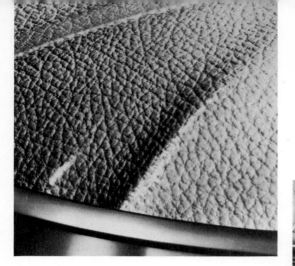

Repairing Wrinkled Vinyl

1. To fix wrinkled (*above*) or torn (*below*) vinyl, first remove the molding metal. Peel back the vinyl about ten inches. Then, with a naphtha-soaked cloth, scour off the old adhesive.

2. Apply fresh trim cement lightly and let it air-dry. Stretch the vinyl back, working out wrinkles. Fasten the edge with drive nails coated with silicone rubber; then, replace the molding.

ing, which would damage the vinyl, hold the dryer 10 to 12 inches from the top and keep it moving in circular sweeps.

If you cannot get a good bond, squirt some trim cement under the vinyl skin with the hypodermic needle and smooth the bubble with your finger. (When you buy the hypodermic needle, explain to the druggist that you need it for your car.)

Wrinkles. Repairing a wrinkle is different from cementing down bubbles. A wrinkle has small, radial folds of slack material that cannot be held down with cement. The excess material must be rearranged.

Remove the chrome molding in the area of the wrinkle. On some cars it is held with Phillips-head sheet metal screws; on others it snaps off. Next, free an area of vinyl top material about ten inches around, being sure to reach to the closest bonded seam. Do that by peeling the vinyl from the metal car top.

Reach in under the vinyl with a cloth soaked in naphtha, gasoline or other petroleum solvent. Do not use carbon tetrachloride; it dissolves vinyl. Clean away the old adhesive thoroughly. Work in a well ventilated area, and keep cigarettes and open flames away.

Repairing Separated Seams

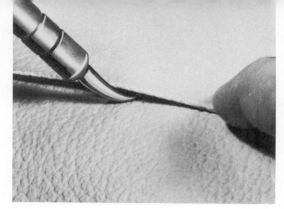

1. Vinyl that has split along a seam can be repaired with a curved soldering iron tip.

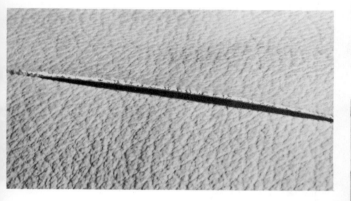

2. Insert the tip and heat both sides of the split, working along the entire damaged area (*above*). Press the heated joint together to bond it. Finish by fusing the edge of the seam. Turn the curved tip face down and move it slowly along the length of the repaired seam (*below*).

Then, apply a thin coat of fresh trim cement to the vinyl backing and top surfaces. Let it dry for several seconds. Now, pull the material tight until all the wrinkles are gone. Fasten the edge of the material with small drive nails, which have screw-like shanks. Put small dabs of silicone rubber over each nail after driving to prevent leaks. Replace the moldings.

Looseness. Vinyl that simply loosens without wrinkling usually appears at padded areas. Padding is found on some makes and models and not on others. If your top has loose areas, fix them as you would fix wrinkles.

Rebonding. A bonded seam that separates, allowing the two layers to come apart, can be fixed by inserting the heated tip of the soldering iron into the seam. Move the tip slowly along the seam, heating both sides of it. Follow the iron closely with your fingers, pressing the seam together and bonding it.

Next, turn the tip of the soldering iron over and heat the seam's edge all along the repair. Move it slowly so that the edge is fully bonded, like the interior of the seam. If you have been careful, no glossy surfaces will show. If they do, dull them as described earlier.

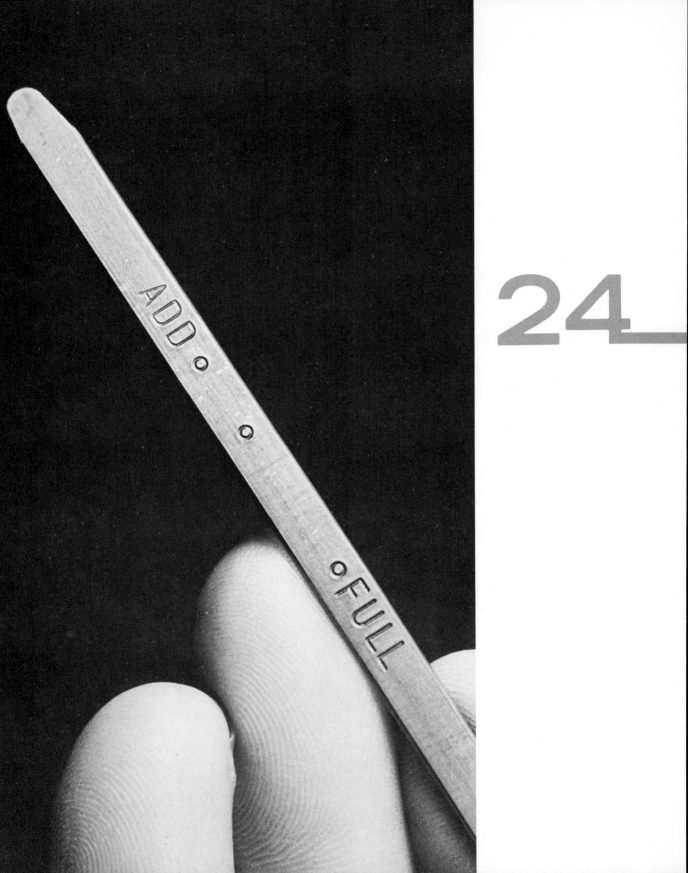

24

Lubrication

The periodic car care covered in this last chapter is probably the most useful of any in the book. It is easy, it is quick, and it does not require much skill. Furthermore, you save on labor, parts, and lubricants — and you extend the life of your car.

This care consists mostly of lubrication of a sort far removed from the simple "grease job" of yesteryear; it also entails some cleaning and the routine replacement of short-lived parts.

Finally, periodic lubrication gives you a chance to regularly examine the underside of your car for problems. Look for signs of fluid leakage at the radiator, engine, transmission, differential, and all four wheels. Examine the brake lines and hoses from front to back. Look at the steering arms and rods for loose or bent parts. Inspect the exhaust system, wiggling the pipes to see that they are not hitting against the chassis.

Tools. The tools and equipment you need for do-it-yourself lubrication can cost less than $125. Spending that much might not pay off too quickly, but you will find so many other uses for the tools that it is worthwhile to have them.

Naturally, if you own a lubricated-for-life car such as a recent Cadillac, a Ford Pinto, or a Chevrolet Vega, you do not need greasing equipment and grease.

But if your car, like most, does have grease fittings, get a high-pressure *greasing outfit*. Do not cut costs by buying a cheap grease gun. A top-quality greasing outfit delivers about 12,000 psi pressure, which cheaper outfits cannot match. With an adapter, such a gun will fit any type of grease fitting, including the plug-sealed type. In addition, a quality gun gives you one-hand operation — a big benefit when you are on your back under the car.

A mechanic's *trouble light* serves as both a light and as a handy, light-duty extension cord. The oil-resistant cord that good trouble lights come with should last a long time. The wire cage surrounding the bulb prevents breakage, and a metal

LUBRICATION EQUIPMENT
(and approximate prices)

Fender cover:	$ 2.00
Lubrication outfit:	$30.00
Chassis lube:	$13.00
Lube gun adapters:	$ 6.00
Oil can:	$ 1.50
Oil filler spout:	$ 2.00
Flex-funnel:	$ 3.00
Oil drain wrench:	$ 2.00
Oil filter wrench:	$ 3.00
Transmission-differential drain wrench:	$ 2.50
Gear lube syringe:	$ 3.50
Wheel ramps:	$20.00
Creeper:	$10.00
1½-ton hydraulic jack:	$12.00
Jack stands, 1 pair:	$ 6.00
Trouble light:	$ 2.50

Products. If your car is still under warranty, use only brands and weights of oil, gear lubricant, grease, and filter elements that are approved by the car manufacturer. Most name-brands qualify, but check the warranty to be sure. Otherwise, you may void your warranty. Keep a record of date of lubrication, mileage, services performed, and the types of lubricants and filter element you used. Also ask for receipts that show brands and weights. Keep the information with your warranty papers, just in case you are ever questioned on a warranty claim.

JACKING SAFELY

Because the bumper jacks that come with most cars are inadequate for your under-the-car safety, a 1½-ton hydraulic jack should be part of your lube center. Do not get under the car, even if it has been raised with a hydraulic jack, until you

shield keeps bare-bulb glare out of your eyes. Its handy hook lets you hang the light almost anywhere. Replacement bulbs for a trouble light should be the kind rated for rough service. Ordinary bulb filaments cannot take the punishment. Though it is insulated, do not risk using a trouble light on a wet floor or around a wet car.

Until that day that you encounter an overly-tightened oil filter cartridge—and if your car engine does not have a spin-on oil filter—you can do without an *oil filter wrench*. And if you already have a wrench that fits your engine's oil drain plug, you can get by without an *oil drain wrench*. Another item you may not have to buy is a *container* for catching drained oil. A low pail, or a can with its top cut off, works well. For most U.S. cars, the container should hold two gallons, with freeboard to spare.

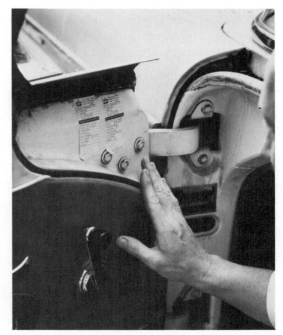

Up-to-date lubrication record on an inner door helps you gauge the need for servicing.

For safe jacking, first raise the car on a hydraulic jack (*left*). Then, position the jack stand (*right*). Finally, unscrew the hydraulic jack release valve; this lowers the car onto the stand.

place a pair of jack stands under the lower suspension arms.

If a hydraulic jack is too short to reach the lift point without excessive travel, screw out the threaded adjusting head on top of the ram. If that does not give enough height, put a block under the jack. If the jack is too tall, try a different jacking point.

Manufacturers publish jack and lift data for their cars. See if your service manual contains such information. Generally, you should jack as follows:

To jack up *one front wheel*, lift under the lower front suspension arm, as close to the wheel as possible. Set the jack stand next to the jack and lock its height. Then, you can release the jack and lower the car onto the stand.

To raise *both front wheels* at once, jack under the heavy member to which the lower suspension arms are attached. Block with jack stands under both suspension arms. Never jack under a steering arm or rod; it will bend.

To lift a *rear wheel*, as when you lubricate the parking brake cables, jack under the rear axle at the point where the springs are attached. Some rear axles should not be lifted inboard of the spring attachment points or under the differential.

To lift *both wheels on one side* of a car with a separate frame, you usually jack under the outside frame member at midbody. Such a lift is useful when you repair an exhaust system on one side of the car or switch front and rear tires. On a unitized-body car, jack only on established lift pads (which often are labeled "lift").

CHASSIS LUBRICATION

Greasing

Some cars need a chassis lubrication with every oil change, others do not.

Before you do such a job, get a copy of the service manual for your car and have its lubrication guide in front of you as you work. That is the only way you can be sure of not missing any fittings.

Typical greasing rig, mounted on a can of grease.

Most grease fittings are on the front steering and suspension parts. Typical places are:

- Above the upper ball joint on each side;
- Below the lower ball joint on each side;
- At both ends of the steering tie-rod;
- At the steering-link to tie-rod attachment point;
- At the idler arm;
- On the front and rear universal joints in the driveshaft.

Preparation. Lubrication can only be performed when the joints will accept grease. This depends on temperature. If the temperature is below about 20°, either park in a heated garage for 30 minutes before beginning, or wait for a warmer day.

Jack and block your car, and have all the tools you will need within reach.

Without fittings. Some ball joints and steering linkage tie-rod ends are lubricated for life. If they have no fittings, you need not grease them.

Regular fittings. Wipe each fitting clean before attaching the grease gun. Otherwise, dirt may be forced into the joint, where it will hasten wear.

Push the grease gun onto the fitting squarely until you feel it snap on. Pump the gun until fresh grease oozes from the joint.

If grease will not flow, the ball check valve in the end of the fitting may be stuck shut. Try probing it with a wire. If the fitting is facing the wrong way, you can turn it with a small open-end or box-end wrench.

Sealed ball joints. Joints covered by sealed rubber boots, often found on front

Before you dolly under the car, make sure that all tools and lubricants which you will use will be within reaching distance.

Inserting wire into a fitting that will not take grease should clean it. If it does not, replace the fitting.

push the adapter into the opening. The adapter is also useful for getting grease into some hard-to-reach universal fittings. Instructions on using it should come with your lubrication outfit.

Grease each fitting until the joint can be felt or seen to swell. This indicates the boot is full of grease. Never over-lubricate —if grease flows from a sealed joint, the boot or seal will have burst.

Replace the plug immediately after greasing each fitting. Never replace such a removable plug with a standard grease fitting. Grease fittings cannot retain the high pressures developed within sealed joints, and you run the risk of having the joint run dry while you are driving.

suspension ball joints, have removable plugs or slotted screws instead of ordinary grease fittings.

To work on them, remove dirt from around the plug and take the plug out. Install an adapter on your grease gun, and

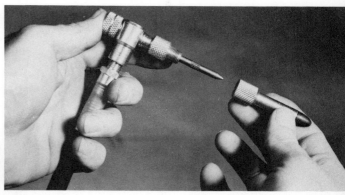

Hard-to-reach fittings are made accessible by a greasing adapter. This accessory snaps onto the grease gun and comes with various points.

Joints sealed by rubber boots should be greased by feel. When you feel the joint swell from grease pressure, stop; such joints can be ruptured by excessive grease.

Before putting away your grease gun, recheck the manual to make sure that you did not miss any fittings.

Other Lubrication

Check through the manual to catch the other, often-neglected lubrication steps. Here is where you can do a more thorough job than many time-pressed professional mechanics.

Lube points. Some car makers call for lubricating such parts as steering arm stops, power steering actuating valve ball stud, transmission shift linkage, clutch shaft, distributor, parking brake cables, and manifold heat control valve.

Body lubrication may also be specified.

In each case, use the recommended lubricant.

Manual steering. Check the lubricant level in a manual steering gear by removing the cap on the gearcase (located at the base of the steering column, under the hood).

Differential gear. While you are under the car, check the level of the differential gear lubricant. Normally, cars keep the same gear lubricant for life. If no drain opening is provided, generally no lubricant change is needed.

To check lubricant level, remove the tapered-thread plug. If it has a square, recessed hole, use a transmission-differential drain wrench or a square socket wrench drive.

If lubricant seeps around the threads before you have removed the plug completely, the level is up. Screw the plug back in.

In checking lubricant level, allow for the fact that when the car is on ramps, the front end is higher than the back. Thus, if the differential fill opening is at the rear of the gearcase, the actual level will be a little lower than indicated. Temperature has an effect, too. When lubricant is cold, its level may be a ½-inch lower than at operating temperature.

If a change is called for, drain the old lube through the plug in the bottom of the gearcase. If you must change the lubricant and no drain plug is provided, remove one of the bottom cap screws on the rear axle housing, and let the old lubricant drain through its opening.

The lubricants themselves vary depending on whether your car has a standard or a limited-slip axle.

Standard axles generally should get an SAE-90 multipurpose gear lubricant.

Limited-slip axles require a special

When you are lubricating, don't neglect such greasing points as the driveshaft universal joint fitting (*left*). In addition, be sure to check such items as steering gear lubricant level, which you perform by removing the plug on the steering gearcase (*right*).

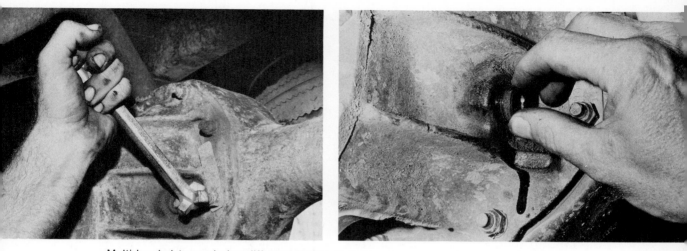

Multi-headed transmission-differential wrench (*left*) makes unscrewing recessed drain plugs easier. When you check for gear lubricant level, remove the plug slowly (*right*); if fluid oozes out before the plug is fully unscrewed, the level is sufficient.

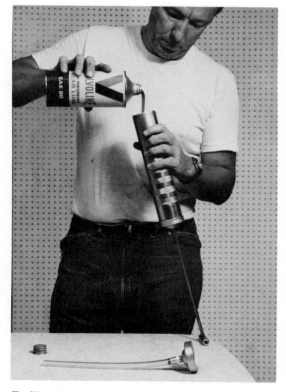

To fill a gear lubricant syringe, remove the end cap and pull out the handle; then, pour in the lubricant.

lubricant with additives. High temperatures or towing a trailer in mountainous country will make the additives wear out fast. Chattering of a limited-slip axle while turning corners is a sign that either a lubricant change is needed, or that a standard lubricant has been used instead of the special one.

If you have to add lubricant, go by the manufacturer's specifications on level. Use a gear lubricant syringe. With the syringe's end plate off and its handle all the way out, pour the correct lubricant into the instrument. Replace the end cap and insert the plastic hose into the gearcase opening. Push the piston handle in slowly until the lubricant reaches the right level. Then, replace the plug and tighten it securely with your wrench.

TRANSMISSION FLUIDS

Manual. Check the manual transmission lubricant level in the same way that you checked differential gear level: by removing the tapered-thread plug.

If you are going to change all the lubricant, draw out as much of the old lubricant as you can with a syringe before adding fresh lubricant.

Make sure that you are using the specified lubricant. Fill with the syringe.

Automatic. Often, the manufacturer's specifications call for the automatic transmission to be at operating temperature, and the engine running with the shift lever in neutral or park position, before the transmission fluid level is checked.

The automatic transmission dipstick usually is at the rear of the engine, near the firewall. When you wipe the dipstick, do not let lint from the cloth catch on the dipstick's sharp edges; lint in automatic transmissions can cause more damage than dirt. The individual marks on a transmission dipstick are usually half-quart marks.

Marks on an automatic transmission dipstick are spaced close together. When adding fluid, do not overfill; sometimes, well less than a quart is needed.

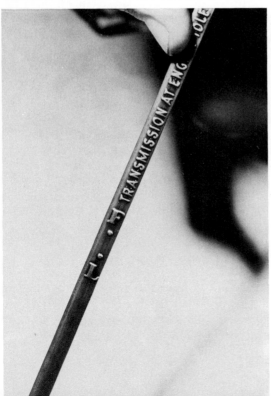

Never run the transmission when it is low on fluid. The shift patterns may become noticeably altered. If that happens, stop driving until you get the transmission filled to the "full" mark. You may have to idle the engine, and shift into each range, to distribute the oil before an accurate level check can be made. If you drive with the fluid level too low, the transmission pumps, bands, and clutches can be damaged. Repair is costly.

When checking the automatic transmission fluid level, also inspect the fluid for color. If you give your automatic hard use, the oil can be scorched or burned to the point where it no longer lubricates the moving parts inside the transmission. It may also be contaminated by particles that have been ground off the bands. If you continue to drive with burned oil, your transmission may soon need a complete overhaul.

Fresh automatic transmission fluid is pinkish, almost clear. Light amber indicates only slight burning; the oil may be used a while longer. If the fluid on the dipstick is brownish, or dark, replace the fluid. Dark fluid with a burned smell indicates the need for immediate transmission servicing. That includes changing the transmission fluid, cleaning out the accessible parts, changing all filters, inspecting the insides of the transmission, and adjusting the bands. Leave the job for a shop. If you continue driving, you risk a repair bill of well over $100.

If the owner's manual calls for a change of automatic transmission fluid at a certain mileage, that should be done whether the fluid is burned or not. The change interval may be anywhere from 6000 to 36,000 miles. Often, it depends on the type of driving you do. Heavy service, according to Chrysler, is more than 50 percent operation in heavy city traffic in hot (over 90°) weather. Police, taxi, limousine, and commercial driving is considered heavy service. So are mountain driving and trailer towing. Transmissions on cars with large, big-bore V-8 engines (over 400 cubic inches) also tend to get heavy service.

Never add engine oil or anything other than approved automatic transmission fluid. Type A transmission fluid, the older Ford-recommended fluid, has been replaced in recent-model specifications by Type F fluid, which is of higher quality. Type F is specified in automatic transmissions in which no changes of fluid are needed.

If Type A is specified, you can substitute the costlier Type F if you wish. But do not use Type A in place of Type F. Moreover, do not use either Type A or Type F fluid in GM cars. They require "Dexron" automatic transmission fluid.

Add automatic transmission fluid through the filler tube, which holds the dipstick. You will need a small rigid funnel or one with a flexible tube. In a pinch, you can make a suitable funnel from a rolled-up magazine cover. Never overfill.

Transmission cooler. This could help eliminate high-temperature transmission problems. Such coolers are available in kit form for most cars; some are offered by auto manufacturers. Order by total weight of the vehicle with trailer, if any.

Some auto makers specifically prohibit installation of automatic transmission coolers on their products, under pain of voiding the transmission warranty. Check with your dealer.

Installation does not require removing or blocking the existing transmission cooling system. The cooler fits in series with the car's present transmission cooler. Follow the instructions that come with the kit.

FRONT WHEEL BEARINGS

All front wheel bearing assemblies are the same on recent rear-drive cars. Two opposing *tapered roller bearings* in each hub resist wheel thrust while allowing the wheel to turn with little friction. The outer bearing is smaller than the inner one because it carries less load. A *grease seal* on the inside of the hub keeps grease

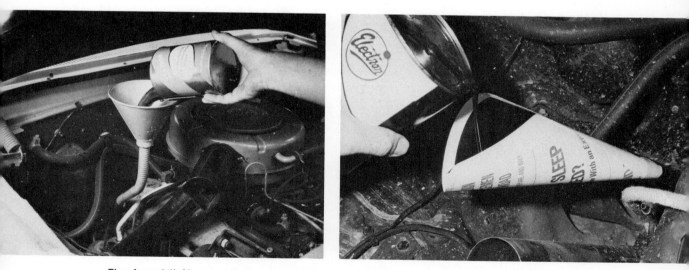

Flex funnel (*left*) or a rolled-up magazine cover (*right*) eases the task of pouring transmission fluid into hard-to-reach filler tubes.

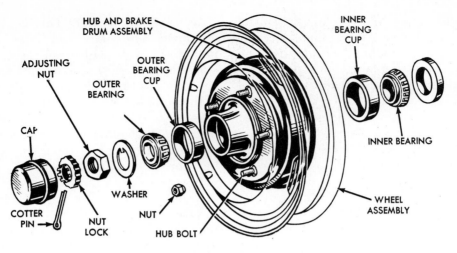

Typical Front Wheel Bearing Assembly

from leaking out onto the brake disc or drum. It also keeps dust and dirt from getting into the wheel bearings.

The entire bearing-hub assembly is held to the front spindle by an *adjusting nut,* which screws onto the threaded end of the spindle. The adjusting nut is castellated, or has a *nut lock* with castellations that are secured by a large *cotter pin.* The pin and castellations keep the nut from turning.

Cleaning and Repacking

Specifications sometimes call for this lubrication job to be done along with each brake relining. Other manufacturers recommend 12,000-mile intervals.

Removal. To do the job, jack both front wheels off the ground and block up the car. Spin the wheels to listen for rough, noisy bearings. If you hear any such noises, look carefully later for abnormal bearing wear. Quiet bearings are probably good.

Remove the hub cap or wheel cover. Then, remove the dust cap from the end of the hub. Start the cap off by driving a large screwdriver into the joint between

it and the hub. Finish by twisting the tip of the screwdriver in the crack. Work all around the cap until it slips off the hub.

Wipe off any excess grease on the end of the spindle. Remove the cotter pin and discard it. With a pair of opened slip-joint pliers, pull off the nut lock, if there is one. Unscrew the adjusting nut. Immerse all of these parts in a can of solvent for cleaning.

Rock the drum or disc from side to side to push the outer bearing and washer off the end of the spindle. Put the washer in the cleaning solvent, and lay the bearing on a clean piece of paper. Dust, dirt, or foreign material in a wheel bearing causes rapid wear. If your work area is dusty, put all bearings in plastic sandwich bags.

Always keep bearings and hubs on the side of the car they came from, so you get them back the same way. Each bearing has already run into its race in the hub. Mark the hubs to be sure.

Replace the clean adjusting nut on the spindle, flush with the end. Take hold of the drum or disc and pull it off toward you. If the car has disc brakes, remove the caliper to allow the disc to come off the spindle.

1. First, brush off accumulated dirt from the hub; this protects the delicate bearing parts.

2. Gently pry off the bearing dust cover with a screwdriver worked into the slot all around.

3. With pliers, unbend and slip out the spindle nut's cotter pin. Discard it.

4. Remove the nut lock (if any) that sits on the spindle nut; soak it in solvent.

5. Unscrew the spindle nut and slip off the large keyed washer that protects the wheel bearing.

6. Pull the outer bearing off and soak it in clean solvent. Keep left and right side parts separate.

7. Partially reinstall the spindle nut; this helps you remove the inner bearing without a special tool.

8. Pull off the hub against the nut; the inner bearing will come off, along with its grease seal.

If drum brake shoes are adjusted too tight, they may hold the drums so you cannot pull them off. In such a case, you have to back off the brake adjustment (see the instructions on page 318).

The adjusting nut should catch hold of the inner bearing and yank it out along with the grease seal. If they do not come off the first time, give the hub several more tugs. Throw away the old grease seal. Place the inner bearing next to the outer one.

Cleaning. Clean all parts with a fresh can of solvent. Kerosene or fuel oil is a good solvent because it is not explosive. Gasoline poses too great a fire and explosion hazard. An engine-oil can with the top removed makes a good container.

First, clean all four bearings, keeping them separated so you remember where they came from. Work the solvent through them and get out all old grease. One reason for removing old grease is that the new lithium-based wheel bearing greases specified by some auto manufacturers are not compatible with the older, sodium-based greases.

Dry each bearing by shaking it. Do not spin it with a blast of air from a compressor. Spinning can throw out bearing rollers and injure someone. Place the bearings aside where they will stay clean while they dry completely.

With your finger, scrape out and discard all old grease from inside the hub. Wipe the hub insides clean with a solvent-soaked cloth. Be very careful not to get any grease or greasy solvent on braking surfaces or brake linings. Keep greasy fingermarks off, too.

Inspect the bearing cone and roller assemblies for scratches, pits, excessive wear, and other damage. If you find any problems, take the bearing and its hub to an automotive machine shop for replacement of the pressed-in bearing race, along with the bearing. Races and bearings always should be replaced as a unit.

With your fingers, wipe grease from the spindles and clean them with a solvent-soaked cloth. Cover each spindle with a clean cloth and brush any loose dust from each drum brake assembly. Afterward, remove the cloths carefully to keep the spindles clean.

Repacking. Use only fresh, clean, wheel bearing grease; it is specially formulated so it will not be flung out. Regular grease may work past the grease seal and get onto brake parts. Get the kind of wheel bearing grease specified for your car.

Fill each bearing with grease by kneading it in your hand with a glob of grease, much like you would work dough. Work the grease into all openings in every bearing. You can keep your hands clean while doing that by putting on a 10-cent polyethylene throwaway glove.

With the glove still on, put a glob of grease into the hub cavity. Use only enough to fill the cavity flush with both bearing races. Using too much grease could allow some to slip past the seal and damage the brake linings.

Spread a smear of grease around each bearing race. Then, insert the inner bearing into its hub. (The small end goes toward the hub.) Take out a new grease seal, and spread a film of grease all around its flexible sealing lip.

Now for the most ticklish part of the job: The grease seal push-fits onto the inside of the hub, and some force must be applied to seat it all the way. But too much force in one spot can bend the seal or damage its lip. In either case, it will leak and ruin your brakes.

Mechanics use a special tool to install grease seals. You can install them with a large socket wrench or piece of pipe or wood the same size as the outside of the grease seal.

Cleaning and Repacking Bearings

1. With a solvent-soaked cloth, clean the inner hub cavity, being careful to keep grease and solvent off all brake surfaces.

2. Pack fresh wheel bearing grease into the hub cavity, leveling the grease with a pencil. Discard the excess grease that clings to the pencil.

3. Knead fresh grease into the solvent-cleaned wheel bearings. This messy task is simplified if you wear a throw-away polyethylene glove.

4. Install the inner bearing (facing it properly). Then, install a new grease seal that has been soaked in lubricating oil for a half hour.

5. To seat the fragile grease seal, tap it in with a socket or a piece of pipe. It must be flush with, or below, the hub edge; inspect carefully.

Start the seal straight in its opening with the flat, smooth side out. Then, push it the rest of the way by tapping lightly on your homemade tool. Be sure the seal goes in and ends up flush with or slightly below the hub.

Examine its sealing lip closely. If it is cut, cracked, folded, or otherwise damaged, remove it and install a new seal.

Make sure that the spindle is still clean. Then, slide the drum or disc on over the spindle. Hold the hub centered as it goes onto the end of the spindle to avoid scratching either the grease seal's lip or the outer bearing race on the end of the spindle.

Install the outer bearing with its smaller end in. Next, slip on the flat washer with its tab, if any, in the groove on the spindle. Finally, screw on the adjusting nut. The rest of the front-wheel bearing repacking procedure is basically the same as for adjusting a front wheel bearing.

Front-Wheel Bearing Adjustment

Front-wheel bearings may need adjustment even before they need repacking. The specified adjusting procedure varies. The one given is for Ford products, but it is usable for other makes, too.

The idea of wheel bearing adjustment is to eliminate preload on the bearing but to leave little or no end-play.

Position a large socket on the adjusting nut and install a torque wrench. Spin the wheel forward as you torque the adjusting nut to 17 to 25 foot-pounds. This seats the bearings. Back up the adjustment one-half turn while pressing in on the hub. Then, remove the socket wrench and finger-tighten the adjusting nut; do not try to force it.

Secure the adjustment in that position. If the bearing came with a nut lock over the adjusting nut, install the nut lock in such a way that a pair of castellations align with the cotter pin hole in the end of the spindle. If the adjusting nut itself has castellations, loosen it just enough to get the cotter pin through the nearest hole in the spindle.

Use a new cotter pin of the right size. Bend the longer leg of the cotter pin around the castellations. Snip off the other leg with diagonal cutters. Be sure that the cotter pin does not rub on the hub dust cap, or the static arrester contact found in some dust caps. Spin the wheel to check for freedom of movement. Install the hub dust cap by tapping with a hammer, and replace the hub cap or wheel cover.

OIL

Probably the most productive operation, in terms of effort spent and dollars saved, is changing your own oil. Though most shops make no labor charge for an oil change, they profit by tacking a healthy mark-up onto the oil itself. The same is true of replacement oil filter cartridges.

If you buy your own oil (preferably by the case) and filters from a store that has no service facilities—and even from some that have—you can avoid that hidden labor charge. And, you can still get name-brand products.

The engine oil you use can make a lot of difference in the life expectancy of your engine. Newer and larger engines require a better oil than older and smaller engines. The type of driving you do also affects your engine's oil requirements, as does the climate.

Almost any decent oil will lubricate the engine and help to cool the moving parts. Oil does not wear out, but it is subjected to engine wastes that create sludge, varnish, and acids. If allowed to accumulate unchecked, these dirts can wreck your engine. Moreover, the oil collects particles of metal and other abrasives that increase engine wear if they are not removed.

Adjusting Front Wheel Bearings

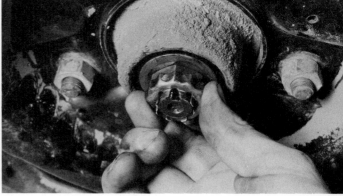

1. Install the outer wheel bearing, washer and spindle nut. Then, spin the wheel forward and tighten the spindle nut to specifications (usually, from 17 to 25 ft.-lbs.).

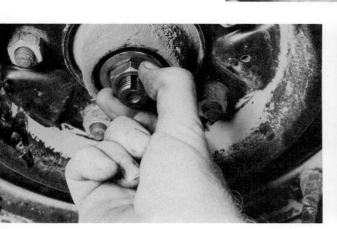

2. Back up the adjustment half a turn (180°). Then, turn the wheel bearing nut finger-tight. This eliminates play without preloading the bearings.

3. When the bearing is adjusted, install the nut lock (if any) so its castellations align with the cotter pin hole in the end of the spindle.

4. Slip a new cotter pin through the lock and hole. Be sure to use a pin of the proper size—and for safety's sake, never reuse an old cotter pin.

5. Finish by clipping off one leg of the pin and bending the other leg around the spindle; this allows you to slip on the bearing dust cover easily.

You can help your oil do its job by the way you drive. When you start a cold engine, do not race it. And do not try to warm up the engine by idling it for several minutes; idling is hard on a cold engine. Drive off right away, but keep the engine speed down to 25 mph for about two to ten miles, depending on whether the air temperature is hot or cold. (Some late-model, emission-controlled engines, when cold, suffer from severe stalling and hesitation. In such cases, you may have no choice but to idle the engine briefly until it warms sufficiently.)

Oil facts

Check your car owner's manual for engine oil service and weight specifications.

Puncturing-type oil filler spout is a good investment.

The brand of oil—as long as it is a nationally-recognized one—is not as important.

Service rating. Oils are tested and rated by the oil makers. The American Petroleum Institute (API) ratings give oils letter designations. Oils classified under the old API system are labeled for various types of service, including ML for light service; MM for medium service; and MS for severe service.

The new API service classifications for oils set up in 1972 are:

SA—For utility gasoline and diesel engines, not for automobiles.

SB—The minimum-duty oil for auto engines operated under mild conditions. No detergents added. (You can do better.)

SC—Meets warranty requirements for 1964 through 1967 passenger car engines made in the U.S. Mild detergent added.

SD—For 1968 through 1970 passenger cars, and some 1971 models. May be used where SC oil is required. Detergent added.

SE—For passenger car engines starting in 1972. Excellent protection against oxidation and high-temperature deposits. A high detergent oil.

SF—A new classification for passenger car engines after 1973 models. Geared to handle the problems of emission-controlled engines of the future.

These newest API designations supersede the older ML, MS designations, even though both may appear on the oil container.

Viscosity. Oils for auto engines also come in 5W, 10W, 20W, 20, 30, 40, and 50 types, often referred to as weights or grades. Those numbers represent viscosity, or flowing ability. The lower the viscosity number, the thinner the oil and the more easily it flows. The "W" in the number signifies a winter-weight oil, tested at

Horror story: this engine went 40,000 miles without an oil change; accumulated sludge resulted in a burned crankshaft bearing.

a low temperature as well as a high one. No "W" in the viscosity indicates a summer-weight oil that has not been tested at a low temperature. The ideal oil would stay at the same viscosity, hot or cold. It has not yet been developed.

Multiviscosity oils, such as 10W-30, contain larger amounts of VI-improvers than single-weight oils, such as 20W. VI, or viscosity-index, improvers have the job of keeping oil from thickening excessively when cold and thinning excessively when hot. Multiviscosity oils come in 5W-20, 10W-30, 10W-40, 20W-40 and 10W-50.

Select oil viscosity according to climate in the area where you will drive the car. The weight should be thin enough for reasonable cold starting, yet thick enough to protect the engine during fast running. If you do much freeway driving, we suggest you avoid multiviscosity oils, because they break down easier at high temperatures. Then, they cannot do as good a job as, say, a straight 30-weight oil. For general all-around city-country driving, however, multigrade oils are fine.

Built-in additives. Oils often contain what is known as an additive package. Different oils contain different packages. Oil additives include antioxidants, corrosion inhibitors, extreme-pressure agents, antifoam agents and VI-improvers.

Oils are also known as detergent or nondetergent types. It is best to use only a high-detergent oil. Sometimes, such an oil will say "HD" on the can. It is no longer necessary to use a nondetergent oil for breaking in an engine, although that had been true in the past.

Mix-in additives. The best advice we can give on extra oil additives—those sold to mix in with your regular engine oil—is: Avoid them. Good-quality oils already contain all the needed additives. Adding something else, even to an old engine, is wasting money. Such additives may not harm your engine, but they probably will not do it any good, either. A Chrysler engineer quoted in POPULAR SCIENCE said about these mix-in additives recently, "We discourage their use as a general policy." Need we say more?

Changing Oil

Frequency. Years ago, auto manufacturers called for changes every 1,000 miles. When you change oil that often in an older engine, you can use the lower-rated, lower-cost Service MM or Service ML oil. The better oils will, of course, perform longer in your engine.

The time between drain periods also determines your engine's oil needs. Many manufacturers now recommend 6,000 miles between oil changes. Under ideal conditions, that is sufficient. But if you drive mostly on short trips or over dusty roads, a 3,000-mile interval may be safer.

Cold weather also calls for more-frequent changes. Low temperatures tend to cause condensation of water in the oil pan, which dilutes the oil.

Depletion of additives; formation of acids, varnish, and sludge; and dilution by raw fuel also can make oil unsafe for the engine after a certain length of time or mileage. Small engine crankcases and the new exhaust recirculating systems bring more contaminants than ever into engine oil, despite filtering protection. Naturally, as those foreign substances build up, the oil's lubricating quality is lessened, and the rate of engine wear increases. Thus, a shorter-than-recommended oil-change interval is needed for severe service.

Preparation. First, drive your car onto a pair of ramps. The ramps should rest on a solid surface. Have someone guide you on so that you will not drive off the ends. Avoid stopping quickly on the ramps, or they may tip over from the momentum; some high-priced ramps have extending arms to prevent tip-over.

With the car solidly positioned, block the rear wheels to prevent the car from rolling off backwards. Set the parking brake. Put an automatic transmission selector in Park; put a manual shift lever in Reverse.

So that you do not forget to add oil later, remove the oil filler cap before you drain.

Now, lay out all the needed equipment under the car. Put everything where you can reach it without getting off the creeper, but where it will not be in your way as you work. You probably will need most of the following: a trouble light; an oil drain wrench; a transmission-differential drain wrench; an oil filter cartridge wrench; an oil drain pail; a new oil filter element; and a cloth for wiping the filter gasket seat and your hands.

The engine should be at operating temperature so that sludge at the bottom of the oil pan can drain. Cold, sluggish oil has little rinsing action. If possible, change the oil immediately after driving the car a few miles.

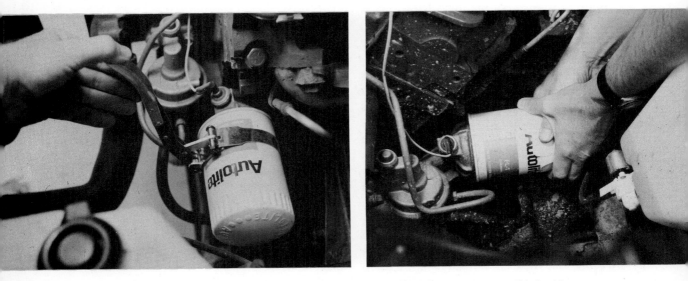

Filter wrench (*left*) easily loosens a spin-on oil filter element. But never use this tool to tighten an element; do that with your hand. If you lack a filter wrench, wrap a layer of double-faced carpet tape (*right*) around the cartridge to get a firm, slip-resistant grip.

Draining oil. Position the drain pail, and loosen the oil drain plug from the bottom of the oil pan with the drain plug wrench. Screw out the plug until the last thread is about to let go (after a few times, you will know when that is). Then, give the plug a quick counter-clockwise half-turn as you pull it out and away. This rapid maneuver keeps hot drain oil off your hand; it also prevents you from dropping the plug into the pail.

After all the oil has drained out, inspect the drain plug gasket (if any) for damage. Wipe the plug clean. Thread it into the drain opening by hand, and tighten it firmly with your wrench.

Changing filters. If the oil filter is due for replacement, move the drain pail under it. Some manufacturers call for oil filter element replacements with every oil change.

Some oil filters are easier to service from above than from below. After loosening a screw-in cartridge with an oil filter wrench, spin the element off with your hand, and catch it as the threads let go. Lower the cartridge gently into the oil drain pail without splashing.

Before screwing on the new filter element, dip your finger into the drain pail and wipe a light film of oil around the filter's rubber gasket. Also wipe off the oil filter seat on the engine with a clean lint-free cloth or paper towel.

Start the element's threads carefully, and spin on the new filter until you meet a little resistance. That is when the gasket first makes contact. Give the cartridge another three-quarter turn. If you tighten further, the gasket may distort and leak. A looser fit will invite leaks. Tighten the new filter element by hand only. Save the wrench for loosening.

Adding oil. Before pouring new oil into the engine, check its crankcase capacity in the owner's manual. When a new oil filter is installed, you usually add one extra quart to replace oil contained in the old filter element. Because the extra quart will not circulate until you start the engine, the oil level should be above the full mark.

After changing your engine oil, start the engine and watch the oil pressure indicator light. If you have changed an oil filter, it may stay red for several seconds while the new filter fills with fresh oil. Then, the light should go out. Fast-idle the engine for three or four minutes. (You can put a business card under the idle-stop.) When the time is up, switch off the engine and roll under the car. Do not get under the car while the engine is running. Examine the newly installed oil filter and the oil drain plug for signs of leakage. If either leaks, tighten it further (if it is the filter, be sure to wipe it clean before checking again).

Disposing of old oil. This is a problem. Pouring it down the drain is out; even if it gets through, the oil will help foul some stream. And burning it only adds to air pollution. Better use what you can of the drainings as a preservative treatment for fence posts, wood patio blocks, and the like. Soak the wood in oil overnight or longer, drain, and use. Save excess drain oil in closed cans. When you fill several of them, give them to a service station to be reclaimed. Or, the next time you take a country drive, bring along your oil and offer it to someone who lives on a dusty, unpaved road. Drain oil is fine for stabilizing road dust.

Imports. Oil changes on some foreign-made cars can be a bit different than in domestic products. For example, Volkswagens do not have oil filters, although most other imports do. The Fiat 850 and the Mercedes-Benz diesel have no external oil filters. Other popular imports have oil filters in the front, middle, or rear of the engine, to one side.

On a Volkswagen, an engine oil change should include removing and cleaning the oil strainer inside the oil sump. New gaskets and new copper washers should be used under the cap screws.

Some Fiat engines without external oil filters need to have the internal filter removed from the oil pump drive pulley and cleaned at 30,000-mile intervals.

If you drive an import, be sure to check your owner's manual for exact oil service needs.

PERIODIC CLEANING

Of course, you can perform many other items of periodic care on your car. Wash the car frequently to remove road salt and other corrosive agents. Do not forget to rinse the undercarriage.

Your car's engine can be kept new-looking and pleasant to work on by periodic cleaning at a jet-spray car wash. To do it, remove the air cleaner. Start with a detergent spray and finish with a plain rinse-

water spray. Be careful to keep water out of the carburetor throat, off hot exhaust manifolds—they may crack—and away from the battery top, where it may spill into the battery cells. While you are at it, clean off the underside of the hood, firewall, brake master cylinder, steering gear, and other underhood parts. Often, the engine will not start after a bath. You will have to remove the distributor cap and wipe off moisture from inside the cap and from spark plug cables. Carry the tools you will need; most useful is a screwdriver.

Periodically check the brake master cylinder fluid level, battery electrolyte, and power steering and cooling system levels. If necessary, fill each with the right fluid.

If your car has air conditioning, peer into the sight glass after the unit has been running for a few minutes to make sure that no foam or dirt is floating in the system.

Fuel filters need periodic replacement. Element-type filters may require a fuel filter wrench to get them off. Do it exactly like removing a spin-on oil filter, as de-

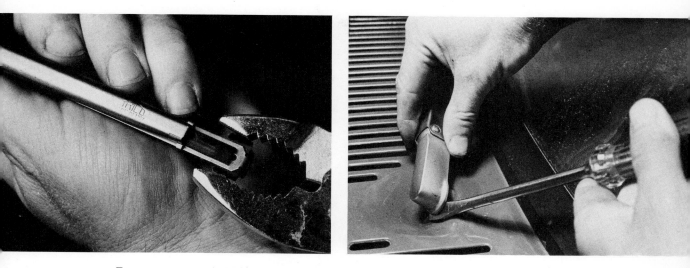

To remove some windshield wiper blades, you depress the red dots that free them; with others, you must pinch the ends with pliers (*left*) and pull. To remove a wiper arm, pull or pry it gently with a screwdriver (*right*).

scribed previously.

Lubrication time is also a good time to service the positive crankcase ventilation system (see the chapter on emission control devices).

Windshield wiper blades need occasional renewal. There are two types: those with a red dot and those without. The two are not interchangeable, and car make and model information is not enough. The best bet is to have an old blade with you when you buy the new ones. Buy refill blades rather than entire new wiper blades; refills cost less.

Red-dot blades come out by pushing on the red button, removing the bows from the wiper arm, and sliding the bows off the blade. The bows can be snapped back into the end of the wiper arm without depressing the red button.

Blades without red dots come out by pinching the larger end with pliers, and pulling. Refills should be threaded into the bow guides, and pushed in until they lock in place.

Some new hide-away wipers have a bell-crank device that makes them harder —but not impossible—for you to service.

The tension springs of wiper arms become weak in time. Weak arms should be replaced. Check wiper-arm tension with a light-duty spring scale, and compare the readings with the specifications. Replacement can be easy or hard, depending on how your car's wiper arms are held to their shafts.

One type is held with a screw or nut that must be undone before you can pull the arm off its serrated drum. Another type is spring-locked to the drum. Simply pry this arm out from under the arm collar with a screwdriver.

Face new arms in the proper direction so they do not hit each other or go off the edges of the windshield when they are operating, and so they park in the proper position.

Most other periodic care has been covered in the chapters relating to specific systems. Look for tips in these chapters.

TUNE-UP AND EMISSION CONTROL SERVICE

Air Filter						
Belts (wear and tension)						
Carburetor Adjustment						
Distributor Points						
Fuel Filter						
Ignition Timing						
Spark Plugs						

Evaporative Controls		
Exhaust Controls		
PCV System		

LUBRICATION

Chassis							
Engine Oil (change)							
Engine Oil Filter (change)							
Fluids:							
Battery (including charge and chemical level)							
Brake							
Coolant (including antifreeze ratio and hoses)							
Transmission							
Manifold Heat Control Valve							
Wheel Bearings							

444

CHASSIS SERVICE

Brake Hoses						
Brake Linings						
Exhaust System (pipes and muffler)						
Headlight Alignment						
Shock Absorbers						
Tire Tread						
Wheel Alignment						
Wheel Balance						
Windshield Wipers						

GASOLINE COST AND CONSUMPTION

Date	Mileage	Number of Gallons	Cost	Date	Mileage	Number of Gallons	Cost

ANNUAL CAR EXPENSES

Gas and Oil				
Minor Servicing (including cost of equipment, lubricants, etc.)				
Major Repairs				
Replacement Equipment				
Insurance Premiums				

Gas and Oil				
Minor Servicing (including cost of equipment, lubricants, etc.)				
Major Repairs				
Replacement Equipment				
Insurance Premiums				

NOTES:

_____

_____

_____

_____

_____

Index